Harvard Studies in Business History XL

Edited by Alfred D. Chandler, Jr.
Isidor Straus Professor of Business History
Graduate School of Business Administration
George F. Baker Foundation
Harvard University

Enterprising Elite

The Boston Associates and
the World They Made

Robert F. Dalzell, Jr.

Harvard University Press
Cambridge, Massachusetts
and London, England

This book is printed on ph neutral paper, and its binding materials
have been chosen for strength and durability.

Library of Congress Cataloging-in-Publication Data

Dalzell, Jr., Robert F.
      Enterprising elite.

      (Harvard studies in business history ; 40)
      Bibliography: p.
      Includes index.
      1. Textile industry—Massachusetts—Lowell—
History—19th century.   2. Textile industry—
Massachusetts—Waltham—History—19th century.
3. Boston Region (Mass.)—Industries—History—
19th century.
I. Title.   II. Series.
HD9858.L9D35   1987   338.4'7677'0097444   86-33649
ISBN 0-674-25765-0 (alk. paper)

For Fred, Jeffery, Victoria, and Alex,
  who will one day build worlds of their own

Editor's Introduction

Robert F. Dalzell's comprehensive, collective biography of the Boston Associates fulfills brilliantly one of the most challenging tasks of business history, that of placing businessmen and their activities in a broad cultural setting. The book that immediately precedes this study in the Harvard Studies in Business History, Steven Tolliday's *Business, Bankers, and Politics*, examines the complex interactions among industrialists, their enterprises, financial intermediaries and the state in the evolution of the British steel industry between the two world wars. Professor Dalzell depicts the evolving activities of industrialists on a different and an even broader canvas. He tells the story of a group of entrepreneurs who profoundly influenced economic, social, and political developments in Massachusetts and even the nation as a whole in the years between the War of 1812 and the Civil War.

The book opens by describing Francis Cabot Lowell's stay in Britain beginning in 1811. There he not only acquired a knowledge of the latest textile technology, particularly the power loom, but also observed the depressing impact of industrial change in Britain on both the rich and the poor. Returning to Boston, he and a few relatives and close friends including Patrick Tracy Jackson and Nathan Appleton built much more than just the first modern factory in the United States. Together they established a wholly new industrial process, "the Waltham system," to provide capital, to recruit labor, to market finished goods, and to purchase supplies—all on an unprecedented scale. Their impressive success at Waltham led these Boston Associates to build an industrial park at Lowell where the provision of massive water power permitted the construction on that site of many mills by several companies, all of which had members of the Associates on their boards of directors. As the Associates expanded to include Lawrences, Lymans,

Cabots, Perkinses, Dwights, Brookses, and other Boston families, they built comparable industrial complexes on the Merrimack at Manchester, New Hampshire, and Lawrence, Massachusetts, and on the Connecticut at Chicopee and Holyoke, Massachusetts.

On the basis of the wealth thus generated, the Associates invested in railways, banks, and insurance companies—activities providing them with essential services ancillary to textile manufacturing. The chapter describing these enlarged and diversified activities is followed by a fascinating discussion of how the Boston Associates spent their money on philanthropy—that is, primarily on socially useful nonprofit institutions, including the Massachusetts General Hospital and its associated McLean Asylum, Harvard University, including the Lawrence Scientific School, Williams College, the Athenaeum, the Lowell Institute, and others. The chapter provides new views on why these donations were made and the way in which the Associates as trustees managed their finances. The final chapter is on the role of the Boston Associates in Massachusetts and peripherally on national politics during the antebellum period.

Professor Dalzell has used archival sources as effectively as any business or economic historian. Yet the greatest achievements of this book are those of synthesis. What is new here is not so much the story of the innovation and development of specific technologies or industrial and business methods, but rather the motives for developing an integrated system and how those motives were reflected in the approach of·the Associates to new industrial and business opportunities. As we follow the story we see how the group responded in ways that helped its members to maintain their identity and their economic and social position in the face of rapid economic and political change. While they began as innovators "on a grand scale," ultimately they hoped, as Professor Dalzell emphasizes, "to check the thrust of change." Although that challenge was too great in the textile industry, they were able to achieve "for both themselves and their descendants, what had always mattered most: a secure and remarkably durable position at the top of the social order." Their approach to the creation of wealth and the institutions they built to maintain and to use that wealth still have a relevance today.

In sum, the study provides an outstanding example of a new and significant approach in the writing of business history by relating the business and economic activities of businessmen to the community in which they operate and by examining and analyzing the complex relations between the two as both change over time.

Alfred D. Chandler, Jr.

Preface

As anyone who has ever traveled in New England knows, Massachusetts abounds in monuments. Some commemorate important events; others aim to depict everyday life in the past. Plymouth Rock, Historic Deerfield, the Freedom Trail in Boston, the homes of famous writers: one can visit them all. And in recent years the historic preservation movement has been active on still other—less traditional—fronts, most notably perhaps at Lowell, Massachusetts. There, thanks to a splendid cooperative effort by the city, the state, private industry, and the National Park Service, it is possible to see and study the physical remains of the nation's first major industrial center. In a handsomely refurbished factory building visitors are introduced to Lowell's development as a preplanned textile manufacturing community. Various walking tours then cross the city, and along the way the canal system, which powered the mills, is explained. Several buildings can be entered, and in one a power loom is demonstrated in full and deafening operation.

An afternoon spent at Lowell is an intriguing experience. Yet like most such attempts to read the past through the tangible bits and pieces that survive, it is also a frustrating one. In Boston the Freedom Trail picks its way along modern paved sidewalks in the shadow of huge skyscrapers built by commercial banks. At Lowell much of the central core of the city was leveled in our own era in the name of urban renewal. Its principal features today are a multilane highway and a number of low-income housing projects. More frustrating still, of the factory buildings that remain, almost all date from the latter half of the nineteenth century. Next to nothing survives from the early years, except the canal system. What then was Lowell really like? And what of the people who planned the town and lived and worked there?

How and why did they come to embark upon the novel world of machines and factories? In its present state Lowell offers some tantalizing clues but not much more.

The problem is further complicated by the fact that few of the builders of Lowell ever lived there. Even the workers in the early years came from elsewhere, most to spend only a short time as textile "operatives." To trace the paths that led the members of both groups to the city one would have to travel to the kind of setting where so many of them began life—a town like Groton, Massachusetts, or New Ipswich, New Hampshire.

The experience of growing up in provincial New England was one that Lowell owners and workers shared, and it marked them deeply, but beyond that their paths diverged, with the owners taking a rather more complicated route. Among the surviving landmarks are the wharves in Boston where the fortunes that went into building Lowell were made. In Boston, too, in impressive array along the streets of Beacon Hill and still looking much as they did then, are many of the houses where the owners lived. Following the route a bit further, one would want to stop at places like the Boston Athenaeum, Massachusetts General Hospital, and Harvard University. A visit to the Longfellow House in Cambridge would also be appropriate. Built and eventually abandoned by a wealthy merchant of Tory sympathies, it served as Washington's headquarters during the first year of the Revolution and, after his departure, was occupied by a succession of owners who one after another fell on hard times. Longfellow first came there as a boarder when he was beginning his career at Harvard. That he was eventually able to purchase and enlarge the house was due to the generosity of his father-in-law, Nathan Appleton, the founder of Lowell.

This book is a study of the lives of those men who, like Appleton, prospered as Boston merchants at the start of the nineteenth century and later invested heavily in the American textile industry. Like Appleton, most of them were not native Bostonians, but because the metropolis became the center of their activities and because the activities themselves were so varied, historians have found it convenient to refer to the group simply as the Boston Associates. I have followed that convention, though it should be recognized that the Associates were never formally organized as a body. Rather they were linked by a host of ties, formal and informal, built up over a period of thirty years and extending not just to the textile industry, but to other key areas of business endeavor, as well as to philanthropy and politics.

Previous studies have analyzed the Associates' role in many of these areas and my debt to the authors of those studies is substantial. Yet no one so far has attempted to tell the entire story, to trace the connections that gave coherence to so many separate initiatives. At most this has been done in the case of individual lives, which means that the corporate character of much of what the Associates accomplished has been obscured. If there is any truth to the notion that the early nineteenth century witnessed a rising tide of "individualism" in America, that development touched Boston's premier business elite hardly at all. The group has long needed a comprehensive, collective biography, and that is what I have sought to provide.

Because the Associates' involvement in the textile industry remains the most striking fact about them, I have begun with Francis Cabot Lowell and the establishment of the Boston Company of Waltham. For those interested in the subject, the early chapters of the book can be read in conjunction with Thomas Dublin's excellent analysis of labor and laborers in the Waltham-Lowell system, *Women at Work*. And for a picture of the early American textile industry as a whole, the reader should compare Dublin's findings and my own with the wealth of material presented by Anthony Wallace in *Rockdale*, a brilliant study of a group of textile manufacturing communities in southeastern Pennsylvania.

Wallace discovered a pattern of development quite unlike the one that shaped places like Lowell. Built by men who were already rich, the Waltham-Lowell mills were the largest American industrial enterprises of the period. At Rockdale, the scale was altogether different: small factories, begun by men of modest means, that grew slowly over the years through reinvested profits. The structure of community was also different at Rockdale. Owners and workers lived and worked side by side, and as time passed—owing largely to the efforts of the owners and their wives—the bonds of community became increasingly intertwined with evangelical Christianity. Most of the Boston Associates, in contrast, never made more than occasional trips to Lowell, and while they did encourage the practice of religion among their workers, most of their efforts to raise the moral tone of society were concentrated in Boston. Finally, in politics the two groups ended up diametrically opposed, with the millowners of Rockdale supporting the Northern antislavery crusade that climaxed in 1860 and the Boston Associates doing their utmost to halt it.

Despite all of the obvious differences, however, there remains a strong element of similarity. At bottom, the world Wallace describes represented a carefully worked out attempt to effect a compromise between modern industrial systems of production and traditional cultural values and patterns of social organization. It is one of the central conclusions of this book that the Waltham-Lowell system, and indeed all the Associates' activities, should be viewed in precisely the same light. As businessmen they were innovators operating on a scale unparalleled in America at the time, yet ultimately they hoped to check the thrust of change—to alter the world they knew only enough to make it secure for people like themselves. Altogether it was a highly complex undertaking, and at least as it involved the textile industry, one destined to fail. But as I have suggested in the Epilogue, that one failure did not mean that the Associates' larger goal had eluded them. In fact it had not.

In a book written some years ago I analyzed in detail the final decade of Daniel Webster's political career. Since the Boston Associates ranked among Webster's chief supporters—financially as well as politically—there was a certain logic in turning next to a study of the group. Nevertheless for someone trained primarily as a political historian the road ahead seemed full of pitfalls, and if I have managed to avoid even a few of those it is thanks in no small part to the help of several institutions and many different individuals.

Work on the present study was begun on a year's leave of absence made possible by a Guggenheim fellowship. During the same year I was fortunate enough to be a fellow at the Charles Warren Center for Studies in American History at Harvard University. The first rough outline of the project was presented at a seminar sponsored by the Center. A revised version of that paper later appeared in *Perspectives in American History*, 9 (1975), 229–268 under the title "The Rise of the Waltham-Lowell System and Some Thoughts on the Political Economy of Modernization in Ante-Bellum Massachusetts." I am grateful to Professor Donald Fleming of the Harvard History Department for helping with the revisions. I also wish to thank the current editors of *Perspectives* for permission to incorporate portions of that article in Part I of this book.

As a single, rather tentative article slowly grew into a full-length study, a number of scholars read all or part of the result. Their questions, criticisms, and suggestions have been invaluable. In this connection I would particularly like to mention Professor Emeritus Fred Rudolph and Professors Patricia J. Tracy and Charles B. Dew of the Williams College History Department; Professors Lee J. Alston and Roger E. Bolton of the Williams College Economics Department; Professor John M. Blum of Yale University; Professor Michael F. Holt of the University of Virginia; and Professor Leo Marx of the Massachusetts Institute of Technology. Professor Alfred D. Chandler of the Harvard Business School and the editor of the series in which the book appears has also been most helpful.

To Professor Michael D. Bell of the Williams College English Department and Professor James B. Wood of the Williams College History Department I owe a special debt. Reading through two and sometimes three drafts of every chapter, they have done all that anyone could ask of colleagues and more. I have not always agreed with their suggestions, but I have invariably found that hearing them out resulted in something better—sharper, clearer—than what I had achieved initially.

Among the benefits of teaching at a small liberal arts college is the opportunity to know and work with colleagues in a variety of disciplines, but the students at such institutions also make an important contribution. To all those young men and women who labored in History 318 over term papers on mid-nineteenth century economic elites in Massachusetts towns; to others who continue to struggle through "The Rise of American Business"—a course that begins improbably enough with a reading of John Hicks's *A Theory of Economic History* and Clifford Geertz's *Peddlers and Princes*—should go credit for helping shape the analytical framework used in these pages. It was before those students that I first tried out many of my ideas, and it was in response to their lively, probing skepticism that the process of honing and refining began and still goes forward.

If scholars writing books had to depend only on their own resources, skills, and energy, there would surely be fewer books written. The Trustees of Williams College have generously approved several semesters of sabbatical leave so the work could continue. The staffs of the Williams College Library; Widener Library, Harvard University; the Massachusetts Historical Society; and the Baker Library of the Harvard Business School have provided vital assistance at many points. Mrs. Sidney D. Ross of Williamstown read the entire manuscript and made innumerable suggestions that improved it. Successive drafts of chapters were ably typed by the Williams College Faculty Secretarial Office under the direction first of Rosemary Lane and then of Eileen Sahady. Donna Chenail did a superb job of preparing the final version of the manuscript. To the editorial staff of the Harvard University Press—and especially to Aida Donald, who took an early interest in the project—I also owe a great deal.

Finally, something must be said about the supple network of kith and kin that has sustained me in various ways through the whole venture. One of the pleasures of my year at the Charles Warren Center was the chance to renew acquaintance with Stephen W.

Botein, a former Williams colleague whose recent death has cost the American historical profession one of its most thoughtful younger members. His initial enthusiasm for this project was crucial in getting it off the ground. Through long summer nights in Maine, conversations with Richard and Kathleen Lyman—old friends and members of the Simmons College faculty—have kept me thinking about the past in new ways. More than the two of them may have guessed, those conversations have had their impact here. To Sarah C. MacFarland of the Williams College Library I am indebted for suggesting a title. Parents who keep asking where "that book" is may seem a nuisance at the time, but we owe them much for their anxious prodding. The names of my four children appear elsewhere, but that can hardly repay them for their cheerful good will and interest in my work over the years, or for all those unattended wrestling matches, soccer games, and cross-country meets. Nor can anything I might say begin to express what I owe Lee B. Dalzell, who has helped with every phase of the work. If marriage today is supposed to be a partnership between equals, no accounting system ever devised adequately values the constant infusions of understanding, humor, and space required to maintain two demanding professional careers. I say that; she knows and lives it.

R.F.D., Jr.
Williamstown
December 1986

Contents

Illustrations

PART I

The Rise of the Waltham-Lowell System

As a problem in historical interpretation the spectacle of people making fundamental changes in the way they come by the necessities and luxuries of life is a little like an iceberg: the changes that one first notices are often but a fraction of those actually occurring. Nor is that the only difficulty. The factors that produce the change, no less than the elements that distinguish it from other, similar occurrences, may seem explicable in relatively simple terms, but the dangers of over-simplification are great. Living in the latter part of the twentieth century we are so familiar with how the process of economic "development" should unfold and where it leads—with what Fernand Braudel calls "the troop of events which have come out on top in the struggle of life"[1]—that we tend to ignore whatever fails to fit the usual pattern.

The Waltham-Lowell system is a case in point. Between 1815 and 1860 the economy of Massachusetts underwent a transformation fully as dramatic as the one that swept across England in the half century prior to 1815. In fact, long before 1860 the state had become the most thoroughly industrialized portion of the globe outside of Great Britain, and on both sides of the Atlantic the leading sector in the process was the same—cotton textiles. Yet as early as 1813, with the establishment of the Boston Company, the first in a long line of Waltham-Lowell ventures, the Massachusetts textile industry moved substantially ahead of its British counterpart in certain respects. For the period, the company carried the basic processes of factory production to an extraordinarily high level of development. Its managers also devised a most unusual system of labor, one that attracted wide-spread and generally favorable notice. Indeed, to many observers at the time it seemed as if the Boston Company of Waltham and the enterprises patterned on it represented a new and singularly benign kind of industrial order.

With good reason, scholars since then have been more skeptical. The tough-minded businessmen who built the great mills at places like Waltham, and later Lowell and Lawrence, meant to make a profit and did. If it suited some of their contemporaries to see them in a different light, a more distanced, dispassionate analysis has depicted them as prototypical industrial capitalists in pursuit of the main chance. According to the standard interpretation, the men in question—the Boston Associates—had as their primary goal increasing the return on capital previously invested, at falling rates, in maritime commerce. The truth is, however, that the facts do not fit this thesis, and part of the purpose of the following three chapters is to suggest an alternative to it.

Necessarily the alternative depends on an analytical framework broad enough to leave ample room for linking social and political factors to economic change. In its day the Waltham-Lowell system represented the greatest single concentration of industrial resources in the United States, yet more than size separated it—even from most early American attempts at industrialization. In many ways the system was unique, and precisely for that reason it seems imperative to cast the interpretive net as broadly as possible, to move beyond models that rely on economic factors alone.

Any analysis of the Waltham-Lowell system must recognize, too, that it grew out of a deliberate attempt at change; on that point the standard interpretation is correct. If the founders of the Boston Company had been content with the world as it was, they would never have bothered with textile manufacturing at all. But that hardly proves that they were simply interested in getting rich, any more than it implies that they wished to engineer something as sweeping as an industrial revolution. For there can be different kinds of discontent— and different degrees of change envisioned as a result.

1.

Yankee Abroad:
Francis Cabot Lowell in Scotland

As the story is usually told, the Waltham-Lowell system had its beginnings in a stunning act of industrial piracy. And so in a sense it did, though the individual responsible probably did not look like a man on such a mission. Instead Francis Cabot Lowell must have struck the people he met as very much what he was: a well-connected, mild-mannered American merchant, traveling in Europe with his wife and young sons. The letters of introduction he carried would have added that the trip had been undertaken for reasons of health—both his wife's and his own—which was true. But there remained, always, that other purpose, known only to a few close friends.[1]

One of those friends—and the only person to have left any record of what happened—was another Boston merchant, Nathan Appleton. Decades later Appleton would recall how he had visited Lowell in Edinburgh in 1810 and discussed in "frequent conversations" with him "the subject of the Cotton Manufacture." In the course of those conversations, Lowell revealed his plan: "he had determined before his return to America, to visit Manchester, for the purpose of obtaining all possible information on the subject, with a view to the introduction of the improved manufacture in the United States."[2]

While anyone reading Appleton's account today might find what Lowell contemplated innocuous enough, both men knew otherwise. The risks were substantial. British law prohibited the emigration of skilled textile workers and exacted heavy penalties for exporting models or drawings of the machinery. By the time Lowell went abroad those measures had already failed to prevent the establishment in America of one phase of the process of mechanized cotton production, with machinery based on British designs. Thanks to the help of Samuel Slater, Moses Brown and his son-in-law William Almy had opened a small factory for spinning cotton yarn in Rhode Island in 1790. During the next two decades the number of spinning mills in New England had grown steadily. Yet the crowning glory of Britain's textile technology—the ingenious power loom, which wove the yarn into finished cloth and which had earned its inventor, Edmund Cartwright, a £10,000 bonus from Parliament—remained beyond the reach of American manufacturers.

Until, that is, Lowell scored his triumph. Leaving the British officials who twice searched his luggage none the wiser, he managed by meticulous observation to memorize the principal features of the power loom well enough to produce his own version of it on his return to Boston.

Considering the complexity of the power loom, it was a remarkable feat, so remarkable that historians have tended to treat it as just that: a kind of extraordinary conjuring trick performed at a particular moment by a man who otherwise is allowed to appear almost totally mysterious. This is unfortunate, because it leaves at least two major issues unresolved. The first is the question of Lowell's motivation. What drew him to cotton manufacturing in the first place? What did he hope to achieve through it? The second issue is the source of his other contributions to the American textile industry, for the Boston Manufacturing Company, which he and his associates founded at Waltham, represented far more than the successful adaptation of a single machine. Everything from the size of the enterprise to the type of labor used was thoroughly innovative, by British as well as American standards. Still, the origin of those innovations remains unclear.

No doubt the entire sequence of events would present less of a puzzle if the principal actors had said more about it. The most complete contemporary account, Appleton's, clearly assigns Lowell the chief role in guiding the Boston Company during its early years, but Appleton rarely bothered to explain why Lowell made the choices he did. Lowell himself was even less communicative. He produced no account of his own, and if he kept a journal, either at home or abroad, it has not survived. Nor do his letters, which deal largely with family and business matters, reveal a great deal.

Yet it is possible to reconstruct Lowell's life in America, as well as something of what he saw in Europe beyond the mills at Manchester. And since he had already decided before leaving on his travels to study the English textile industry, the factors influencing that decision probably lay on this side of the Atlantic. As for the rest—the particular form the Waltham venture assumed under his direction—there the European experience appears to have been crucial, though not in any simple or obvious way. We know who Lowell was and what he saw while he was abroad; what he made of what he saw and how it influenced him we can only infer.

II

The mere fact that Lowell could afford to spend two years traveling abroad with his family says something about him. Had his affairs not been in good order he never could have been away so long. On the other hand, the fact that he considered such a trip desirable, even necessary, seems to point to a different conclusion. People who are fully and comfortably engaged in the normal day-to-day activities of life are seldom willing to leave them for great stretches of time. From the beginning, then, there was a hint of something amiss.

Yet exactly what it was would have been difficult to guess. In the early years of the nineteenth century the American social landscape— or at any rate that part of it centered on Boston—offered few redoubts more secure than the one Lowell occupied. His forebears had seen to that: several generations in commerce in Newburyport, a noted clergyman for a grandfather, and a father who had been a distinguished lawyer, first in Newburyport and later in Boston. Upon graduating from Harvard, where he excelled in math, Lowell himself had gone directly into commerce and prospered. By 1810 he was already quite well off.[3]

It was, after all, the sort of tidy saga that had long since become familiar in New England. The region's physical characteristics had always made the creation of great landed estates impractical. If substantial fortunes were to be accumulated other means had to be found, and commerce early on proved the most reliable alternative. By the eighteenth century every seaport along the coast boasted its group of leading merchants, who, with their associates in the professions, regularly indulged in a certain amount of frank aristocratic pretension. This was especially true in Boston, the economic and political capital of the region, where success in commerce or law could be translated into a connection with the imperial establishment. In the years before the Revolution, families like the Hutchinsons and Olivers—both of which owed their initial rise to trade—had come to fill many of the colony's major offices, and as befitted their dignity, they managed to live in considerable state. Though the result would hardly have satisfied European tastes, it constituted a fair facsimile in American terms of aristocratic status and power.[4]

As a result of the Revolution, of course, not a few leading families— including the Hutchinsons and Olivers—fled to England, leaving distinct gaps at the top of Boston's social order. But eventually those gaps were filled by other families. Some, like the Adamses, Otises, and Warrens, already had associations with the city and owed their prominence in part to the role they played in the struggle with Great Britain; others gravitated to Boston from elsewhere in New England. While often in the confusion of those years the move was necessary to repair declining family fortunes, those who came from positions of consequence in their native towns and prospered were accepted readily enough. The Lowells were just such a family.

Yet if for Francis Lowell, and others like him, access to the upper levels of Boston society proved relatively easy—given the requisite degree of financial success—what they found there was often something less than the secure haven of colonial days. And ironically, the source of the difficulty was the Revolution itself. For in the end independence had done far more than remove a few families from power; it had created an entirely new set of economic, political, and social conditions—one that made it much more difficult to live the kind of life successful Boston merchants had once taken for granted.

In its economic dimension the problem could be stated quite simply: commerce, though it continued to provide impressive financial returns, had become in other ways a burdensome occupation. Working within the British Empire, colonial merchants had benefited from long-established trade routes and the protection afforded by imperial regulations. After independence, with those advantages gone, the entire American economy suffered a sharp decline. In time Boston's merchants sought out new markets and suppliers around the globe, and as war spread across Europe neutral trade came to offer splendid opportunities for gain. Profits rose steadily; but so did the attendant risks. Whether in the newly opened trade with the Orient or in more conventional exchanges of American staples for European manufactures, painstaking attention to the details of every transaction was imperative. In a sense each voyage represented a new undertaking. For those who prospered luck was essential, but equally important were sound accounting methods and reliable sources of information, both of which made unrelenting demands on time and energy. To reduce risks partnerships were formed, yet that only added to the burden of work and involved the parties in each other's affairs in a way that carried risks of a different sort. A merchant could be ruined as surely by standing security for someone else's debts as through the failure of his own enterprises. And for every outright disaster there were a dozen narrow escapes.[5]

As it happened, such matters were much on Lowell's mind while he was abroad. Early in 1811 the firm of Joseph and Henry Lee failed.

The Lees were relatives and business associates of Patrick Jackson, Lowell's wife's brother, and the failure of the firm nearly wiped out Jackson's own fortune.[6] For several months Lowell thought he might have to return to America to salvage his brother-in-law's affairs. Then, with the storm weathered, he wrote frequently, offering advice. He was particularly distressed to learn that Jackson, undaunted by his brush with bankruptcy, was once again engaging—in a large way— in business.

In an eleven-page letter, written in November 1811, Lowell spelled out his fears in detail. " 'Making too much haste to grow rich' is the great stumbling block of enterprising men," he wrote, "I consider you among the class of enterprising men and that what you have to guard particularly against is being tempted to extend your business beyond all reasonable bounds." This Lowell took to be a cardinal principle at all times but he felt it was especially important at that moment. "The hazards of business are much greater now than they even were in my day." It was essential, therefore, to exercise restraint, and to that end Lowell proposed a hard-and-fast formula: "You ought to fix some ultimatum for your debts and when you have come up to that nothing ought to tempt you to go beyond it. Let the speculation be ever so good even if you are sure of 100 percent profit you ought not to be tempted. For it is better to forego now and then a certain good profit than break a rule which ought to be kept so sacred." And the same policy should cover not only Jackson's own debts, but all "endorsements or responsibilities in any shape for others." That had been the cause of his recent trouble, which Lowell regretted had neither "calmed" nor "cured" his brother-in-law.[7]

Whatever Jackson made of Lowell's advice, the truth was that implementing it as precisely as he intended would have been difficult. Iron-clad debt ceilings, and the regularization of business activities they implied, were not always possible. Some ventures had to be entered into quickly, without full knowledge of the extent of the commitment, otherwise the opportunity would be lost. And enough lost opportunities could mean the elimination of all income, since idle mercantile capital earned nothing, as Lowell himself well knew.

In the years before his trip abroad, he had been trying more or less systematically to limit his own involvement in trade. Having accumulated a modest fortune he could afford to do so, and he did manage to find a few attractive investment opportunities. In financial terms the most significant was India Wharf, which he built in partnership with Uriah Cotting. Completed in 1808, India Wharf was the second-largest docking and warehouse complex in Boston and promised to pay substantial returns, but it remained tied to commerce, and there was a limited need for similar projects. From time to time Lowell also bought and sold large tracts of land in Maine, yet there too difficulties arose. Land speculation rarely provided income on a regular basis; it involved much the same risk that commerce did and was hard to carry on at any distance. As a result Lowell found himself while abroad, engaged in the usual types of mercantile activity. The same letter in which he urged Jackson to limit his commercial obligations contained instructions for purchases of juniper berries and wheat for Lowell's own account. The wheat was to be shipped to Liverpool or Bristol where a profit seemed likely, but then the proceeds had to be reinvested promptly because of the monetary situation in England. "The little chance there is of any fall in the price of gold and high probability of a greater rise should induce you if you have any dealings with this country not to let your money lay here long."[8]

More sound advice, as events proved, but the sense it gives of the pressures commerce entailed is telling. To be faced with a lifetime of such stress cannot have been comforting, and Lowell clearly did not find it so. The evidence is that his weakened health—the announced reason for his trip abroad—was the result of anxiety over business.

More to the point, the same anxiety almost certainly explained Lowell's interest in textile manufacturing. Investment in manufacturing had the potential of paying regular returns, and unlike India Wharf, it could be expanded to accommodate additional capital. Also in time, if all went well, the day-to-day chores of management could be left to others. That would be especially true the more thoroughly routinized the business became. Given measured increments of capital, regular business practices, established markets, and above all the maximum use of machine technology, the result itself might become a kind of great humming engine, which could be kept in motion with nothing more than occasional adjustments.

The benefits, then, would be financial, but only in part. Equally important would be the freedom gained from constant involvement in business, which someone in Lowell's position had good reason to value, because the existing situation told in half-a-dozen ways, small and large. It told in the tedium of long hours spent poring over ledgers or trying to arrange credit and insurance for a few thousand dollars worth of goods. It told in chronically poor health and in relatives and friends scattered around the globe, overseeing commercial operations that no one else could be trusted with. But most of all, perhaps, it told in the failure of Boston's merchants, as a class, to fulfill the role in society their predecessors had.

Through their domination of political and cultural life, the city's pre-Revolutionary merchants had functioned as a traditional elite.

Money alone was never enough; it had to be paired with an appropriate measure of public service. And since 1776 the terms on which such service was to be rendered had changed. Before the Revolution the elite had governed as a matter of course, but in the deepening struggle with Great Britain, power and place—especially when they seemed to become the property of a small clique bent on maintaining their positions at any cost and passing them on to sons and nephews—had become a major target of the patriot movement. As a result traditional notions of deference, while not discredited, were tempered. Candidates for office labored longer and worked harder to persuade larger numbers of people. Republican politics took more time.

Republican government also took more time and paid less well. In Massachusetts, legislative sessions lasted longer than during the colonial period, and any involvement in national government meant spending months in Philadelphia or New York and later Washington. A lawyer might serve in Congress and still practice his profession— arguing before the Supreme Court, for example—but a merchant could not. He found no business at the seat of government and was forced to suspend activities or leave them in the hands of others. Had the likelihood of gain from some other source matched the sacrifice, it might have been less burdensome. Service in colonial legislatures had brought the chance of appointment to any number of offices, some quite lucrative. The chance still existed, but official salaries rarely amounted to enough to support a gentleman and his family. Then there was the annoying impermanence of political results under the new order. When, in the closing hours of John Adams' presidency, Lowell's father had been appointed chief justice of the first circuit court of the United States, it must have seemed an appropriate reward for his legal talents and many services to the Federalist party. But within a year Congress had abolished the court at Jefferson's urging. Fortunately, the senior Lowell had his own lucrative law practice to fall back on.[9]

The truth was that a merchant like Francis Lowell, dependent on commerce for a living, could not afford to play a large role in politics, and though there were other forms of public service, they too posed difficulties. In a society where government concerned itself only to a limited extent with the welfare of its citizens, opportunities for private philanthropy abounded. It was possible to be of service and never have to stand for election or spend time in Washington. Yet most significant philanthropic projects lay beyond the means of a single individual or family. Groups had to be formed and commitments secured for continuing support—commitments that many merchants were reluctant to make, knowing as little as they did of the funds they might command six months hence, let alone in as many years.

Lowell's father and older brother John had each served as members of the Harvard Corporation in the years when the college was becoming increasingly reliant on private sources of support. The younger John was also active in founding the Boston Athenaeum and the Massachusetts General Hospital, two highly worthwhile organizations. But unlike his father and brother—lawyers both—Francis Lowell had yet to participate in such ventures. Great philanthropic institutions were not built with resources snatched from a life already overburdened with the workaday demands of counting house and exchange.

Somehow that burden had to be lightened, and if not immediately, then at least for the next generation. As matters stood, Lowell had little more to offer his sons than a share of the family capital, a few connections, and a lifetime of the same risks and pressures that he had known. Without the latter there was scant hope of preserving the capital, and without capital nothing was possible. While many a poor farm boy might have envied such a heritage, its drawbacks were palpable.

Here too, then, was a problem that investment in textile manufacturing might solve: a steady income from mill shares could provide both the money and the time to pursue activities outside the narrow realm of business. But as Lowell himself well knew, there were likely to be other, far less attractive, by-products. In England the social costs of industrialization had been high—staggeringly high by some accounts. Lowell described the situation succinctly in the letters he sent home from abroad. While he discovered much to admire in England, there were also "shades to this picture." Thus he noted, "We found the manufacturing towns very dirty."[10] And later he remarked with unwonted feeling on "the great corruption of the highest and lowest classes, and the great number of beggars and thieves."[11]

At such moments Lowell was responding much as other Americans had when confronted with the spectacle of England in the throes of the Industrial Revolution. No one wrote more eloquently on the subject than Thomas Jefferson, yet even as un-Jeffersonian a figure as Nathan Appleton was prone to thinking it a stroke of good fortune that America had thus far avoided the grip of change. A decade before he sat down with Lowell in Edinburgh to discuss the prospects of a new manufacturing venture, Appleton had written from England, "Tis true that in this country money will purchase a thousand conveniences and attentions we are without in America—but as these are in great measure the consequence of the debasement of the lower classes of society—for the happiness of our country at large I could wish it long without them."[12]

Dirty towns, corrupt and debased lower classes, beggars and thieves: the list was enough to challenge even the most hopeful estimate of the benefits of investing in manufacturing. Merely recognizing how many of their countrymen shared their feelings must have led Lowell and Appleton to wonder what it might take to alter attitudes on the subject, to demonstrate that the British reality was not the inevitable outcome of using machines to do work previously done by hand. Without such a change, any attempt to conduct large-scale industrial operations in America was bound to produce opposition. But that could be dismissed as a matter of public relations. Ultimately the problem went deeper.

For what Lowell and Appleton thought they saw in England was a society moving perilously near a state of critical disorganization. As the rich became richer, the poor seemed to be growing poorer and, as Lowell found them, more "jealous." If that continued, it could only be a matter of time before a major upheaval occurred. In America the gap between the rich and the poor was much narrower than in England, so the initial danger might not be as great. Yet England also afforded its upper classes a far more elaborately developed set of defensive bulwarks; there everything from the king's army to time-honored patterns of deference stood between the rich and the specter of popular discontent. Such safeguards—if they existed at all in America— were too weak to rely on.

And safety, at bottom, was the issue. Someone as cautious as Lowell had not achieved all that he had in order to risk it in the wholesale disorganization of society. He had reached the point where he could reasonably hope to enjoy the gains he had won, to devote his life to something more than money-getting. But if the effort to do so brought him into open conflict with those beneath him in the social order, if it led to a need for constant vigilance and endless maneuvering to protect his interests, then the game would hardly have been worth the candle.

Thus simply building a textile mill, or even a whole string of them— however well financed and managed—would not be enough. Fully as important was checking the dangerous potential of industrialization to undermine the peace and traditional order of society. European technology might be used, but whatever threatened to produce discord and division would have to be eliminated, or at least as thoroughly neutralized as possible. The result, in short, could only be quite unlike anything Lowell saw in the very factories where he stood for hours studying the power loom. But with the mills of Manchester offering little beyond technological know-how, where else might he have turned for ideas?

III

One appealing answer involves Robert Owen's activities at New Lanark, Scotland. Owen, who later founded New Harmony in Indiana, was then managing the large textile mill that his father-in-law had built on the banks of the Clyde not far from Glasgow. Having begun a decade earlier to implement a series of reforms aimed at improving the morals and developing the character of his employees, he had already made New Lanark something of a tourist attraction.[13] Appleton, in his journal, described a visit there, though he stayed only part of a day and never mentioned meeting Owen.[14]

If Lowell was familiar with the place, there is no record of it. Nevertheless, the similarities between New Lanark and the Boston Company make it tempting to think he might have been influenced by Owen. Both enterprises used waterpower, in rural settings, to manufacture cotton cloth. A conspicuous concern for the living conditions and moral character of its labor force did play a prominent part in the Boston Company's operations, and Owen at the time was just beginning to give wider publicity to his views on those subjects. He had yet to build his school or the famous "Institute for the Formation of Character"—a kind of grand community center for the workers and their families—but talk of such projects was making his partners increasingly anxious about the future of their investment, so anxious that they had begun to consider selling out. In defending himself, Owen would come to speak more and more openly of the importance of mixing business and philanthropy, a line of argument that led eventually to his rejection of the capitalistic system. But that lay several years in the future. In 1811 it was still possible that New Lanark could have offered Lowell an attractive model for a novel kind of industrial development. The idea that business should be combined with what Owen would shortly be calling an "experiment . . . for the general happiness of society"[15] had a fine ring to it, and Lowell was not uninterested in larger social issues.

On the other hand, like Owen's original partners, Lowell tended to value profits above answers to abstract philosophical questions, or at any rate it is difficult to imagine him pursuing the latter at the expense of the former. Nor, beyond the details of technology and setting and an unusual concern for the workers' welfare, was there ever much to connect the Boston Company and New Lanark. And if it seemed otherwise, a more convincing explanation involves a broader—and far more significant—pattern of change occurring throughout Scotland during those years. In the long run Owen's enterprise was but a single, rather eccentric, product of that larger phenomenon, and

Lowell may never have seen New Lanark. Scattered across Scotland, however, were literally scores of examples of just the sort of development that might have interested him.

Originally Lowell had hoped to spend much of his time traveling in France, but with Napoleon invading Russia and Wellington battling French forces across Portugal and Spain, the vagaries of war intervened. British officials refused to allow foreigners to cross the channel and return to England. Under the circumstances, the Lowells did the best they could and set up housekeeping in Edinburgh.

From a practical standpoint, the choice of Edinburgh made excellent sense. Several years earlier Charles Lowell, Francis's brother, had been a student at the university there and as a result had come to know a number of people, including that group of bright young Scots who had just founded the *Edinburgh Review*. Later when John Lowell—another brother—passed through the city, he was introduced to those friends and others and subsequently entertained Francis Jeffrey, the *Review*'s first editor, at the family home in Roxbury.[16] Similarly, for Francis Lowell the capital of Scotland offered a ready-made set of acquaintances. In his luggage he carried a closely written, four-page "memorandum respecting people in Edinburgh" from his brother Charles.[17]

With friends to look after the children, the Lowells were able to take several shorter trips outside of Scotland. For much of the winter of 1811–12—leaving the younger boys with Mrs. Anne Grant, an author with a wide acquaintance in Scottish literary circles—they traveled in England. It was then that Lowell visited the cotton mills of Lancashire. As important as the experience later proved to be, however, he much preferred Scotland to anything he saw in England. "Of all the places we have been in we admire Edinburgh the most," he wrote his uncle, William Cabot, from London.[18]

Lowell's fondness for Edinburgh was in part a tribute to its people, who he felt were "as attentive as the French and have as good morals as the English."[19] But the city had other attractions, even as a substitute for Paris. No great armies marched through it; indeed the Niagara of events overtaking the rest of Europe must have seemed scarcely nearer than Boston. Yet Edinburgh, together with the country it still served as a legal and cultural center, offered another sort of drama, for in 1810 Scotland stood at the end of a century of extraordinary change.[20]

Much of what had happened mirrored earlier developments in England; the difference was the speed with which change occurred in Scotland. The heart of the process was the transformation of the country's rural, agricultural economy. Increasingly after 1800, farming and those dependent on it were drawn away from subsistence and into the market. At the same time traditional patterns of land tenure were radically altered. Relationships defined in fixed, cash rents came to replace those based on kinship and mutual service.

Starting in the Border country and the Lowlands, the revolution in Scottish agriculture moved steadily northward. After 1745, with the final defeat of the Jacobite cause at Culloden, the way was opened for the spread of the process throughout the Highlands. By the end of the century that was an accomplished fact, except in a few isolated regions of the far north. Meanwhile, at villages along the coast commercial fishing and kelp gathering were occupying more people every year, as were linen spinning and weaving in the interior. Most of the workers were displaced tenants and agricultural laborers from newly enclosed estates. Such people also found their way to the rapidly growing cities and larger towns. Glasgow in particular underwent a marked expansion, becoming the commercial and later the industrial center of Scotland. For years its merchants specialized in American tobacco, but when the Revolution ended that trade, the enormous capital reserves it had created flowed into manufacturing, especially cotton textiles.

As these developments gathered momentum, other changes occurred as well. A pronounced shift in both the birth and the death rates kept population levels rising everywhere. In a country half of which had never before known wheeled vehicles, the entire communications and transportation network was altered along modern lines, as was the educational system. The Presbyterian church also became distinctly more moderate in doctrine and structure. And finally, to cap the entire achievement, there were the glories of Scottish intellectual life: the great universities, the brilliant literature, and the names associated with both—Adam Smith, David Hume, Dugald Stewart, Robert Burns, Walter Scott.

In short, the country Lowell saw was vastly different from what it had been a hundred or even twenty-five years earlier. From a condition barely removed from the Dark Ages, Scotland had assumed a position in the forefront of European economic and social development. In 1810, riding the crest of a wave of inflated profits resulting from the Napoleonic Wars, the country's agriculture and its infant industries had never offered more promising prospects. On every front change, expansion, and high hopes seemed to be the order of the day.

Obviously there was much to be learned from such a place; the optimism, the constantly rising rents and profits were proof of that. But the lesson did not end there; for, to a remarkable extent, the changes affecting Scottish life were the product of conscious planning and effort. In region after region, the revolution in agriculture and the reform of rural society, the establishment of commerce and industry, the building of roads and harbors, the restructuring of kirk and school were carried out according to carefully conceived, clearly mandated policy. Quite often programs in one area were shaped to support those in others, so that the result acquired a unity of design that made it doubly impressive. As landholdings were consolidated and tenancies eliminated, the displaced population was not, in many instances, simply left to wander off but encouraged to settle on different land, taught new techniques of farming, or provided with other skills. At the same time incentives were given to southern tradesmen and artisans to relocate in Scottish villages, and transportation facilities, inns, markets, schools, and churches were planned to service the whole developing system.

Upon occasion such an approach could be quite overbearing. At its core lay the notion of "Improvement" and all that term implied to the eighteenth-century mind. Improvement meant not just change for the better, occurring randomly; human reason and human will were to provide the essential motive power. But Improvement in Scotland also had its darker side. Time would demonstrate that the momentum of the change could not be sustained, and in the short run the social costs sometimes rose to alarming heights. Tenants did not always want to leave the land they farmed, however inefficiently, and when they resisted force had to be used to evict them. In her *Letters from the Mountains*, Anne Grant, who cared for the Lowell's children in Edinburgh, had called the "clearance" of the rural population "the only real grievance Scotland labours under" and had written movingly, if briefly, of the plight of people left with "neither language, money, nor education, to push their way anywhere else."[21]

Yet such scenes gave scant comfort to anyone, including the planners themselves. They assumed that Improvement would benefit the many as well as the few. If some segments of the population had to be made to conform to the larger design against their will, the necessary coercion was considered reasonable only if those coerced would gain in the long run. And on that point the periodic famines that continued to afflict unimproved regions—as opposed to the obvious prosperity of the rest of the country—seemed to offer compelling testimony.

Still, Improvement was undeniably the policy of some Scotsmen and not others, and anything more than a passing interest in the subject would have led one to wonder who had played the dominant role and why. From Lowell's standpoint the answer was potentially quite significant.

Of considerable importance was Scotland's legal profession—centered in Edinburgh—and its university establishment, both of which favored Improvement and participated in a variety of ways. But the major responsibility rested with neither group. That distinction belonged to the country's landed aristocracy. As a class it took the initiative in planning the development of agriculture, transportation, commerce, and industry on hundreds of estates, large and small, throughout the country. Its needs as a class, too, stamped the movement indelibly from its inception onward.

It could hardly have been otherwise. Before the eighteenth century Scotland was a poor country, but the aristocracy controlled what resources there were: land and the people entitled by ancient right and service to the laird to eke out a meager existence upon it. Most often the service had been military. Notorious for quarreling with one another, Scottish nobles were among the most contentious in Europe. For centuries, disputes between rival chieftains, against the Scottish—and later the English—monarchy, and over religion had consumed the best energies of the class and everything else its members could throw into the balance.

But gradually after 1700 the upper class grew less warlike and more interested in other activities—chief among them the development of previously neglected estates. By the second half of the eighteenth century the role of improving landlord had become one of the principal avenues to prestige within the Scottish aristocracy. Typical in that respect was David Steuart Erskine, the Earl of Buchan, whose name Charles Lowell had given his brother accompanied by instructions to convey "the homage of my most profound respects."[22] Buchan combined a minor role in Scottish politics with a keen interest in his country's history and antiquities. He was also intrigued by America. In 1811, while Lowell was in the city, the Earl published "An Address to the Americans at Edinburgh on Washington's Birthday," stressing the importance of peace between Great Britain and "the Infant States of America," where, he felt, "the mirror of true national grandeur and happiness is likely to be held out for ages, to adjust the ornaments of European policy."[23] Yet it was neither as a scholar nor as an advocate of peace that Buchan first made his mark. He had begun life by devoting himself to the improvement of his estates, which at the time he inherited them were burdened with debt. Instituting a policy of long leases to encourage his tenants to try new methods, he became a wealthy man.[24]

Of the various factors that turned Scottish aristocrats from their customary pursuits to careers like Buchan's, none was more important than Parliamentary Union with England, imposed in 1706. By removing Scottish government to London, union brought representatives of the nobility to Westminster to sit in Parliament, thereby drawing them into the mainstream of English society. Union meant contact with new ideas and, what mattered as much, new modes of aristocratic life. Suddenly a drafty fortress in the Highlands had to be measured against the convenience and elegance of a townhouse in Park Lane, or, at the very least, in St. Andrews Square, Edinburgh.

Yet elegant townhouses were not so easily come by. Whatever its drawbacks, the Highland fortress had one great advantage—it was cheap. It could be built, maintained, and defended by one's tenants in return for their use of the land. Most of the tangible items that defined the position of an English peer, on the other hand, had to be paid for in cash. In that world, power and place went to those with liquid assets. Money was essential, and Scottish estates had never produced more than a trickle of cash.

To further complicate matters, money was never the only requirement. Aristocratic status still depended finally on two things: the ownership of land and service to society. That much had not changed. Thus the land could not be parted with, nor could moneymaking be allowed to take precedence over the hereditary obligations owed by the laird to the people entitled to his protection. Otherwise, in the act of increasing their incomes, Scottish aristocrats stood to lose the traditional marks of their position. And this was but one facet of a larger problem. Without sweeping changes of almost every kind, the goals of the aristocracy were unlikely to be achieved; yet at all costs the country's basic social order had to survive intact. The class at the top of that order could scarcely have stipulated anything else.

Out of this mixture of paired requirements and qualifications, then, grew the collection of initiatives known as Improvement. Motivated by aristocratic self-interest tempered by customary notions of service and responsibility, it seemed for a century and more to fill the bill admirably. The society it produced was unmistakably different from the one that preceded it, but never so different as to threaten the power and prerogatives of the dominant class. Hundreds of thousands of acres were made productive, whole communities were eliminated and others founded, industries were encouraged, and roads, schools, and churches were built where none had been before; still the Earl of Buchan and those like him could be satisfied that nothing had been sacrificed in the process.

The key was selectivity. As much as anything else that quality provided the tactical thrust of Scottish Improvement. A great deal was accomplished in a short period, but some things were studiously avoided. Energies were concentrated on a variety of projects, yet the range was never without limits. Particular kinds of projects, too, tended to absorb an inordinate share of available resources.

In all of these respects perhaps the most revealing creation of the movement—and certainly the most impressive to visitors—was the planned village. One study estimates that as many as 130 such villages were founded in Scotland between 1730 and 1830 and divides them into four categories: agricultural villages, fishing villages, villages based on small rural industries, and factory villages. Of the 130, the greatest number fell into the first category; the least into the fourth.[25]

By building villages Scottish landowners simultaneously attacked a broad spectrum of problems. The characteristic Scottish rural settlement was a hamlet, consisting of a cluster of huts inhabited by tenants who farmed the surrounding land in common, generally at or very near the subsistence level. The village model, imported from England, assumed both a larger population and modern economic activities. The initial intention was often to establish a market where tenants could exchange surplus produce for cash, thereby enabling them to meet the landlord's demand for rent and incidentally increasing their own living standard. In addition, villages—particularly those with some industry—could provide employment for tenants "removed" from elsewhere to accommodate large-scale commercial agriculture. Finally, there was another purpose, less tangible, but fully as important. If village life promised to make people prosperous, it would also, the hope persisted, make them virtuous. The old peasant hamlets were presumed to have fostered indolence and a dozen other vices, and the inhabitants of the larger cities seemed, in their poverty and unruliness, threatening enough without increasing their number. As one advocate of village-building remarked, "It is from the temperate and healthy family of the country labourer or tradesman and not from the alleys and garrets of a town that the race is to be sought who are best calculated to cultivate our fields or defend our properties from danger . . . villages are in general contented and unambitious."[26]

Indeed, as a device for combining economic change with maintenance of the traditional social order, the planned village seemed to have everything to recommend it. The usual pattern saw the landowner assume responsibility for laying out the site and specifying the type of construction. Tenants, who were expected to build their own dwellings according to the designs provided, were encouraged to come by grants of long leases and reduced rents. As a rule, major public buildings were financed by the landowners, who took the initiative as well in attracting tradesmen and manufacturers.

When Lowell visited Scotland, dozens of planned villages had been operating successfully for a generation and more. Within half a day's ride from Edinburgh there were at least six such communities, including the admirable Ormiston. Founded by John Cockburn in 1738, Ormiston was developed around the linen industry and had become a model of its type, providing the impetus for many similar villages. In laying out the place Cockburn had concerned himself with every detail down to the size of windows and doors, stipulating that the latter should not be made so small that "nobody can go in or out without breaking their heads except the(y) remember to duck like a goose."[27] A second example not far from Edinburgh was Athelstaneford, built as a market town, of which one observer remarked, "There is no village where of late years the inhabitants have improved more in comfort and convenience."[28] The orthodox minister of Athelstaneford, a Mr. Ritchie, was another of the people Charles Lowell had suggested his brother visit in Scotland.[29]

In 1811, too, the greatest single program of village-building—and Improvement—was just getting under way. It involved the vast landholdings of Elizabeth, Countess of Sutherland and Baroness of Strathnaver. The countess's Scottish estates, which at one time totaled more than a million acres, constituted the largest private landholding in Great Britain. Situated in the extreme northern Highlands, the property had been left undeveloped throughout the eighteenth century and might have remained so had it not been for the countess's marriage to George Granville Leveson-Gower, second marquis of Stafford. In addition to his own family's property, he had inherited through his uncle the income from the Bridgewater Canal, making him the richest Englishman of his day, a veritable "leviathan of wealth," as one contemporary described him.[30] With his enormous resources Stafford maintained a huge London townhouse, embellished several palatial country residences, held up the family political interest, and acquired one of the largest art collections in Europe, which Lowell, through a mutual acquaintance, arranged to see while he was in England.[31] For two decades a significant part of Stafford's fortune also went toward improving his wife's Scottish estates.

A dramatic increase in the price of raw wool—sixfold between 1770 and 1810—and the fact that the Sutherland holdings were admirably suited to raising sheep and little else, made that the most attractive way of using much of the land. To establish sheep walks it was necessary to move people from the interior, forcing them to abandon their homes and communities. The result was the notorious "Sutherland Clearances," in which several thousand tenants were evicted. Yet at the same time, those affected were to be elaborately provided for elsewhere on the estate, through what one historian has described as "a remarkable experiment" involving "simultaneous creation of vigorous coastal settlements which would generate a diversified range of employment opportunities . . . for the population."[32]

The villages in question—including Brora, Helmsdale, and Port Gower—were located along the North Sea coast. As the Sutherland planners envisioned the future, such places were to become centers for kelp gathering and commercial fishing. A colliery, as well as a brickworks, a barrel-making enterprise, salt pans, and a brewery were also established. By 1821, in Helmsdale alone, two thousand people— the great majority of them resettled from the interior—were employed in fishing. In addition to financing the new industries, the landlord built roads and inns, improved harbors and provided docking facilities, and initiated a packet service. The expense was enormous. One estimate placed the outlay between 1808 and 1833 at more than a million pounds, most of which was concentrated in the period 1809 to 1820.[33]

At the time, it was assumed that much of this investment would be returned; that having provided, in the words of his chief agent and planner, "the great sinews of improvement," the landlord could expect outside capital to flow into the region and complete its development. But such was not to be the history of the Sutherland estate. Improvement brought it within the larger market economy of Great Britain, and in the general decline in prices following the Napoleonic Wars the infant industries of towns like Brora and Helmsdale suffered severely. Nor did they ever fully recover, forced as they were to compete with producers better located to the south. Thrown back on local markets, the estate's fishermen and the merchants and entrepreneurs who had been attracted to the new villages made do as well as they could, or left. By 1821 Lord Stafford was calling for retrenchment. Yet despite the outcome, there is no gainsaying the sweep of the original vision, or the seriousness with which it was pursued, as the imposing freestone buildings—many displaying the Sutherland coat of arms—that survive along the coast bear witness.

When Lowell was in Scotland the Sutherland villages had barely been laid out. In any case it is unlikely that he would have seen them. Even after Scott's novels had made a Highland tour all but mandatory for visiting Americans, only the most intrepid ventured beyond Inverness to the wilder regions of the north. But there were other ways Lowell might have heard of the project. In August 1811, John Henderson, an agricultural reporter, produced a lengthy, favorable account of the scheme that was republished in book form the following year.[34]

At the same time the Countess of Sutherland was writing to Sir Walter Scott of her "great hopes . . . of considerable improvements being effected in Sutherland and without routing and destroying the old inhabitants, which contrary to the Theories respecting these matters, I am convinced is very possible."[35] And Scott was a leading figure in the circle of writers and intellectuals to which Lowell's friendship with Anne Grant and his brother's introductions had gained him access.

Still another connection involved James Loch, who in 1812 became superintendent of the Stafford-Sutherland properties. Serving in that capacity for forty-three years, Loch oversaw most of the family's Scottish improvements and was responsible for a good deal of the planning.[36] Labeled by one of his critics "the Sutherland Metternich," he was a Lowland Scot who had read law in both London and Edinburgh. He had also been a student at the university in Edinburgh between 1797 and 1801, a member of the Speculative Society, and part of the group that founded the *Review*. Given those associations he must have known Charles Lowell, who was on familiar terms with several members of the same group. Certainly the two men were in Edinburgh at the same time, and during those years Loch—in addition to his legal studies—was already trying his hand at estate management by superintending improvements for his uncle, William Adam.

While at the university, Loch studied Smithian political economy under Dugald Stewart, whom all of the Lowells, but particularly Francis, came to know and admire. In Loch's case the experience proved decisive. Throughout his life he remained wedded to free trade, but in other ways, his thinking was flexible and nondoctrinaire. Though he made a gospel of efficiency and was to the core of his being a liberal rationalist, he devoted most of his life and his very considerable talents, as a recent student has noted, to maintaining "the most traditional of Britain's institutions"—the power and prestige of the landed aristocracy.[37] His employers' decision to devote the bulk of their resources to land improvement schemes, when other forms of investment promised higher returns, Loch fully supported. He also believed it "fit and proper" that men like Lord Stafford should demand less than the full amount of rent they might receive and set rates accordingly. In explaining such policies he remarked: "The property of a great English Nobleman must be managed on the same principle as a little kingdom, not like the affairs of a little Merchant. The future and lasting interest and honour of the family as well as their immediate income must be kept in view—while a merchant thinks only of his daily profits and his own immediate life interest."[38]

IV

When Loch wrote these words Lowell had been back in America for four years and the factory at Waltham had been a going concern for two. In another year the directors of the Boston Company would vote to pay the corporation's first dividend. From being, in Loch's phrase, a "little merchant," Lowell had become the guiding spirit of the largest and quite possibly the most successful manufacturing concern in the United States. But while the magnitude of the enterprise alone might have made it tempting to search for similarities, seeing the Boston Company as a "little kingdom" in the sense that Loch used the term would have required considerable imagination. The company owned only a few acres, could claim nothing more in the way of a tenantry than several hundred mill girls, and, though its paid-in capital would shortly amount to $400,000—a very large sum for the time—the figure was still far less than the Marquis of Stafford's annual income.

If a parallel existed at all, it lay beyond the realm of concrete detail. Upon occasion Scottish aristocrats did support textile manufacturing on their estates, and several planned villages were created around such undertakings. At one point Lord Stafford's son participated, in a small way, in a cotton spinning venture—established at "Spinningdale" in Sutherland—but the mill proved unsuccessful and was never rebuilt after it burned in 1806, leaving a picturesque ruin with graceful Palladian windows.[39] Later, when Loch hoped to encourage linen weaving in the estate's coastal villages, nothing came of the plan. Other landowners, like Archibald Campbell of Jura, who put up part of the original capital for Robert Owen's New Lanark, had better luck with textiles. But the number who tried in the first place was not great, and those who did were unlikely to involve themselves in the operation of the enterprises they sponsored. Providing land and perhaps capital, they left to others the work of planning and management. Lowell proceeded quite differently.

Yet along with the obvious differences, a close examination might have revealed several surprising similarities between the Boston Company and the projects that Loch oversaw. Certainly there was about the company's design much of the same kind of careful selectivity, the precise adjustment of means to ends, and the restraint—shaped always by a broadly conceived sense of self-interest—that Loch tried to build into the Sutherland improvements. Some observers even went so far as to label the Waltham enterprise utopian, which it assuredly was not. But Lowell and his associates did seem willing to forego at least some of the financial return they might have had for the sake of other objectives. Later, all of this would become clearer, when the

Waltham group went on to expand operations—in a series of towns specifically designed for the purpose that in several respects bore a marked resemblance to the planned villages of Scotland. By then Lowell was dead, but the basic principles of the system remained his, as Nathan Appleton pointed out.[40]

Of course similarities do not prove influence, and Lowell said no more about Scottish Improvement in his letters home than he did about most other things he encountered abroad. As usual he kept his impressions to himself. Possibly he was afraid that his correspondence—if it said too much and fell into the wrong hands—might reveal the secret purpose behind his travels. Perhaps, too, like the conservative businessman he was, Lowell felt more comfortable letting his actions speak for him.

If so, the sequel would indeed suggest that he had been influenced by many of the values and ideas then transforming Scotland in the name of Improvement; that there if anywhere he found a model for a different kind of industrial development. Nor should this seem especially surprising. For while Lowell, good republican that he was, unquestionably would have balked at having his ambitions labeled aristocratic, he did share one pressing problem with Scotland's ruling class. At a certain point in his life he found himself at the top of a particular social order without a satisfactory means of maintaining his place there. Having passed through the tangled world of "daily profits," he needed some way of securing what Loch referred to as "the future and lasting interest and honour of the family." In that situation the new industrial technology offered a promising solution, but only if its grimmer consequences—so appallingly visible in England—could be eliminated. It was a question of controlling the process of change, of channeling its direction so that it did not simply sweep everything before it.

And nowhere else in Europe, during those years, could one have seen that done with better effect than in Scotland. In the long run the Scottish results were mixed: highly impressive at the outset, but much less so later on. It remained to be seen—as Lowell sailed for America on the eve of the War of 1812—whether he and his associates would fare any better.

2.

The Boston Company of Waltham

On October 20, 1813, those present at the first directors' meeting of the Boston Manufacturing Company voted to assess $100 on each of the company's 100 outstanding shares of stock. Twelve days later the "proprietors"—as the stockholders of the company were called—met and passed an identical resolution. Then, later the same day, the directors met again to annul their own earlier assessment, "the same having been this day voted by the proprietors at their meeting."[1]

If all this seemed to imply a certain tension between the proprietors and directors of the Boston Company, in fact no such tension existed. It was simply a question of the confusion always likely to plague a new and complicated undertaking. The company's bylaws stated that assessments were to be voted by the shareholders, at duly called meetings, and then implemented by the directors. The directors had merely jumped the gun a bit. It was a mistake they did not make again.

Nor, in the months that followed, would any similar misstep mar the Boston Company's progress. At carefully staged intervals its capital was paid in, up to the authorized limit of $400,000, and promptly paid out again to erect the handsome stone and brick buildings on the banks of the Charles River at Waltham and fill them with the wonderful new machinery Lowell had designed. Later Appleton would assert that from the first successful operation of the power loom in Lowell's Boston workshop in the autumn of 1814 there was never the slightest "hesitation or doubt about the success of this manufacture,"[2]—a judgment the company's own records amply support. No victorious army ever marched through conquered territory with greater precision or confidence.

II

Lowell had thought of everything. When adaptations in existing technology were required by his design for the power loom, he and Paul Moody, the brilliant mechanic he had hired and would later make a stockholder of the company, provided them. A new kind of dressing machine, the double speeder for making roving, a method of spinning filling directly onto bobbins, and finally the intricate adjustments necessary to suit each to the waterpower available at Waltham were the result.

As important as these developments were individually, their major significance lay in the ability that they—together with the power loom—gave Lowell to engineer a far more striking innovation. The formal "Articles of Agreement between the Associates of the Boston Manufacturing Company" signed on September 4, 1813, and later incorporated in the company's bylaws, cited weaving as the stockholders' "principal object of attention." The same document, however, also mentioned, as "connected with this," the spinning of cotton yarn.[3] At that point no manufacturing firm in the United States and few, if any, in England had gone as far as combining the entire process of mechanized cotton textile production—from the raw material, ginned and baled, to the finished cloth—in a single factory. Yet that was Lowell's goal and had been from the beginning. As early as their meetings in Edinburgh he had confided his plans to Appleton, who was soon writing on the subject of cotton manufacturing that "a large establishment with all the branches connected would be sure to do well."[4]

What Appleton did not add was that such an establishment was also likely to prove very expensive to create, but there too every possible contingency had been anticipated. On the basis of its authorized capital, the Boston Company was almost ten times larger than the average Rhode Island cotton mill would be a full two decades later. Actually only a portion of the $400,000—about a quarter, Lowell estimated—was required to build and equip the first mill. The rest would go toward providing a safe operating margin of liquid assets. It could also be used to finance expansion, if conditions warranted. Beginning in 1813 shares were offered for subscription three times— 100 on each of the first two occasions and 200 on the third. The price per share was $1,000, but subscriptions were collected in installments, most often of $100 each, as the money was needed. Altogether it took over five years to reach the $400,000 limit.

Building up the enterprise's capital in measured increments gave stockholders both an inducement and the opportunity to evaluate the progress of their investment closely. They were, to be sure, charged interest on the uncollected balance, but the arrangement still made sense. It constituted a kind of protection for everyone concerned, and considering the amount of money involved such safeguards were important. Still another safeguard—and one that in the long run would have an even greater impact—was the organizational form Lowell and his associates had chosen for their venture.

British textile firms and the smaller American concerns established up to then were, with few exceptions, organized as individual proprietorships or partnerships.[5] In their own commercial operations, merchants like Lowell and Appleton had found the same forms convenient enough, even when substantial sums of money were called for. In this case the capital in question was not only large, but would have to remain committed to the enterprise over a long period. This was so both because of the new and untried character of the undertaking and because of the nature of the investment itself. Commercial assets were divisible more easily and on far shorter notice than a fully equipped textile mill. At the same time investors needed assurance that they could liquidate their holdings if they wanted to.

Together all of these considerations argued for the wisdom of the joint-stock arrangement the organizers of the Boston Company had adopted. The men themselves could retire or die, shares could be sold or willed away, and the company's capital would remain intact. Not content with those guarantees, however, the group had taken the added precaution of applying to the state for a charter of incorporation. In 1813 some of the more attractive features of incorporation—including statutory sanction for limited liability—still lay in the future, but there were other benefits. An official act by the commonwealth would make the enterprise seem that much more secure. It also carried with it a special sense of quasi-public responsibility. Since then the corporate form has largely lost this connotation, but at a time when state governments could claim few resources to devote to larger social purposes, they often had little choice but to rely on private citizens in accomplishing a wide range of ends. Acting through incorporation, such citizens became, in effect, arms of the state in everything from building turnpikes to caring for orphans. Massachusetts had been particularly active in this regard, and the founders of the Boston Company were clearly both conscious of that tradition and eager to associate themselves with it.[6] Thus, in petitioning the General Court, they described at length the details of their project but spoke, too, of a desire to "secure the establishment of manufactures upon a more permanent foundation than has hitherto been found practicable in this commonwealth."[7] Anchored in such a context the Boston Company was not to be lightly abandoned.

Still, a charter of incorporation was only a piece of paper. And even the Boston Company's meticulously drawn articles of association offered Lowell no assurance that his experiment would be fairly tried unless the men who joined him as coinvestors were determined to see it through. Much would depend on who those men were, so Lowell had chosen them with great care. The list of subscribers to the Boston Company's first hundred shares contained the names of only a dozen individuals. Most were already men of substantial wealth, and every one was well known to Lowell through either family relationship or previous business connections. He himself was the second largest subscriber with fifteen shares. His brother-in-law, Patrick T. Jackson—whose tangled affairs had recently been set right—took twenty shares and became the company's largest single shareholder. Two of Jackson's brothers, James and Charles, were down for another fifteen shares between them, giving the family, together with Lowell, 50 percent of the outstanding stock. John Gore and Israel Thorndike Senior and Junior each subscribed to ten shares, and the remaining twenty were divided in smaller lots, with Uriah Cotting, Lowell's partner in India Wharf, taking five and Nathan Appleton the same number.[8]

No doubt Lowell could have found other investors if he had wished to, but the small size of the group promised to help ensure harmony—and commitment. The sums involved were not negligible, Appleton had been asked to subscribe to ten shares but declined, offering instead to put up half the amount requested and "make no complaint under these circumstances, if it proved a total loss."[9] This was venture capital in the purest sense. Yet for those who invested more the situation was different. Ten to fifteen thousand dollars was an amount of money no one would want to lose. If, too, the business gave signs of prospering, those amounts were likely to double and redouble on subsequent subscriptions to the point where they might come to represent a sizable portion of one's total wealth.

The determination to hold the number of investors to a minimum persisted, at least through the next two subscriptions, which raised the remainder of the Boston Company's authorized capital. In both instances the stockholders voted beforehand to limit the new shares each person could acquire to the number he already owned, thereby ensuring that no single holding would increase in size relative to the others. At the same time no lower limit was set, so some fresh capital could have come into the enterprise. In the event, almost everyone chose to take the full number of shares allowed, and as a result only one new member, Paul Moody, the company's chief mechanic, joined the group. In a forerunner of modern corporate stock-option plans,

Moody—having been put down for four shares on the second subscription and eleven on the third—was then permitted to postpone
payment, without interest, as long as he wished and in the meantime
have his dividends credited to the unpaid balance. Apart from the
provision for Moody, the only other changes involved the absence of
James Lloyd (who had been down for five shares initially) from the
second subscription list and of Lloyd, Uriah Cotting, and John Gore
from the third. Since Appleton had purchased Cotting's shares and
Lowell Gore's and both chose to increase their holdings proportionately on the third subscription, the net effect was to leave the Boston
Company—once its capital had been fully paid in—with one less
stockholder than at the outset, or a total of only eleven.[10]

By then the small group of proprietors had ample reason to be pleased
with their investment. Several had made substantial commitments
indeed—Lowell and Jackson $80,000 each and Charles Jackson and
the two Thorndikes $40,000—but in return they had been receiving
regular dividends from profits on cloth sales for two years. Meanwhile a second mill had been built, along with a superintendent's
house and a store, and the company had begun to sell machinery,
made in its own machine shop, to other textile manufacturers. Yet
before any of these developments could occur, it had been necessary
to solve three additional problems. A decision had to be made about
the kind of product the Boston Company would manufacture, a
means of marketing that product had to be found, and finally some
system of labor had to be established.

Of the three problems, the question of the product had proved the
simplest to resolve. Without elaborate technological modifications—
including the addition of a printing process—Lowell's system was
not capable of producing what housewives and storekeepers alike
referred to as "fancy goods." Nor was the American demand for fancy
goods as large as it was for coarser, cheaper grades of cloth. For more
than a decade the market for cheap cloth had been supplied from
abroad, principally with Indian cotton textiles; in fact, that trade had
netted any number of Boston merchants substantial profits. But if
Indian goods were both inexpensive and profitable for those who
imported them, they also tended to be flimsy and uneven in quality,
which gave Lowell his opening. A type of cloth that was durable and
consistent, yet still relatively low in price, stood a good chance of
selling well. The result, which thereafter bore Lowell's name, was
described by Nathan Appleton in 1858 as "precisely the article of which
a large portion of the manufacture of the country has continued to

consist; a heavy sheeting of No. 14 yarn, 37 inches wide, 44 picks to the inch, and weighing something less than three yards to the pound."[11]

Entering an established market with a superior product had obvious advantages, but capitalizing on those advantages still presented problems, at least initially. With the first power loom in operation, Lowell had the goods delivered to a shop in Boston, only to discover that they languished there unsold. At that point Nathan Appleton offered to have B. C. Ward and Company—the commercial firm in which most of his own assets were invested—try to effect a sale. The outcome was a transaction in which B. C. Ward sold the goods to an auctioneer, who in turn auctioned them off "at something over thirty cents" a yard. Charging a 1 percent commission on the sale, Appleton's firm thereafter became the sole selling agent for the Boston Company.[12] Under the terms of the agreement the manufacturer retained ownership of the goods up to the point of sale and the 1 percent commission was fixed as a standard rate. Relieving the company's management of the burden of having to deal with a host of separate agents and jobbers, this procedure was both more efficient and freer from risk than other methods would have been. It also netted substantial profits for B. C. Ward, for though the commission rate was low, as the output of the mills at Waltham rose, a fraction of a cent a yard multiplied hundreds of thousands of times over became a very respectable sum.

Afterward Appleton was inclined to congratulate himself for devising such "a desirable and profitable business."[13] No doubt his pride was justified, but the result also owed something to happenstance and in that respect was uncharacteristic of the Boston Company's founding. Elsewhere careful planning made the difference, and certainly nowhere more so than in the area that had, from the beginning, represented the greatest challenge facing Lowell and his associates: the company's labor system.

As disturbed as both Lowell and Appleton had been by the plight of English factory labor, it was only to be expected that everything about the work force at Waltham should have been, as Appleton put it, "deeply considered." What caused the "degradation" so readily apparent in factories abroad? Was it "the result of the peculiar occupation"—working in close quarters at routine tasks—or were "other and distant causes" involved?[14] In England millowners employed large numbers of young children, all too often recruited from poorhouses. Since this work force was already pauperized and paid barely enough to survive, it was difficult to tell what part of the sorry result was attributable to the work itself.

Neither was the evidence provided to date by the American experience with manufacturing particularly conclusive. The smaller yarn mills in southern New England drew their unskilled workers primarily from local farm families no longer able to support themselves on marginal land and unwilling or unable to move on to newer areas opening up in the West. People of all ages worked in the mills, but millowners preferred families with at least four or five children. Though wages were higher than in England, even large families—paid as they generally were in credit at company stores—found it difficult to maintain positive balances for any length of time.[15] Again the results were discouraging. While not in a strict sense paupers, and certainly unlike the frightening denizens of Manchester, such workers still impressed contemporary observers as "often very ignorant and too often vicious."[16]

Thus far, then, the record was bleak, but in both England and America industrialization had brought into the factories the most vulnerable members of the community. Who could tell what might happen if sturdier material were chosen? On the other hand, implementing such a proposition posed grave difficulties, the first and most daunting of which was that labor of all kinds commanded a premium in the United States. Even in New England, with the traditional agricultural sector of the economy showing signs of strain, existing mills employed impoverished farmers and their children because other workers had no need to accept the modest wages millowners offered. There were too many better-paying jobs, too many other opportunities—in the South or West, if not at home—that offered brighter prospects. If the founders of the Boston Company wanted to attract a different type of labor, they would have to pay more for it. Nor would the added cost be a matter of higher wages alone. Workers drawn to factories by something other than grim necessity were likely to be less docile than the average industrial "operative." In time, of course, that spirit could be bent, but not without costs of another sort. Sullen, dispirited workers were sure to be inefficient and might fall prey to dangerously radical ideas.

At every turn, in short, a careful balance had to be struck. Higher wages would have to be paid, but not so high as to weaken the financial soundness of the enterprise. Control would have to remain in the hands of management, but that control would have to stop short of becoming in fact, or appearance, too oppressive. Workers would have to submit to the routine of factory organization, without exploiting the uses of organization to further their own, as opposed to their employers', interests. In a sense it was a discrete version of the larger problem industrialization posed—at least for someone in

Lowell's position: how did one combine the benefits of the process with a wholesale blunting of its more ominous tendencies? In fact the solution Lowell arrived at did just that, as thoroughly as anything could have.

Paying its skilled male laborers well above the going rate, the Boston Company employed as the bulk of its unskilled work force young, unmarried women. Since many more were needed than the area around Waltham could supply, they were recruited throughout New England, and once hired they lived in company-owned boardinghouses. The boardinghouses were operated by matrons who leased the premises from the company and charged a fixed amount for room and board. After the charges were deducted, the girls received the rest of their pay in cash, usually twice a month. Though most wages were calculated on a piecework basis and varied from job to job, they tended to be significantly higher than in other textile mills. Meanwhile, in addition to paying and housing the girls, the company assumed, with a good deal of fanfare, responsibility for their moral well-being. Standards of decorum in behavior and dress were enforced, and weekly church attendance was required.

Thus provided for, Appleton noted, "the daughters of respectable farmers were readily induced to come into these mills for a temporary period."[17] They came in numbers so large, indeed, that the Boston Company maintained a waiting list. Many things brought them. Working at Waltham offered a release from the tedium and isolation of rural life. It promised a certain measure of freedom from parental and community supervision. But by all accounts the major attraction was the chance to earn wages paid in cash. Cash wages were still relatively rare in America, and for women, unlike their male counterparts, employment opportunities of any sort were limited. Domestic service—ill-paying and low in status—was one possibility, teaching another. The pay was better in teaching, but positions seldom lasted longer than a few months, leaving the hapless incumbents to fend for themselves during the rest of the year. A good many women also earned a bit of extra money at home spinning, or weaving, or making braid for straw hats, yet none of these paid a living wage.

Nor was mere self-support—even if it had been possible in such cases—the goal of most of the workers at Waltham. As daughters of "respectable" farmers, few would have gone without the necessities of life had they remained at home. Rather their hope was to save at least a portion of their wages, and many did so. The money was used for a variety of purposes; as a dowry, or a way of paying for a few terms at normal school, or sometimes for financing a brother's college education. Even allowing for boardinghouse costs and other expenses, a careful girl could "set by" half her pay and in a few years have earned the amount she needed. This, in turn, gave working at Waltham a characteristic at least as important as its respectability: it was, as Appleton observed, a "temporary" kind of employment.[18]

The hours in the mill were long—at least twelve a day, six days a week—and the conditions, by modern standards, were poor. Summoned at dawn by the relentless bell, the girls worked all day breathing stale, lint-filled air and surrounded by clanging machinery, in long low-ceilinged rooms. For the most part the tasks were not physically difficult, but breaks were few and rigidly supervised. The records show that all this proved too much for some workers. Yet at the first sign of strain they were free to return home, just as the company was free to dismiss anyone who chose to make an issue out of some part of the arrangement. Those who left, or were let go, would lose the opportunity to earn money for whatever purpose had brought them to Waltham in the first place, but that was all. Meanwhile, those who stayed could look forward to their own departure, a year or two hence, with a tidy accumulation of savings.

The plain fact was that such a work force had few if any of the makings of a depressed, angry industrial proletariat. If the girls were exploited—and in the ordinary sense, surely they were—that exploitation never threatened to become a permanent feature of their lives. Hence the attitude or, as Lowell and his associates would have said, the "character" that such exploitation produced had little chance to develop. And without that attitude, the responses it engendered—everything from the "dull dejection" observers noted in the faces of workers at places like Pawtucket to the more fully articulated forms of labor unrest—seemed unlikely to materialize. It was, in sum, a system that promised owners and managers the maximum degree of security and control and society at large a minimum amount of disruption.

Yet from a financial standpoint none of it came cheaply. Indeed, the willingness of the Boston Company's founders to bear the considerable costs involved was itself testimony to just how seriously they took the threat they saw implicit in industrialization and how anxious they were to neutralize it. Higher wages alone would doubtless have brought Waltham a "better class" of family labor than existing textile mills attracted. Payroll costs might have been greater in that case, but there would have been substantial savings in other respects. The owners, for example, would have been spared the expense of having to provide moral supervision for such workers, to say nothing of housing them. Or if housing had been provided, more could have been charged for it. As it was the company's investment in boardinghouses generated a return below the current rate of bank interest, which meant—as businessmen at the time calculated such things— that it was unprofitable. A more permanent labor force, too, would have netted significant savings in training costs.

Accounting systems were much less sophisticated in 1814 than they are today. Nevertheless potential savings of this magnitude could not have escaped the notice of Lowell and his associates. Engaged in an enterprise they knew would compound dividends only out of minuscule sums multiplied time and again in the continuing operation of the business, they constantly had to make choices, each of which had a price that up to a point could be determined readily enough. In this case the choice was to pay a premium in the short run for an arrangement that promised certain obvious long-range benefits.

It was even possible to see those benefits stretching beyond security and control and the promise of harmony between labor and management. The jobs created at Waltham would put money in the hands of people who previously had had none. Not only was this desirable in a general sense, but the specific ways the mill girls were likely to spend their savings also had advantages. The westward spread of settlement had left New England's farmers at a disadvantage. Would this not be a way of directing resources back to the region's family farms, of shoring up its traditional economy at a vulnerable point? Granted, the wages of a few hundred mill girls could not, alone, rescue New England's agriculture; at least the money would not be spent, as Americans like Lowell feared it often was in Europe, enriching grogshop owners or spawning a steadily growing horde of pauper children.

Precisely how far in this direction the thinking of Lowell and his associates extended is difficult to tell. Perhaps for the moment it was enough that they had found "a fund of labor, well educated and virtuous."[19] In later years, however, they did discuss the merits of the system in terms like these. Four decades after the founding of the Boston Company a mill agent at Lowell could still greet with hearty scorn the assertion by a Fall River agent that he saw his own workers as "part of my machinery . . . What they do or how they fare outside my walls I don't know, nor do I consider it my business to know."[20] Managers at Waltham were obliged both to know and to care. It would be a mistake to think they did so out of charity. Their concern was not philanthropic; they were manufacturing cotton cloth that they expected to sell for more than it cost to produce, which meant keeping labor costs in line with other expenses. But the line could be drawn in more than one way. It did not have to become a simple matter of maximizing dollar profits at every turn, as the founders of the Boston Company demonstrated when they created a labor system that no simple business calculation could have explained. And if, in the bargain, they sought to return to the hillside farms of New England something in exchange for what they took, it would not have been inconsistent with the rest of their vision or with the hopes and anxieties that shaped it.

III

With all the necessary factors of production in place, the enterprise at Waltham forged ahead. In January 1816 Nathan Appleton wrote his brother describing the Boston Company's second subscription for shares and noting, with obvious pleasure, "*no* new subscribers have an opportunity of coming in."[21] Doubtless Samuel Appleton concluded— as he was meant to, in the spirit of friendly rivalry between the brothers—that the business was thriving. Later the same year Lowell and Appleton traveled to Rhode Island to survey the textile industry there, only to find that "all was dead and still."[22] Peace with England had deluged the American market with quantities of cheap British cotton goods, forcing domestic manufacturers to cut production or close down altogether. In response they demanded that Congress enact drastically higher tariffs at once. But Lowell, in Washington for the debate and aware of how well the Boston Company was doing, argued successfully for a more moderate rate—though one, to be sure, that still excluded Indian cotton goods from the United States.[23]

Lowell's role in shaping the tariff of 1816 was to be the last of his many services to the Boston Company. Having never really recovered his health, he died late the following year. The evidence suggests that at the time he was concentrating on developing the market for power looms.[24] If so, the result would have disappointed him, for though the Boston Company did make a lucrative sideline of selling textile machinery, the technology proved too valuable—indeed was too essential to the survival of the American textile industry—to remain the exclusive property of one company for long. While Lowell was touring Rhode Island, at least three millowners there were at work on their own designs for the power loom.[25]

Thus the major activity of the Boston Company—and the chief source of its profits—continued to be the manufacture of cotton cloth. Lowell's stock passed to his heirs. The management of the mills at Waltham had already been placed in the capable hands of Patrick Jackson, who was by then receiving an annual salary of $3,000, having agreed—in deference, no doubt, to Lowell's fears about his brother-in-law's recklessness—to "enter into no commercial speculation, or other business, that may take from the just and necessary attention to the duties of his office."[26] A few months after Lowell died the directors voted to raise Jackson's salary to $5,000.[27] Meanwhile Lowell's own place in the company went unfilled. In truth, none of the other principals could have done all that he had. But it was possible to parcel out his responsibilities, and increasingly Nathan Appleton came to play a dominant role in long-range planning.

Together Jackson and Appleton were an effective team. The same driving energy that had earlier led Jackson into business ventures of dubious soundness made him invaluable as field commander of the company's operations. His skill at supervising construction and managing labor was unsurpassed. He also had a talent for tapping available sources of credit in Boston and so was given the task of raising the short-term loans the company occasionally required, though always with the specific approval of the directors.[28] Appleton, by contrast, was inclined to move cautiously and deliberately. Born into a respectable New Ipswich, New Hampshire, family of only modest wealth, he had entered commerce in Boston with fewer advantages than either Lowell or Jackson. Working closely with his brothers, he had nevertheless managed to develop a very profitable business and was already, at the age of thirty-two, considering "what course to take to avoid the necessity for laborious personal attention to business for which I am becoming intolerant"[29] when Lowell approached him about cotton manufacturing. His initial investment was small—only a fraction of his total wealth—but from the beginning he had taken a keen interest in the Boston Company and by 1817 was ready to devote a major portion of his attention to it, a circumstance for which his fellow stockholders had cause to be grateful. Less of an innovator than Lowell, Appleton traveled most comfortably along roads others had pioneered. Yet few Americans had a surer grasp of the basic business conditions of the time or knew better how to weigh conflicting risks and opportunities.[30]

During the next few years those abilities manifested themselves decisively at Waltham. Between 1817 and 1820 the postwar economic crisis in the country at large deepened steadily as the inflationary boom that had begun in 1815 first accelerated and then collapsed. In the midst of the boom, with costs of all kinds rising, most New England textile manufacturers consistently failed to undersell English cottons. When the crash came, even stronger firms found themselves pushed to the wall. Little aided by the nation's prostrate banking system, they made do as best they could, scrambling to meet obligations with promises to pay later and dumping quantities of finished goods on the market for whatever they would bring. Yet from it all the Boston Company—protected by its comfortable margin of uncommitted capital—emerged unscathed. In the depths of the crisis the company did resort to borrowing more often than usual, but arrangements were also being made to expand the enterprise, proof enough of the stockholders' confidence in its fundamental soundness.

Planning for expansion during a depression that nearly ruined one's competitors had Appleton's stamp on it. So too did the decision to wait to begin until the storm had passed. Even more characteristic was the careful dovetailing of the new arrangements with all the built-in sources of security that had served the Boston Company so well up to then. Early in 1820, just as the economy began to right itself, the stockholders petitioned the legislature to authorize an increase in the company's capital from $400,000 to $600,000. With rising profits to pay off any added debt, borrowing might have served as well to finance the expansion, but that would have added to the company's fixed obligations, whereas relying on equity capital let individual stockholders continue to bear the risk. To avoid penalizing the original owners, whose stock had appreciated significantly in value, 50 of the 200 new shares were given outright to them. The remaining 150 shares were then sold "at a fifteen percent advance," with the $150-a-share premium also going to the original stockholders.[31] In effect this levied a rather stiff tax on those purchasing the new stock, but there was no apparent shortage of subscribers. Seven were new to the Boston Company, forming a group in which Christopher Gore, who took forty shares, was the largest subscriber. Of the original stockholders, the two Thorndikes together were down for thirty-five shares, and Appleton himself took another fourteen.[32]

The new mill—the third at Waltham—built with the capital thus raised substantially increased capacity. By the time construction began, the company was producing more than half a million yards of cloth a year. In 1820 sales reached $260,658. At the same time dividends were rising. Between 1817 and 1821 they averaged 19.25 percent a year, and in 1822, with the new mill in operation, they came to fully 27.5 percent.[33] Meanwhile the demand for "Lowell sheeting" continued to grow as fast as the supply, despite the fact that new companies were entering the field every year.

All of this ought to have suggested the wisdom of expanding the Boston Company's operations even further. And indeed it did, but the addition of the third mill had exhausted the potential of the water-power at Waltham. Consequently a new site had to be found, and the need to take that step raised any number of questions. How much of an expansion could the market sustain? How was the new venture to be financed and organized? What would its relation to the existing company be? Also, as tempting as it might have been to suppose that the Waltham system could be duplicated quickly—and perhaps even at less cost—somewhere else, Appleton had good reason to think otherwise. To his certain knowledge it had been tried before, with dismal results.

In 1803 Appleton had married Maria Theresa Gold, the daughter of Thomas Gold, a wealthy resident of Pittsfield, Massachusetts. At the time the trip between Boston and Pittsfield took several days, but the two families kept in close touch. In 1818, when the Agricultural Bank of Pittsfield was organized, Nathan Appleton and his cousin William put up a sizable portion of the capital and Gold became the bank's first president.[34] Gold also knew, of course, of his son-in-law's association with the Boston Company and evidently had thought enough of its prospects to become involved in a similar venture himself. Incorporated in 1814, the Pittsfield Woolen and Cotton Factory was financed on a joint-stock basis with shares having a par value of $1,000 each. Its $130,000 authorized capitalization made it smaller than the Boston Company, but it dwarfed, by comparison, all other manufacturing concerns in Berkshire County or anywhere else in western Massachusetts. In short order an impressive brick mill was built and filled with spinning machinery, and the business got under way. At first it was operated as only a yarn mill, but its founders no doubt expected in time—through Gold's connection with Appleton—to adopt the power loom.[35]

Then, in the aftermath of the War of 1812, the Pittsfield company fared no better than most other American textile firms. By the middle of 1817 matters had so far deteriorated that the directors levied a 5 percent assessment on each share of stock to pay the company's outstanding debts, but even that failed to save the business, at least organized as it was. Later the same year the directors voted to lease the mill to Lemuel Pomeroy, one of their number and the sole member of the group with any prior experience in manufacturing. Subsequently Pomeroy bought out his fellow shareholders and did manage to make a success of the business.[36] Yet his gain was their loss, and a considerable one. Any hopes they had of matching the kind of return, or the security, that stock in the Boston Company brought its owners had come to nothing.

There were several obvious lessons to be learned from the history of the Pittsfield Woolen and Cotton Factory. Here was telling proof—if any was required—of just how essential the power loom and integrated production had been to the Boston Company's success. The entire sequence also strongly emphasized the importance of the com-

pany's continuing ability to attract the very substantial sums that
went into creating the enterprise at Waltham. Large as the Pittsfield
Company's capital had been, it proved inadequate. And when more
was needed, the owners had balked, apparently preferring to lose
money rather than accept any additional risk.

Still another problem was management. Of the Pittsfield group,
only Pomeroy involved himself to any great extent in the daily conduct of the business. The other incorporators—prosperous landhold-
ers, merchants, bankers, and professional men—chose not to. In that
respect, of course, they were like most of the large investors in the
Boston Company, who left to Lowell, Moody, and Jackson the burden
of building and running the mills at Waltham. But such an arrangement was costly. Not only was Jackson's salary quite high, but the
company provided him with a house. Moody also had to be paid, and
on top of his salary there was the cost of his stock, most of which the
company bore.

So it came down to money again. Competent, paid management
was expensive, and paying the added costs—especially after the flush
of wartime prosperity in the textile industry had ended—meant making a greater financial commitment with a diminishing hope of profit.
Always, too, the return had to be weighed against the rewards generated by the region's traditional investment opportunities. With Berkshire County still expanding, albeit more slowly than in the past,
agriculture, commerce, and professional activities continued to produce profits, particularly if one had already accumulated significant
wealth. And the thirteen men who, with Thomas Gold, backed the
Pittsfield Woolen and Cotton Factory were among the richest in the
county. For those who wanted more money, there were surer ways of
making it. For those content with what they had, the size of the
commitment required by manufacturing, whether of capital or personal participation, evidently proved too great. Perhaps if their fortunes had been larger—or smaller—they might have been willing to
hazard more, as Pomeroy alone chose to.

Certainly the sequel demonstrated that Pomeroy was right. In time
Berkshire County did develop as an industrial center, and some people grew rich as a result. A list of the county's wealthier manufacturers drawn up a half a century later, too, would have included only a
handful who had any connection with the elite of 1815. Meanwhile
the descendants of men like Gold, or those who still lived in the
county, were not often poor, yet neither were they to be found—as
their fathers and grandfathers had been—at the top of Berkshire's
economic and social order.[37]

But in 1821 it would have been enough for Appleton to note that the Pittsfield Woolen and Cotton Factory had floundered for want of sufficient capital. Large amounts of money were essential. As for why more money had not been forthcoming in Pittsfield, the evidence indicated that much depended on the personal characteristics of the men in question: who they were, what their experience had been, and what conclusions they drew from it. Such factors were also likely to prove vital in any attempt to duplicate the enterprise at Waltham.

Weighing them, Appleton could take comfort in the fact that his own wealth—and the wealth of most of the other Boston Company stockholders—was such that efforts so far had only partially tapped the most obvious source of additional capital. The same men could afford to finance at least part of the expansion. Another hopeful sign was the ease with which the Boston Company's capital had been enlarged to $600,000. At the time seven new individuals had joined the group, and a list of stockholders dated April 1821 included the names of seven more, for a total of fourteen. Yet fully half of the fourteen were related to one or more of the original stockholders, so the circle had expanded less than the numbers implied.[38] In fact the indications are that purchasing Boston Company stock had early assumed the character of being let in on a good thing. But whether the same would be true of an entirely new venture remained to be seen, because there were also compelling reasons why the sort of investor Appleton needed might have preferred to stand aloof from any further development of the textile industry.

The capital that created the Boston Company had been accumulated in foreign commerce, and since all but a few of Boston's larger private fortunes had similar origins, commercial wealth remained the logical place to turn for fresh capital for the textile industry. Yet most of the city's merchants tended to oppose all domestic manufacturing schemes. By reducing foreign imports, domestic manufactures cut into the volume and hence the profits of trade. The success of the Boston Company in the market once largely supplied by Indian cottons was a case in point. In addition, manufacturers favored the tariff, which further hampered trade. In 1820 the issue was joined head-on. In a *Report of the Committee of Merchants and Others, of Boston; on the Tariff*, leading members of the commercial community detailed their grievances at length. Not only was the system of protective tariffs unfair, they argued, but the factories supported thereby damaged the nation by raising prices and by employing less labor and capital than they displaced in foreign trade.[39]

When the *Report* appeared many merchants were suffering from the effects of the crash and its aftermath. Part of their anger resulted from the fact that commerce revived more slowly than manufacturing. Two years later, with credit available and cargoes circulating again, tensions were less acute. Still, the tariff continued to divide men long accustomed to agreeing about most things, and however often Appleton and his associates pointed out that they had asked for only a moderate rate, their allegiance was clear: they had joined the ranks of the manufacturers.

In such a situation, offering the opposition a chance to purchase shares in the Boston Company or some similar venture might have been a promising tactic. Stock paying as high as 25 percent a year in dividends was no mean olive branch. Of course it was impossible to guarantee future profits. And even if it could have been done, there remained, in addition to the tariff, all those long-standing fears about the broader social effects of industrialization—fears that Appleton himself understood only too well. Some changes had occurred. As early as 1816 Jefferson had written Benjamin Austin of Boston, "Experience has taught me that manufactures are now as necessary to our independence as to our comfort."[40] In 1821 a congressional committee pushed the argument even farther, declaring: "That manufactures tend to destroy the morals of those engaged in them is an objection which, it is believed, has not arisen from the experience of their effects among us."[41] Yet the very fact that the committee took pains to so record itself indicated that many people still thought factory production threatened the peace and moral fiber of society. Ultimately, too, reaching the men Appleton had to persuade would require more than politicians' rhetoric. Tough-minded businessmen, they based decisions on what they could see and know from firsthand experience. What kind of a case could be made in those terms?

The answer was, a remarkably strong one. In less than a decade the Boston Company had hardly produced enough evidence to dispel all anxieties about the social consequences of industrialization, but a labor force of clear-eyed young women, working temporarily to earn money for useful purposes, leading regular, well-supervised lives constituted an affront—or a threat—to no one. Even the solidly built mills at Waltham, surrounded by neat boardinghouses and presided over by the handsome mansion of the superintendent and the church the directors had voted to build in 1820, were reassuring. Here was no grim, despoiled landscape, no "foul sink of corruption," of the sort found abroad. On the contrary, visitors were already remarking that what they saw of the novel experiment had much the air of a prosperous rural college or academy. And if that seemed improbable, there was the traditional New England town as a model—the village setting, with its time-honored ways of making physically manifest the religious, social, and economic order that governed all men. In Scotland improving landlords had been forced to rely on English precedents in creating such an environment. In Massachusetts the basic materials came more readily to hand. Firmly rooted in the past, they were part of the heritage of everyone involved, from Lowell and Appleton to each newly arrived loom operator. With so many familiar components, it would have been surprising if the result had not been calming.

Sketched in these terms, indeed, the enterprise at Waltham was likely to strike even the most conservative potential investors as appealing. And there was another point to consider as well. Given the steady expansion of the American market the factory system was bound to spread. Surely, therefore, it was important to have the right people overseeing that growth. Though the prevailing democratic ethos afforded little enough protection against those jealous souls who—in their headlong rush at the future—seemed interested only in catapulting themselves into the seats of power, it was at least possible to stake a claim to the future before they arrived in force. For the moment the advantage lay with those who already had money and power: only the rich could command the capital necessary to build mills as large and well-equipped as those at Waltham. Yet that could change. How much wiser to move before it did.

Turning the expansion of the Waltham system from a threat to Boston's commercial elite into a means of defending it against the dangers of change was a kind of alchemy not easily accomplished. But the magic, if such it was, lay in the system that Lowell had designed. While apparently exacting few if any of the usual social costs, and still handsomely rewarding its owners, it succeeded in being the most thoroughly modern engine of industrial production in America. That ought to have been evidence enough to convince any skeptic. And if it was not, one could always add the striking fact that, for all the benefits—tangible and otherwise—that they received, only three or four of those owners had to bother with the business at all. Beyond attending an occasional directors' meeting, they were free to spend their time in other ways.

No doubt even with so many splendid inducements there would still be holdouts: men who refused to join Appleton and his associates because of the tariff, or simply out of a settled opposition to change.

Nevertheless by the beginning of 1822 Appleton himself was sufficiently confident about the outcome to have begun planning in earnest
for a major expansion of the Waltham system. The full measure of
what would be accomplished over the next quarter century he probably did not foresee, but then neither could he have predicted all that
had followed from his conversations with Lowell in Edinburgh, just
ten years before.

3.

Expansion

In 1842 Charles Dickens visited the United States. During the weeks he spent traveling from Boston to Virginia and then westward to St. Louis he found much that annoyed and discomforted him. The climate, the rude, improvised character of most American cities, the smug self-satisfaction of many of the people he met, their fondness for chewing tobacco, and the deplorable consequences of their poor aim while indulging in the habit were all described at length in his *American Notes*. It was not a flattering portrait. Yet there were some things Dickens did admire, and he was generous in his praise of those. One was the town of Lowell.

Originally part of East Chelmsford, Lowell had grown up along the Merrimack River around the point chosen by Nathan Appleton and Patrick Jackson in 1821 as the site of their next major venture in textile manufacturing. Noting that the town was "only just of age," having reached "barely one-and-twenty years," Dickens found it already "a large, populous and thriving place." Its youth, to be sure, made for a certain amount of "quaintness"—a newly built church, for example, lacking both paint and a steeple, so it looked "like an enormous packing-case, without any direction upon it." Yet somehow the vigor everywhere apparent at Lowell made such oddities seem less jarring. "The very river that moves the machinery in the mills (for they are all worked by water power), seems to acquire a new character from the fresh buildings of bright red brick and painted wood among which it takes its course."[1]

But what most impressed Dickens were the workers in the mills. Seeing them first just as they were going to their noontime meal, he discovered scores upon scores of healthy, clean, well-dressed young women. Later he could not remember "or separate one young face that gave me a painful impression; not one young girl whom . . . I would have removed from those works if I had had the power." And if that fact seemed calculated to surprise his readers, he added others even more startling. Many of the boardinghouses where the workers lived boasted joint-stock pianos, and, when not busy playing, the girls read—"nearly all . . . subscribe to circulating libraries"—or wrote for *The Lowell Offering*, a magazine they themselves published, which Dickens thought would "compare advantageously with a great many English annuals." Meanwhile, 978 of the girls had accumulated deposits in the Lowell Savings Bank estimated at $100,000.[2]

Surely nothing could have been more commendable, but there was also just the barest hint that Dickens remained skeptical. Through much of his account he refrained from obvious contrasts between Lowell and Britain's industrial centers—"those great haunts of desperate misery"—yet toward the end he did touch on the difference, describing it as nothing less than one "between the Good and Evil, the living light and deepest shadow." Then, after a brief plea for reform at home, he concluded the chapter with a paragraph on his train trip back to Boston. While his usual style was anything but symbolistic, it is tempting to speculate about the possible meaning of the final image he left his readers. Pretending to sleep in order to escape his companion's discussion of "the true principles on which books of travel in America should be written by Englishmen," he spent the time studying "from the corners of my eyes" the effects of the engine's wood fire, "Invisible in the morning" these were "now brought out in full relief by the darkness: for we were traveling in a whirlwind of bright sparks, which showered about us like a storm of fiery snow."[3] It was almost as if Dickens were suggesting that, having seen and admired what he had been taken to Lowell to see and admire, he still sensed behind all the rushing, purposeful energy of the place some uncontrollable, even destructive potential that time alone would reveal. But if that was true, as a visitor it would have been rude to say so, especially without a shred of evidence to offer.

Something of the same ambiguity would characterize another, if less notable, description of Lowell during those years. Lucy Larcom missed seeing "Boz" when he came, but she was one of several girls working in the mills whose efforts for *The Offering* marked the start of a serious literary career. After her years at Lowell she moved west, studied to be a teacher, taught for awhile, and then returned to Massachusetts to write poetry. *A New England Girlhood*, written in her old age, contained several chapters on life in the mills. Most of her memories were happy ones. In fact, having left Lowell temporarily to care for a sick sister, she described herself as only too eager to go back.

"I did not like to feel the horizons shutting me in. I must be where my life could expand."[4] Yet running through the account was another strain. Had she been too independent, shown too little regard for essential human obligations? In her preface she implied as much, saying that in retrospect she found the young girl she had been "undisciplined" and given to "cowardly shrinking from responsibility."[5]

Irresponsibility and lack of discipline were not encouraged at Lowell, but sometimes they reared their heads, wanted or not. Working in the mills was a liberating experience for Larcom. She regularly chose undemanding jobs, at lower pay, which left her free to read and think. In her move west she went unaccompanied by any homesteading husband, and afterward she pursued her literary career with singular determination. Yet if all this seemed to her credit, her employers at Lowell might not have found it so and even she had misgivings. The new industrial paternalism was apparently no substitute for the old. Significantly Larcom's fondest recollections were neither of Lowell nor of her later achievements, but of Beverly, her birthplace, a town which, she noted, "we children felt as if we belonged to . . . as we did to our father or our mother."[6]

II

According to the census taken in 1840, two years before Dickens' visit, Lowell already had a population of 20,000, making it the second largest city in Massachusetts.[7] By then nine separate textile manufacturing firms were located there with a combined capital of more than $8 million, a figure that would grow over the next decade to $12 million. In 1837 eight of those firms had employed some 6,000 women and 1,800 men to produce cloth at a rate just short of a million yards per week.[8] Yet the same place in 1821, the year the site was selected, had contained only a dozen houses—a dozen houses and the Merrimack River, which at that point fell a full thirty feet.

The process by which, in the intervening years, that impressive source of waterpower had been developed, first by a single company and then made available to others as they came along, was an orderly one, running through several stages, each carefully planned. It was also, at least as far as the planners were concerned, a process singularly free of whatever doubts people like Dickens and Larcom may have felt later about the result.

In many respects the pattern had been set at Waltham. With the site chosen, a small group, all stockholders of the Boston Company, began to buy up land. In order to secure waterpower rights it was also

necessary to acquire a majority interest in the nearly defunct Pawtucket Canal. Couched in secrecy to prevent any sudden rise in the
price of either the land or the canal shares, the necessary steps had all
been taken by the beginning of 1822. Meanwhile articles of association
were drawn up, calling for the creation of a corporation, to be chartered by the state, named the Merrimack Manufacturing Company.
Authorized capital was set at $600,000, with shares costing $1,000
apiece. The articles of association listed only five stockholders, but a
week later nine more joined the group, including seven men whose
names had not previously appeared on the Boston Company's lists.
Among them were William and Eben Appleton, who together took
forty shares, and Daniel Webster, who took four. Shortly afterward
the group was further enlarged when—as the result of a complex
series of stock transfers and cash payments to compensate them for
agreeing to share their patents and the services of Paul Moody—the
stockholders of the Boston Company were granted the right to purchase shares in the new venture. In all, twenty-seven chose to do so,
giving the Merrimack Company a list of subscribers three times as
long as the one the Boston Company had started with.[9]

Thus launched, the Merrimack Company began an extensive building program that saw the Pawtucket Canal widened and deepened at
a cost of $120,000, and a large textile mill erected, as well as a separate
machine shop and housing for the workers. The company also built a
number of roads and allocated $9,000 for an Episcopal church. The
unlikely choice of Episcopalianism was made by Kirk Boott, one of
the principal stockholders and the person who would play at Lowell the role Jackson had at Waltham. An Episcopalian himself, Boott
was "desirous of trying the experiment whether that service could be
sustained." In due course St. Anne's Church, an imposing stone
building done in Gothic style, was dedicated by Bishop Griswold.[10]
But some people apparently felt obliged to cover the company's bets,
for as Appleton noted, "Liberal grants of land were made for other
places of worship, and subscriptions freely made by the stockholders
for different religious societies."[11]

The wheel of the Merrimack Company's first cotton mill began to
turn in September 1823. Two years later the company paid its first
dividend. In the meantime its authorized capital had been increased
to $1,200,000, with the additional money used to build three more
mills. A separate corporation had also been set up to own and manage the machine shop and the land and waterpower not needed
by the parent company.[12]

The establishment of the so-called Locks and Canals Company as
an independent concern in 1824 marked the start of the second stage

of development at Lowell. It grew from the conviction, expressed by Appleton in 1821, that despite the very substantial sums of money already invested in textile manufacturing, it could still absorb more. "It is true a good deal of capital is going into this business, but so wide is the field before us that I think it will not soon be overdone."[13] Proof of the accuracy of that prediction was not long in coming.

The year after the Locks and Canals Company was formed, it transferred a portion of the land and waterpower rights at its disposal to the Hamilton Manufacturing Company, a new firm organized to manufacture cotton textiles. Three years later, in 1828, similar arrangements were made with two other new companies, the Appleton and the Lowell. In 1830 three more were added: the Suffolk, Tremont, and Lawrence Companies. The Boott followed in 1835 and the Massachusetts in 1839. In every case the terms were the same: the land was sold outright while the waterpower was leased. And the services of the Locks and Canals Company did not end there. It also provided full sets of every type of machinery required and laid out and built whatever roads or other improvements were needed, including the mill buildings themselves and housing for the workers. The Locks and Canals Company, ownership of which had passed to the stockholders of the Merrimack Company on a share-for-share basis, had thus assumed the function of selling what amounted to complete, prepackaged textile mills to groups of interested investors.[14]

This aspect of the development of Lowell—its dual nature, manufacturing *cum* real estate promotion—differentiated it sharply from the Boston Company. Other changes also set the two increasingly apart. One involved management. At Waltham there had been no precise division of authority. Appleton described Francis Lowell as the "informing soul," who "gave direction and form to the whole proceeding,"[15] but it was Jackson as "Superintendent" who managed the day-to-day business. In the case of the Merrimack Company, Kirk Boott, taking on the same task, received the double title of Treasurer and Agent. The presidency of the corporation went to Warren Dutton, a minor investor, who functioned largely as a figurehead. That pattern persisted. Presidents called meetings of the directors, presided at them, and did little else. The duties Boott performed, on the other hand, were subsequently divided between two individuals, each of whom had a good deal of responsibility. Working in Boston, the treasurer set the broad outlines of company policy, handled its financial affairs, purchased its capital goods and raw materials, and negotiated the sale of its output. In effect the treasurer served as the chief executive officer of the company, while the agent, who reported directly to the treasurer, assumed responsibility for managing the factory itself, including supervision of the labor force. All Lowell corporations used this system, which was, for its time, quite sophisticated.[16]

Equally innovative was the variety of textiles manufactured at Lowell. Each company tended to specialize in a different type of cloth. With high tariffs for the moment providing ample protection, the Merrimack Company led the way by turning out fancy calicoes. The Hamilton Company followed with flannels, drills, and dimities, and the Appleton and Lawrence companies added underwear and stockings, while the Boott mills produced cassimeres. To develop methods of manufacturing the new products, skilled mechanics and examples of various kinds of machinery were liberally imported from England, sometimes at considerable expense. John D. Prince, for example, a native of Manchester who oversaw the Merrimack Company's printworks, demanded a salary of $5,000 a year—$2,000 more than Boott. Meanwhile, in addition to manufacturing their specialties, most of the mills retained the capacity to shift to other types of production if market conditions changed.[17]

The chief advocate of the growing diversity of Lowell products was Nathan Appleton, and as at Waltham, he designed the system used to dispose of the mills' output. By 1829 the business had become too large for B. C. Ward and Company, a general commercial firm buying and selling a broad range of merchandise. With an eye to remedying the situation, Appleton terminated the partnership and entered into another with James W. Paige. The new partnership dealt exclusively in domestic textiles. The services it rendered included taking on consignment and selling the entire production of individual manufacturing companies. Drawing on its partners' extensive knowledge of the market, the firm also provided specifications for new products and employed patternmakers to create designs for printed fabrics. Upon occasion, it purchased raw materials, and, in a complex series of credit arrangements, both borrowed from the large cash balances it held for the companies it served and advanced them short-term loans for operating expenses. In addition, the partners regularly endorsed notes for bank loans to the same companies. Carrying out all these functions required an investment in Paige and Company itself of several hundred thousand dollars. The firm's profits came in large part from the commission it charged on sales—initially set at 1 to $1\frac{1}{4}$ percent, but substantially increased over the years.[18]

As the number of companies at Lowell grew, other firms entered the business alongside Appleton's, most notably A. and A. Lawrence and Company and James K. Mills and Company. Together the selling houses were tireless and singularly successful at seeking out new markets during the thirties and forties. Shipments to the American West and South rose almost every year, and to those prime sales areas were added South America and Mexico, and later China. Lowell cottons also found their way to the West Indies, Turkey, and Africa, and beginning in 1840 to India and Russia. In many foreign markets quality and price combined to give American manufacturers an edge over British as well as local producers. The profits on export sales, too, were usually higher—especially in the China trade, which, after the opening of the treaty ports in 1842, absorbed over a million dollars worth of American textiles annually. Given the dramatic expansion of the market and a general tendency for prices to fall, sales continued to climb. Between 1832 and 1846, for example, Paige and Company increased its business for the Hamilton Company from $354,319 to $921,000, or a full 260 percent.[19]

For someone like Appleton who was willing to take the added risk and invest in a selling house, the commission on sales in effect compounded earnings from mill stocks. But most people who put money into Lowell corporations preferred a simpler arrangement. They invested in manufacturing alone and looked to returns from that source to compensate them for the capital they ventured. How large were those returns?

Of the various ways of measuring, profits and dividends remain the most obvious, and though it is impossible to tell much about profits during the early years at Lowell, there is a fair amount of information about dividends. They fluctuated a good deal—in some years there were none at all and in others they rose to well above 15 percent. Yet at no point did the rate match the Boston Company's 1821 dividend of 27.5 percent—a level of return which remained unequaled even by that company in the years before 1861. Nathan Appleton's accounting shows that for the period 1824 to 1831 "Waltham Dividends" averaged 17.36 percent a year. Over the next seven years the figure dropped to 11.53 percent and between 1838 and 1846 stood at only 5.16 percent. By comparison the Merrimack Company's first dividend, paid in 1825, was 10 percent, and Appleton's records put the average for the next decade at 10.75 percent. For the years 1836 to 1845 his figures show a marked increase—all the way to 14.9 percent. The rates for other Lowell companies seem to have been slightly lower, though not dissimilar. In general dividends were rising during the early thirties but declined in the depression of the latter part of the decade. Slow to recover thereafter, they shot upward again in 1844.[20]

As time passed, the records kept by treasurers' offices became increasingly elaborate, making it possible to follow some of these developments in greater detail. The results of one study of eleven companies for the years 1838 through 1846 are summarized in table 1. Modern accounting methods were used, and the sample includes both the Boston and Merrimack Companies as well as four others at Lowell. In the case of profits the high came in 1844 at 19.1 percent and the low in 1843 at 2.3 percent. Dividends, on the other hand, rose from a low of zero in 1838 to a high of 22.32 percent in 1846.

As might be expected, fluctuations in both profits and dividends reflected changing conditions in the economy in general and the textile industry in particular. But the figures also suggest that over time the relationship between profits and dividends itself changed significantly. In 1838, when profits were down, the companies in the sample paid no dividends at all; yet five and six years later, when profits fell even lower, dividends were continued. Further, in the recovery of 1844–1846, rising profits were reflected in dividend increases more promptly—and emphatically—than before.

The altered relationship between profits and dividends reflected in the data became, in fact, standard practice for all Lowell corporations. In the long run they tended to pay out an ever higher portion of their profits in dividends. During good years dividends would be only a little less than total earnings, while in bad years payments to stockholders might well exceed the amount a company had received above

Table 1 Profits and dividends of eleven textile companies, 1838–1846

Year	Profits (percent of net worth)	Dividends (percent of paid-in capital)
1838	3.7	0
1839	14.1	8.03
1840	4.2	7.45
1841	7.9	7.36
1842	3.2	8.50
1843	2.3	2.89
1844	19.1	12.20
1845	17.1	16.99
1846	18.2	22.32

Source: Paul F. McGouldrick, *New England Textiles in the Nineteenth Century: Profits and Investment* (Cambridge, 1968), pp. 81, 251.

what it needed to meet expenses. Between 1842 and 1846 the average rate of profit (net earnings) for the companies in the sample remained a bit higher than the average dividend rate, but over the longer period from 1838 to 1861 the two proved to be identical. Both were 7.9 percent, suggesting that ultimately dividends came to absorb every dollar of earnings.[21]

Such generosity to investors was and is striking. It effectively sets Lowell companies apart from the great majority of American business enterprises, past as well as present. Certainly it is in sharp contrast to modern corporate practice. It also conflicts with the standard view of entrepreneurial behavior. For Lowell companies to have conformed to either model, at least a portion—preferably a substantial portion—of earnings should have been retained, if for no other purpose than to facilitate future capital spending. Plainly that did not occur.

The companies did, to be sure, invest from time to time in improvements that increased capacity or lowered costs. Mills were expanded, even completely rebuilt, and machines that wore out were replaced with others of better design. But when such projects reached major proportions, new stock was usually sold to cover the cost. All of the companies tried to avoid long-term debt. For financing smaller projects—barring retention and use of earnings—there were two possibilities: short-term borrowing or withdrawals from working capital. Upon occasion both were used, but borrowing remained the preferred choice. At the same time, conservative financial policies set limits on the extent to which either approach could be used. Just as the Boston Company's managers had before them, Lowell treasurers studiously maintained the large reserves of working capital paid in by investors at the outset and kept total debt low relative to liquid assets.[22]

Throughout the years when the Lowell mills were being built, Massachusetts banks refused as a matter of policy to lend money to manufacturing firms, which no doubt helps account for the high priority given liquid reserves. Without ready cash, in times of economic dislocation companies might have had trouble raising needed funds except by assessing individual stockholders, who remained legally liable for corporation debts up to 1830. But no similar considerations influenced the treatment of earnings. Boards of directors were free to allocate whatever portion they wished to dividend payments, making the Lowell pattern in this respect doubly significant, and difficult to explain.

Still another reason—in addition to financing capital spending—why present-day businesses hold onto earnings, rather than disbursing them all as dividends, is that doing so increases the total worth of an enterprise. This too was a goal Lowell managers might have pursued but apparently chose not to. On the other hand, modern tax laws have tended to give such a strategy an appeal it would not have had in 1840. At present, earnings paid out in dividends become taxable as income; retained they will be taxed, if ever, at the rate applied to capital gains, which until very recently has been much lower. The tax liabilities in question, of course, are those of the shareholders in the company. It is their financial interests that are being sheltered when earnings are retained, and investors in the early nineteenth century needed no such shelter; taxes were not a problem.

But this puts the issue squarely on the doorstep of the stockholders, which is where in all likelihood it belongs. If every dollar earned by a Lowell corporation became a dollar in dividends it must have been because the stockholders—or more accurately those of them in a position to exercise control—wanted it that way. And evidently they preferred such a policy despite the obvious constraints it placed on future growth. The question is why.

In this connection it is interesting to note several other features that came to characterize Lowell enterprises—features which, when taken together as a response to changing conditions in the industry, form a distinct pattern. As more companies, in and out of Lowell, embarked on the business of manufacturing cotton cloth and as the capacity of older mills was increased, the growing quantity of goods tended to lower prices, even in the face of rising demand. As long as prices did not fall too far it was still possible to make a profit, but higher levels of profit invariably called forth new increases in industry capacity, higher levels of production, and hence downward pressure on prices. Furthermore, for technological reasons it was difficult for individual textile mills to scale down production at any point. In effect the choice owners had, when confronted with falling earnings, was to shut down completely or to continue to operate at, or close to, capacity. Most tended to stay in operation unless earnings fell so low they failed to cover out-of-pocket costs. Indeed many companies actually increased output while earnings were dropping, behaving quite like wheat farmers in an elementary economics textbook.[23]

Yet there was an alternative, at least at Lowell, where—as closely allied as they were—the companies should have been able to cooperate to restrict output. In fact such a scheme was tried. In 1842 all of the mills, by prior agreement, made a concerted effort to cut back production in the face of falling earnings. But the experiment lasted less than a year, and at the time it was abandoned prices were still declining; it was also not repeated.[24]

A second area in which Lowell companies tended to act independently of one another, despite both the pressures and the opportunities for cooperation, was wages. As at Waltham, most workers were paid on a piecework basis, yet company managers only occasionally joined forces in setting rates. Nor did such arrangements ever last long. Again, there were technological problems: the capacity of mills and machinery dating from different periods, and therefore labor productivity, varied widely, making it difficult to set uniform piecework rates. Still, the establishment of the whole Waltham-Lowell system had involved the solution of so many technological problems that it remains something of a wonder that more was not accomplished. Presumably if the company managers had wanted to work together on a regular basis to limit output or set wages they could have found a way to do so.

But cooperation went untested to any significant extent. And the same conservative tendency manifested itself in other ways. Up to 1830 the mills at Lowell had been in the forefront of development in the American textile industry; after that date the pace of innovation slowed substantially. Capacity was expanded and productivity raised, often through requiring higher levels of output from labor. Experience over time and the benefits of "learning by doing," too, made a significant contribution to productivity.[25] Yet increasingly, important technological changes were pioneered at places other than Lowell. Also, the basic structural characteristics of the system remained unaltered. No attempt was made, for example, to integrate the marketing function into the manufacturing companies themselves. Nor was there any move toward merging individual companies. As a result they remained much the same size as one another and were managed according to quite similar principles, proceeding along parallel, yet essentially separate, tracks. Anything else would have represented a departure, and after a certain point a brake seems to have been put on departures of all kinds at Lowell.

Of course people who have discovered a formula that works are often reluctant to change it, but businesses that resist change seldom remain successful for any length of time. Certainly a team of modern management consultants studying the Waltham-Lowell system would point out that the policies which appear to have governed it are not those generally associated with long-run profit maximization. And in truth the conservative financial practices of the companies, their failure to retain earnings, and finally the slowdown in the rate of innovation after 1830 all imply a rather unusual order of priorities.

Conservative financial management and lack of innovation would seem to point to security as a primary goal, while the high rate of payout of earnings suggests a paramount desire to reward stockholders with current income. In other words, if the attempt was being made to maximize anything in the Waltham-Lowell system, it was the safety of investors' capital and the size of their dividends.

Ultimately, of course, such things—having value—qualify as profit, just as gains in net worth do, but the assumption is that there must be some trade-off between the two types of benefits; that emphasizing one will necessarily exact a price in terms of the other. In this case the precise values of the equation are less important than what such priorities suggest about the motives of Lowell investors. What did they hope to gain from involvement in the textile industry? Looking at the results they actually achieved, the answer could well be a way of investing money that was above all safe and productive of steady income. At the same time they seem to have been far less concerned about the possibility of any long-range increase in the value of their holdings. While parallels do exist, this was no ordinary set of investment objectives. But then there was nothing ordinary about the individuals who—along with the early promoters like Appleton and Jackson—came to dominate the ranks of Lowell stockholders.

III

A glance at any list of major investors in Lowell enterprises indicates two things they had in common, both with one another and with members of the much smaller group that initiated developments at Waltham: almost all were already wealthy by the time they bought into the textile industry, and most had made their money as merchants. Boston's great commercial fortunes had always been the logical source for Appleton and his associates to tap in their search for fresh capital to expand the Waltham system, and plainly whatever inducements they offered the individuals in question worked.

Simple numbers tell part of the story. In 1813, when the Boston Company was founded, there were 12 shareholders, four of whom held a majority of the stock. Seven years later—with four people still holding a majority interest—the number had risen to 24. By 1828 there were 74, and the largest single holding had dropped to fifty shares. Over the next eight years the number of stockholders rose to 110, while the largest holding fell to twenty-five shares. In 1822, at the time the Merrimack Company was organized, it had only 5 stockholders; in 1842 it carried 390 on its books. And where the Boston and Merrimack Companies led, others followed. A marked dispersion of financial interest became a standard feature of all the Waltham-Lowell corporations.[26]

Yet the spread of ownership was never a random affair. It took place in two quite purposeful and controlled ways. In many cases shares were given or willed away by the original owners to children or other relatives. Thus, of the 118 stockholders of the Boston Company in 1846, 43 by name were members of eight families, and at one point no fewer than 14 Appletons owned stock in the Hamilton Company. Not all multiple holdings within families were the result of gifts or inheritance, but many seem to have been. At various times between 1831 and 1855, for example, Nathan Appleton gave three of his children a total of thirty-six shares in the Boston Company, and in addition he transferred shares in five other textile companies to his son-in-law, Henry Wadsworth Longfellow.[27]

The second means by which ownership became dispersed was through sales of stock. Once an enterprise was established as a going concern, the owners generally sold part of their investment. Because such sales were almost always private, it is difficult to tell whether they netted a profit, or how large the profits might have been. What became of the proceeds, however, is clear. The same names appear time and again as new companies were founded, suggesting that money taken out of one venture was promptly reinvested in another. In this way—since only rarely was all of the equity liquidated when capital was moved from an established company to a new one—individual holdings could become quite diversified, with all the added security that implied.[28]

For those who wished to sell stock, there were a variety of potential buyers. Some shares even ended up in the hands of the mill workers, but as a rule sales involved substantial blocks of stock taken by people already associated with or at least well known to the sellers. Moreover, once an individual acquired an interest in the industry in this fashion, a steadily growing involvement often followed. A large holding might bring a seat on the board of directors. Investment in an established mill could lead to a role as founder of another, or that sequence could be reversed, as in the case of the Lawrence brothers, Amos and Abbott. Though they had begun as importers of British goods, by the early 1820s the Lawrences were marketing domestic textiles. A decade later they appeared as incorporators and major stockholders of the Tremont Company, and finally in the late forties they went on to develop—as a carbon copy of Lowell—the town on the Merrimack that bears the family name to this day.[29]

In a variety of ways, then, the group that planned and developed the Boston Company and the facilities at Lowell grew larger. Each new venture tended to attract new investors: the Merrimack Company brought in William and Eben Appleton; Samuel Appleton was an incorporator of the Hamilton Company, as were G. W. Lyman, John A. Lowell, John Lowell, Jr., and William Sturgis; T. H. Perkins became a founder of the Appleton Company; and Henry Cabot joined the group when the Suffolk Company was established. At the same time stock in older companies was gradually being sold. Yet at no point was there anything like a public offering in the modern sense. As had been true since the early days at Waltham, it was essentially an insider's game.[30]

As a result, control over the companies remained highly concentrated, despite both the dispersion of ownership and a management structure that, for the period, separated the owning and managerial functions to an unusual degree. Today such developments have rendered most corporations of any size more or less immune to the wishes of ordinary stockholders. This was not so at Lowell, at least through 1845. Increasingly large numbers of people owned stock in individual companies, yet power remained in the hands of a small group of men who spoke for consolidated family interests and wielded, by proxy, the votes to back up their words. Salaried managers established and implemented company policy, but always within guidelines determined by others.

Though it seldom happened, disagreements within the controlling group could and did arise. The most notable example occurred in 1842, at a time when the earnings of all the companies were depressed. Allied on one side were the Lowells, the Jacksons, Nathan Appleton, and the Lawrences, against a "reforming party" made up of large investors with no immediate role in managing the companies. The reforms proposed—and to some extent accomplished—included lowering inventories of raw cotton, reducing salaries and wages, and the single attempt on record to cooperate in cutting production. But a year later, with prices and profits up slightly, Henry Lee, one of the reformers, concluded that the campaign had run out of steam. "The improvement and prospect of better prices have already quieted so many of our side that I fear we can't gain any more advantages."[31]

The same controversy may also have affected dividend policy. The tendency to reward stockholders with a steadily rising share of earnings did become pronounced at about this time. On the other hand, only Nathan Appleton seems to have questioned the wisdom of the practice. And any doubts he had cannot have been very strong, for he continued to invest the bulk of his wealth in textile manufacturing, just as a growing number of his friends did.

As for what led so many of Boston's prominent commercial families to invest in Waltham-Lowell ventures, the answer—then and afterward—appeared obvious: the amount of money to be made in cotton manufacturing. The fact, too, that those controlling the system guarded access to it so closely lends weight to such an interpretation. Yet in most other respects it seems singularly inadequate. How well, for example, does it explain the preference of the same investors for security and dividend income over capital gains? Indeed, how useful is any interpretation which relies so heavily on considerations of profit, when in the long run the return on money invested at Lowell averaged only 7.9 percent a year—less than 2 percentage points above the legal rate of bank interest? The truth is that the issue of motivation here is more complex than simplistic notions about profit maximization and entrepreneurial behavior imply. Much continued to depend, as it had since the Boston Company was founded, on who the individual investors were, what their experience up to then had been, and what alternatives in the economic realm they had.

There is little to suggest, for instance, that Boston merchants were following a general trend in shifting their resources so decisively from commerce to manufacturing. No similar shift occurred in New York City. But there the economic elite was more thoroughly entrenched—contained more individuals who were members of families at the top of pre-Revolutionary society—and hence tended to be more conservative in outlook.[32] Fifty years after the Revolution the social structure of Boston remained almost as fluid as it had been when families like the Lowells first settled there.

Yet by the same token, Waltham-Lowell investors failed to fit another stereotype—the early industrial capitalist as a new man, making his way in opposition to those above him in the social hierarchy. In Boston there was no need for aggressive strategies. If the Appletons and the Lawrences came from the hinterland and entered business without so much as a single Harvard degree to their credit, let alone an established position in the community, those advantages were still relatively rare among the people with whom they would be associating. Nor were the few families that could claim some sort of long-standing prominence prepared to exclude the newcomers. They might grumble about questions of taste from time to time, but that was all. The groups intermarried freely, sat on the same boards of directors, and supported the same worthy causes. Just as Robert Winthrop—one of the few legitimate representatives of pre-Revolutionary elite status—would eulogize Abbott Lawrence at the time of his death as the most important man in Boston,[33] so when Francis

Lowell had wanted help in founding the Boston Company he had no qualms about turning to Nathan Appleton. By then Appleton's position was in every way secure, socially as well as financially; he may have been a man on the make, but he was also a man who already had it made.

None of this is to say, of course, that such men might not have wanted to enlarge their fortunes still further, and it was possible to do so in the textile industry. As a result of the losses he had suffered up to then, Patrick Jackson could claim assets worth only $13,000 in 1810, but during the next twenty-five years he increased that amount to almost $400,000.[34] While there were several ways of achieving such results, one of the most lucrative turned out to be the promotional side of the Lowell venture. After the Locks and Canals Company was established as an independent concern, it continued in existence until 1845. By then the mill sites had all been taken up and the directors had sold the machine shop to a separate group of investors. The company had also liquidated its miscellaneous land holdings in the town. The profits were high. The owner of a share of Locks and Canals stock worth $500 in 1825 would have received $3,004 in earnings over the next twenty years.[35]

Often too, there was even more money to be made buying and selling Waltham-Lowell stocks than by simply sitting tight. William Appleton regularly described such activities in his diary and was quite successful at them. In 1836 he wrote: "Under the belief that the present Congress would modify the tariff, or at least attempt it, I sold in the course of the last summer a large part of my Manufacturing stocks, with an intention to purchase when the prices should get down."[36] The practice of disposing of stock when it was high and buying as the price fell was one that Appleton continued throughout his life. In the aftermath of the Panic of 1857 he was delighted to purchase shares in one company for $400 apiece, noting, "I have in the same concern that which I paid one thousand dollars for . . . they have been years in declining, but will advance rapidly; I expect the stocks I now purchase at four hundred dollars will sell for six in one year and eight in two years."[37]

Appleton's speculations and the dramatic increase in Jackson's wealth indicate that there were indeed large sums of money to be made in the Waltham-Lowell system, yet both men were unusual. Over a long career Appleton showed himself to be more willing than many of his associates to live with substantial anxiety resulting from his business activities. The same was true of Jackson, who remained to the end the plunger he had been as a young man. In the mid-1830s—evidently restless with the returns he was receiving—he liquidated almost his entire interest in the mills. The proceeds went into a series of real estate ventures that turned out disastrously, leaving him with less than a quarter of his initial stake.[38]

There were one or two other such stories, but no more. For most large investors the Waltham-Lowell system seems to have been a place to put money and keep it. Unlike his cousin William, Nathan Appleton never speculated in the securities of the enterprises he backed, though he occasionally sold shares to finance new ventures. His estate on his death contained stock in twenty-four different textile companies worth approximately $800,000.[39] Similar—and possibly more typical, since he played no managerial role—was John Cushing's investment record. Returning to Boston in 1828 after twenty-five years spent in Canton as a merchant, Cushing continued his trading activities for a while longer but in 1831 was ready to retire from business altogether. Over the next few years as his commercial holdings were liquidated, the proceeds were systematically reinvested. A portion went into notes and personal loans, a portion into bank, insurance, and railroad stocks, and some into bonds and real estate. However the largest amount—just under a third of the total—was invested in manufacturing, principally New England textiles. From the meticulous ledgers that survive it is clear that the purpose was to produce regular income from dividends. Cushing bought shares only in large, well-established companies or those of solid promise, and with few exceptions he still owned the same securities at the time of his death in 1862.[40]

The careful building of an investment portfolio that would yield modest but steady returns is not in itself, perhaps, an unusual activity. Yet for someone like Cushing, whose fortune had taken root and grown in so exotic and lucrative a field as the China trade, it seems an odd move. To exchange the "benefits" on tea, or for that matter East Indian spices and French wine, for 7.9 percent a year in Lowell dividends must have required strong inducements.

Of course, if those "benefits" were drastically declining the individuals may have had little choice in the matter. That, in fact, is the usual explanation for the transfer of so much Boston capital from trade to manufacturing in the second quarter of the nineteenth century. Put succinctly the theory holds that "The failure of commerce to employ merchants' earnings operated directly to make capital available for industry."[41] To support such an interpretation historians have catalogued at length the disasters that befell Massachusetts commerce during the Embargo and War of 1812. Something is generally said too about the advantages that later accrued to the port of New York as a result of the Erie Canal, and finally reference is made to the Boston Company's 19.25 percent average dividend rate between 1817 and 1821.[42] Less often mentioned is the fact that 19.25 percent was a level of return not again achieved in the New England textile industry until 1863.

Unquestionably the Embargo and the War of 1812 did hurt the Bay State's commerce, but neither lasted forever. After 1815 commerce revived, slowly at first yet unmistakably. That year T. H. Perkins sent his first shipment of opium to Canton, and by 1819 his firm had ventures under way involving a combined value in cargo of more than $750,000. In a single voyage the *Augusta*, freighted with 120,000 pounds of Turkish opium, earned a profit of $50,000, and that was considered little better than average. Nor was opium the only commodity in which such sums were to be made. By 1824 a contract with the Hudson's Bay Company of nine years standing had netted Perkins and his partners a profit of $90,000 plus a 5 percent commission on all sales in China and America.[43] And returns in other types of trade could be just as high. During the same period, Henry Lee later recalled, ventures to Calcutta and Madras "were pretty certain to obtain 10, 15, or 20 percent profit" and on one voyage in 1821 the advance had run as high as 60 percent on some articles.[44]

As commerce continued to move toward prewar levels of prosperity, even merchants who had invested heavily in manufacturing kept up their commercial activities. Patrick Jackson and Nathan Appleton both did so for varying periods, as did T. H. Perkins, while William Appleton—despite heavy investments at Lowell—remained a trader as long as he lived. Presumably if commerce had become a losing proposition those personal investment histories would have been different. But the evidence from family papers and business records is at best spotty. Ultimately a more general measure of the ability of commerce to attract investment capital after 1815 is needed, and one reliable index of that ability is the record of ship tonnage owned in Boston and Massachusetts during the period.

Ships represented, after all, the major item of fixed capital in the kind of maritime commerce that had made fortunes for men like the Appletons, Jackson, and Perkins. Over time, as a result of increasing specialization among Boston's merchants, firms owning ships tended to become separate from those dealing in cargoes; but the issue, again, is how those activities fared—regardless of organization—in attracting investors' dollars. Table 2 lists the percentages of increase or decrease in tonnage owned for nine intervals between 1789 and 1860. For purposes of comparison the appropriate percentages for New York City are also given.

Table 2 Percentage change in tonnage of shipping owned in the customs districts of Massachusetts, Boston, and New York City, 1789–1860

Period	Mass.	Boston	N.Y.C.
1789–1800	+ 7.5[a]	+19.3[a]	− 5.8
1800–1807	+38.8	+24.1	+ 48.4
1807–1810	+10.3	+24.8	+ 25.5
1810–1820	−10.8[a]	−15.3	− 13.9
1820–1830	+ 4.2	+ 6.9	+ 11.0
1830–1840	+62.8[a]	+63.1[a]	+ 61.7
1840–1850	+27.8	+45.6	+101.5
1850–1855	+42.9	+70.3[a]	+ 54.1
1855–1860	−14.7	−15.0	+ 13.6

Source: Based on data in Samuel Eliot Morison, *The Maritime History of Massachusetts, 1738–1860* (Boston, 1921), p. 378.

a. Periods in which tonnage owned rose more or fell less, proportionately, in Massachusetts or Boston than in New York.

The most striking thing the figures reveal is the extent to which shipping in Boston and Massachusetts generally continued to expand. Taking the five intervals after 1820, in only one—the last—did tonnage in either the city or the state decline. In every other interval after 1820 the total rose, usually by a substantial percentage. Even when the results are compared with those for New York City, the picture of commercial health is hard to challenge. In the long run New York's natural advantages were bound to tell, and the city on the Hudson did outstrip Boston commercially. Yet taking again the five intervals after 1820, it is interesting that in two of them, 1830–1840 and 1850–1855, tonnage owned in Boston rose more, proportionately, than in New York. And in a third, 1820–1830, while the figure for Boston is lower, the difference was not great.

Thus the facts do not support the view that the traditional activities of Boston merchants failed to attract and employ capital after 1815; if anything they suggest the reverse. Consequently it makes little sense to argue that the money invested at Lowell gravitated to manufacturing by default. The shift was a matter of choice, and as such it must have been undertaken with certain clear objectives in mind. Recognizing, too, that those objectives were unlikely to have been the obvious ones—since investors waited longer for returns at Lowell, and even then the rate of return was no higher and may well have been lower than in commerce—what could they have been? In the end the standard explanation is not completely wrong. The answer does lie in the comparative benefits of investment in industry over investment in commerce and navigation, but only if those benefits are defined in the broadest possible terms.

Though commerce continued to expand after 1820, that did not mean it had become any easier—as an occupation. The pressures, the uncertainty, the draining anxiety were no different in prosperous times than Francis Lowell had found them in the worst of the embargo and war years. Even a cursory reading of the journals and diaries of Boston merchants makes this clear. In 1826, at the end of a two-year period during which Amos Lawrence had "added much to my worldly possessions," he still felt moved to complain of his *"overengagedness* in business," adding, "I now find myself so engrossed with its cares, as to occupy my thoughts, waking or sleeping, to a degree entirely disproportioned to its importance."[45] Resolving to curtail his business activities in the future despite whatever loss of income might be involved, Lawrence concluded: "Property acquired at such sacrifices as I have been obliged to make the past year costs more than its worth; and the anxiety of protecting it is the extreme of folly."[46]

As further proof of the pressures inherent in commerce, being a Boston merchant tended to be a young man's game. Those who did well often retired—sometimes even before the age of thirty. Nathan Appleton was just thirty-two when he first began considering "what course to take to avoid the necessity for laborious personal attention to business for which I am becoming intolerant,"[47] and John Cushing retired at forty-four. Other successful merchants rejected early retirement, then found the decision difficult to live with and continued to dream of escaping the cares of trade. William Appleton debated the subject endlessly in his diary. "I am so much excited by business concerns that I have very little pleasure,"[48] he remarked in 1822, adding a few days afterward, "The distress among the merchantile [*sic*] community has almost sickened me of business."[49] Almost, but not quite; thirty years later he was still engaged in commerce and still unhappy at the consequences. "I attribute much of my anxiety the last few years to my business which has been profitable beyond the natural income . . . May I have less hazard and no misgivings of duty."[50] By 1856 Appleton seemed at last to have settled the issue and vowed "to withdraw wholly or nearly so from commerce the coming year."[51] Yet in this case the "or nearly so" provided the clue. The final month of his life found him speculating in saltpeter and pepper in an attempt, as he explained, "to show the younger part of the Merchants that an old man of seventy-five has energy left."[52]

There were many reasons why an individual might choose to continue in commerce. Apart from the desire to impress his juniors, William Appleton tried half a dozen other explanations for his own failure to retire, though often the result only added to his anxiety. "I want no man's money, but it gives me an unpleasant sensation to have others more successful than myself," he wrote in 1835. "These are feelings I am ashamed of and I endeavor to correct them."[53] As time passed Appleton discovered a more acceptable reason for remaining in trade, commenting in 1858 that he did so because he had sons-in-law who were similarly engaged and wished "to aid them by my advice."[54] T. H. Perkins, who also resisted retirement long past the point when he had accumulated ample means, offered the same explanation. "After an active merchantile [*sic*] life of nearly half a century," it was only natural, as he wrote, "that I should incline to retire altogether from business concerns." But inclination was one thing and duty another; Perkins would stay on with his firm "to give continuance and support to my sons-in-law, Mr. Cabot and Mr. T. B. Gary."[55]

Concern for younger relatives involved in commerce may have been an acceptable reason for keeping one's own hand in, but it also implied a significant increase in the attendant strains. Stretching from generation to generation and growing as the family circle expanded, such stress could come to seem wearisome indeed. Understandably, Boston merchants were not always eager to steer their children toward careers in commerce. Thomas Gold Appleton, the only one of Nathan Appleton's sons to survive to maturity, was admitted to the bar but never practiced law, preferring instead to devote his time to travel and the arts.[56] Some fathers actively discouraged their offspring from following the parental example. "I have no wish that you pursue trade," wrote Amos Lawrence to his eldest son "I would rather see you on a farm, or studying any profession."[57]

In such remarks, and in the kinds of activities merchants engaged in after retirement, there is also more than a suggestion that—in addition to the other problems it entailed—commerce struck those involved as unduly narrow; that it failed to fulfill any larger sense of purpose. Thus at the same time Lawrence advised his son against becoming a merchant, he praised a life devoted to the full realization of one's God-given talents.[58] The theme occurs over and over again in his correspondence, and he worked at putting it into practice in his own life. Having finally retired from business in 1830 because of what seems to have been a psychosomatically induced ulcer, he spent the next twenty-two years giving away thousands of dollars to rural colleges and academies and making up packages of religious tracts and used clothing to send to impoverished clergymen. The contentment such pursuits brought was in marked contrast to his earlier, often depressed, emotional state. "The situation I occupy is one that I would not exchange, if I had the power, with any man living," Lawrence wrote his wife in 1833; "it is full of agreeable incidents, and free from the toils and anxieties, frequently attendant on a high state of prosperity."[59] A decade later he confided to his diary in much the same vein, "My life seems now more likely to be spared for a longer season than for many years past; and I never enjoyed myself more highly."[60]

The particular objects of Lawrence's philanthropy and the intense pleasure he derived from it may have been unusual, but the fact that scores of charitable and cultural institutions throughout New England owe their existence to men in similar positions suggests that the deeper impulse behind the philanthropy was not unusual. There were also the benefactions that left no tangible trace, to say nothing of the time spent in civic and political activities. Much of this might be dismissed as a form of expiation, yet on the record it is difficult to do so. Men like Amos Lawrence seem to have been operating out of a thoroughly coherent vision of society and their role in it. That vision may have imposed many obligations upon them, but it never required that they atone for anything.

Before the vision could become reality, however, life had to be put on a secure basis. Above all, one needed money and leisure and the assurance of being able to transmit both to one's descendants. And though commerce offered the first of these, it could not provide the other two. Nor, even as late as 1840, were there many ways of making up the deficit. Banking and real estate still posed most of the same problems they had in Francis Lowell's day—the risks and the constant uncertainty. For a time it seemed that money invested in the quasi-public ventures sponsored by the state, such as turnpikes and canals, might be both safe and productive of steady returns, but in most cases the profits proved lower than expected. The monopoly privileges claimed by the promoters of those projects were also coming under increasing political pressure. What was needed, indeed, was something as far removed as possible from the instabilities of politics. But that left, again, private business, where the number of undertakings capable of absorbing large amounts of capital—and meeting the other requirements at issue—was decidedly limited.

Surveying the situation in 1833, Amos Lawrence had seen only one solution. Asked by a friend for advice "upon the subject of investing some money," he wrote: "There is a demand for money, on pledges of collateral security, and for a period of 12 or so months, but it is not easy to invest a large sum at 6 *per cent interest* for a series of years, in real estate, or any other perfect security." All things considered he thought the best course was to purchase "manufacturing stocks." There alone could one expect with *"reasonable* assurance" that the investment would not, as he put it, "be worth less than cost, allowing 6 per cent, and deducting dividends for the next five or seven years."[61]

The advice was apt. Not only had Lawrence himself invested almost his entire fortune in the textile industry just before retiring in 1830, but the logic behind such a move was inescapable. None of the traditional business strategies would have enabled him to live as he wished, nor were minor modifications likely to render them any more serviceable. What the situation required was nothing less than a totally new form of business enterprise, and that Francis Lowell had provided at Waltham. The next step has to take the basic model and expand upon it—something that worked so smoothly in practice precisely because the needs of the men who underwrote the expansion were the same ones that had moved Lowell to create the system in the first place.

IV

Thirty years after its founding, then, the Waltham-Lowell system remained the curious hybrid it had been at the outset: a strikingly modern combination of resources and techniques, yet one devoted to the support of a traditional group of public-spirited *rentiers*. Far from the production of wealth in the usual sense, the goal was the preservation of fortunes already made, positions already won. And though from a twentieth-century standpoint the result had much the look of a textbook case of blossoming industrial capitalism, in several important respects it neither functioned as one nor was intended to.

Such, at any rate, were the motives that caused the original $600,000 invested at Lowell to grow by a factor of twenty in little more than two decades. The same motives, too, went far toward explaining the curious anomalies that continued to surprise visitors to Lowell—everything from joint-stock pianos and the *Lowell Offering* to the oriental rugs neatly stored in the attic of the town's hotel when not in use at stockholders' meetings. Like the rugs, many of those anomalies required a fair amount of assiduous care and upkeep. A case in point was the *Offering*. As testimony to the owners' continuing concern for the welfare and personal development of their labor force, and the price they were prepared to pay to foster both, the *Offering* performed an invaluable service. Yet few readers probably knew that the price included regular payments by Amos Lawrence to Harriet Farley, the publication's editor.

Nor was someone spending only a day at Lowell and glancing through an issue of the *Offering*, as Dickens had, likely to discover much about a distinctly different kind of response to conditions in the mills. In the thirties, with the exception of two brief "turnouts," Lowell workers had stood above the developing American labor movement. A decade later some of them seemed to be changing their minds. In the intervening years there had been steady pressure both to increase the number of machines tended by individual workers and to speed up the rate at which the machinery ran. In response, in 1844 the Lowell Female Labor Reform Association was founded with Sarah Bagley as its president. An employee of the Hamilton Company who had been an early contributor to the *Offering*, Bagley was a leader of great energy and determination. In 1845 through the Female Labor Reform Association she launched a campaign that collected over 2,000 signatures on petitions favoring a law limiting the working day to ten hours. Thereafter, out of work in the mills, she extended her efforts to other factory towns and before long could be heard denouncing Harriet Farley as "a mouthpiece of the corporations." Under Farley's management the *Offering* consistently favored moral suasion—as opposed to Bagley's more direct tactics—in the cause of reform. The goal was to "do good by stealth." But if that approach satisfied Amos Lawrence, it apparently held less appeal for other readers. Subscriptions fell off, and late in 1845 the *Offering* quietly published its last issue.[62]

The demise of the *Offering* was a milestone of sorts, but other changes occurring at the same time left an even more noticeable mark on Lowell. As initially laid out, the mill and housing complexes—with churches and shops tucked about—seemed to represent a fine example of planned development. Neither the plan nor the rationale behind it, on the other hand, envisioned the growth of a full-fledged city. Urban facilities of every variety had to be jammed into odd corners, and while the Locks and Canals Company did for a while continue to control where and how new mills were built, other kinds of change became increasingly haphazard.[63]

Historians would later argue that what happened at Lowell was predictable, given the utilitarian, business-oriented character of the venture.[64] A more accurate view would be that the plan suffered not from an overdose of practicality but from the reverse: from too strenuous a determination to counteract the economic logic inherent in the situation. With their horror of crowded urban industrial settings, the Lowell promoters had gone to great lengths not to create one. The buildings continued to have a distinctly collegiate look. In the original plan each mill with its surrounding housing formed a separate, self-contained quadrangle. Strung out along the canals, one after another, they were to constitute in effect a series of independent, nucleated units. It would be Waltham duplicated, not on a grander scale, but over and over again. The impracticality of such a design, taking into account the physical requirements of modern utilities, commercial arrangements, and transportation facilities—to say nothing of the needs of the thousands of people drawn to Lowell to service those systems—is obvious to our eyes. Yet it may well not have been clear in 1822, when a city the size of Boston still had no organized police force of its own. In any case, by 1845 the result had become a moderately cramped and inconvenient place, complete with areas that candor would have labeled slums. Though this was still above the norm for factory towns, the gap had narrowed perceptibly and there was little likelihood the trend would be reversed. When the Locks and Canals Company auctioned off its remaining landholdings that year, the period of planned development at Lowell had come to an end.[65]

With the workers organizing and Lowell looking more like any other industrial city, two impressive early achievements of the Waltham-Lowell system stood in jeopardy. There were other changes, too, as the protracted depression of the late thirties and early forties gave notice. In 1819 the Boston Company's technological superiority and hefty capital reserves had insulated it all but completely from the normal operation of the business cycle. Twenty years later that turned out to be less true; even the strongest Waltham-Lowell companies suffered some damage.

It was a simple matter of supply and demand. The nation's output of cotton goods had grown to the point where it much more nearly matched the demand for them. As a result anything affecting demand—such as a general economic downturn—was reflected more emphatically in prices and hence profits. At the same time the competitive advantage that wealth gave Lowell and his associates in setting up the enterprise at Waltham was shrinking. By 1830 the cost of building and equipping an integrated cotton mill had fallen sharply and would continue to decline over the next twenty-five years. Consequently new textile factories kept appearing, despite the growing pressure on prices and profits.[66]

In the face of the steady expansion of the American cotton industry, Waltham-Lowell investors had reason to be wary on economic grounds alone, but ultimately the problem went deeper. Not only did the increased capacity threaten earnings; a fair share of the enterprises responsible for the increase were products of a completely different pattern of industrial development. The truth was that the Waltham-

Lowell system had few imitators, even in the textile industry. The use of the corporate form, the high rate of payout of earnings, the conservative financial policies, and the increasing resistance to innovation all remained highly unusual until after the Civil War. The major difference, however, was size. Most firms began as small, individual proprietorships or partnerships and depended on reinvested profits for capital. Such was the case, for example, in Adams, Massachusetts.

Located in the far northwestern corner of the state, Adams was blessed with abundant waterpower and developed early as a manufacturing center. The principal industry was textiles, and by 1837, according to the state census of that year, the town boasted roughly the same number of mills in each branch of production as Lowell. Thereafter all resemblance between the two places and the enterprises in them ceased, as table 3 indicates. In cotton printing and woolens the average capitalization of mills in Adams was only a fifth as large as at Lowell. And where the technology at Lowell was most fully developed—in cotton goods—Adams mills were capitalized at barely more than a twentieth of the equivalent figure for the city on the Merrimack.

Results so dissimilar can only have been achieved by processes that were themselves quite different. And if the processes were different, the goals that shaped them must have been too. A few of the millowners of Adams eventually made modest fortunes producing textiles, but to a man they did so after, not before, becoming manufacturers. Just starting out on the road that had long since been traveled at Waltham in a single giant stride, they had everything to gain from change. Indeed the principal danger they faced was that too much of the old order might survive intact, not that too little would. The builders of the great mills at Lowell, on the other hand, were at bottom conservative. They may have been committed to change of a sort, but the broadest possible interpretation of that commitment would not have seen it as anything more than a very partial, and selective, affair.

Table 3 Average capitalization of textile mills in Lowell and Adams, 1837

Type of Mill	Number		Total capital		Average capital	
	Lowell	Adams	Lowell	Adams	Lowell	Adams
Cotton	23	19	$6,167,000	$295,725	$280,318	$15,564
Printing	3	2	700,000	86,000	233,333	43,000
Woolen	5	4	580,000	114,000	116,000	28,500

Source: Data are from John P. Bigelow, *Statistical Tables: Exhibiting the Condition and Products of Certain Branches of Industry in Massachusetts, for the Year Ending April 1, 1837* (Boston, 1838), pp. 31, 105.

It was on that score, as much as any other, that the constantly rising rate of industrial expansion posed a problem. Whereas smaller manufacturers were likely to conclude that continued, even accelerated, economic development was in their interest, Waltham-Lowell investors—with their dividends safe and their gnawing fear of the consequences of unbridled industrialization—were sure to balk. Translated into the political arena such differences could become the stuff of genuine controversy. Thus everyone agreed that the state should help finance a railroad between Boston and Albany, and by 1841 the project was complete. But that still left manufacturers in northern and western Massachusetts clamoring for a four-mile tunnel beneath the Berkshire barrier to insure even easier and cheaper access to the expanding national market. From Boston, thanks to the influence of Nathan Appleton and others, the answer came back emphatically: enough was enough.[67] Yet every time the members of the Waltham-Lowell group took such a stand it cost something. Even if the result was only to reveal a division that had always been there, that still did not bode well for the security of the whole elaborate system that had been so carefully built up since 1813.

But whatever dangers lay ahead, in 1845 the system itself still struck its designers as eminently sound—so sound, indeed, that they were contemplating yet another major expansion of it. Some additional development, financed by members of the group, had already occurred at places like Chicopee, Massachusetts; Manchester, New Hampshire; and Saco, Maine. Yet none of those equalled Lowell in size or scope. That distinction would fall to Lawrence, the town that the Essex Manufacturing Company was formed in 1845 to build and promote. The prime mover behind the venture was Abbott Lawrence, brother of Amos, but the capital came from all of the other usual sources as well. And two years later a second, closely allied group would make similar plans to develop the part of West Springfield that later became the town of Holyoke.[68]

Conceived at a moment when profits in the cotton industry were near record levels, the new undertakings involved an almost imperial breadth of vision. Every one of the corporations at Lawrence was to be capitalized at over a million dollars, and to ensure adequate water-power the promoters bought rights to all of Lake Winnepesaukee. At Holyoke a masonry dam a thousand feet long and thirty feet high was needed to harness the enormous power of the Connecticut River, and when the first one proved inadequate and washed away, another was completed in less than eleven months, despite an epidemic of cholera among the workers.[69]

Obviously the risks involved in ventures of this magnitude were substantial, but against the risks could be weighed the achievements of the system. Above all it did what it was designed to do. Every year directors met and duly voted dividends, secure in the knowledge that they themselves, their relatives, and their friends would continue to enjoy the benefits and the responsibilities of wealth without the grinding anxieties it had once entailed. For the adventuresome, or those who wanted a little more money, there were partnerships in the selling houses. Or for the son or nephew interested in trying his hand at business, a comfortable berth as an agent in one of the mills could always be found—a far cry from the old days when starting a career often meant long years at sea serving as a supercargo. Granted, all this exacted a toll in lower rates of dollar profits than might have been earned otherwise; the rewards were worth it. One could take comfort, too, in those aspects of the system so admired by the public at large and thoughtful foreign visitors: its imaginative solution of the labor problem, the solidly impressive buildings at Lowell, the extent to which in fact most of the drearier consequences of European industrialization had been avoided. Time might have dimmed the luster of those accomplishments somewhat, but they still seemed to offer ample testimony to the foresight and wisdom of the founders.

It must have been pleasant as well for those same men to know that their own children had so much cause for gratitude. After all, they were meant to be the principal beneficiaries of the system, and not surprisingly they tended to be very grateful indeed. Writing in 1835 Amos A. Lawrence had said only what many others could have. The son of Amos Lawrence and the nephew of Abbott, he was at that point about to graduate from Harvard and, contemplating the future, observed: "My present design is to be a merchant, not a plodding, narrow-minded one pent up in a city, with my mind always in my counting room, but (if there be such a thing possible) I would be at the same time a literary man in some measure and a farmer." How was such a varied agenda managed? "If I have mercantile tact enough," Lawrence wrote, "to carry on the immense though safe machine my father and uncle have put in operation, it will turn out gold to me as fast as I could wish." The gold, to be sure, imposed obligations, but Lawrence could afford to take a much happier view of the subject than his father had as a young man. "They say riches are a burden that harass the soul and lead into temptation: so they are to the miser who is in constant fear of losing his acquisition . . . A good man will willingly endure the Labor of taking care of his property for the sake of others when he can do so much benefit by it."[70]

The vision of aristocratic noblesse oblige energized by the right measure of "mercantile tact" might have implied a certain confusion in Lawrence's mind. Nevertheless, he did manage to live a life that met his own standards well enough. Marrying the daughter of William Appleton, he had a successful business career, was active in politics, and contributed at least as generously as his father and uncle had to dozens of worthy causes. The thing that made it all possible, too, was what he predicted would: that "immense though safe machine"—a creation which in the end even the Countess of Sutherland might have admired, so much more efficient was it than any means of support available to her.

PART II

Perfecting the Immense Machine

Striding across the hills and valleys of New England, buying up vast stretches of land and water, and plunking down whole cities where none had been before, men like Abbott Lawrence offered a dazzling lesson in the potential inherent in the combination of modern technology and large amounts of capital. But that had never been the only role such men imagined for themselves. In the great scheme of things, as Lawrence's nephew testified, the textile industry was nothing more than a convenient investment vehicle—a means to other ends. And even it required a carefully constructed network of supporting enterprises: not just selling houses, but banks, insurance companies, and railroads as well. So over the years various members of the Waltham-Lowell group remained—or became—active in those fields.

Still, in their eyes the true test of the system lay outside the realm of business altogether. As the burden of care and attention once imposed by commerce was lifted, they looked forward to playing that larger, more satisfying role which presumably came as the duty and prerogative of wealth. There were many forms the role might take: John Cushing built an elaborate house in the country and made a scientific study of exotic fruit trees; Amos Lawrence sent packages to needy clergymen and donated a library building to Williams College. And as time passed such undertakings became even grander. Significantly, 1847—the year that saw the town of Lawrence a going concern—was also the year Abbott Lawrence contributed $50,000 to found the Lawrence Scientific School at Harvard, and the year too when he was first prominently mentioned as a possible candidate for the vice-presidency of the United States. In the long run Lawrence's ambition, no less than the magnitude of his generosity, set him apart from most of his Waltham-Lowell associates, but the difference was mainly one of scale. Year by year, as the cotton mills rose on the banks of the Merrimack, other members of the group continued to move just as energetically in new directions on different fronts—to develop fresh strategies in their larger quest.

Because the activities in question were so varied, a certain amount of separation in analyzing them is unavoidable. Yet most previous studies have gone no further than piecemeal analysis, which unfortunately distorts the reality. The similarities in values and goals as one moves from business to philanthropy to politics, the institutional ties that both expressed and reinforced those similarities, and the fact that so many members of the group were active simultaneously in two and often three different fields, all argue for a more comprehensive approach. Ultimately the Lawrences and their friends tried to shape the world not in pieces, but as a whole. And while the actual result may not have represented quite the seamless web they intended, it nevertheless achieved an impressive coherence in purpose and style—at least for a time.

4.

Transportation, Banking, and Insurance

People who live and work side by side, who invest in the same enterprises and contribute to the same charities, whose families exchange visits daily, and whose children marry one another with almost predictable regularity seldom need labels to identify their common bond. But for historians such labels are a convenience, and it was an historian, writing almost a century after the fact, who first used the term "the Boston Associates."[1] The choice was one that would have appealed to the men Vera Shlakman was writing about. Beyond implying the existence of a relationship and locating it geographically, the phrase revealed little.

As Shlakman used the term, it signified a loosely formed coterie of men whose primary commitment in the field of business was to textile manufacturing. The role its members played in establishing the factory system at places like Lowell—and later Chicopee, Manchester, Lawrence, and Holyoke—gave the group its identity. Yet for many of the individuals, and hence for the group as a whole, power over the great cotton mills seemed so nearly matched by power everywhere else in the region's economic life as to create an impression of dominance unparalleled in antebellum America.

To a point the impression was accurate enough. Depending on how membership is defined, by 1845 the group came to contain about eighty men with interests in thirty-one textile companies. (See the Appendix.) Together those companies controlled 733,981 cotton spindles, or one-fifth of the total capacity of the American industry in 1850. Meanwhile, in 1848, seventeen of the same individuals served as directors of seven Boston banks commanding over 40 percent of the city's authorized banking capital. A similar situation existed in insurance and railroads. In 1846–47 the directorates of six Massachusetts insurance companies, carrying 41 percent of the state's marine insurance and 77 percent of its fire insurance, included twenty Associates. At about the same time, eleven members of the group were serving on the boards of five railroads operating in New England, and a decade earlier, when the Western Railroad was organized, its seven-member board had included two Associates. Also, James K. Mills, another of the Associates, had been the largest individual subscriber to the Western's first stock issue.[2]

Aside from being a partner in one of the major textile selling houses, Mills was involved in manufacturing companies at three different sites and would eventually become the prime mover behind the Hadley Falls Company's development at Holyoke. In addition to the Western, he was an active investor in at least two other railroads, the Boston and Providence and the Taunton Branch, and in 1848 he was listed as a member of the board of the Merchant's Bank. With its paid-up capital of $3 million, the Merchant's was the largest bank in Boston.

Even excluding figures like Abbott Lawrence and Nathan Appleton—who, according to his biographer, served as president or director of no fewer than twenty-two companies in the textile industry alone[3]—Mills's varied business activities and the breadth of influence they implied were by no means unusual among the Associates. Ebenezer Chadwick combined an interest in four textile companies with positions on the boards of the Suffolk Bank, the Merchants Insurance Company, the Massachusetts Hospital Life Insurance Company, and the Boston and Lowell Railroad. An officer or principal stockholder of eleven textile companies, G. W. Lyman was also a director of the Boston and Lowell, as well as of the Columbian Bank, and a vice-president and later president of the Massachusetts Hospital Life Insurance Company. Ignatius Sargent, whose interests in the textile industry paralleled Lyman's, served simultaneously as a director and member of the finance committee of the Massachusetts Hospital Life Insurance Company, president of the Globe Bank, and director of the Boston Insurance Company and the Connecticut River Railroad. Equally active in the management of the Massachusetts Hospital Life Insurance Company, William Sturgis added to that responsibility an interest in six textile companies, directorships of both the Boston and Lowell and the Boston and Providence railroads, and a partnership in a mercantile firm still engaged in the East Indian trade as late as 1840.

If all this overlapping on key boards of directors appeared to concentrate power to a striking degree, it is tempting to argue that the effect was even further compounded by the sturdy network of family ties that bound so many of the Associates together. On the basis of surnames alone, thirty-one members of the group belonged to only eleven families, with the Appleton, Lowell, and Lawrence clans boasting the largest representation of four apiece. Only slightly less numerous were the Cabots, Jacksons, and Brookses, who contributed three members each to the group. Considering, too, that kinship through marriage already linked the Lowells with the Amorys, the Cabots, and the Jacksons, as well as to Benjamin Gorham and Warren Dutton, and more distantly to the Thorndikes, and would in time draw families like the Appletons and Lawrences into the same circle, the apparent consolidation of economic power becomes formidable indeed.

But surely there is a chance that appearances here were deceptive, or at any rate that the conclusions most likely to be drawn from them might misrepresent the reality. Thus, while the constantly ramifying business and family relationships of the Associates could have been aimed at concentrating ever-greater quantities of power in the hands of the group, was that in fact the purpose? Just how much control over the economy of Massachusetts or New England was actually achieved, or exercised, or sought, and for what ends? Lists of directorships and family connections may imply a particular type of motivation, but by themselves they hardly prove that the world of Nathan Appleton was a prototype of the one J. P. Morgan created sixty years later.

In their business activities outside the textile industry, the Associates did favor many of the forms that had worked so well at Waltham and Lowell. Almost without exception the enterprises were organized as corporations chartered by the state. Those corporations also tended to be both heavily capitalized and conservatively managed. Yet the amount of energy expended varied from area to area. In the case of railroads, the Associates' involvement was highly selective and came to less, perhaps, than their impressive array of directorships implied. In banking they made more of an effort and consequently accomplished more, but the result still fell short of undisputed sway over the region's currency and credit, if that was the goal. In insurance the record was similarly mixed, though it may have seemed otherwise because the company that mattered more than any other to the Associates—the Massachusetts Hospital Life Insurance Company, the largest financial institution in New England—had been granted in its original charter a monopoly of life insurance sales in the state. On the other hand the Massachusetts Hospital Life never did more than a small fraction of its business in life insurance, writing as few as sixty-five policies between 1851 and 1860 and only one after that date.[4] There, as elsewhere, the real achievement was not what a cursory review of the evidence might suggest.

Ultimately, companies like the Massachusetts Hospital Life owed their existence to a complex series of investment decisions made over a period of more than thirty years, and without reconstructing those decisions in detail it is impossible to understand how such companies functioned—let alone why they functioned the way they did. With substantial sums to invest and a variety of outlets from which to choose, the Associates allocated resources differently at different times, but the choices were hardly random. Through the years a definite pattern did emerge, implying an equally clear range of objectives. Unquestionably, too, one of the objectives was power, yet never power for its own sake, at least in the eyes of the men themselves. Rather their goal was more precise: above all what they wanted was to protect and perpetuate those gains already achieved in the textile industry. Everything began and ended with the Waltham-Lowell system.

II

By the time the Associates purchased their first railroad shares, a characteristic model of joint public and private action with regard to transportation had already evolved in Massachusetts. In that sense there was less room for innovation than in other sectors of the economy, but the model did allow individuals to vary the level of their participation: they could invest as much or as little as they chose. In the Associates' case a decision to hold investment in turnpikes and canals to a minimum preceded a much heavier—if still limited—commitment to railroads.

Broadly speaking, the commonwealth's approach to transportation projects left to private investors responsibility for taking both the initiative and the risks. In return, the government granted such investors, through charters of incorporation, certain valuable powers—typically the right to take land by eminent domain and permission to charge tolls. In some cases the powers extended farther and included monopoly privileges over specified routes or the right to operate lotteries to raise money. In the bargain it struck with private investors, the government also sacrificed much of the control it might have exercised over the expanding transportation network. Charters of incorporation did impose standards of quality in construction and usually set time limits within which projects had to be completed; upon occasion they even regulated tolls and profits. But exceptions were almost always granted if the original terms proved too confining. And as time passed the tendency was to require less in the first place, if only to save the trouble of negotiating new terms later.[5]

In all of this the state gave away a great deal in return for an uncertain and ill-defined promise of gain. Equally questionable was the fundamental equity of the policy. Instead of relying on private investors, the government could have developed the transportation network itself, covering the costs out of tax revenues. Such an approach would not have gone unopposed: memories of Shays' Rebellion—when an overly heavy burden of taxation had very nearly toppled the social order—ran deep in Massachusetts. Still, in electing not to finance transportation improvements through the tax system, the state was making a choice which, as Morton Horwitz has pointed out, "had major consequences for the distribution of wealth and power in . . . society."[6] Presumably the commonwealth's goal was to facilitate economic development in the interests of all of its citizens, yet its manner of doing so stood to benefit some citizens more substantially—and far more directly—than others.

Nevertheless in practice such issues often seemed secondary to the more tangible results of the state's policy. Thanks to scores of bridge, turnpike, and canal-building ventures, a growing portion of the population was linked to the expanding market economy. Though not all sections or regions benefited equally, most gained at least something. Nor did the investors whose capital financed the effort necessarily reap great rewards. Up to the beginning of the railroad era, profits were generally much lower than expected. Indeed from that standpoint the commonwealth—and beyond it the average citizen—appeared to fare rather well.[7]

The first privately financed transportation facility incorporated by Massachusetts was a bridge spanning the Charles River between Boston and Charlestown. Granted in 1785, the charter went to a group of investors led by Thomas Russell, a wealthy Boston merchant. In the legislature Russell's group had won out against another, organized by the Cabots of Beverly, proposing a different route. Two years later the Cabot group was granted a charter to build the Essex Bridge across the Merrimack at Salem, and in the same year the legislature incorporated the Malden Bridge over the Mystic River. All three bridges lay in the path of major routes northward from Boston, and traffic was heavy from the beginning. As a result investors found themselves handsomely rewarded, and several profited as well from the increased value of adjacent real estate holdings and the opportunity to sell construction materials to the companies in which they were stockholders.[8]

But while a few other bridge projects paid similarly high returns, most did not. And the record was even less prepossessing in the case of the next two innovations in the transportation system: turnpikes and canals. A bridge carrying a significant volume of traffic could be built for as little as a few thousand dollars; turnpikes and canals cost far more. Chartered in 1793 as one of two pioneering canal projects in the United States, the Middlesex Canal took ten years to construct and cost over $500,000. When complete, it ran, via a system of twenty locks, for twenty-eight miles from Boston to a point on the Merrimack River just above the future site of Lowell. The project's backers hoped that a sizable portion of the commerce passing along the river would thus be drawn away from Newburyport to Boston. In time that vision was realized, particularly after the mills at Lowell went into operation. But during the years the Middlesex carried its greatest volume of traffic—between 1833 and 1837—dividends averaged only $30 on stock that had cost $740 a share, or a return of 4 percent. Meanwhile the Salem turnpike never paid more than 3 percent a year, and it was reputed to be the most profitable private road in Massachusetts.[9]

Forced to pay the high costs their ventures entailed, turnpike and canal backers faced similar difficulties in trying to turn a profit. Often such projects were built in anticipation of, rather than in response to, any pressing need for them. They could and did play a crucial role in developing the areas they served, thereby adding to their own business, but only when tolls were kept at a level which encouraged use. That level generally proved to be too low to reward stockholders with adequate dividends. Later, as the transportation network expanded, competition worked to keep proceeds down. Turnpikes vied with one another, and canals competed with turnpikes, while a greatly improved system of free public roads took business away from both. With a growing range of choices, shippers and passengers—farmers, merchants, and manufacturers—benefited, but stockholders suffered.

And when their ventures did pay satisfactory returns, they faced yet another problem. In such instances it became much more difficult, if not impossible, to ignore questions of equity, as the *Charles River Bridge* case proved. Like most investors in transportation projects, the proprietors of the Charles River Bridge assumed that their charter, though it contained no explicit guarantee of a monopoly, granted them a "vested right" in the traffic between specified points. Thus in 1791, when a proposal for a second toll bridge across the Charles came before the legislature, they protested vehemently. They did receive some compensation from the state, but the competing bridge went up in spite of their protest. By 1816 two more had been added. Then in 1828 the legislature chartered another, a scant few hundred yards away, to operate without charging any toll at all. At that point, arguing that the latest grant rendered their own charter worthless, the Charles River Bridge proprietors took the issue to court. Unable to resolve the case, the Massachusetts Supreme Court left it up to Chief

Justice Taney's tribunal in Washington, which in 1837 upheld the legislature's action.[10]

Unless it specifically so stated, a charter of incorporation could not be construed as granting monopoly privileges: that was the gist of Taney's decision—the epilogue of the Charles River Bridge dispute. Yet in Massachusetts the issue had been more broadly defined. Obliged to act in the public interest, the General Court was finding itself deluged with appeals to do whatever seemed necessary to foster continued economic expansion. At the same time voters were expressing growing resentment against any special privilege that appeared to enrich the few at the expense of the many. Even if many people stopped short of challenging the ultimate justice of the state's approach to transportation projects, it was easy enough to understand that by 1828 the original investment in the Charles River Bridge had been returned to the proprietors many times over. In that situation the least the General Court could do was treat all comers alike, and not even the judiciary afforded any protection. Despite the eloquence of Daniel Webster's arguments before the Supreme Court, the Charles River Bridge proprietors lost their case and subsequently had to abandon their investment to the state. But by then the public's enthusiasm for transportation improvements had found a new focus—the railroad—though hardly one that settled many of the relevant issues.

At the outset it would have been difficult to predict what role the Boston Associates might play in constructing New England's railroad system. One of their number, Thomas H. Perkins, had been largely responsible for first demonstrating in America the feasibility of hauling heavy freight significant distances over rails. Completed under his direction in 1826, the Quincy Granite Railway used horse-drawn cars, a masonry roadbed, and wooden rails to move cut stone for the Bunker Hill Monument three miles from the quarry in Quincy to a wharf where it could be shipped to Charlestown.[11] The entire undertaking stood as an imaginative solution to a difficult problem and attracted a great deal of attention. Whether, on the other hand, it prefaced any broader commitment on the part of Perkins and his friends remained to be seen. The Bunker Hill Monument had long been a favorite project of theirs, and except for the Quincy Granite Railway they had taken little part in the many transportation ventures that flourished—or failed to flourish—around the region.

A few of the Associates did have family or business connections with some of the promoters of the earliest bridge and canal projects, but many were too young to become investors themselves in the 1780s and 1790s, and others, like the Appletons and Lawrences, had yet to arrive in Boston. Later the low rate of return in all but a handful of instances would have gone far toward dampening interest. Even during the 1820s, when the completion of the Erie Canal sparked a renewed boom in canal building, most of the Associates continued to hang back, and with good reason. By then Lowell mill stocks represented a more attractive investment opportunity; they were both safer and more profitable. In the growing debate over special privilege, too, they carried with them less need to defend unpopular positions than transportation shares did. Except for machinery patents, no Waltham-Lowell corporation ever asked for a monopoly. In place of the dubious security such favors brought, stockholders had been able to rely on the technological and financial superiority of the enterprises themselves. For the moment those things guaranteed protection enough against competition.

Still, the Erie Canal was a fact, and as investors whose substantial interests remained almost exclusively concentrated in New England, the Associates might have been expected to be concerned about the threat posed by New York's great achievement. At the time newspapers in Boston were full of dire predictions about the fate awaiting the city, its commerce, and the enterprises dependent on both unless steps were taken to meet the danger. The image used most often was that of a great race between Boston and New York City, one Boston was on the verge of losing forever. Any number of petitions to the legislature took such a line, and not surprisingly—with so much evidence available—most historians have ever since.[12] As early as twenty years afterward the notion that New Englanders in general, and Bostonians in particular, had uniformly succumbed to a state of depression as a result of the opening of the Erie Canal, was all but taken for granted. "Between the close of 1825 and the beginning of 1831 gloom and despondency seemed to settle upon Massachusetts," wrote Elias Derby, the great railroad promoter, in 1846. "The grass began to invade the wharves and pavements of her commercial centers and the paint to desert the front of her villages . . . She seemed to stand at the ancestral tomb, sorrowing that she could not partake of the progress of the age."[13]

But apparently there were some quarters where such emotions never penetrated, regardless of what later observers thought. Writing to his son in January 1831, Amos Lawrence was pleased to report: "Our local affairs are very delightful in this state and city . . . the prosperity of the people is very great. In our city, in particular, the people have not had greater prosperity for twenty years."[14] Of course there was always a chance New York's canal might end the happy situation Lawrence described, which was exactly the specter

that transportation enthusiasts raised, when they were not arguing that the process of decay had already begun.

Whatever the reality, their arguments proved singularly effective.
By the end of 1831 Massachusetts stood committed to the construction
of a railroad that would run from Boston to Albany, thereby—the
plan's supporters claimed—stealing a march on New York City in the
great scramble for commercial advantage. Behind that commitment
lay several years of heated debate in the legislature, first over the
comparative virtues of canals versus railroads, with the railroad
emerging victorious, and then over how such an undertaking should
be financed. Because of the size of the project, many people maintained that nothing would be done unless the commonwealth itself
built the railroad. But as in the past, fear of taxes settled the issue in
favor of a private effort, aided by the state through its powers of
incorporation. Actually there were to be two charters and two separate companies. One would build a railroad as far as Worcester, and
once the practicability of that much of the plan had been established,
a second corporation would extend the line the rest of the way to
Albany. Chartered in 1831, the Boston and Worcester was opened in
1835, while the Western, chartered in 1833, took all of eight years to
inaugurate full service over its route.[15]

In order to make the two railroads as attractive as possible to private
investors, both charters contained provisions guaranteeing investors
freedom to set rates and the right to a monopoly along the routes
specified for thirty years. Thus was a repetition of the Charles River
Bridge disaster to be avoided. In addition, stockholders were granted
limited liability, and finally, to encourage even people of modest
means to participate, the par value of a share of stock was set at $100.

Ultimately the enormous expense involved in building the Western—over $7 million by 1841—compelled the commonwealth to de-
part from its time-honored practice by agreeing to aid the line with
substantial stock purchases and loans. But the Boston and Worcester
did manage to raise all of its capital privately. In response to the
legislature's generous grant of privileges, 238 individuals and firms
subscribed to the corporation's first issue of 10,000 shares. And the list
did contain the names of many of the Boston Associates, suggesting,
on their part, a hearty endorsement of the scheme.

Nor was the Boston and Worcester the only railroad that attracted
the Associates' support. Several of the group were even more conspicuously involved in the Boston and Lowell. Chartered a year before the
Boston and Worcester, the Boston and Lowell was designed to do
exactly what its name implied: provide a more serviceable link between the great textile mills and the coast. Until then both raw mate-

rials and finished goods had been shipped, weather permitting, along
the Middlesex Canal. Obviously the railroad promised to destroy
much of the canal's business, and in due course stockholders in the
older facility protested—to no avail. With the General Court's blessing and Patrick Jackson to supervise construction, work on the railroad began at once, and by mid-1835 it was open for its entire
twenty-six-mile length. To inaugurate it Jackson, using his largest
locomotive, took a party of two dozen directors and stockholders up
to Lowell. Making the trip in an hour and seventeen minutes, they
dined on salmon brought along for the occasion and then left for
Boston again, arriving an hour and twenty-three minutes later. As the
train sped by "the country people" gathered "on the bridges and
banks," one of the travelers wrote afterward, "the Track labourers
swung [their] hats with huzzahs."[16]

Altogether it was a pleasant initiation into the wonders of the railroad age. Yet it may also have promised more than the sequel delivered, at least as far as the continuing participation of the Boston
Associates was concerned. To be sure, they supported both the Boston and Worcester and the Western, adding their names to the appropriate subscription lists with considerable fanfare. But the role they
played in those instances was quite different from the role they played
in building the Boston and Lowell, an enterprise they continued to
dominate for decades, providing the company's entire slate of directors year after year. In the case of the Boston and Worcester, most of
the Associates originally down for shares—including Harrison Gray
Otis, Nathan, William, and Samuel Appleton, and Patrick Jackson—
sold their rights within a year. Usually the sales netted a small profit,
but Jackson was so anxious to get out that he took a $600 loss at a
point when the corporation seemed to be having difficulty getting
under way.[17]

And when the Western's turn came, the same pattern developed:
an initial flurry of activity followed by a period of withdrawal. At the
outset the Associates went to even greater lengths than they had in
behalf of the Boston and Worcester. After subscriptions to the Western's first stock issue proved virtually impossible to raise, a mass rally
was organized at Faneuil Hall with Abbott Lawrence in the chair, and
when that failed to drum up a sufficient number of pledges, a door-to-
door campaign was mounted. Serving with Edmund Dwight, an Associate, as one of the Boston solicitors, Josiah Quincy, Jr. thought it
"the most unpleasant business I ever engaged in." Everyone made
excuses. "Some think the city is large enough and do not want to
increase it. Some have no faith in legislative grants of charters
since the fate of the Charlestown bridge."[18]

Eventually, with men like Dwight, Lawrence, and Nathan Appleton to tout the project, enough stock was sold for construction on the Western to begin. Among the Associates down for 100 shares or more were Appleton, Thomas H. Perkins, and the Lawrences and James K. Mills through their firms. Several of the same men were also instrumental in working out the series of state stock purchases and loans that made the line's completion possible. Nor did as many of them immediately rush to sell their shares. But buyers were probably few and far between, at least for several years. By 1845 the company's records would reveal that it had sustained every bit as sweeping a change in ownership as the Boston and Worcester. Only 12 of the 111 original stockholders who had purchased fifty or more shares—a group in which the Associates figured prominently—still held so much as a single share.[19]

All this suggests a rather complex set of motives. In a new field where the risks are high, investors will normally proceed with a combination of caution and patience. When the Associates sold their stock in the Boston and Worcester and the Western, neither company had started paying dividends. Still, there was every likelihood they would do so in time, and in the long run investment in both lines proved quite profitable. The Boston and Worcester paid its first dividend in 1835. Though the directors set the rate at a mere 2 percent, by 1837 they felt able to pay four times that. Thereafter the return never fell below 6 percent, and between 1845 and 1862 it averaged 7.28 percent. Slower to offer stockholders any return, the Western waited until 1845 to pay its first dividend. Two years later the rate, which had been set at 6 percent, rose to 8 percent, and over the whole period from 1845 to 1862 the Western's average return of 7.39 percent actually exceeded the Boston and Worcester's.[20]

At 6 to 8 percent, railroad dividends compared well with the return on money invested in Lowell mills. From 1838 on, in fact, the comparison distinctly favors the railroads in many years. Yet there is nothing to indicate that they ever acquired the importance, as investment outlets, in the calculations of the Associates that, for example, an enterprise like the Hamilton Company enjoyed from the start. If railroads mattered to the group at all—and clearly they did—it was for other reasons.

At the time subscription lists were being circulated for the Western, there was a good deal of talk about patriotic duty. Without describing grass covering the wharves of Boston, Nathan Appleton could still speak of the "enlightened public spirit" he hoped would lead his fellow "capitalists" to support such projects.[21] Doubtless Appleton was sincere, but he also had the better part of $1 million invested in textile mills that would benefit directly from improved transportation facilities. The bulk of his capital was tied up at Lowell, so he must have been especially eager to see a railroad built there. But other men, with whom he shared many interests, had large investments at Chicopee, which the Western would serve. Edmund Dwight and James K. Mills were both in that category. Why not, then, join forces and back one another's pet ventures? After an early show of support, with all the weight it would carry considering its source, any unwanted shares could be put up for sale quietly. Even if no purchases materialized, a loss of $10,000, or twice that—the most any of the Associates invested—would still be relatively minor. Meanwhile the railroads would get built. And that has what counted.

As for why such a strategy was not revised later, once investment in railroads became profitable, there were several good reasons, most having to do with a single, prominent feature of railroad corporations: the low par value of their stock. The $100-a-share figure—as against $1,000 for Waltham-Lowell ventures—did broaden participation and hence dilute the risks involved. But increasing the size of the stockholder group also made it more difficult to maintain control, a problem that the high visibility of railroads and the general public's stake in their operation simply compounded. More stockholders, too, meant a greater volume of stock sales at any point, which in turn encouraged speculation in railroad shares.

All of these pitfalls became clear in the first decade of the Western's operation. For years a bitter dispute raged between those stockholders who wanted high-to-moderate freight rates, in order to enable the corporation to meet its obligations to the state and begin paying dividends, and an opposing party, led by Elias Derby, demanding low rates to improve Boston's commercial position. With ownership spread among several thousand individuals and the commonwealth the largest single shareholder, the contending points of view were endlessly aired in the press, in the legislature, before special investigating committees, and in numerous stockholders' meetings, many of which came to look more like political conventions than orderly gatherings of investors going about their business. Also disturbing was the spectacle of the managements of the Western and the Boston and Worcester openly quarreling over the division of fares between the two lines.[22] And finally there was the singular conduct of Addison Gilmore as president of the Western.

The fourth person to hold the office, Gilmore served from 1846 to 1850. Unlike his predecessors—T. B. Wales, Edmund Dwight, and George Bliss—he had no connection with the Boston Associates. In fact, having made his stake in the drug business and selling liquor, he was very much an outsider. But despite his dubious credentials,

Gilmore proposed to make money out of the Western and did just that. While he was president, firms in which he was interested earned substantial profits selling construction materials and equipment to the railroad. He also used his insider's knowledge to buy and sell the company's stock at a dizzying rate. When he took office he owned 200 shares, an amount that grew to 409 over the next year, just as the Western was about to increase its dividend to 8 percent. By 1848 he had reduced his holding to a mere 7 shares, only to increase it again to 350 the following year. Busy as he was with such pursuits, Gilmore managed to initiate few changes in the railroad he ran, yet given the Western's steadily increasing business it scarcely mattered. Just as when $235,000 worth of rails purchased from the Tremont Iron Works—in which Gilmore was a large investor—proved to be of inferior quality, or when, in 1850, an audit revealed that the treasurer had embezzled almost $70,000, the company seemed to weather the storm handily enough.[23]

But even if Gilmore's activities did no lasting damage, one could still find in them ample reason to doubt the wisdom of tying up money in railroad shares. Irresponsible management was a danger in any corporation; when it occurred in a situation characterized by diffuse ownership and a high degree of public involvement, the threat was one no thoughtful investor could ignore, especially if there was an alternative. And of course for all of the Associates there was an alternative. From the beginning, their own model of corporate organization could not have been less like Addison Gilmore's Western. Closely held and tightly controlled, Waltham-Lowell companies were managed with the utmost discretion. They were also managed as far away from the glare of publicity as possible. With such a safe harbor in which to anchor their capital, the Associates had no need to invest in companies like the Western.

So they confined themselves to a promotional role: plugging this or that railroad project if it promised a more efficient way of transporting raw cotton or finished goods. Because they threw themselves into the effort with such enthusiasm, it was easy to miss the point. The truth was that only in the case of the Boston and Lowell was there much beyond an initial burst of activity, and significantly, the Associates took steps to ensure that the Boston and Lowell functioned quite differently from other railroad corporations. If it cost only $100 to become a stockholder in the Boston and Worcester or the Western, the par value of a share of Boston and Lowell stock was set by the company's charter at five times that amount.[24]

The entire sequence, to be sure, could be seen as something of a lost opportunity. Having managed to write the necessary terms into the Boston and Lowell's charter, the Associates might have tried the same tactic with the other railroads. Had they then bought and held onto a sufficient quantity of stock, they could have acquired both a profitable investment and effective control over the region's transportation system. But did the Associates want such power? In the end their behavior suggested that they did not. Some developments in transportation were most unlikely to occur without their involvement—a railroad to Lowell, for example. It was important too, although less so, that other railroads be built. And in a minor way the group also supported the policy of high freight rates and prompt payment by the railroads of all financial obligations, despite the adverse effect on the port of Boston.[25] But that was all. At stake was no sweeping campaign for ultimate power, only a series of limited initiatives, most of them directly related to the Waltham-Lowell system.

III

Much the same sort of approach characterized the role the Associates played in banking. Few fields of business endeavor were more beset by risk and confusion in America during the antebellum period than banking, and no other so agitated voters and politicians at every level. Because the paired issues of money and credit—how much, controlled by whom, and for whose benefit—appeared so central to economic growth, any action became the subject of instant controversy. The federal government sponsored two national banking systems between 1789 and 1861, only to dismantle each in turn, and had recourse at other times to a dozen different expedients. The states, meanwhile, created banks of their own at a frantic clip—just as the banks themselves created the notes that remained the nation's principal currency. It was not, in short, a milieu calculated to attract men with an interest in stability and security. But it was also not one that could be ignored. Too much depended on what shape the resulting financial system would assume. Perforce, then, the Associates were concerned with banking, and by proceeding largely outside the political arena, they managed to fasten certain patterns of order on banking in New England—patterns, in fact, that made the region something of a model.

In several respects the history of commercial banking in Massachusetts paralleled developments in transportation. Assigning, through charters of incorporation, valuable privileges to groups of private individuals, the commonwealth sought both to encourage efforts it chose not to undertake itself and to exercise a measure of control over what was done. In the long run, however, it proved easier to encourage than to control, and the balance steadily shifted toward the former.[26]

The Massachusetts Bank, the first such institution sanctioned by the General Court, received its charter in 1784. Its powers included the right to issue notes bearing the commonwealth's seal, with harsh penalties imposed by the state in cases of counterfeiting. The bank was further entitled to hold deposits and make loans and was to function as the commonwealth's fiscal agent. Though the charter contained no explicit grant of a monopoly, the stockholders doubtless assumed the bank would continue to enjoy its unique status. Yet that assumption proved no more valid than the similar hopes of the proprietors of the Charles River Bridge.[27]

By 1792 pressure from many quarters for more money in circulation and opposition to the special privileges of the Massachusetts Bank combined to force the chartering of a second "state bank"—the Union—which, in turn, fueled demand for others. Between 1795 and 1803 eight new banks were added, and over the next nine years at least a dozen more were created. At the same time the state did what it could to impose restraint. Except in Boston, the General Court refused for a while longer to charter more than one bank in a community and prohibited unincorporated groups from operating in the field. The state also taxed bank capital, limited note issue to twice the amount of capital, and made it illegal for bank directors to serve on the boards of other banks. But all the while the number of banks continued to grow. By 1829 there were 66 and eight years later 129, with a combined capital of $38 million.[28]

Under the circumstances investment in banking involved considerable risk. Dividends were high in some cases, but so was the element of uncertainty. Thus while many Associates owned bank stock at one time or another, most held their commitments to a fairly modest level. Nathan Appleton invested in several banks between 1804 and 1823 and then, over the next two years, sold almost all his shares. After 1831 he again began buying limited amounts of bank stock. Except for those at Lowell and Lawrence, the banks he chose tended to be both large and conservatively managed. At the time of his death his bank shares had a book value of $92,000—a substantial sum, yet far less than the $827,000 he had invested in the textile industry.[29]

The relative size of Appleton's commitments to banking and textiles gave some indication of how he assessed the attractiveness of each as an investment outlet; so did his decision to liquidate his bank stockholdings in the mid-1820s, just as the mills at Lowell were going up. At that point, too, there were more than the usual number of warning signals along the banking horizon. By law all bank charters in Massachusetts were scheduled to come up for renewal in 1831, and there was always a chance the legislature might decide to take back some of

what it had given away so freely. In the event, the system survived
intact. Not a single bank failed to win recharter, and as a result investors like Appleton reentered the field.[30] There was also by then an
added protection: an institution capable of controlling the worst banking abuses, though hardly one the state had created.

For anyone doing business in Boston, the chief problem posed by the
unending proliferation of banks was the flood of currency that resulted, much of it sound, but some of it not. Notes from country
banks inevitably gravitated toward the coast, and bankers there were
at a loss as to how to proceed. Their own sound notes were driven out
of circulation, and it sometimes proved impossible to get the country
paper redeemed. Merely distinguishing good notes from bad took
more time every year. For a while there was talk of chartering a state
agency to act as a clearinghouse, but the project never came to anything. The country banks had no interest in it, and certain traders in
Boston made a profitable business out of speculating in discounted
bank notes; together the country bankers and the speculators defeated the drive for state regulation.[31]

There matters stood until the Suffolk Bank came into being in 1818.
While nothing in its charter distinguished it from any other Boston
bank, the Suffolk from the outset took on a series of unique functions
that made it, in effect, the central bank of New England. Inviting
deposits of $5,000 or more from country banks, it offered, upon re-
ceipt of such deposits, to begin accepting the notes of those banks at
no additional discount. At the same time it announced that it was
prepared, "as the directors may hereafter order," to present for immediate redemption in specie, all other out-of-town bank paper that
came its way. By thus combining the carrot and the stick, the Suffolk's
officers hoped to bring order out of chaos. In 1824 the system was
further refined when six of the major Boston banks agreed to maintain
deposits at the Suffolk and have it act as their sole agent in redeeming
country notes.[32]

As might be expected, the Suffolk Bank was unpopular in not a few
quarters. Its agents were relentlessly efficient in pursuing country
bankers reluctant to make good on their notes, and the added clout
the arrangement acquired with the inclusion of the other Boston
banks made it doubly offensive. Charging undue coercion and unfair
monopolistic practice, opponents referred to the "Holy Alliance" or
the "Six-Tailed Bashaw" and appealed to the General Court for relief.
Still, the system worked—it did stabilize the currency. In time the
notes of almost all New England banks came to circulate at par. And

recognizing that the Suffolk had accomplished what they themselves were powerless to do, the legislators seemed disposed to leave it alone, at least for the present.[33]

Creating a central bank without official sanction took energy and imagination, as well as substantial financial resources, and while others might have met those requirements, in the end it was the Boston Associates who chose to make the effort. From first to last the Suffolk Bank was their project. Seven of its first eleven directors were members of the group—including Patrick Jackson, Kirk Boott, Nathan and William Appleton, and Amos and Abbott Lawrence. Thirty years later the number had fallen to five out of twelve, but the Suffolk still drew a higher percentage of its board from the ranks of the Associates than any other bank in Massachusetts.[34]

Apparently, too, they were pleased with the result. In the 1820s, the Second Bank of the United States stood ready to perform many of the same functions the Suffolk system did, and with William Appleton running its Boston branch, the BUS did exert a salutary influence. But when Andrew Jackson's attack on the bank led its president, Nicholas Biddle, to retaliate with drastic measures of his own, the Associates became increasingly disenchanted with the whole idea of national banking. Deploring Jackson's crusade, they liked Biddle's tactics no better and were furious when their attempts to reason with him were dismissed with "the merest commonplaces."[35] In the aftermath, Henry Clay got little help from Boston in his attempt to have a new bank chartered by Congress. Writing in 1841, Abbott Lawrence remarked that, in his opinion, the country was better off *"without* than *with* a Bank unless we can have one of the good old fashion Alexander Hamilton character"* and doubted, as did Nathan Appleton, whether stock in the proposed institution would sell.[36] Both men fully supported John Tyler's veto of Clay's bank bill. The truth was that banking and politics were a dangerous combination. In New England—thanks to the Suffolk Bank—matters were more satisfactorily arranged.

Yet even the Suffolk system required a constant public relations campaign. If published together, the anonymous newspaper articles and pamphlets written by Nathan Appleton on banking during the late thirties and early forties would have filled a fair-sized volume. In paragraph after paragraph readers were shown the virtues and benefits of a sound currency, circulating at par and redeemable in specie on demand. Often signing himself "Bullionite," Appleton left no stone unturned in endeavoring to prove that any other system was "merely a broken promise."[37]

At such moments Appleton could have been seen as a conservative businessman with the same stake in stable values that any very wealthy man had. The fact that part of his fortune was tied up in banking gave him an added reason for speaking out. On the other hand, bank stocks never accounted for more than 6 percent of his total holdings, and there were men in Boston at least as rich as he who felt no need to lecture the public on banking—who seemed content to let others bear the burden of maintaining the Suffolk system. What, then, moved Appleton and his friends to act? The answer is that they were involved with the banks not just as investors, or out of a general interest in financial stability, but also as borrowers. The connection was indirect; they did not need the money themselves. The mills at Lowell did, and in increasingly large amounts.

At first glance this might seem surprising, since keeping debt levels low continued to play an important part in the Waltham-Lowell system. But even the most conservatively managed companies occasionally require cash, and Waltham-Lowell companies were no exception. As a rule, their working capital was tied up in inventories and accounts due from selling houses. At particular times of the year—when dividends had to be paid, for example, or when raw cotton purchases had to be financed—borrowing often proved easier than drawing on other resources. Though such loans rarely ran for longer than twelve months, they could be quite important, especially during periods of economic stress.[38]

Originally, much of this sort of short-term credit had been provided by the selling houses themselves. But as the volume of business grew the amounts involved became larger, and the backers of the principal houses were reluctant to commit the extra capital to their firms. After 1830, Nathan Appleton devoted much less time to the affairs of Paige and Company, and in a series of revised partnership agreements systematically limited his financial exposure. As anxious as ever to spend time in other ways, he apparently had doubts about the ability of his partners to carry on the business without him, doubts their performance during the depression of 1837–1842 did little to allay. In that situation—drawing heavily on Appleton's credit—the firm made it through, but not without some difficult moments.[39]

Obviously it would be better to be spared such moments altogether, and the banks provided a ready alternative. They still required an added endorsement before lending money to manufacturing corporations, but company officers or directors could cosign notes when the selling houses chose not to. That way all commitments would be kept in line with available resources. Meanwhile, for their part, the banks would be acquiring—as major borrowers—a group of companies with a capital structure that made any loan to them virtually risk-free.

But for the arrangement to function properly, it was essential that the banks themselves remain sound. Weak banks would call loans at the first sign of distress, and it was just at such times that Waltham-Lowell companies were likely to want to increase—not reduce—their borrowing. Thus anything that contributed to instability in banking was to be avoided, and above all a disordered, unmanaged currency. The system was only as strong as its weakest link. If country banks were allowed to turn out paper at will, every bank in Boston stood in jeopardy. Hence the "Holy Alliance" with its elaborate mechanisms for enforcing responsibility: it ensured that New England's banking business would be conducted on a sound basis, and in the process it guaranteed its organizers an adequate source of short-term credit—one they used with increasing frequency. A study of the borrowing practices of eight Waltham-Lowell companies estimates that between 1840 and 1860 commercial banks provided 63 percent of all loans running from six months to a year. In the case of loans running from thirty days to six months the figure was even higher—86.9 percent.[40]

By substituting bank loans for their own capital the Associates could have been freeing resources for projects outside the textile industry, yet that does not seem to have been their objective. The money Appleton withheld from his selling house went to buy shares in the manufacturing companies themselves.[41] The capital remained in the industry, but without the added elements of risk and uncertainty that came with investing in selling houses. In the Waltham-Lowell system ordinary stockholders could not be asked for commitments of money—or time—they preferred not to give.

As for the time involved in managing the affairs of the Suffolk bank, surely the work was pleasanter than hounding country storekeepers who had fallen behind in payments for cloth shipments. The one could be seen as a service to society; the other was nothing more than the workaday routine of commerce. Since, too, the goals Appleton and his colleagues sought to achieve through the banking system were limited, there could be limits to the resources of all kinds that they devoted to the effort. And such limits remained important. By tailoring a broader strategy to a more complex problem, the Associates accomplished more in banking than they did with the railroads—a greater degree of control, a tighter rein on a vital sector of the region's economy. Still, their overriding concern was the same in both cases: refining and protecting their stake in the textile industry.

IV

But even with the railroads and a sound banking system in place, the structure stood only partially complete. Faster, more reliable access to markets offered no protection against the danger of fire along the way, or in the mills themselves. An abundant supply of short-term credit hardly guaranteed that manufacturers could borrow money for longer periods if they wished to. And finally, neither the iron horse nor the "Holy Alliance" provided any solution at all to another pressing problem. Capital invested in industrial corporations could pass readily enough from one generation to the next: gifts or simple inheritance would convey the appropriate stock certificates to children and grandchildren. Yet that did not necessarily mean they would continue to enjoy the same benefits their parents had. Considering the intricacies of the Waltham-Lowell system, a more elaborate means of transmission seemed essential.

When the Boston Company was founded, fire insurance was still a novelty in Massachusetts, but at least the form existed. No financial institution at that point extended long-term credit to manufacturers, and the law governing inheritance remained in a primitive state. In each of these areas the Associates made significant contributions, encouraging and sometimes initiating—as they did elsewhere—developments that were at once far-reaching in effect and peculiarly adapted to their own immediate needs.

In colonial New England disasters like fire tended to be seen as acts of God against which people could do little to protect themselves, but it was possible to deal with the consequences. When buildings burned, individuals suffering losses were often helped by voluntary contributions from the community at large. Since the contributors could reasonably expect that the favor would be returned if they found themselves in similar straits, this amounted to a crude form of insurance, and for a merchant with a few rooms full of goods it usually proved adequate. An enterprise with hundreds of thousands of dollars invested in buildings and machinery was another matter, and the danger of fire in textile mills ran high.

The earliest prepaid insurance available in Boston covered losses in maritime commerce. Offered by individuals and groups on a voyage-by-voyage basis, it helped spread risks over the merchant community as a whole and became increasingly common after 1800 as the hazards of commerce grew. Fire insurance developed more slowly. Though its title implied otherwise, the first incorporated insurance venture in the state—the Massachusetts Fire and Marine Company, which received its charter in 1795—confined itself to maritime underwriting. Then, in 1798, the General Court agreed to charter the Massachusetts Mutual Fire Insurance Company provided that its directors secured pledges for $2 million in property coverage before beginning business. Eventually a vigorous campaign, stretched over an entire year, produced the necessary pledges.[42]

With one company operating successfully, others soon entered the field. Most early fire insurance policies were written on commercial and industrial property, and from the start all Waltham-Lowell ventures were heavily insured. As solidly financed as they were, not one of them could have afforded the loss of two-thirds of its capital. Choosing only the largest insurers, the Associates tended to divide their business among a limited group of companies—in particular the Merchants', the Manufacturers', the Firemen's, and the National. The same companies, in turn, regularly listed the largest number of Associates as directors. In a complex field it was important to keep track of the latest developments. A growing body of experience made it possible for insurers to gauge risks with considerable precision and set rates accordingly. In time a system of slow-burning construction was developed for textile mills, which came into general use at places like Lowell. Initial costs were higher, but the savings in insurance premiums more than justified the added expense.[43]

Investment in insurance companies also proved quite profitable in some cases. The $200 Nathan Appleton put into the Merchants' Insurance Company in 1822 had grown—with the dividends used to purchase new shares—to $15,000 by 1850, and the following year the company paid what he described as a "whopping dividend of 15 percent." But the risks in insurance were high. Appleton lost money in several such ventures, and at his death his total insurance holdings amounted to only $67,740 at market value—less, even, than his investment in banking.[44]

Still another way the Associates used the insurance business was as a source of loan capital for textile enterprises. The same eight Waltham-Lowell companies that came to rely so heavily on the commercial banks for short-term credit also borrowed from insurance companies for periods running from thirty days or less to over a year.[45] But the frequency of such borrowing was never great. Other lenders were better equipped to operate in the field: commercial banks and, for intermediate-term credit, savings banks.

Organized as a way for the "working poor" to secure a portion of their earnings against the perils of modern economic life, savings banks accumulated substantial resources before the Civil War. The first savings bank in Massachusetts—the Provident Institution—

received its charter in 1817 and by 1856 there were eighty-four in the state, with combined deposits of more than $27 million. Investing heavily in mortgages, the savings banks also lent money to larger, well-established industrial corporations, and because savings deposits were more stable than those of commercial banks, such loans ran for relatively long periods. Of the loans contracted for over a year by the eight textile companies in the sample, savings banks accounted for more—39.7 percent—than any other type of institution.[46] Among their other activities, too, various Associates routinely served on the boards of savings banks and so were in a position to influence their lending policies.

But individually the savings banks could only extend credit to the limit of their modest holdings. A far richer institution—and one in which the Associates played a much more prominent role—was the Massachusetts Hospital Life Insurance Company. In 1836 it had resources half again as large as the twenty-eight savings banks in the state combined. Over the next decade the savings banks pulled ahead in terms of total deposits, yet as compared to the $10,681,000 controlled by thirty-eight of them together, the Massachusetts Hospital Life—alone—administered a fund of $7,703,000.[47] And between 1845 and 1855 the company's loans to Waltham-Lowell ventures grew from $311,000 to $3,927,000, or very nearly half its total resources.[48]

The Massachusetts Hospital Life did not make its first loan to a Waltham-Lowell corporation until 1826. In the beginning the benefits envisioned had been of an altogether different sort. As John Lowell—the brother of Francis Cabot Lowell and one of the founders of the company—remarked in trying to convey some sense of its unique function: "It is *eminently* the *Savings bank of the wealthy.*"[49] Though obviously the kind of saving Lowell meant bore little resemblance to setting aside a few dollars each month to buy a home or educate a child, at bottom his description was accurate. Like a savings bank, the Massachusetts Hospital Life Insurance Company assumed as its primary duty the preservation of the capital entrusted to it. But because the sums were large, they required rather special management. Also important in determining the company's character was the particular set of contingencies against which its depositors hoped to protect their money.

In one sense those contingencies affected all New Englanders—not just Lowell and the other Associates who took such a large hand in the company's affairs—for they were all subject to the practice of partible inheritance. Mandated by law and custom, partible inheritance had been in force since the seventeenth century. It dictated that property passing from one generation to the next would be divided equally within families; that children would share alike in the estates of their parents. The rule held even when the division produced individual portions of little value. A farm that supported a family comfortably could become worthless as four or five separate parcels of land. Dividing the capital needed to carry on commerce successfully might leave heirs with sums quite inadequate for that purpose. Division also invariably disrupted the normal operation of the business. Still, tradition and the courts granted little leeway when the time came.

The problem of disruption had partially been taken care of in the Waltham-Lowell system by the use of joint-stock corporations. When a partner of an unincorporated commercial firm died, its assets had to be valued and appropriate portions conveyed, in some form or other, to his heirs. The process might take years, and all the while the firm would remain in a kind of limbo, unable to function on anything like the usual basis. Corporate holdings, on the other hand, had established values and could be distributed to heirs by simply reregistering the shares in a different name. As a result the business would continue with its capital intact and the same family interests represented.

Unless, of course, the heirs decided to sell their stock, which, under ordinary circumstances, they were free to do. And clearly, from the Associates' standpoint that possibility posed serious difficulties. Sudden sales of large blocks of stock were likely to lower prices, damaging the position of other Waltham-Lowell investors, many of whom were relatives or friends. Such sales also threatened to bring unwanted strangers into the group. In the case of new enterprises especially, either or both could prove disastrous.

The very energy with which the Associates urged their children to follow careers outside business only compounded the dangers on this score. Beyond the dividends they received, there would be little to bind those children to the companies their fathers had founded. What if, in a time of crisis, dividends were reduced? Or what would become of the individual who refused to live within the income provided? The truth was that lacking expertise in financial matters, the same children for whose sake the system had been so carefully designed might be all too prone to making rash investment decisions. And given free rein, they were in a position to harm not only themselves, but others— indeed the entire group.

The obvious solution was an arrangement that guaranteed heirs the appropriate benefits—in the form of income—but prevented them from determining how the principal would be treated. Something like this could be accomplished through guardianship for those unable to manage their own property, such as minor children. Yet on reaching the age of twenty-one, children normally came into full possession of their inheritances. Massachusetts law did not cover situations in which those writing wills, or otherwise disposing of property, preferred to limit a beneficiary's discretion in the absence of any notable incapacity.

Nevertheless, by the end of the eighteenth century a number of people, particularly merchants, were taking the first tentative steps in that direction. The result was the practice of transmitting property in trust, under terms that bound those receiving it—the trustees—to provide certain benefits, including income, to designated individuals. Depending on the terms of the arrangement, a person so designated—the *cestui que trust*—might in time be given the property itself, but it was also possible to postpone that step by a generation or more. Thus widows could be granted an income during their lifetimes, and the assets thereafter conveyed to children. Or the life interest might go to children, with grandchildren receiving the property.[50]

Even without any solid legal basis, such practices were common enough by the second decade of the nineteenth century to have come before the courts on several occasions. But lacking equity jurisdiction judges could do little. The common law, on which they were obliged to base their decisions, applied to specific acts of transgression. It did not extend to questions of justice or fairness in complex relationships involving long-standing obligations. Then in 1817 the legislature finally granted the Supreme Judicial Court jurisdiction in equity cases, and from that point on a body of legal doctrine developed that provided the necessary underpinning for trusts. Over time the tendency was both to grant increasing latitude to trustees in the performance of their duties and to surround the assets they managed with a mounting barrier of protective sanctions. To satisfy judges a trustee had only to demonstrate that he treated funds as other "men of prudence" in the community did. Meanwhile he was empowered to hold principal sums inviolate against almost every kind of claim, including those of both the beneficiary and the beneficiary's creditors. Only on the issue of the duration of trusts were the courts inclined to impose strict limits. Early on it was established that no trust could remain in force for longer than a life or lives in being at the time of the testator's death, plus twenty-one years, plus the normal gestation period.[51]

By preventing trusts from becoming perpetuities, the courts blocked their use as a full-fledged substitute for aristocratic entail, but lives in being plus twenty-one years and nine months was still a long time. While it might not have guaranteed all the security and control the Associates wanted, it went far enough to promise substantial stability. For up to three generations family capital could be preserved intact, and the enterprises it funded would not have to face—unless knowledgeable trustees thought it appropriate—the risks inherent in sudden changes of ownership.

In practice the trust-making activities of the Associates followed two patterns. The first involved individual trustees; in the second the functions of the trustee were performed by institutions overseeing large aggregates of capital. Many Associates used both approaches simultaneously. Though the role of the trustee varied little from one to the other, institutional trustees often received assets well before the death of the person making the trust, whereas private trustees rarely did. In time each approach generated a classic model representing how, at its best, the system was meant to function. In the case of private trusteeships, it was "the Boston trustee," a paragon of conservative financial wisdom, who guided and preserved family fortunes down through the years. And for institutional trusteeship the model became—almost from the moment of its founding—the Massachusetts Hospital Life Insurance Company, that "savings bank for the wealthy," which John Lowell was also pleased to call "the best institution on earth."[52]

As its title implied, the Massachusetts Hospital Life was organized in part to help fund Boston's first modern health care facility. According to the company's charter, it was to pay one-third of the profits from its life insurance business to the Massachusetts General Hospital. Granted in 1818, the charter was not acted upon until 1823, because of the financial dislocation of those years. At that time—though they were under no obligation to do so—the directors voted to extend the hospital's profit-sharing rights to all of the company's activities. From the hospital's standpoint this was fortunate because the company's foremost commitment, always, was to trust management, not life insurance. In less than seven years its trust deposits grew to almost $5 million as against only $67,000 outstanding in insurance policies and annuities.[53]

While the Massachusetts Hospital Life pooled all sums deposited with it in a single investment fund, it offered several different types of trust contract. Money could be deposited in an individual's own name or in someone else's, with the interest either paid at regular intervals or allowed to accumulate as principal. Some contracts were renewable every five years by the depositor; others were written to remain in force during his lifetime with instructions that the principal be paid thereafter to his estate or to some designated party or parties. Or the beneficiary so designated might be granted only the interest, with the principal going in turn to his or her heirs. In this fashion the so-called strict male and strict female contracts as well as the deferred annuity in trust made it possible to secure sums through an entire generation and beyond, without hazarding dissipation of the principal. And if the person making the trust wished, a further inalienability clause could be added in the case of women beneficiaries stating that the income was "for her separate use, free from the debts, control, or interference by any husband she now has, or may hereafter have."[54]

In the fifty-page booklet of *Proposals* the company published in 1823, it offered services designed "to accommodate persons in almost every age and situation in life." Young men with little property could purchase annuities for their old age or protect their families with life insurance. Widows without enough money to live on could exchange their capital for life annuities. Trusts, on the other hand, were explicitly described as a device "for persons of moderate property and for the rich."[55] A glance at a list of the company's trust accounts a few years later would have shown how very accurate that description turned out to be. The names were indeed those of the rich, and among them the names of the Associates were strikingly prominent. In 1830 the company maintained as many as seventy-nine separate trusts for members of nine Associate families. There were twenty-one in the name of Perkins alone, with seventeen in the name of Appleton, nine in the name of Cabot, and eight each for the Lawrences, Eliots, and Searses. Trusts made by and for members of Associate families also tended to cluster in those categories involving the tightest restrictions and the largest amounts of money. Thus the Lawrence and Perkins families together accounted for fully half of the strict male trusts then in force.[56]

Whatever the offspring who would one day benefit from these arrangements thought of the system, their elders were obviously committed to it. They also had no intention of letting control over any part of it slip from their hands. Only carefully selected individuals were given the opportunity to subscribe to Massachusetts Hospital Life stock, and a provision in the company's bylaws obliged all stockholders selling shares to offer them first to the directors at cost. The directors would then sell the shares "to such persons, not Directors, as shall appear to them, from their situation and character, most likely to promote confidence in the stability of the Institution."[57]

Even more closely guarded was access to the company's inner councils. The list of its officers and directors read like a Who's Who of Boston's business and professional life, and again the Associates were present in force. Of the thirty-six vice-presidents who served before 1850, fifteen were Associates, while in the case of the directors the ratio was higher still: twenty out of thirty-four. And on the crucial Committee of Finance, all three members—through most of the period—were Associates, with Amos and Abbott Lawrence, Patrick Jackson, Daniel Parker, Nathan Appleton, William Sturgis, and Ebenezer Chadwick each serving for various lengths of time.[58]

The particular responsibility of the Committee of Finance was to advise the Actuary—as the company's chief operating officer was titled—on investment policy. The first actuary, the brilliant mathematician and navigator Nathaniel Bowditch, met often with the committee and followed its advice closely, a precedent all of his successors adhered to. Decisions involving millions of dollars placed with the company for safekeeping were not to be made lightly, and apparently even the board itself was considered too casual a forum for that purpose.

The broad outlines of the company's investment policy, as described in the 1823 *Proposals*, came to a simple point: to keep "always in view the safety of the Capital, rather than the greatness of the income." The charter of incorporation further limited investment to mortgages on property within Massachusetts, loans on collateral, and purchases of securities, with the latter two restricted to the indebtedness of the United States and the commonwealth, and the stock of either the Bank of the United States or banks chartered by the state. While all this seemed to leave little enough room in which to maneuver, the Committee of Finance did manage to stretch the terms in several significant ways. During the early years the company committed its funds primarily to mortgages and, until 1834, commercial bank deposits. In the middle thirties a substantial sum was also invested, for a brief period with highly satisfactory results, in the stock of the Second Bank of the United States. But increasingly, money from the Massachusetts Hospital Life went to finance activities distinct from banking and real estate. And, as might be expected, the activities—and enterprises—so favored tended to be those in which the men managing the company's affairs had a particular interest.[59]

Often the procedures were, of necessity, rather complicated. Since the company could not, for example, accept textile manufacturing stock as collateral, loans to such companies were endorsed by private individuals, usually directors, who themselves put up the required bank shares or government securities. In this respect the arrangement resembled the one used by commercial banks for textile loans, but the Massachusetts Hospital Life made a point of being even more accommodating than the banks. For the company's first loan to a textile manufacturer—in the amount of $20,000 for the Boston Company— the members of the Committee of Finance accepted a mere five shares of Suffolk Bank stock as collateral, and a few years later they were approving loans to the Dover Manufacturing Company totaling $200,000 backed by as little as fifteen shares of bank stock. There were, of course, other guarantees: the signatures of Nathan Appleton and Patrick Jackson on the note in the first instance and an additional pledge of Dover Company stock in the second. Yet the fact remained that neither the signatures nor the added stock met the terms of the Massachusetts Hospital Life charter.[60]

The company was equally flexible in other ways. Textile loans were regularly made on a "demand" basis, with no fixed date for repayment as long as the interest was paid and the collateral did not decline in value. And the same leeway was afforded the individual borrowers who comprised another growing outlet for the company's funds. Most were officers or directors, and several carried loans over considerable periods, using the money—the evidence suggests—to finance further development of the textile industry. William Appleton borrowed from the company no fewer than thirty times before 1840, and David Sears twenty-two times. In dealing with such individuals it was sometimes necessary to be very flexible indeed. Not only were the rules governing collateral often relaxed, but in the midst of the Panic of 1837 the company permitted a number of borrowers to regain their collateral, sell it, and with the proceeds pay back their loans. Since the value of the collateral exceeded the amount of the loans, the company was in no danger of losing money. Still, under normal circumstances the officers would have demanded more collateral and then, if it were not forthcoming, conducted the sale themselves.[61]

In 1839 the company petitioned for and was granted an amendment to its charter that regularized at least one of its more unusual practices. By loosening collateral restrictions, the amendment made it possible—a full ten years after the Committee of Finance had begun doing so—to lend money on a wide variety of securities, including manufacturing stocks. For a while thereafter textile loans increased slowly but then, beginning in 1845, shot dramatically upward. Over the next decade the company made 407 loans, of which 168 went to the textile industry. The first large borrowers were Lowell enterprises using the money to expand, but Massachusetts Hospital Life funds were also much drawn on later to develop Lawrence and Holyoke. Of the loans outstanding in 1855, those to companies at Lawrence totaled $572,000, with the Hadley Falls Company owing another $90,000. At the same time individuals active in promoting Lawrence and Holyoke were also borrowing sizable sums. This was especially true of members of the Lawrence family, six of whom in 1855 were on the Massachusetts Hospital Life's books for a total of $538,000 in loans.[62]

Had such figures been publicly available they might have provoked searching questions. Between loans to the Lawrences and loans to enterprises in the town of Lawrence, better than a million dollars were involved. Was this the result the company's Committee of Finance had envisioned when it began to invest so heavily in textile loans? It would have been difficult to tell, but the basic policy was clearly a matter of deliberate choice. For several years before 1845 the company had a substantial investment in government bonds. Much of the money that went into textile loans came from the sale of those bonds in a very weak market. All told the loss amounted to over $100,000.[63] Since, too, the rate of return on the loans was no higher, and the bonds if held to maturity would have been refunded at par, the Committee of Finance was taking a singularly unusual step. At that point its membership consisted of William Sturgis, Nathan Appleton, and Abbott Lawrence—all Associates. Was their behavior prudent? Were their decisions made by keeping "always in view the safety of the Capital"? Perhaps not, but that phrase had a rather special meaning in this case, for the capital the members of the committee—and the rest of the company's directors and officers—appeared to be treating so cavalierly was, after all, their own.

Their purchases of Massachusetts Hospital Life stock had brought the company into being, and their money, placed on deposit, had created the tremendous pool of resources, so much of which eventually flowed into the textile industry. It is worth noting, as well, that the same men were also investing large sums directly in the ventures they supported with Massachusetts Hospital Life funds. If the company's portfolio was weighted in a particular direction, so were theirs. In that respect they were simply bringing management of the company's affairs more in line with the principles they followed in managing their own. The difference was that they, and they alone, controlled what happened to Massachusetts Hospital Life funds. The death of any one of them, the inevitable replacement of one generation by another, the irresponsibility or lack of interest of heirs; every eventuality had been provided for. Widows, sons and daughters, children and grandchildren, would benefit from the assets accumulated and invested in their behalf, but the capital itself would not be disturbed—would remain committed to the industry and the system that had been so painstakingly designed with just that goal in mind.

From their own perspective, then, the Associates were behaving with the utmost probity. If moving Massachusetts Hospital Life funds out of government bonds and into textile loans resulted in a significant financial loss, so be it. The gain in other respects was worth far more. The matter of timing was also important. During the years when the Massachusetts Hospital Life held the bulk of its resources in mortgages, bank deposits, and bonds the company was still a new venture, as was the Waltham-Lowell system. The two grew side by side, at least until the early forties. Up to 1845, indeed, there was even a rough parity between the amounts of capital invested in each, suggesting that funds deposited with the company may have functioned initially as a kind of hedge—a way for the Associates to cover their collective bet on industrialization. If so, their determination to shift the company's funds so decisively into textile loans after 1844 gave notice that they considered the experiment a success and no longer needed the protection of an alternative investment vehicle.

By 1845, too, most of the Associates were well past the age of fifty. The next decade would surely see many of them in their graves; the time had come to tie up loose ends. Those members of the group who were left would have to carry on for those who were not, and the Massachusetts Hospital Life provided the perfect mechanism for that purpose. It both empowered and enjoined the survivors—and whoever they might select to share the responsibility—to continue to act in the best interests of the group as a whole, and enabled them to do so with a minimum of fuss. It stood as their joint pledge to one another that what they had created in the textile industry would endure. It was in fact the final embellishment on the structure Francis Cabot Lowell had begun to build thirty years earlier at Waltham.

V

The final embellishment—but also, perhaps, something more. In the days when Boston merchants sent cargoes out across the ocean never knowing what the result might be, it rarely seemed wise to make long-standing commitments or to pledge more than a portion of available resources to any one project. In that world, survival meant placing in the balance against every risk an appropriate measure of security, and since the risks were many and the means of protection few, ventures tended not to grow beyond a certain size. They also failed to generate stable patterns of organization. Most arrangements were made on a voyage-by-voyage basis because anything else threatened to tie up capital in ways that could suddenly become unprofitable. At bottom the system remained fragmented, impermanent, and highly personalized. Its only fixed component was the traditional family unit, and the only principle that could be relied on, absolutely, to guide it was the importance attached to augmenting and preserving family capital.

By comparison, the environment in which the Boston Associates moved—and of which they were the chief architects—appeared to be an economist's dream of rational organization. Through use of the corporate form, an extensive network of institutions had been created, each of which had a precisely defined function. Those institutions were both permanent and so arranged as to complement one another at every turn. They also nicely checked any tendency toward dissension within the group. Whereas before, individual family interests were as likely as not to conflict, the pooling of resources made possible by incorporation nurtured a steadily growing sense of common purpose and identity.

Pooled resources and rational organization had other effects as well. In combination with one another they did indeed produce an unprecedented concentration of economic power—and one capable of extraordinary impact. Thus Boston banks sharing directors with the Massachusetts Hospital Life were almost guaranteed survival during the depression of 1837–1843, while not a few banks lacking such connections failed. And just as it supported the Waltham-Lowell system with massive loans after 1844, the Massachusetts Hospital Life also gave a major boost to the Western Railroad at a critical juncture. In 1843, when sales of the bonds issued by the commonwealth to help finance the line seemed to be flagging, the company quietly invested $641,000 in them.[64]

Exercised impersonally, with no goal other than the pursuit of profit, such power and the structures that underlay it might well have led to constantly expanding horizons of economic involvement. By 1850 fields as diverse as shoe manufacture, paper production, ready-made clothing, and mining were fully as ripe for development as textiles had been a generation earlier. Within a decade more, food processing, retail merchandising, iron and steel manufacture, and petroleum would be added to the list. In each case technological innovation, an expanding national transportation system, and rising levels of demand made the investment of large amounts of capital not only feasible but highly profitable. To say that fortunes were there for the taking might not have been accurate, but the rewards for the right combination of resources and imagination could be, as events proved, substantial.

Yet clearly the Associates were not interested in such an effort. From the first their goal in areas like transportation, banking, and insurance had been to meet the needs of the Waltham-Lowell system. Even the vast cache of resources once squirreled away at the Massachusetts Hospital Life as a contingency fund eventually found its way into the textile industry. If there was money to be made in other ways, the Associates appeared content to let the opportunity pass them by—however well adapted the structures they had created might have been to fresh bursts of adventure in the economic realm.

And nothing else so clearly revealed the nature—and the limits—of their thinking. Tightly controlled rational organization, extending from a region's leading industry, throughout its banking and insurance systems, and touching at key points its developing railroad network, seemed to imply a determination to follow wherever the twin lures of higher profits and greater power led. But in the Associates' case the focus of concern remained as narrow in 1850 as it had been a quarter of a century earlier. It was as though, finally, some enormous vessel, richly freighted with cargo, had been launched upon the waters to circle round and round the globe. With the wind blowing steadily behind it and the waves calmed before it, the vessel would stop—ever on schedule—at carefully selected ports to engage in trade, the terms of which had been fixed for all time. And once a year, always on the same day, it would sail into Boston Harbor to distribute the profits, in predetermined amounts, to the merchants gathered on the wharf, awaiting its annual visit. If it seemed unlikely that such a vision could have animated men who gave every outward appearance of having transformed themselves into modern captains of industry and finance, it remained, nevertheless, a fair approximation of what the Associates hoped to accomplish.

Which is to say that even in fields outside the textile industry, the impressive range of structural innovations pioneered by the group occurred without any corresponding change in motivation. In this case modern corporate organization neither followed from nor led to the development of modern corporate mentality. Rather the new structures—in all of their finely tuned, overlapping, interlocking complexity—represented a method of achieving goals still highly personalized, still centered ultimately around traditional family concerns. This did not mean, of course, that the potential for further change inherent in the system had been eliminated. As long as Abbott Lawrence and Nathan Appleton continued to dominate the Massachusetts Hospital Life's Committee of Finance, the company's investment policy was bound to reflect their interests and their sense of what best served those interests. But there was always a chance that the men who came after Lawrence and Appleton might see things differently, and they would be free to use the power at their disposal in any way they wished.

Still, for the time being the policy remained set, and in practical terms it dictated that the resources available to the Associates would be handled in what had become the customary manner, with the lion's share going to the textile industry. For the group as a whole this amounted to pursuing security, steady income, and effective control over management at the expense of higher rates of return on invested capital. The same equation could have been carved on the cornerstone of the first mill at Waltham. Applied as it was in 1845, however, the equation had implications far beyond any it might have had in 1814—implications, too, that cannot have been lost on the Associates.

A single, highly innovative venture in a new field is easily seen as a bold initiative, a step in the onward march of progress. To repeat the step over and over again becomes a very different sort of undertaking, especially when, with each repetition, another sizable portion of a region's investment capital is pledged to the effort. For that is exactly what happened. Even if the Associates' banking connections and their control of the Massachusetts Hospital Life's vast funds had not assured them preferential treatment in the New England money market, Waltham-Lowell companies—by virtue of their size and success—would have ranked among the prime borrowers of their day. Using that leverage as freely as they did to develop places like Lawrence and Holyoke, the Associates were also, perforce, diverting funds away from other projects. From there the consequences rippled outward in ever-widening circles. New ventures of all kinds would have to scramble that much harder to find adequate financing, or make do with less, and multiplied often enough, such instances could shape the way an entire economy developed. Given a sufficient degree of pressure, diversification—even growth itself—might be curtailed.

In this case, too, applying the pressure involved no shift in direction, much less anything as open as a public political debate. It was necessary only to keep on doing—albeit at an accelerated rate—what one had been doing for the past two decades. Few people were likely to interpret a fresh spurt of mill building at half-a-dozen sites as part of a campaign to retard the pace of economic change in New England. Yet it may well have been just that.

Emerging from the long depression of 1837–1843, the region stood on the brink of what promised to be a period of dramatic growth and development. Technology, the nearly complete railway network, a favorable tariff, and a labor force already swelling in a mounting tide of foreign immigration: everything pointed to a greatly accelerated rate of economic—particularly industrial—expansion. As exciting as this prospect might have seemed to many people, however, the Associates can only have greeted it with mixed emotions. If their own ventures prospered, well and good, but what of their old fears of uncontrolled industrialization? Surely nothing had happened to diminish them. Why not, then, try to lay hold of that burgeoning potential for growth and direct it along safe and familiar paths? The same line of reasoning had doubtless come into play during the move from Waltham to Lowell. This time the energies to be contained were stronger, but the Associates were also in a position to throw far more into the balance on behalf of whatever policy they favored. All the power they preferred not to use in pursuit of fresh gains in new fields could be directed instead toward keeping the larger system—the economy itself—as stationary as possible. It was a more subtle strategy, though hardly a less ambitious one.

Was it in fact the choice the Associates made? Certainly they themselves never said so and would have resisted such an interpretation if confronted with it. It smacked, after all, of a kind of class consciousness few members of the group could have acknowledged with anything but anxiety. They were accustomed to thinking of themselves as prosperous merchants with important common interests. In their quest for security for themselves and their children the perils they confronted had been those of the marketplace—impersonal and anonymous. They asked for few favors; they wished no one ill and were generous to a fault in fulfilling what they took to be their broader social obligations. They even, for the present, continued to admit newcomers into their ranks with surprising frequency.

Compared with all this the picture of a threatened, potentially embattled group bent on defending its position at the expense of others was, to say the least, unappealing. But year by year since Waltham the reality had also moved farther from a simple matter of shared interests and occupations. As joint ventures grew in number and scale, as the mechanisms of collective control bound members of the group more and more tightly together, and above all as plans were made to transmit the benefits—and the power—to subsequent generations, something very like a distinct class had evolved.

Moreover, the sequence of events does suggest that by 1845 the Associates had settled on a policy of using their resources to block, insofar as they could, the further development of New England's economy; that having themselves contributed in major ways to the work of change, they wished to call a halt. Admittedly such a conclusion rests less on what they said than on what they did—and in particular on the investment choices they made—but it is not unsupported by other evidence. Much the same progression can be seen in the two areas outside of business that remained of greatest interest to the group: philanthropy and politics. There too one discovers an initial burst of innovation on a grand scale; yet there too, beneath all the bustling activity, lay a rather narrow range of concerns—concerns which, as time passed, seemed increasingly both to set the Associates apart and to channel their energies toward defining ever more precisely their own particular position in society.

1. Francis Cabot Lowell. A plain silhouette is the only known likeness of Lowell.

2. Nathan Appleton. In this portrait, done in 1846 by George Peter Alexander Healy, Appleton is shown in front of a calico printing machine.

3. The Boston Manufacturing Company of Waltham, painted in oils, ca. 1830, by an anonymous artist.

4. The Merrimack Mill and adjacent workers' housing, Lowell. In 1849 this engraving appeared on the cover of the *New England Offering*.

5. A pair of Lowell power loom operators. Although this design for a bank-note vignette implies otherwise, the ratio of workers to looms in Lowell mills was never as low as one to one.

6. The city of Lowell after ten years. By then all of the major mills were in place, though they continued to expand in later years.

7. The first train on the Boston and Lowell Railroad. The corner vignettes of this decorative rendering are as interesting as the picture of the train itself.

8. Amos Lawrence, as painted by Chester Harding in 1846.

9. Abbott Lawrence, from a portrait done in 1832, also by Harding.

10. The Appleton family home, Ipswich, Massachusetts. The house built by Isaac Appleton III in New Ipswich, New Hampshire, closely resembled this one.

11. Nathan Appleton's Beacon Street house, Boston. Designed by Alexander Parris, #39 (center building in the photograph with the entrance on the left) was actually the second house Appleton owned on Beacon Street. He lived there from 1819 until his death in 1861.

12. Massachusetts General Hospital, Boston. Pictured here, in an engraving done by Abel Brown from a drawing by J. R. Penniman, is the hospital's first building, designed by Charles Bulfinch and completed in 1823.

13. McLean Asylum, Somerville. McLean was housed originally in a complex of buildings—including the former Joseph Barrell mansion and two connected wings added later to accommodate patients. All three buildings were designed by Bulfinch.

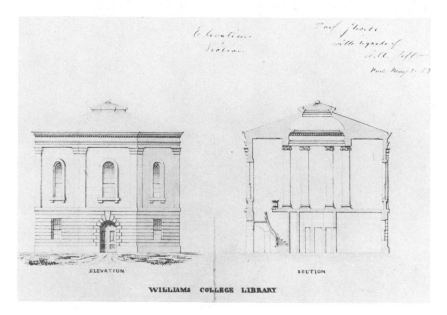

ELEVATION   SECTION

WILLIAMS COLLEGE LIBRARY

14. Lawrence Hall, Williams College. The design for the building was provided by Thomas A. Teft, working in collaboration with Charles Coffin Jewett, the eminent American librarian. This drawing was done by Teft.

15. Amos A. Lawrence, photographed in old age, at Nahant.

HARPER'S WEEKLY.

A JOURNAL OF CIVILIZATION

VOL. IV.—No. 160.]   NEW YORK, SATURDAY, JANUARY 21, 1860.   [PRICE FIVE CENTS.

Entered according to Act of Congress, in the Year 1860, by Harper & Brothers, in the Clerk's Office of the District Court for the Southern District of New York.

RUINS OF THE PEMBERTON MILLS, AT LAWRENCE, MASSACHUSETTS, THE MORNING AFTER THE FALL.—[FROM A PHOTOGRAPH BY WHIPPLE, OF BOSTON.]

16. The Pemberton Mill disaster, as depicted on the cover of *Harper's Weekly*, January 21, 1860.

5.

Philanthropy and the Uses of Wealth

In 1810 James Jackson and John C. Warren, two of Boston's leading physicians, circulated a letter among the "wealthy inhabitants of the town" describing the need for a hospital to receive "lunatics and other sick persons." Unlike the recently established Boston Dispensary, or a traditional almshouse, "a well-regulated hospital" would provide systematic care on the premises, if necessary over long periods of time. On the face of it nothing could have been more straightforward than this approach to what the doctors described as "the first of duties . . . in Christian countries"—healing the sick. "When in distress," the two declared, "every man becomes our neighbor."[1]

But if Boston had ever been a "town" where simple neighborliness and Christian duty could be counted on to handle problems like illness and insanity, much had changed, and Jackson and Warren clearly recognized that fact. Their letter, after all, appealed to the wealthy as a distinct class. Similarly, the intended beneficiaries of their philanthropy remained anonymous members of generalized groups: "the poor"; those who had acquired "a competence" but no extra resources to meet emergencies; men who lived in lodgings; "women who are either widowed, or worse than widowed"; journeymen, mechanics, and servants. Often confined when ill to some "miserable habitation . . . a garret or a cellar," such people could not even rely on relatives or friends to bring their plight to the attention of the public.[2] Many of them had neither family nor friends in the city. Newcomers and strangers, they lived alone and constantly ran the risk of sinking out of sight of anyone who might have cared for them.

The social reality thus depicted—Boston as a place inhabited by significant numbers of nameless, faceless people existing outside the network of traditional institutions—was a disturbing one. And by

113

implication, the argument for a hospital turned on precisely that point. Here was a way of restoring to the community some measure of its vanishing social cement. Thirty years later Jackson and Warren might have discussed more openly the dangers inherent in the situation they described. From social disorganization to social conflict was a short step, and obviously the rich stood to lose much if things moved in that direction. Yet writing in 1810, the doctors chose a more positive approach. Rather than emphasizing the growing gulf between rich and poor they worked to minimize it, just as they worked to minimize the discrepancy between the ideal of neighborly community and the actuality of urban alienation.

As tempting as it might be—in retrospect—to dismiss the resulting appeal as an exercise in mere sentimentality, it would be a mistake to do so. Too much in the subsequent history of the Massachusetts General Hospital suggests that Jackson, Warren, and the other prominent Bostonians who contributed so heavily to the institution did indeed interpret their actions in terms very like those of the 1810 letter. They were building a modern health care facility to serve an expanding urban population, yet somehow old-fashioned notions of neighborliness survived at the heart of the enterprise. Organized as a corporation like those at Waltham and Lowell, the hospital had a board of trustees that routinely designated a committee of its members to visit the patients in person.[3] Funds were solicited for "Free Beds" for the poor, but the board rejected as "very distasteful to patients" the suggestion that plaques with donors' names be placed above those beds.[4] And when a proposal to display a list of all contributors in some central location was approved, no further action was taken. Instead the names were kept in a plain, bound volume.[5]

These of course were points of style, but style in such matters can be important. In this case it helped define a particular approach to organized philanthropy, and one that shaped not only the Massachusetts General Hospital but dozens of other institutions as well. At every point along the way, too, the role played by the Boston Associates was crucial. Investment in the textile industry had given them both the leisure and the steady income to function as benefactors, and they responded with gusto. Someone like Amos Lawrence even made what amounted to a second career out of philanthropy, investing in it—along with a sizable portion of his income—all of the energy and attention that had once gone into checking on the progress of cargoes around the globe.

In building Boston's great philanthropic institutions, the Associates seldom acted alone, but increasingly they came to dominate the important committees and boards. Dr. James Jackson was the brother of

Patrick T. Jackson, and Francis Cabot Lowell was elected to the Massachusetts General Hospital's first board of trustees. Over the next four decades fully twenty-seven Associates served as hospital trustees.[6] And even more impressive was the group's financial participation. Between 1811 and 1851 its members contributed one out of every four dollars raised for the hospital. Including the amounts donated annually by the Massachusetts Hospital Life Insurance Company, which the Associates controlled, the total came to just over $300,000, the equivalent of an entire year's return, at the legal rate of bank interest, on all the capital invested in Lowell cotton mills up to 1837.[7]

Such generosity—matched as it was in not a few other areas—clearly represented a major commitment. But as with so much else the Associates undertook, the commitment remained a highly selective one. Certain projects were singled out for lavish attention, while others were ignored altogether. Like the style, too, the choices seemed to express several rather different—even contradictory—impulses. Tradition was alternately venerated and abandoned; echoes from the past coexisted with much that was decidedly modern. And on a deeper level still lay a tangle of motives in which generosity and self-interest were so thoroughly mixed as to render separation of the two almost impossible.

Or at any rate all of this was true initially. In time, the Associates' approach to philanthropy changed in important ways, so that it is possible to see one kind of effort being made up to 1845 and another after that date. As a result, some of the contradictions apparent in projects like the Massachusetts General Hospital receded. In effect, as philanthropists, the Associates came to embrace more fully the imperatives of modern urban life—at least modern urban life as viewed from a position at the top of the social order.

But that was only after 1845. In the beginning the contradictions abounded, and to understand why, it is necessary to turn to the world from which so many of the Associates came in the first place—to provincial New England at the end of the eighteenth century. It was a world where people still equated home with community and where, in the ideal community, life went forward on terms of mutual respect and harmony. Yet by those very standards, it was also a world in deep disarray—as many of the Associates knew from firsthand experience.

II

Through the years it would become part of the legend surrounding the Lawrence family that Amos, the first to leave home, had arrived in Boston with only twenty dollars in his pocket; Abbott, who followed soon afterward, is supposed to have had less than three. But Amos also recounted later that when he was setting up in business on his own, his father traveled from Groton to Boston with $1,000 to lend to his son. The money had come from mortgaging the family farm. Altogether, according to Lawrence's estimate, his parents were worth "perhaps four thousand dollars"—an impressive sum for that day.[8] The Groton farmer who lived to see no fewer than three of his sons leave home to make their fortunes was not a poor man.

So it was with many of the Associates. If few of their fathers were truly wealthy, most could have been described in Lawrence's phrase as "comfortably off." In addition, they tended to be men of standing in the places where they lived. Some were professionals or merchants; others were farmers, though not of the usual sort. Living in foursquare "mansions" on main roads, near the center of town, they raised their crops on substantial holdings of prime land. Their fellow townsmen regularly chose them to fill important local offices, and when worthy projects were organized to benefit the community their names invariably appeared on the lists of subscribers and trustees. At an earlier date, many had been singularly forthcoming in the patriot cause, especially during the harrowing days of 1775. Several had fought at Lexington and Concord, while others showed up soon afterward and stayed to participate in the following summer's engagements against the British—a fact that doubtless helped account for the extraordinary energy some of their sons later poured into building the Bunker Hill Monument.

Typical of the Associates' fathers in many of these respects was Isaac Appleton III, who provided the group with three of its most distinguished members: Samuel, Nathan, and Eben. One of the original settlers of the town of New Ipswich, New Hampshire, he took up his farm in 1750 at the age of nineteen and prospered thereafter. In a 1763 assessment for the minister's salary, he ranked among the wealthiest 5 percent of the town's taxpayers. Active in church affairs, he served for so long as deacon that the title, duly capitalized, almost always precedes his name in records and documents. But in 1775 it was Lieutenant Isaac Appleton who helped raise the local militia and accompanied them in their dash to join the minutemen forty miles away at Concord.[9]

After serving with the army a while longer, Appleton returned home and devoted the next three decades to farming, local politics, and a variety of schemes aimed at improving life in New Ipswich. His favorite project was the town's academy, founded—like so many others in New England at the time—to provide an adequate secondary education for local youth. Appleton was one of the original backers of the New Ipswich Academy, pledging a £35 bond to see the experiment fairly tried.[10] In Groton, Samuel Lawrence, whose career paralleled Appleton's at many points, was similarly active in behalf of his town's academy. Later the sons of both men would become generous contributors to the schools their fathers had helped establish. Meanwhile, Isaac Appleton—after a long and busy life—died in 1806, leaving an estate valued at $7,500.[11]

By any standard, it was a heritage to be proud of. If little distinguished Appleton's career from hundreds of others, at least it partook of all the best traditions of the time and place. In England it would have assured his sons a respectable position as members of the lesser gentry, and even in New England it brought advantages that many might have envied. Yet the sons themselves were probably less aware of those advantages—particularly as young men—than of certain limitations touching their own immediate interests. The truth was that in one very important respect Deacon Isaac Appleton had failed. Despite his substantial achievements, he was never able to offer his children the same start in life he had enjoyed. In a sense the consequences were obvious: sons who see appealing prospects at home rarely go off to make their way elsewhere. But the process at work was more complicated than this implies, and considered in detail it reveals a great deal, not only about the Appletons, but about the changing character of the society in which they lived.

Isaac Appleton II, the father of Isaac III, the Deacon, belonged to the fourth generation of the family to live in Ipswich, Massachusetts, and from the beginning the Appletons had played a prominent role in town. Over the years they acquired large landholdings and were enterprising in other ways. In addition to farming, various members of the family operated a brewery, a sawmill, and an ironworks. Nevertheless by the fourth generation the problem of divided inheritance had become acute. It was the familiar story: split too often, even the most ample accumulation of assets could become worthless. In traditional fashion Isaac I had received one-quarter of his father's lands, but any further division would have produced portions too small to farm. Fortunately, Isaac II was an only son, so he came into his father's entire share. But then he himself had eight sons.[12]

In the second half of the eighteenth century the difficulties facing the Appletons were by no means unique. Recent historical scholarship suggests they were typical of a general "crisis" affecting much of New England.[13] As long as towns had surplus land to distribute, successive generations could be accommodated in spite of the practice of partible inheritance. Yet sooner or later the land ran out, producing pressures that strained and finally altered forever the life of the community. Year by year the gap between haves and have-nots tended to widen, with all that did to erode individual and community peace of mind. Fathers who had hoped to die surrounded by handsomely provided-for, grateful offspring, saw that dream fade. Ministers and town officials, trying to govern as they always had through consensus, found it increasingly difficult to win agreement on even the simplest points. Since, too, the old ways were so intimately bound up with everything that gave life in New England its special purpose and meaning, the result for many people was an abiding sense of loss.

Still, in individual cases adjustments were possible. In coastal towns especially, commerce and the professions offered brighter prospects than farming. Thus several of the Associates could claim forebears who had moved from the land at an early date—the Lowells and Jacksons, for example.[14] But evidently someone like Isaac Appleton III preferred a more traditional existence: he wanted to farm. In that situation it was up to his father to make the necessary arrangements, and Isaac II managed very well. Unable to provide land in Ipswich for all his children, he did the next best thing and acquired valuable holdings in several areas just opening up for settlement. Two sons remained at home and the youngest was given a college education, but off to New Ipswich, New Hampshire, went Isaac III, another son, and a daughter.[15]

For those Appletons who made the move, the circumstances—if not ideal—were still quite promising. As a result of their father's efforts, they went to fill secure places at the top of a social order quite similar to the one they had known. Except, presumably, some of the pressures and tensions that had of late troubled the waters in Ipswich would be absent in the new community where land was still plentiful. In Ipswich it had taken four generations to bring things to a point where migration had become imperative. By that reckoning any similar crises in New Ipswich lay decades in the future.

But during those years everything had a way of moving more quickly, including the process that transformed new communities into mature ones. There were several reasons for this. In towns settled in the seventeenth century, the land—held jointly by the inhabitants—was distributed rather slowly; in towns settled later it tended to be owned by a small group of promoters anxious to realize a profit on their investment. The result was a more rapid division, and one that depended on cash sales rather than periodic grants to heads of families. At the same time, the agricultural economy itself was changing, as more and more farmers sent their surplus produce to market, thereby putting an added premium on owning as much land as possible. And with land already becoming scarce and the cash nexus growing, the concentration of wealth would have continued apace, making for many of the same divisions found in older towns.

Moreover it was against this background that the conflict with Great Britain developed, raising new issues and giving fresh meaning to old ones. For some people, perhaps, the struggle for independence represented a way of purging society of all that threatened its peace and stability—a chance to return, via restoration of the twin bulwarks of local autonomy and unity, to earlier, more traditional patterns of community life. For those at the top of the social order, on the other hand, involvement in the patriot cause offered a different kind of opportunity. Increasingly challenged from below, a beleaguered elite needed ways of justifying its authority, and revolutionary politics provided a handy forum for that purpose.[16] Still other people may simply have wanted to preserve access to the political process on something like the existing basis.

Which—if any—of these camps Isaac Appleton belonged to is not clear. He did support the patriot cause, but in the years after the Revolution he seems to have been primarily concerned with cultivating as many options for himself and his children as possible. His efforts on behalf of the local academy implied a sense of the world as a changing place, one in which the knowledge and skills that came through education could prove vital. In financial matters, too, flexibility was his guiding principle. While he continued to farm, he became involved in a glass-manufacturing venture. He also kept a good portion of his assets liquid. At the time of his death only half his estate consisted of real, as opposed to personal, property.[17]

With the intervening years bringing no letup in the rate of change—whatever hopes the Revolution might have kindled—such strategies made sense. But they were not without drawbacks. A little education sometimes begot a taste for more; nor was it enough for a career in one of the learned professions. In the end Appleton felt compelled to send two of his sons on to Dartmouth after they had completed the course at New Ipswich Academy.[18] Keeping a ready supply of liquid assets also posed problems. If one expected to live on the income, the assets could not fall below a certain level. How, then—short of dying—was one to provide for sons just setting out in life?

Facing these problems, Appleton did the best he could, but often his efforts had about them a groping, uncertain quality. Things proceeded in fits and starts, and the result—when all was said and done—looked more like a structure hastily knocked together out of whatever came to hand than the product of any consistent plan.

The two sons at Dartmouth both graduated the same year, and by then the older one was twenty-seven. In the meantime another son, Samuel, had tried farming in Maine for several summers, with stints at teaching school in between, and after that a partnership with a merchant in Ashburnham, Massachusetts. Though he preferred merchanting to farming, Samuel made no money in Ashburnham and so returned to New Ipswich to open his own store. Two years later he left home again, this time for Boston. There he found business better but soon decided he needed help and asked if his younger brother, Nathan, could join him. At that point Nathan, a promising scholar, was just finishing his course at the academy and had already passed the examinations for Dartmouth. His entrance fee had even been paid, yet Isaac decided to send him to Boston anyway.[19]

So it went. One of the two sons who graduated from Dartmouth died a few months afterward, and the other went off to practice medicine in Waterville, Maine. Several years later Eben, the youngest, followed Samuel and Nathan to Boston. Another son took up farming in Dublin, New Hampshire. That still left one at home, but Isaac II had managed to keep two sons in Ipswich and in the bargain had provided farms elsewhere for each of his other children. In a single generation life in New Ipswich had passed through and beyond a cycle that took over a century to complete in Ipswich.

And in addition to the tangible costs, there remained what the town itself had become and all the ways it fell short of the ideal. As communal harmony waned and cooperation grew more difficult, even simple charity posed problems. Compared with their neighbors the Appletons had not done badly. Many families fared far less well, yet as matters stood little could be done to help them. In New Ipswich, "devil take the hindmost" had become a maxim that scarcely anyone could afford to ignore. During the closing years of the century the practice of formally "warning out of town" most newcomers—especially those "in indigent circumstances"—became increasingly common. In 1789 Dr. John Preston, the physician charged with caring for the town poor, had to bring suit to recover payment for his services. And in 1791, when an attempt was made to raise money for a town library, it failed. Only after the project had been put on a subscription basis, with use of the books limited to subscribers, was any headway made. Finally, in 1802, the town academy, once the focus of so many high hopes, had to close its doors for a full two years due to a lack of funds. Thereafter the school limped along for a decade or so—until, in fact, a group of former citizens of the town, among whom various Appletons figured prominently, combined to rescue their alma mater.[20]

III

No doubt in later years the Appletons of Boston preferred to think of the situation they had confronted in New Ipswich as a useful training ground for the successful men of affairs they became.[21] Certainly, too, the lives they led beyond New Ipswich gave them little cause to regret having left when they did. Still, it is difficult not to conclude that the whole experience marked them deeply. And the same was true of other Associate families. Almost all had roots running back to communities left behind as much out of necessity as choice—the Lawrences in Groton, the Dwights in Springfield, the Cabots, Francises, and Thorndikes in Beverly, and the Jacksons and Lowells in Newburyport. Even when the family's position seemed more secure than the Appletons' ever had, sooner or later shifting economic realities forced a move. The Jacksons were a case in point. Jonathan—the father of Patrick T. as well as of Dr. James, Charles, and Francis C. Lowell's wife, Hannah—had been one of the wealthiest men in Newburyport before the Revolution, but afterward he lost most of his fortune and finally followed his children to Boston in 1796.[22]

For the Jacksons to have remained in Newburyport, or the Appletons in New Ipswich, would have meant forcing the entire family to live in steadily declining circumstances, and for the next generation the outlook was bleaker still. Somehow life had to be started over again somewhere else, and this time the cycle had to be made to operate more slowly—much more slowly. Having watched their fathers try, and fail, to provide economic security for their children, the Associates would remain very much committed to the same goal. As time passed, too, they tended to set their sights even higher, allowing the vision of family security to stretch on almost indefinitely into the future.

What made it possible to think in such terms, of course, was the creation—in the Waltham-Lowell system—of a satisfactory investment vehicle. Something the Associates' fathers had failed to accomplish in a lifetime of trying, their sons managed in only a few decades. In that respect, as in so many others, it was a remarkable achievement. But it was also not quite the unalloyed triumph it might have seemed. The major problem facing the previous generation—family security—had been solved. Yet if the past was any guide, every foot gained on that front was likely to exact a price of a different sort.

Simply stated, the price was a continuation of all those tendencies that had so disturbed the unity of New England's once stable, peaceful towns. In that world the growing scarcity of resources had forced people to scramble, as individuals, after benefits formerly enjoyed by the community as a whole. In such a situation one man's victory almost always required someone else's defeat, and the victory of an entire group could only mean that many people would suffer. The specter of an entrenched aristocracy—selfishly enriching itself at the expense of the rest of society—was palpable enough during these years to find frequent expression in political rhetoric at all levels. And from the beginning the larger enterprise in which the Associates were engaged had certain characteristics that fit the stereotype all too closely. If Francis C. Lowell could take as his model for a new kind of industrial development the improvement schemes of Scottish aristocrats, it was because his own needs closely resembled theirs. Most of those who followed his lead as heavy investors in the Waltham-Lowell system were already wealthy men, yet they continued to pursue the goal of family security as long as they lived. Not infrequently referred to as "Cotton Lords," presiding over a constantly expanding network of industrial and financial institutions, dominating year after year one of the state's two major political parties, and all the while marrying off their children to those of other members of the group—what were such men, if not would-be aristocrats?

What indeed! But the fact remained that the Associates themselves took a different view. They understood only too well the threat to the existing order of things that a too-open display of aristocratic pretensions would pose. America was not Europe; it had a different past, different traditions, and—one hoped—a different destiny. Traveling in England, Francis C. Lowell had remarked on "the great corruption of the highest" as well as of the "lowest classes."[23] And Amos Lawrence was careful to advise a son studying abroad: "Bring home no foreign fancies which are inapplicable to our state of society." America was quite unlike Europe; "and our comfort and character require it should long remain so."[24] Precisely which "foreign fancies" Lawrence had in mind he left to his son's imagination, but the general point was one he made time and again. "An idler, who feels that he has no responsibilities . . . can find no comfort in staying here. We have not enough such to make up a society. We are literally all working men."[25]

Work and responsibility: those were the proper preoccupations of an American gentleman, and in every way possible the face he presented to the world ought to reflect that fact. In Newburyport old John Lowell had built an imposing three-story mansion, next door to and closely resembling that of his friend Jonathan Jackson. To John Adams the place seemed "A palace like a nobleman's."[26] But in Boston the Associates preferred a plainer style, and never again, according to the family historian, would any Lowell build or buy a house "with the idea of impressing."[27]

Along with other Associate families, the Lowells tended increasingly to cluster in the area around the Common and Beacon Hill, where the houses, insofar as physical structures could, admirably bespoke a commitment to measured restraint in all things. Harrison Gray Otis, a member of the group and the principal developer of Beacon Hill as a prime residential district, was inclined to build houses for his own use that were a trifle grand, allowing Charles Bulfinch, his architect, to create facades at least as wide as they were high.[28] But Otis set no trend among his neighbors. Instead he found himself surrounded by buildings that occupied a minimum of ground space. People built upward, and except for rounded fanlights over doorways and an occasional wrought-iron balcony, left exteriors largely unadorned. The result resembled the better sections of Georgian London, as foreign visitors sometimes noted with approval.[29] But there were differences. Rarely was the attempt made to work a row of separate dwelling units into a larger, more palatial architectural composition, something commonly done abroad. On Beacon Hill individual houses were recognizable as just that, and if they could not have been described as modest, neither were they—with their taut brick surfaces and strictly rationed detail—meant to be in any way ostentatious.

From such houses the Associates issued forth on a round of duties that left as little room for frivolous pleasures as the buildings themselves gave to unnecessary ornament. When the day's routine permitted, a quiet hour or two spent reading at the Athenaeum was acceptable, but that in itself marked yet another of the group's careful choices. Responsible men of means in every society had always supported culture—those myriad forms of activity that give rise to man's finest achievements. To the Associates, however, culture meant almost exclusively literary culture. In America, where a higher portion of the population could read than anywhere else in the world, this must have seemed appropriate. The culture of the printed word excluded few men, at least in theory, and its development could only benefit the citizens of a democratic republic.[30]

So the Associates supported literature. They bought books, and—while few members of the group were as assiduous in that regard as Abbott Lawrence, who owned, next to Theodore Parker, the largest private library in Boston—many were serious readers. Except on practical matters, they did not write a great deal themselves, but they were eager to know those who did. There, old friends like George Ticknor and Edward Everett proved invaluable allies. To family connections with Boston's business community, both men added ties to Harvard and, beyond it, the larger world of letters in America and abroad. If, too, one wished to meet those awkward souls like Thoreau or Hawthorne, who were just beginning to sound so many new notes in American literature, there was always Nathan Appleton's son-in-law, Henry Longfellow, or his successor at Harvard, James Russell Lowell, to arrange the introductions.

Yet for the average Associate the most enduring testimony to the group's commitment to serious literature remained the Boston Athenaeum itself. Founded in 1807 by the members of the Anthology Society—which also published the *Monthly Anthology*, the predecessor of the *North American Review*—the Athenaeum quickly became the richest private library in America and grew richer with each passing decade. By 1849, the year it moved to its final location on Beacon Street, its assets totaled more than $400,000, which included $161,000 in real estate, $152,000 in "productive property," and almost $90,000 worth of books, statues, and busts. The statues and busts betokened a certain interest in the fine arts, but from the start the Athenaeum devoted itself primarily to literature. As the "Memoir" of 1807, which first announced the scheme to the public, had made clear, "the Reading-room and Library" were to be the "leading objects and chief departments" of the new institution.[31]

The 1807 "Memoir" also explained at length why such an institution ought to recommend itself "to the friends of improvement" in Boston. There were a number of lesser reasons: it would be "a place of social intercourse," it would be "ornamental to the metropolis," and it would "confer honor on its patrons." By assembling large and diverse collections, it also would appeal to a wide variety of visitors. Thus, while "the man of business" would find "the means of intellectual activity and enjoyment, without any injurious interruption of his ordinary pursuits," members of the learned professions could, under the same roof, "derive important assistance, in their respective pursuits," and scholars would discover "facilities in study, hitherto not enjoyed; but highly desirable and even necessary." Women and children, too, would "have more than an indirect share in the advantages of the Athenaeum."[32]

In short, the institution as planned offered something for almost everyone. But above all, the signers of the "Memoir" claimed, the Athenaeum would be "a source of rational enjoyment"—a phrase the meaning of which became clear in an ensuing capsule-history of human society. As "affluence and prosperity" grew among men, so did the "passion for amusement and pleasure in their diversified forms." For the sake of "security to public and private morals" it was imperative to "correct and regulate this passion." That, in turn, entailed checking not only the tendency to dissipation in its more blatant forms, but also "less exceptionable modes of pleasure"—the desire for "show and equipage, convivial entertainments, festive assemblies, and theatrical exhibitions." And one way of doing this was to foster "a relish for the pleasures of knowledge." Such pleasures would "subdue, not inflame the passions," would be "friendly to cheerfulness and the social virtues, and serve to disengage the feelings from ignoble gratifications."[33]

While all this might have made literary culture seem roughly the equivalent of a cold bath, the "Memoir" accomplished its purpose. Duly incorporated by the legislature, the Athenaeum raised $45,000 on its first subscription. Shares to be held in perpetuity cost $300, and life subscriptions sold for $100. With no one individual allowed to own more than three shares, the resulting membership was relatively large, but the price still limited participation to a narrow segment of the city's population.[34]

Among the original subscribers, the Associates were already quite prominent. More than half of the stockholders of the Boston Company bought shares, and subsequent subscriptions brought in still other Associates to the point where fully 90 percent of the group could claim the privilege of membership in the Athenaeum.[35] Indeed, the dates of those later subscriptions coincided to a surprising extent with the points at which major increases in capital were being sought for the textile mills, suggesting that the two may even have been related in some way. Since Athenaeum shares descended through families and were rarely available on the open market at any price, the only way of enlarging the membership was through new subscriptions. Could this have been a means of rewarding those men willing to invest their money at Lowell, or Lawrence and Holyoke? Possibly, but whatever the connection, membership in the Athenaeum became a much-coveted badge of status.

Membership also provided practically the only means of access to the institution's collections. Whether the founders intended this is not clear. One version of the 1807 "Memoir" referred to "occasional visitors" as well as subscribers.[36] The rules adopted by the trustees in 1808, however, specified that "No inhabitant of Boston, or of any town or place within twenty miles of Boston, who is not a proprietor or subscriber to the institution, or a member of the family or a proprietor or life subscriber, bearing their ticket, shall be allowed access to the library or reading-room, unless by consent of the trustees or of their committee."[37] The Boston Athenaeum, in other words, was not to be in any sense a public library.

In thus restricting access to the institution, the trustees no doubt had in mind several British models described in the 1807 "Memoir": the Liverpool Athenaeum and two similar libraries in London. These were also private organizations that refused admission to the general public. The men involved in founding them—William Roscoe, for example, who had made a fortune as a merchant in Liverpool and gone on to cultivate both a talent for vivid historical prose and a large circle of friends whom he entertained lavishly at his country estate— might in themselves have seemed apt models for Boston's merchant princes.[38] On the other hand it remained unclear where such exclusiveness left the Athenaeum's mission to foster public virtue by encouraging "rational" culture. Perhaps, considering the magnitude of the task they faced, the trustees decided to concentrate first on shaping the tastes of those with $300 to spend on subscriptions, leaving the rest of the population until later. But how and when was that broader mission to be fulfilled? For all the earnestness with which they raised the issue, the founders failed to resolve it. As time passed, too, the problem became more—not less—acute.

Still, in some ways the scheme worked remarkably well in practice. Several significant works of scholarship were produced within the Athenaeum's walls. Membership did become the mark of a Boston gentleman, whether he taught at Harvard or kept an office in State Street, and meeting in those lofty, well-appointed chambers the two groups could easily imagine that they worked toward the same goal, shared a common purpose—which in most cases was true enough.

Yet for the Associates the full bill for such quiet pleasures still had to be met. Even with its subtle austerities and devotion to higher cultural values, life as it was lived on Beacon Hill and in institutions like the Athenaeum inevitably looked too narrow—and too aristocratic—for comfort. In a sense this was the natural result of copying European models which were themselves the product of aristocratic pretensions. In translation the details were altered, but never completely. So, while one might belong to the Athenaeum, duty and responsibility were hardly satisfied thereby. If Boston was ever to be the kind of community the Associates' fathers had hoped to preserve in towns like New Ipswich and Groton, other ways of binding up the social fabric would have to be found. And there institutions like "the Hospital" seemed to provide the answer.

IV

On July 4, 1818, with the governor and his council in attendance, as well as the selectmen and board of health of Boston and "a great concourse of citizens, who assembled to witness the ceremony," the cornerstone of the Massachusetts General Hospital was laid, in proper Masonic form, by the Grand Lodge of Massachusetts. Josiah

Quincy, Sr., delivered the principal address. Speaking for the hospital trustees, after the usual pleasantries, he took occasion both to thank all those present for the extraordinary "liberality and favor" already lavished upon the institution and to solicit continued support for "a charity destined to confer lasting blessings on future times, as it has already conferred immortal honor on the present."[39]

In offering so many individuals a share of the "immortal honor," Quincy was not exaggerating. The imposing brick and stone building that would rise on Allen Street over the next three years was in fact the result of hundreds upon hundreds of donations large and small. The government of the commonwealth had contributed with singular generosity, and so had the rich—those individuals Quincy described as "distinguished at once for wealth and liberality." But no less important were scores of more modest gifts. In the end what the trustees had seen, and what Quincy wished to take special note of, was the happy spectacle of "all classes of . . . citizens combining and concentrating their efforts." Here was the entire community at work, "and the irresistible force of public opinion applied, not as has happened in other countries, to destroy, but to found and erect institutions destined to be the refuge of the afflicted."[40]

The full dimensions of the phenomenon Quincy described were to be formally recorded—a decade later—"in a beautifully neat style of penmanship" in the hospital's "Donation Book." By then the two branches of the institution, the hospital itself and the McLean Asylum for the Insane, were solidly established and almost twenty years had passed since Doctors Jackson and Warren first circulated their appeal on behalf of the project.

The initial response had come from the state. Voting to incorporate the hospital in 1811, the legislature at the same time granted it the Province House Estate—the former residence of the royal governor— with authority to sell or lease the property and use the proceeds as the trustees saw fit. But as was so often the case with the commonwealth's generosity, there were strings attached. It would take effect only after $100,000 had been raised from private sources, and for that to happen the legislature set a time limit of five years, adding a second five-year term in 1813 in recognition of the economic dislocation caused by the War of 1812. In the event, the trustees came close to meeting the original deadline. With several large contributions already in hand, the board mounted a door-to-door campaign, manned by committees in each ward in Boston and by representatives in most nearby towns. The results were striking. Within three days over $78,000 poured in, and by January 5, 1817 the total had swelled to $93,969.[41]

In writing the hospital's first official history, Nathaniel Bowditch analyzed with characteristic precision all gifts recorded in the Donation Book up to 1843. By then the hospital had received—exclusive of bequests and contributions for free beds and other special purposes—$131,269.21 in individual donations from private sources. In monetary terms large gifts made up the lion's share. With the "magnificent" Phillips family donation of $20,000 topping the list, more than half the total came in amounts of $500 or more. On the other hand, the average size of the 1,189 donations recorded was only just over $110, and even that figure is misleading. By Bowditch's count fewer than three hundred of the donations were as high as $100. The rest—fully 75 percent—fell below that amount, including 556 of $10 or less and 60 of as little as one or two dollars.[42]

In short, though the rich may have borne a disproportionate share of the burden, they were hardly acting alone. And this became one of the chief hallmarks of Boston philanthropy during those years. Projects benefiting the community were regularly designed to involve as many people as possible. The city might have become a place of strangers, but the hope does seem to have persisted that relationships other than purely economic ones could dispel the feeling of personal isolation, join people together, and remind them of their collective responsibility for one another's welfare. Invariably, too, lest the corporate nature of the enterprise be compromised, the wealthy took pains to minimize their own role. Hence the resistance of the hospital trustees to plaques honoring the donors of free beds. Even names were significant. To have failed to recognize John McLean's extraordinary bequests—ultimately totaling over $100,000—by naming the asylum after him would have worked a serious injustice, but the hospital remained simply the Massachusetts General Hospital.

Eager to acknowledge the contributions of others while marking their own generosity with modest memorials—or no memorials at all—Boston's philanthropists were unusual in another way: they seemed content to limit their activities to a quite narrowly defined geographical area. What mattered was the city itself; the nation, the region, even the state, were all much less important. Of course new methods used at the hospital and the asylum, or places like the Perkins Institution for the Blind, another favorite charity of the period, ultimately helped thousands of people outside Boston—as, for example, when the hospital pioneered in the use of ether during surgery, or when Samuel G. Howe perfected techniques for teaching the blind to read at Perkins. But the good accomplished in the larger world was a by-product of the system, never its reason for being.[43]

In 1810 so exclusively local an outlook was perhaps to be expected. Yet already, a decade and a half later, a very different way of managing worthwhile projects could be seen in organizations like the American Sunday School Union, the American Home Mission Society, and the American Society for Promoting Temperance. Each of these was national in scope and organized hierarchically, with paid "agents" doing much of the work, a central office, usually in New York, and a network of regional and local branches. Functions were carefully delineated both within and among individual organizations. Whether to keep the masses from the demon rum, lead their children to Sunday School, or free the slaves, the great benevolent societies were designed to achieve their purposes with impressive efficiency. And if reams of paper in printed pamphlets, the size of annual budgets, or numbers of members were any indication, the entire effort was a rousing success.[44]

It was also part of a much broader phenomenon. Increasingly throughout the nineteenth century large-scale organization and standards of rational efficiency would come to dominate American life. The area most completely transformed was business, and significantly the benevolent societies owed much to the support of wealthy New York merchants like the Tappan brothers. But in the short run no process of cultural change ever operates with absolute uniformity. Reaching out to the future with impressive boldness on one front, people will often hang back on another, apparently oblivious to the contradictions their actions pose.

So it was with those who oversaw Boston's philanthropic ventures during the early years of the nineteenth century. As businessmen they seemed quite comfortable with the new scale of things and hardly shied away from national enterprises, but philanthropy was another matter. Working through a network of manufacturing corporations and marketing firms that were easily the largest of their day, the Boston Associates conducted a business in cotton textiles that spanned the continent, indeed the globe. Yet in due course, decade after decade, the leaders of the group took their places as trustees of the Massachusetts General Hospital, and in good times and bad their pledges and checks kept the institution handsomely supplied with funds. Meanwhile, only a handful of the Associates played any role at all in mounting the sundry crusades of militant Protestantism across the United States.

Men so reluctant to cast their nets farther than they could see from their own front doorways were bound to appear conservative, and in that sense Boston's philanthropists were conservative. But in other respects they proved themselves remarkably innovative. Though anxious to use their generosity to foster a sense of common purpose among their fellow citizens, they also meant to get their money's worth in more obvious ways, and incidentally to reap something of a private return on what remained a very substantial investment. On both counts imaginative solutions were plentiful.

During its first three decades, the Massachusetts General Hospital admitted over thirteen thousand patients. Of those, four out of five were listed as "well" or at least "relieved" on discharge, an excellent record.[45] Similarly, the McLean Asylum managed to discharge as "recovered" just under half the 3,341 patients it accepted up to 1851.[46] Both institutions applied unusually high standards of treatment and care. Annual reports were full of attention to sanitary conditions, diet, and ensuring proper ventilation. As the number of patients grew—from 18 at the hospital in 1821 to 870 in 1849—so did the number of people caring for them. By 1846 the hospital staff included a board of consultation made up of four doctors, six additional visiting physicians, six visiting surgeons, and an admitting physician. All appointments were renewed annually, with the trustees carefully screening the credentials of new candidates. In addition, the trustees settled major questions of policy and, through weekly visits to the wards, satisfied themselves that everything was running smoothly.[47]

But the trustees also recognized that there were limits to what they could or should attempt. As one of their number, Samuel A. Eliot, remarked in a report defining the duties of the staff: "Much must be left to the discretion of those who hold responsible stations." In practice this meant that "having expressed their general views of the subject—having stated, as it were, their theory of the government of the institution—the Trustees must leave the application of them to the good sense and good feelings of the present incumbents."[48]

For 1834, Eliot's statement has a surprisingly modern ring. Once the trustees had established policy, qualified professionals were to exercise effective control over the day-to-day operation of the institution. To be sure, there had to be standards on which to base judgments, guidelines within which to frame policy, and even then trustees and professional personnel might disagree, but at least they would be talking the same language, giving weight to the same factors. Some sense of the issues involved may have been brought home in 1825. Late that year the trustees were informed that "certain persons" were in the habit of visiting the hospital on Sundays in order to conduct religious services. No doubt the staff deplored a practice "often producing . . . excitement in the patients." No doubt, too, some of the trustees would have liked to supplement bodily healing with a measure of spiritual balm. Yet early the following year a report was adopted forbidding all such services.[49] Professional health care was just that; other agencies, with appropriately trained personnel, could minister to other needs.

Left unresolved, disagreements between trustees and managers could sap the energy of everyone concerned and finally paralyze even the best of organizations. By all accounts Boston's philanthropic institutions managed to steer well clear of that danger. Like the question of religious services at the hospital, most issues were quickly and amicably settled, with the professionals carrying the day more often than not. Nor was agreement on standards the only reason for this. As important was the good sense of the individuals themselves; they meant to get along and did. Yet good sense—and the good relations it fosters—is usually easier to find among people who have something in common in the first place. And here the common bonds were very strong indeed. For when trustees voted to vest substantial authority in the professionals they appointed, those so favored were rarely strangers. On the contrary, many were close friends or relatives.

Not surprisingly, Doctors James Jackson and John C. Warren became the hospital's first chief physician and the first chief surgeon, respectively. Chosen by the trustees in 1817, the two continued to serve for decades thereafter. Meanwhile, by 1846 the hospital had come to include among its visiting physicians and surgeons both a second Jackson and a second Warren, as well as two Bigelows, a Shattuck, a Hale, a Bowditch, a Parkman, and Oliver Wendell Holmes, Sr.—all names associated with Boston's leading business and professional families. A full century later there was still a Warren on the staff—representing the sixth generation of his family to serve—and still, after five generations, a Shattuck.[50]

For a handful of families to have provided a major hospital with so large a portion of its medical personnel over such a long period was unusual, to say the least, but there is little evidence that the quality of care at the hospital suffered as a result. The standards established at the outset were steadfastly maintained thereafter, and having a position on the staff meant conforming to those standards. It was also true, however, that anyone of sufficient intelligence with the proper training could qualify, including the relatives of trustees. And if they happened to qualify, why not give them preference, since doing so contributed to the institution's smooth functioning? Much the same logic governed the hiring of agents at Lowell textile mills. In this instance, too, there was an added reason for choosing one's own, because it helped solve a problem that faced many of Boston's wealthier families: what to do with offspring who had neither the taste nor the ability for careers in business.

In New Ipswich, Isaac Appleton, struggling to equip his children for life in a changing world, had discovered limits to what he could accomplish. Unwilling to insist that his sons do as tradition dictated and follow his own occupation, he had to seek out alternatives, or urge them to, with such resources as could be spared for the effort. By no means free of worry on the same score, Boston's rich managed with far greater—in fact with spectacular—success. Like Appleton, they encouraged their children to pursue a variety of careers, but unlike him they were able to make the alternatives singularly attractive and rewarding.

It was a complex process, in which institutions like the hospital played an important part. As a result of their growing need for professional personnel, not a few sons of founders and donors managed to enjoy highly satisfying careers. The work was respectable, interesting, and significant—in every way suited to individuals whose financial security freed them to concentrate on goals like community service. Of course professional training remained essential, and men who had made fortunes in commerce and reinvested them in manufacturing were in no position to provide that themselves. But they could and did turn to Harvard, so it too became a link in the chain, though the Harvard in question was necessarily a far cry from the college of colonial days.

In 1780 virtually no professional training was available in any American school. The best that could be hoped for was a trip abroad or an apprenticeship with somebody already practicing in the field. Then three years later Harvard opened its medical school, and by 1820 the process of setting off the theology department as a separate school had begun. That year the university also conferred its first Bachelor of Laws degrees. Slow to take hold at the outset, legal education finally came into its own at Harvard in 1829, when Joseph Story accepted the newly created Dane Professorship. Meanwhile the medical school had become a thriving institution, thanks in no small part to the broad clinical experience available to its students at the Massachusetts General Hospital.[51]

In effect these changes created across the river in Cambridge the prototype of a modern American university—an undergraduate college surrounded by a cluster of distinct schools, each offering training in a different professional field. From one perspective the pattern simply evolved, but there had always been alternatives. The professional schools could have been founded as separate institutions. In that event none of the special standing that came from their association with traditional liberal learning would have developed. Yet so it might have turned out, had it not been for two earlier changes at Harvard: one affecting its governance and the other its finances.

Originally composed of the teaching faculty of the college after the English model, the Harvard Corporation had gradually, in the latter half of the eighteenth century, become a board of external trustees. According to Samuel Eliot Morison the transformation entered its final phase in the decade 1779–1789. Thereafter vacancies were filled by "public-spirited lawyers and businessmen of Greater Boston—with an occasional clergyman or man of letters."[52] In fact it is possible to be even more specific than that. During the presidency of John T. Kirkland, which lasted from 1810 to 1828 and during which the schools of law and theology were added, no fewer than six of the eighteen men serving—including almost the entire "business" contingent—were members of Associate families.[53]

At the same time, the same men, and others like them, were becoming increasingly important to Harvard as a source of funds. After 1750 there was a tendency for grants from the General Court to diminish, and in the early years of the nineteenth century the trend became pronounced. From the end of the Revolutionary War until 1858 the only major gift from the commonwealth was $100,000, paid from the tax on banks, to benefit the medical school. In general, Harvard's cause was not popular with the public, which saw it as too liberal in religion and too aristocratic in everything else. Also, though their own parsimony was largely to blame, the legislators came to resent the corporation's growing independence.[54] In the words of one contemporary observer, "The legislature ceased to cherish an institution, which it could no longer control."[55] But what the General Court had ceased to cherish, others—in return, as it proved, for an ever-increasing voice in the university's affairs—flocked to support. As government aid declined, private gifts rose dramatically. A conservative estimate puts the total for the period 1827–1857 at $858,000.[56]

The money came in many forms: outright gifts, bequests, and also—inevitably—subscriptions, making it possible for larger groups to share the burden of major projects. The Massachusetts Professorship of Natural History, a professorship of mineralogy and geology, another in pulpit eloquence and pastoral care, and the Astronomical Observatory were all funded through subscriptions. So too, in large part, was the Theology School. Though the amounts contributed by most people were modest—usually between $100 and $200—the presence of the same names on list after list suggests how seriously the effort was taken.[57] Israel Thorndike was a case in point. A merchant who had moved his business from Beverly to Boston, he was one of the original backers of the Boston Company at Waltham, as well as other textile ventures, ultimately investing in them, according to Josiah Quincy, "a greater amount of capital . . . than any other individual in New England."[58] Thorndike's name appears on three of the five subscriptions mentioned. In addition, he served as an organizer of the subscription for the Theology School and in 1818 donated the Ebeling Library—a large collection of materials relating to American history for which he had paid $6,500—to the university.[59] Coming from someone who had never received more than a grammar-school education, such generosity to Harvard might have seemed surprising, except for the fact that the story was repeated time and again during these years. Only slightly better educated than Thorndike—and certainly not at Harvard—the Appletons and Lawrences were at least as generous.

In all of this there was, to be sure, a certain element of social ambition: giving to "the College" was an eminently acceptable way to display one's wealth. But hardheaded businessmen were also likely to want something more tangible for their money, and what the university gave them—or rather their children—was solid preparation for a growing variety of useful careers. Under the watchful eyes of such men Harvard would continue to expand and diversify, ultimately taking on, as the Overseers' visiting committee of 1849 claimed, "all the characteristics of a national institution, in the grandeur of its objects, and its powers to carry them into operation."[60] Yet the same institution would also remain, for another half century at least, dependent on the generosity of a relatively small circle of Boston families, some of whose "objects" were more limited. For dozens of sons freed from the necessity of having to earn their living in State Street offices, a Harvard education marked the beginning of richer, more fulfilling lives than their fathers had known. In that regard the pattern at Massachusetts General Hospital was typical, and eventually even Harvard itself came to boast an impressive array of faculty members and administrators drawn from the familiar circle.[61]

Such a system—with its elaborate network of interlocking family and institutional connections—could have seemed quite thoroughly closed, but that was never the intention. Every one of the institutions in question continued to find room for bright young men from the provinces. It was rather a question of the choices trustees would make, all other things being equal, which made it, in turn, yet another example of the way in which modern structures and methods could be adapted to traditional goals. No hospital in America set higher professional standards than the Massachusetts General, but nowhere else would one have discovered so many personal ties linking donors, board members, and practicing physicians. Both circumstances were the result of careful planning, and achieving both simultaneously required even more forethought—plus, from the beginning, a firm conviction that any conflict between the two could be kept to a minimum.

Something like the same combination of elements was revealed in the way philanthropic institutions in Boston handled money. As time passed and donations continued at the customary pace, assets mounted steadily. A certain portion went into buildings and equipment, but that generally left considerable sums to be used at the discretion of the trustees. Had they wished, the money might have been paid out to meet current expenses, thereby lowering the cost of services to the community. Most trustees, however, would have found such an arrangement dangerously haphazard. Far better to husband surplus resources, investing them to earn additional income, and use that to help defray expenses. Meanwhile the funds—like the hefty balances of working capital maintained by Waltham-Lowell corporations—would provide security against the uncertainties of the future.

To these ends, many charitable organizations in Boston accumulated substantial endowments over time, and investing those endowments became one of the chief functions of trustees. It was a grave responsibility, presenting genuine, if not altogether unfamiliar, problems. Prudence dictated that priority be given to preserving capital; income was of secondary importance—or so most trustees concluded. They also tended to conclude that the safest investment outlets were those they themselves regularly used for their own surplus funds.

This meant, more often than not, the Massachusetts Hospital Life Insurance Company. By the terms of its charter, the company was obliged to share its profits with the hospital, so a connection already existed there, which the hospital trustees chose to strengthen by subscribing to $50,000 worth of the company's stock—an investment that was yielding 9 percent in dividends within a few years.[62] The company also maintained a special category of "institutional deposits" that was much used by charitable organizations. The services were the same as those provided private customers, and the money went into the same investment fund. In time the list of endowments handled in this way came to include those of the Boston Athenaeum, the Boston Female Society, the Boston Marine Society, the Boston Dispensary, the Boys Asylum, the Bunker Hill Monument, the Massachusetts Medical Society, the Massachusetts Charitable Eye and Ear Infirmary, Harvard College, the Handel & Haydn Society, the American Academy of Arts and Sciences, the Franklin Fund, and the Greene Foundation.[63]

   Given the standing of the Massachusetts Hospital Life Insurance
Company—its enormous resources and the expertise of its managers—it would have been difficult to fault a trustee who saw it as
an ideal investment vehicle for the funds in his care. The fact that
the money would augment a pool of capital which he himself—or
firms in which he was interested—might simultaneously be drawing
upon for loans complicated matters, perhaps, but not unduly. In all
likelihood the same trustee had on deposit with the company funds of
his own that were being treated in the same way, and the money he
invested as a trustee was often in no small measure the product of
his generosity.

Thus did the complex interrelationships among institutions in Boston
continue to multiply decade by decade. One gave money to support
education or heal the sick, only to borrow it back from the Massachusetts Hospital Life and invest it in the textile industry, the very place
from which the money had probably come in the first place. Meanwhile the community found itself provided with valuable services,
and in addition to involving people from many different walks of life,
the effort created a number of highly attractive career opportunities
for those with the right training—and connections.
   Though it might have been an interesting issue to debate, who
could have said with any precision where self-interest left off and
philanthropy began in such a system? In effect, the men who designed it were creating a new social calculus, one that involved turning over to corporate institutions a broad range of functions that had
traditionally been lumped together under family or community control—everything from furthering knowledge and training the young
to caring for the needy. At the same time similar institutions were
pooling and protecting family capital in the economic realm. How
logical, then, to merge the two systems. Historians have often pictured Jacksonian America as a world of self-reliant individuals, single-
mindedly struggling to rise, but for Boston's leading families the
reality was quite different. Joint ventures remained the rule in business, and the new corporate forms—at once sturdier and more flexible than traditional kinship alliances—had made it feasible to spread
both the risks and the rewards of business to ever-larger groups. As a
result the ties uniting the rich had grown immeasurably stronger. In
a real sense an institution like the hospital seems to have been run, at
least initially, along similar lines; except that now it was all society
—Boston itself—which was to be transformed into a kind of vast,
harmonious joint-stock company, with as many people as possible
contributing and benefiting according to their respective resources

and needs. In these terms, too, the more difficult it became to distinguish between pure and "interested" generosity, the more successful the enterprise was. Too finely drawn, such distinctions, along with an excess of individualism, had shattered the peace of places like New Ipswich. Here was a way of avoiding that sad denouement.

Yet the fact remained that achieving social harmony in a modern city was far more complicated than manufacturing cotton cloth. Even if the institutional framework could be expanded to fit the task, there was always a danger that the new corporate structures might prove less accommodating—less amenable to change—in society at large than they were to the quiet comings and goings in State Street offices and Beacon Hill drawing rooms. What then? How at that point would the costs and benefits be calculated? And whose interests would receive priority?

In 1825, or even as late as 1840, these questions were unlikely to have occurred to anyone. But soon afterward philanthropy in Boston began to shift course. Subtle enough at first, the changes gradually grew more distinct, and as they did, so too did a whole range of issues that had earlier been left conveniently vague.

V

The shift coincided with the general improvement in business conditions that occurred after 1842. As a result of the economic dislocation of the preceding five years, Boston's philanthropists had tended to hold the line on fresh initiatives. Few new organizations were founded and those already in being had to make do with existing resources and facilities. But once business improved, purses were opened as generously as ever and the old patterns reasserted themselves. Or at any rate they seemed to; in truth a change was evident even then.

On January 12, 1844 the trustees of the hospital voted to add two new wings to the Allen Street building. Though the cost was estimated at $50,000, the moment seemed well chosen for the institution's second major fund drive. Once again an address to the public was drawn up and published both in the newspapers and in a pamphlet of fourteen pages—"a beautiful specimen of typography." Yet this time there was no door-to-door campaign. Instead, the entire business was handled at a single meeting with Thomas H. Perkins in the chair and Abbott Lawrence, among others, offering appropriate resolutions.[64] The results, too, were quite different.

While subscriptions proved more than adequate for the purpose, they tended to come in larger amounts—and from many fewer sources. All told 200 individuals and firms contributed $62,550. Between 1811 and 1843, by comparison, total subscriptions, in dollars, had run more than twice as high, but the number of individual contributions had been just short of six times greater. The average subscription in 1844 was about $300, or roughly triple the size of the average subscription during the earlier period. And completely absent from the list in 1844 were the proceeds from ward collections—as well as the contributions from benevolent and religious societies and outlying towns—that together had swelled the original total by over $15,000. Similarly in 1844 there were only 2 donations of less than $50, as opposed to the 786 listed earlier.[65]

A glance at figure 1 will indicate just how sharply different the patterns were. Only 24.8 percent of the original subscribers had contributed $100 or more. The corresponding figure for 1844 is more than three times as high—79.5 percent. And with so few small contributions to balance the larger ones, the latter acquired far greater relative weight. From 1811 to 1843, for example, subscriptions of $500 or more totaled forty-two, as against fifty-eight in 1844—not a great difference, perhaps. Still, such subscriptions amounted to less than 4 percent of those on the original list, compared with 29 percent of those recorded in 1844.

To have duplicated the tremendous outpouring of communitywide generosity that led to the founding of the Massachusetts General Hospital might not have been possible a generation later. Also, the amount of money needed in 1844 was smaller, and certainly it was more efficient to do without a door-to-door campaign if the goal could be met by other means. But if the trustees were in fact thinking in such terms, much had changed since 1818. In that year Josiah Quincy had spoken with pride of "all classes of . . . citizens combining and concentrating their efforts," and a list of subscriptions that ranged from $20,000 to 25¢—"the gift of a poor black"—gave palpable meaning to his claim.[66] The original hospital trustees had gone to great lengths to cultivate an image of partnership, to involve "persons of all conditions of life." The abandonment of that effort—even if only for efficiency's sake— represented something more than a modest reshuffling of priorities.

And whether, in fact, efficiency was the sole consideration is unclear. From the beginning there had always been a notable drawback to communitywide participation. In effect it was a two-sided coin: though it did distribute in useful ways both the costs and the benefits of philanthropy, it could also be used to justify a similar diffusion of authority. At the time the hospital was founded, the General Court— in return for its donation of Province House and $30,000 worth of convict labor to quarry stone for the Allen Street building—had ac-

Figure 1. Comparative distribution, by size, of donations to the Massachusetts General Hospital, 1811–1843 and 1844. Data are from Nathaniel I. Bowditch, *A History of the Massachusetts General Hospital (to August 5, 1851), Second Edition, with a Continuation to 1872* (New York, 1972; Arno Press reprint), pp. 432–438.

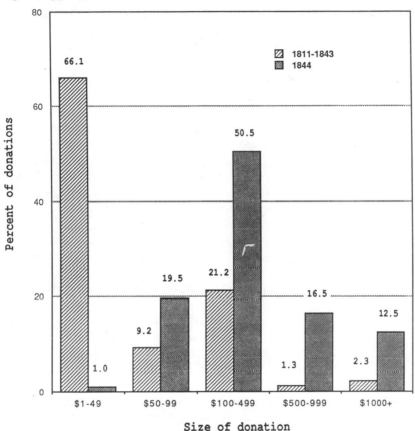

quired the right to appoint a Board of Visitors, made up of state officials, which in turn chose four of the hospital's twelve trustees.[67] Significantly, in their fund-raising efforts, the trustees of 1844 bypassed not only the less well heeled portions of the community but the state government itself. Perhaps with their own private interests so intimately bound up with the hospital, it seemed best to keep the reins of control more firmly in hand than ever. If so, restricting giving to a narrower circle made sense. Within a very short while, too, events were to provide an even more compelling rationale for such a strategy.

*   *   *

In the history of "social Boston," as Oscar Handlin has demonstrated, 1845 stands as a major point of demarcation. After that year what had been a steadily mounting trickle of Irish immigration turned into a flood, sweeping thousands of desperately poor human beings in upon the "startled and scarcely prepared" city. In 1840 fewer than 4,000 immigrants had reached Boston from Ireland. By 1849 the number had risen to almost 29,000. According to the census taken the following year, fully 35,000 of the city's inhabitants—more than a quarter of its population—were Irish by birth.[68]

More driven than drawn to America's shores, the Irish altered and would continue to alter life in Boston in countless ways. Lacking skills, they took whatever jobs were available—most often as manual laborers and household servants. Yet for many there was no regular work at all. As the statistics suggest, a sizable number left to find places elsewhere, but more remained, living from hand to mouth, crowded into hastily improvised, wretchedly cramped, and unsanitary quarters. In time those who stayed managed—principally through banding together to help one another—to achieve a measure of order and security. But in the late forties any sign of that development would have been difficult to detect, particularly from outside the city's spreading Irish slums. Instead, what most Bostonians saw was the poverty, the disease, the vice, and the crime, which those neighborhoods seemed to breed at a rate that completely swamped existing agencies charged with handling such problems. And no less troubling was the attitude of the Irish themselves. Deeply conservative, and forced in any case to live lives that made a mockery of the characteristic American faith in progress, they often appeared to accept their lot with a kind of grim fatalism.[69]

Indeed, the difference in attitude probably struck at the sensibilities of Boston's native-born Americans more deeply than anything else. Poverty and its consequences had always been part of life, but in this case the traditional remedies simply did not work. Those in need responded grudgingly if at all when helped, and attempts to combine support with lectures on the virtues of self-improvement regularly met with stony indifference. Such behavior conformed to no existing system of social theory, and those displaying it seemed destined to remain on the other side of an unbridgeable gulf.

In short, the Irish were not just strangers; they were outsiders. In that respect they constituted a fundamental challenge to the assumptions which had shaped philanthropy in Boston since the early years of the century. In first appealing for funds for the hospital, Doctors Jackson and Warren had spoken of helping young men "of good and industrious habits" made ill "by the very anxiety and exertions" of their efforts to succeed in life.[70] Those young men might have been newcomers to Boston, but otherwise they seemed—or could be made to seem—quite like the rest of the population. Sharing the same values and goals, they required nothing more than support through a temporary crisis; beyond that point the road ran smoothly onward to full participation and membership in the community. None of this applied to the Irish. They were not part of the community, and there appeared to be no way of drawing them into it.

In the decades ahead, that view would acquire the force of a settled conviction—a conviction, too, which the obvious preference of the Irish for those charitable institutions they built themselves simply strengthened. Long before then, however, Boston's native-born philanthropists had managed to redirect the thrust of their own efforts. If it no longer made sense to think in terms of projects benefiting the entire community, there were other ways of spending "charity's share," some quite attractive.

At established institutions goals were already set, but even there adjustments could be made—and were. Nor were they always confined to minor matters. Upon occasion what began as a modest program of tinkering ended by becoming something far more sweeping. A case in point was the McLean Asylum.

As a distinct "department" of the hospital, McLean had always fared well with wealthy donors. The rich, when physically ill, were treated at home in the nineteenth century, but serious mental disorders posed problems that defied solution even in the best-run households. Often there was nothing to do but lock the unfortunate patient in an attic room with whatever "care" might be available from servants. A familiar theme in literature, such cases were not uncommon in real life, and anxiety about them haunted many people. Also, though psychiatry was still in its infancy, there was a growing recognition that certain mental disorders were related to home or family situations in a way that made it impossible to cure patients without a change of environment.

In the treatment of the insane McLean represented, from the start, a bold departure. Not only was the institution very generously funded, but the trustees and staff for their part had responded by developing a truly remarkable system of care or, as they liked to refer to it, "moral management." As much as possible patients were left free of the usual restraints. In place of chains and straitjackets, they were given meals and rest at scheduled hours and were required to exercise daily on the asylum's spacious grounds in Somerville. Attendants were forbidden to strike patients "even in self-defense," and "amusements" of all kinds, including reading, games, and carriage rides, were encouraged. In 1835, during Dr. Thomas G. Lee's tenure as physician, weekly dancing parties were added to the program, as well as regular work assignments: for men on the asylum farm and for women in the laundry and kitchen.[71] Not all of Dr. Lee's innovations survived, however, and the reason given at the time—accurately enough, it turned out—was a marked change in the institution's clientele.

Originally, McLean had drawn its patients from every walk of life, but by 1840 that was ceasing to be true. Instead, the poor were turning in growing numbers to recently opened public institutions like the State Asylum at Worcester or the Boston Lunatic Asylum. The major factor was cost. Though the care was decidedly inferior at such places, most charged little or nothing at all, whereas the trustees held McLean's rates to between $2 and $20 a day, depending on ability to pay. Some people were always carried at the lower figure, but with no change in the basic rate structure, the proportion of "lower-rate patients" continued to decline, while the number of those paying the full cost rose.[72] Inevitably the difference affected the way the institution was run. During the early 1840s the rooms were embellished with "carpets, wallpaper, mirrors, mantels and better furniture" so that the patients "might not miss their home surroundings."[73] It became necessary, as well, to abandon Dr. Lee's work assignments since "the class of patients . . . received at McLean was not accustomed to such manual labor and refused to do it."[74]

All of these changes, of course, involved decisions made by the trustees: had they wished to they could have lowered rates and spent less on wallpaper and mantels. No doubt at first there was a certain amount of genuine regret. Unquestionably something had been sacrificed, and the board did greet with notable enthusiasm William Appleton's donation in 1843 of $10,000 "for the purpose of affording aid to such patients in the McLean Asylum as who from straitened means might be compelled to leave the institution without a perfect cure."[75] Duly deposited with the Massachusetts Hospital Life Insurance Company, "the Appleton Fund for the Relief of the Insane" helped support patients unable to pay even the lowest rate.[76]

But in the long run the trend at McLean was away from gestures like Appleton's. Costs continued to rise, as did the social and economic standing of the patients. Meanwhile, the physician of those years, Dr. Luther V. Bell, remarked at some length in his 1848 annual report on the large number of vagrants, paupers, and insane persons coming to America from abroad. Not a few of them, he felt, were being sent by their native countries simply "to rid themselves of their care."[77] Did it matter that only a handful of such people would ever see the inside of the McLean Asylum? Bell was silent on that point, but he himself did little to reverse the trend. On the contrary, one of his first recommendations was that rates should be increased.[78] And even William Appleton, in time, seems to have accepted the new order of things. In 1851 he made another major donation to the asylum, this time of $20,000. As he requested, the money—combined with an earlier gift from the Lee family—was used to erect and furnish two buildings "designed especially for such patients as shall have previously dwelt in residences of a spacious and cheerful character, and with the view of affording, as far as possible, to this the wealthiest class of our inmates the accustomed comforts and conveniences of home."[79] Finished in 1853, the new buildings together accommodated sixteen patients, providing each with a suite of three appropriately decorated rooms.[80]

In their resolution thanking Appleton for his second "munificent gift," the trustees commended his "enlarged philanthropy" which had "thus provided for the equal relief of rich and poor."[81] Still, as even they must have sensed, the meticulous balance they praised was exactly that and nothing more. And it left the broader vision which had sustained both the hospital and the asylum at their founding—if it survived at all amid the luxuries of "Appleton House"—so thoroughly altered as to be unrecognizable. Far from bridging divisions in the community, McLean had come to mirror them. In fact, with its charity cases maintained by special funds, or through surplus revenues from "full-rate patients," who in turn stayed in comfortable enclaves of their own, the institution reflected quite accurately the developing social reality of Boston. In that scheme, too, there could be little doubt about who benefited most. By 1853 McLean had become a place supported and run by—as well as largely for—the rich.

VI

With all of its components so neatly focused, philanthropy could appear very narrow indeed. Yet the pattern at McLean was only one of several to emerge as Boston's leading citizens searched for worthwhile projects to support after 1845. Some people—quite possibly uncomfortable with the particular kind of balance William Appleton settled for—were prepared to venture farther afield in attempting to fulfill their obligations in an altered world. One was Amos Lawrence.

Few men were as "giving" as Lawrence, and perhaps no one else in Boston thought harder about what the objectives of large-scale private philanthropy ought to be. From the beginning, in his quest to "Do with thy might what thy hand findeth to do," he contributed generously to places like the hospital and Harvard, and as long as he lived his name continued to appear on all of the appropriate subscription lists. But Lawrence also developed a number of highly individual enthusiasms, such as undertaking—often with very little help from anyone else—to complete the Bunker Hill Monument.

Begun in a flush of patriotism in the 1820s, the massive obelisk of Quincy granite that was to memorialize the first full-scale battle of the Revolution stood, a decade later, less than half finished and sorely in need of funds. Without Lawrence's help, many more years might have passed before the final stone was laid. Yet he himself always considered the way the project was accomplished at least as important as the result itself. In 1830, when the directors of the Bunker Hill Monument Association applied to the legislature for lottery privileges to raise money, he was furious. "I opposed the measure in all its stages, and feel mortified that they have done so."[82] Happily, the bill was defeated, whereupon Lawrence offered to subscribe $5,000 if an additional $50,000 could be raised from other sources. Two years later he repeated the offer, this time asking the Massachusetts Charitable Mechanic Association to conduct a campaign for the $50,000. Finally in 1839, with the necessary funds still not in hand, he proposed to increase his contribution to $10,000 if the Mechanic Association could raise $30,000 from the general public. In that form—and helped along by an additional $10,000 donation from Judah Touro, a wealthy New Orleans merchant—the plan succeeded.[83]

Afterward Lawrence remarked that if he had wished, he and a small group of friends—including Edmund Dwight, "three Appletons, Robert G. Shaw and us three Lawrences"—could have financed the completion of the Bunker Hill Monument "without saying 'by your leave,' to the public."[84] But going to such lengths to involve other people, when a stroke of the pen might have served as well, was important. Indeed in this case Lawrence seemed to see in it a significance that transcended even the logic that had shaped projects like the hospital. For if a few rich men were to assume sole responsibility for the monument, it would never, he felt, become a true "nucleus for the affections of the people."[85] And only as it drew and held people's affections would the monument continue to remind them, generation after generation, of that most essential component of the great American experiment in self-government: "character."

By "character" Lawrence presumably meant the sort of courage and self-sacrificing dedication patriot volunteers had shown under British fire. He never defined the term in so many words, though he did worry constantly about "the downhill tendency in the standard of character."[86] As time passed, too, the slide downhill seemed to accelerate. Certainly the completion of the Bunker Hill Monument—celebrated with a great procession from Boston over to Charlestown and an address by Daniel Webster that concluded on the theme of character—did little to halt it.[87] But Lawrence was not a man easily discouraged, so the years after 1843 found him busy with half-a-dozen new projects, all directed more or less to the same end.

Most had to do with education, which as a means of molding character had the virtue of being both more direct and more systematic than monument building. Typically Lawrence saw no solution to the Irish problem "but to educate the children."[88] The thing most to be feared was "that ignorance which will bring everything down to its own level, instead of that true knowledge, which shall level up the lowest places, now inundated with foreign emigrants." Nor could there be any doubt about the consequences of inaction: "if we do not educate and elevate this class of our people, they will change our system of government within fifty years."[89]

For all Lawrence's concern for educating the Irish, however, the two institutions on which he lavished most of his time and money could hardly have been farther removed—in every sense—from the slums of Boston. The first was the local academy in Groton, Massachusetts, his boyhood home. By 1847 he had given it over $20,000, including the cost of a new library that he hoped would be "second to no other in the country except that of Cambridge."[90] He also encouraged his brother William to contribute, which netted the school an additional $45,000 and led the trustees, in recognition of the family's generosity, to rename the place Lawrence Academy.[91] Meanwhile, Lawrence himself had become the principal benefactor of Williams College, and it was in that role that he both made his greatest efforts and seemed to take the keenest satisfaction during the last decade of his life.

When Lawrence took it under his wing, Williams had been a going concern for just under half a century. Located in the far northwestern corner of Massachusetts, it owed its establishment to a bequest from Ephraim Williams, a member of the large clan that had dominated western Massachusetts during the final decades of the colonial period. Over the years the college had received sporadic grants from the General Court, but in 1844 Williams was in debt with no certain means of relieving its difficulties. Yet in Mark Hopkins it could claim a president distinguished enough to be invited by the Lowell Institute to give a course of lectures, which was how Lawrence became interested in the college.[92]

The general purpose of all Lowell Institute lectures—as set forth by John Lowell, Jr., the son of Francis Cabot Lowell, whose bequest of over a quarter of a million dollars had made them possible—was to demonstrate "the truth of those moral and religious precepts, by which alone . . . men can be secure of happiness in this world and that to come."[93] It was a mission with which Lawrence heartily sympathized, and Hopkins' personal interpretation of it struck just the right note. Nominally a Unitarian, Lawrence had long deplored the tendency among his coreligionists to "sink" Jesus "to the level of a mere human teacher."[94] Thus when Hopkins, in his opening lecture, steadfastly clung to the divinity of Christ as the principle uniting all Christians, he found both a ready listener in Lawrence and—what mattered more—a ready source of funds for Williams. Before leaving Boston, he received a visit in his hotel room from Amos A. Lawrence, who came bearing his father's offer to donate $5,000 to the college.[95]

That proved to be but the first of many gifts. Six months later Hopkins was happy to accept a check for a second $5,000, which ended the college's indebtedness.[96] The next year there was a donation of $10,000, and in 1846 Lawrence assumed the entire cost—some $7,000—of a new library. The graceful octagonal building was both more elaborate and more expensive than the modest structure Hopkins and the Williams trustees originally envisioned, but Lawrence was emphatic: "Prepare such a building as you will be satisfied with & as will do credit to your taste & judgement fifty years hence."[97] In the same spirit came $1,000 to enlarge the college grounds in 1852, as well as $1,500 for a new telescope for the observatory. And to those smaller amounts, Lawrence over the years added $2,000 to establish scholarships for graduates of Lawrence Academy, plus an annual check for $100, to be used at Hopkins' discretion "for the aid of needy students in those emergencies which often arise."[98]

Including miscellaneous art works and books for the library, "the expense of which I know nothing," Hopkins estimated that Lawrence gave Williams "between thirty and forty thousand dollars."[99] He also gave without any of the condescension—or the insistence on having his own way—that too often characterized those in his position. "He seemed," remarked Hopkins, "to place himself in the relation, not so much of a patron of the college, as of a sympathizer and helper in a great and good work."[100] In turn Hopkins responded with genuine affection. The two became fast friends, corresponded frequently, and exchanged—each according to his means—a constant stream of personal gifts and mementos.

In short, Lawrence was, as Hopkins' biographer Frederick Rudolph has observed, "a model benefactor."[101] But he for his part always felt that he got far more than he gave: "The reports of & from your college," he wrote Hopkins in 1850, "make me feel that my labours in

getting it on 'its legs,' have been repaid fourfold."[102] Ultimately, however, Lawrence looked for returns far more significant than any personal satisfaction he, as a donor, received. Referring to Lawrence
Academy and Williams together at one point, he remarked: "There is
a pleasant vision which opens to me when I look forward to the
characters that the academy and the college are to send forth for the
next hundred years." Surprisingly, the vision was inspired by his old
home in Groton "and the great elm in front." The tree had "a teaching
and a significance" that he used in "training" his own grandchildren.
"How important, then," he added immediately afterward, "that our
places of education be sustained, as supplying the pure and living
streams that shall irrigate every hill and valley of this vast empire, and
train men to know and do their duty!"[103] The Amos Lawrence that
Hopkins knew was never just a practical businessman: "He built
air-castles, and they vanished, and then he built others."[104]

But whether Hopkins noticed it or not, the "air-castles" of those
years—no less than the solider structures that resulted from
Lawrence's generosity—all tended to conform to a single basic design. Rural colleges and academies, religious conservatism, character
forged in the citizen-military-revolutionary mold, the Bunker Hill
Monument itself: each was yet another step leading ineluctably out
and away from the hurly-burly of Boston and its distressing social
dilemmas—leading, in fact, to the past.

And so it was with Lawrence's lesser charities, including the countless barrels of books and bolts of calico that descended on the Hopkins
family in Williamstown and so many other clergymen and academi-
cians across the country. Two and sometimes three rooms in Lawrence's house were needed to store the articles used for such
purposes. There, on rainy days, he would personally assemble the
contents of every package, keeping careful track of the value of each
item, after which the "small hay-cock"—containing, perhaps, a
"dressing gown, vest, hat, slippers, jack-knife, scissors, pins, neck-
handkerchiefs, pantaloons, cloth for coat, 'History of Groton,' lot of
pamphlets"—would be neatly bundled up and shipped out by the
family coachman. What the recipients made of their good fortune is
difficult to guess. To Mary Hopkins and her children Lawrence became "Uncle Amos"; many of those so favored had never met him.
The packages and barrels simply arrived out of the blue, as if sent by
some wonderful country merchant, who, miraculously, had no wish
to be paid. For that indeed was the role Lawrence appeared to be
playing: down to the minutely kept "accounts," the steps in the process were all the ones he had gone through day after day as a clerk in
the Groton store where his business career began, except that he and

he alone paid. No bills were ever rendered, and for good measure he usually slipped in "a note containing from five to fifty dollars in money."[105]

In praising Lawrence after his death, Hopkins observed that one notable "peculiarity" of his generosity was "the personal attention and sympathy which he bestowed with it." Those qualities, Hopkins believed, were the very warp upon which the fabric of society was woven. "Only this sympathy it is that can establish the right relation between the rich and the poor . . . can neutralize the repellent and aggressive tendencies of individuals and of classes and make society a brotherhood."[106] Little that his friend might have said would have pleased Lawrence more. As a philanthropist he did try to avoid the starker—and at bottom, split—conception of society that motivated gestures like William Appleton's gifts to the McLean Asylum. He worked at eliminating barriers, not at erecting them. Still, with each passing year the "brotherhood" Hopkins referred to—at least as Lawrence envisioned it—seemed to slip further back in time. As a paradigm of social harmony, a college where the president personally joined in conducting religious revivals had a certain charm. It was also, like the tasseled velvet cap Lawrence affected late in life—so similar to the ones in which Copley had often painted Boston's pre-Revolutionary merchants—emphatically the property of an earlier era. And by 1850 it was in danger of becoming merely quaint. Yet none of this appeared to bother Lawrence. Rooted in the past and his own personal values, his vision of a better society kept him busy and happy until the day he died.

What Lawrence found so satisfying, however, evidently held limited appeal for his friends. The truth was that most of them were content with existing channels of philanthropy. The increasing narrowness of those channels and their growing divergence from past principles may have bothered some people, but they were in the minority. Far more typical was Lawrence's brother, Abbott, who made of philanthropy an instrument that operated with all the force and efficiency of a drive shaft in one of the Essex Company's huge new mills on the Merrimack.

Above all Abbott Lawrence was a realist. He tailored his values to life as he found it, not as he thought it ought to be—or might have been. Good at games as a boy, he never stopped competing and was easily the most ambitious of the Lawrence brothers. "He still grasps at money though he has more than a million and is the richest man of his age here," commented his nephew, Amos A. Lawrence, in 1842. "He loves power too and office. He does not grow better nor happier as he gets older."[107] Less harsh in his judgment, Amos Lawrence objected only to his brother's perennial political hopes, and the objection was more to the thing sought than to the seeker himself. "If my vote would make my brother Vice President," he wrote at one point, "I would not give it, as I think it lowering his good name to accept office of any sort, by employing such means as are now needful to get votes."[108]

But whatever his family thought, Lawrence continued on course, determined if not precisely serene. As a philanthropist, too, he seemed to have few qualms about trimming the terms of his gifts to fit his view of the world. In 1844 he gave $2,000 to the Boston High School to establish a fund for the purchase of prizes to be distributed annually among those students "who may excel in the various branches of learning taught in that valuable institution."[109] That life was a race in which victory went to the swiftest was not a lesson to be postponed. The following year a like sum went to the Latin School to reward "good conduct in general, embracing moral rectitude and gentleman-like deportment."[110] Of course, there was always a danger that "gentleman-like deportment" might mask some fatal flaw in character, but Lawrence left to others the task of chasing will o' the wisps like "character." No doubt it was in the same spirit that he declined to subscribe anything for the establishment of the Theological School at Harvard. His name did appear on the list of donors to the university's astronomical observatory, and in 1844 he contributed $2,000—twice the amount his brother Amos gave—to the fund for enlarging the General Hospital, an institution he had earlier served as a trustee.[111]

In addition to these and the school prizes, there were other donations for equally sound projects—money for the Congregational Church in the town of Lawrence and $1,000 to assist in endowing the Franklin Library—making the record an altogether respectable one.[112] Yet to those who knew Lawrence it must have seemed an imperfect measure of the man's true capabilities. Certainly from the standpoint of size, his benefactions in no way distinguished him from a dozen other members of the Associates group, at least up to 1847. Then, in one fell swoop he remedied all that by making over to Harvard a larger sum of money than the university had ever received before from a living donor.[113]

In describing the uses to which his gift was to be put, Lawrence noted that Harvard already had "special schools of Theology, Law, Medicine, and Surgery," but where, he asked, "can we send those who intend to devote themselves to the practical applications of science?" It was training of that sort he wished to encourage, and to that end he was prepared to offer "for the acceptance of the President and Fellows of Harvard College, the sum of fifty thousand dollars."

Specifically, the money was to be used to erect and equip a building or buildings "including an extensive laboratory" and to help support two new professorships, one in geology and the other in engineering. All of this, too, was to be accomplished "with as much expedition as may be consistent with economy."[114] And so it was, with the result appropriately named—by vote of the Harvard Corporation—the Lawrence Scientific School. Meanwhile, words of praise had poured in from everywhere, including an especially warm note from Amos Lawrence. "Dear Brother Abbott,—I hardly dare trust myself to speak what I feel, and therefore write to say that I thank God I am spared to this day . . . This magnificent plan . . . is a better investment than any you have ever made." It was also—or so an "affectionate" brother could not resist adding—"more honorable and more to be coveted than the highest political station in our country."[115]

No one reading Amos Lawrence's note could have doubted his sincerity, but even he must have sensed the gulf separating his brother's generosity to Harvard from his own to a place like Williams College. The whole point of giving money to Williams was to keep it as it was—to preserve it from change—whereas the Lawrence Scientific School promised to move Harvard decisively forward into the future. Lawrence's gift to Harvard also seemed calculated to tie the university yet more closely to the interests of the men who had become its principal benefactors. When he said "Let theory be proved by practical results," he probably had in mind the prodigies accomplished by someone like Charles S. Storrow, a Harvard graduate of the Class of 1829 who had studied at the Ponts et Chaussées in Paris. After serving as chief engineer of the Boston and Lowell Railroad, Storrow turned his hand to an impressive array of projects, including the waterpower system for the town of Lawrence.[116]

In the long run Lawrence's plan to graft onto Harvard a full-fledged modern school of engineering proved only partially successful. Appointed professor of zoology and geology in 1847, Louis Agassiz stole the show for pure science, thereby leaving it to M.I.T. in later years to dominate the "practical" field.[117] Still, what Lawrence had intended remained very much of a piece with the prevailing pattern of philanthropy in Boston during those years—as did his later charitable donations. In his will he left an additional $50,000 to the Lawrence Scientific School and an equal amount to underwrite the construction of model lodging houses for Boston's poor. According to the terms of the second bequest, three trustees were to oversee the building of the houses, collect rents, and distribute any excess income to other worthwhile charities in the city. In practice the scheme worked remarkably well, but then Lawrence must have known it would, having already seen something very like it in England, where he had served as American minister from 1849 to 1852.[118] A similar system of model lodging houses for the poor ranked among the favorite projects of Albert, the prince consort.[119]

So in the end Lawrence chose to strike the same sort of careful balance that William Appleton had at the McLean Asylum. With calculated precision he lavished his princely generosity alike on Harvard and "the poor." And just to ensure that the accounts remained absolutely equal, he even included in his will, in addition to the two large bequests, several smaller ones—to places other than Harvard—which together exactly totaled $50,000 and thus neatly matched his earlier gift to the university.[120]

VII

A rough computation of all the money spent for philanthropic purposes by the first generation of Lawrences in Boston would have put the figure somewhere near one million dollars. Amos, who kept better records, probably spent more, but it was Abbott who, on his death in 1855, was eulogized in Faneuil Hall by Robert Winthrop as "the most important person" in the community.[121] If he gave less, his gifts were bulkier, more visible—loomed larger. This too was becoming characteristic of philanthropy in Boston. The cooperative efforts of the past were giving way before a spate of individual projects that inevitably assumed the air of personal monuments—the Lowell Institute, the Lawrence Scientific School, Appleton Chapel at Harvard. On one level the explanation was simple: after 1840 someone like Abbott Lawrence had more money to spend than he or anyone else had had thirty years earlier. But the impression created was also quite different, and communicating it seems to have called for more than ordinary eloquence. Thus Winthrop could think of no better way of summing up Lawrence's contribution to life in Boston than to quote Edmund Burke's "beautiful words" about Sir George Saville: "When an act of great and signal humanity was to be done, and done with all the weight and authority that belonged to it, this community could cast its eyes on none but him."[122]

Of course not all philanthropic projects could be managed by lone individuals. Some continued to require collective action. Yet even in those cases the results were fundamentally different from what they would have been a generation earlier. Distinctions were drawn publicly that had once been mentioned, if at all, only in private, and if a few purses were opened more widely than ever, there was also a growing willingness to let other agencies—including government—shoulder more of the burden in some areas.

A notable example of all these trends was the Boston Public Library, founded in 1852. Among Abbott Lawrence's smaller bequests, $10,000 was earmarked for the library, and by then it had also received $10,000 from Jonathan Phillips, as well as several even larger donations from Joshua Bates, starting with one for $50,000 in 1852.[123] Bates had begun his business career in Boston, but most of his adult years were spent in England as a partner of Baring Brothers. The truth was that years of trying to win support for a public library from Boston's rich had netted only modest returns. Nor was the issue one of money alone. What the library's backers wanted more than anything else was some arrangement that would have opened the collections of the Boston Athenaeum to the general public, thereby providing a nucleus for the new institution. On that score they met solid opposition from the Athenaeum's proprietors.

Solid, but never quite unanimous—so the issue was at least fairly joined, producing, if nothing else, a highly revealing debate. The leader of the pro-merger forces was George Ticknor, who was both an Athenaeum proprietor and the individual who more than any other saw to it that the Boston Public Library became a reality. German-trained scholar, Smith Professor of Modern Languages at Harvard from 1819 to 1835, author of a massive treatise on Spanish literature, Ticknor was the foremost American man of letters of his generation. In addition he could claim impeccable social credentials and the wealth to go with them.[124] "The arch devil of the aristocracy," Theodore Parker called him.[125] Yet Ticknor also hoped, as Martin Green has pointed out, "to establish a decent society in which a man of letters could feel himself fully a citizen—both as democrat and as aristocrat."[126] And an important part of that effort was his campaign—begun as early as 1826—"to unite into one establishment" all the smaller libraries of Boston "and then let the whole circulate, Athenaeum and all . . . open to the public."[127]

Since Ticknor was serving as a trustee of the Athenaeum when he first formulated his plan, it must have received more than passing consideration, but apparently he failed to win many converts, for the next such proposal came from a very different source.[128] In 1841 Alexandre Vattemare, a French ventriloquist, who improbably had chosen to make a personal crusade of public libraries, visited Boston and aroused enormous enthusiasm for his ideas. Public meetings were held, with resolutions passed and a committee appointed.[129] In due course letters went out to determine whether "a union of the principal literary associations and those for the promotion of the arts and sciences, could be effected . . . to make their various collections as available to the public of Boston as can be."[130] In their reply the Athenaeum's trustees were blunt. "There are insuperable objections to the adoption of this measure by the Boston Athenaeum," they noted, adding "these objections [we] do not think it necessary to state in detail."[131]

The next time the subject came up was in 1848. By then the city government itself, under Mayor Josiah Quincy, Jr., was giving serious thought to establishing a public library. Among other things Vattemare—having lost none of his passion for libraries in the intervening years—had made a practice of shipping over collections of French public documents, which the city had no place to store. But Quincy also favored a library for its own sake, and in addition he was treasurer of the Athenaeum, which at that point was having difficulty finding the money to complete its new building. The result was a plan—this time fully approved by the Athenaeum's trustees—that called for giving "to the public the use of the Library in as full a manner as it now is, or hereafter may be enjoyed by the shareholders."[132] As its part of the bargain, the city was to provide a lump sum of $50,000 plus an annual subsidy of $5,000, gaining in return the right to appoint four of the ten directors of the reorganized Athenaeum. Yet if all this satisfied the Athenaeum's trustees, the reaction of the proprietors was anything but favorable. Late in 1848, five hundred of them attended a special meeting to consider the proposal, at the end of which "on motion, the whole subject was indefinitely postponed."[133]

In the aftermath Ticknor reappeared on the scene and—with the help of Edward Everett, who in 1850 offered to donate his personal collection of more than a thousand volumes of American public documents—finally worked out a plan that committed the city to going ahead on its own with a public library. By the end of 1852 the necessary steps had all been taken by the city council and Bates's initial gift of $50,000 was in hand, as well as several smaller ones for the purchase of books.[134] Ticknor personally drafted the new library's regulations, which stipulated that the great majority of books should "circulate freely . . . to create a real desire for general reading."[135] That had always been his goal. He firmly believed that the opportunity for such reading "ought to be furnished to all, as a matter of public policy and duty, on the same principle that we furnish free education, and in fact, as a part, and a most important part, of the education of all."[136] Many people had misgivings about some of the more liberal features of the plan, including Everett, who doubted whether the public could be trusted to care for the books properly. But in the end Ticknor carried the day, and encouraged by his success, he decided early the following year to have one more go at the Athenaeum's proprietors.

The occasion was the appearance in the Boston *Daily Advertiser* of a letter, signed simply "Shareholder in the Boston Athenaeum," favoring union.[137] Styling himself "An Old Proprietor of the Athenaeum," Ticknor wrote a few weeks later heartily endorsing the idea. Land had recently been purchased as a probable site for the city's library—then temporarily located in quarters on Mason Street—which would have placed it only a stone's throw from the Athenaeum. The result, according to Ticknor, would be an inefficient and needlessly expensive duplication of facilities. His principal point, however, had to do with the reasons for the Athenaeum's existence—or rather his view of those reasons. "Four-fifths of the proprietors of the Athenaeum," he wrote, "regard and have always regarded, their interest in it as a public rather than private one."[138] Many of those proprietors, Ticknor felt, would gladly give their shares to the city, provided the others could be sold at market value.

Signed by seventy-seven respected proprietors, Ticknor's letter was republished in pamphlet form and for a while seemed to be making headway. Then a major stumbling block arose. One of the city councilmen, who was also a trustee of the public library, was reported in the newspapers as having said "the Athenaeum must soon play second to the Boston Free Library, and the owners are perfectly willing now to sell out at half what they charged at first."[139] In the ensuing furor, the voice that spoke with greatest authority belonged to Josiah Quincy, Sr. Signing his *Appeal* "The Sole Survivor of the First Five Subscribers to the Athenaeum," the venerable former president of Harvard and mayor of the city of Boston (not to be confused with his son, Josiah Jr., who also held the latter office), argued strenuously against any change in the Athenaeum's status. His reasons were two: first the Athenaeum's founders had "intended it to . . . remain in all time to come a memorial of those who created and endowed it"; and second, it would be "unjust, unwise, and unprincipled" to vest control of the institution in "a political body, annually shifting its members, and changing principles and policy with every turn of party or passion."[140]

If Quincy was right, Ticknor had to be wrong. Either the Athenaeum was and ought to remain a private "memorial," or it represented and always had a "public" interest. It was up to the proprietors to decide. And at a special meeting held March 28, 1853, they came down resoundingly on the side of Quincy's interpretation. With six hundred people in attendance, Ticknor's proposals were rejected by an overwhelming majority; union had become a dead letter.[141]

It is sometimes suggested that if Councilman George Warren had kept his opinions to himself, the outcome might have been different. But at no point had a majority of the Athenaeum's proprietors favored union. Even when the trustees supported it, as they did in 1848, it failed to pass. The only thing that changed was the candor with which the reasons for opposing union were discussed. By 1853 Quincy was willing to say it all; not only to defend the Athenaeum's special status, but to base his defense on the separate and distinct status of "those who had created and endowed it" as a "memorial" to themselves. And though in later years the public library flourished, the Athenaeum would continue its charmed existence, as its members wished, inviolate—the exclusive preserve of that class Quincy had so tellingly described. Perhaps no better example could have been found of what philanthropy in Boston had become than the two institutions, equally prosperous, moving forward side by side along separate tracks.

VIII

Ironically it was also Josiah Quincy, Sr., who, thirty-five years earlier when the cornerstone of the Massachusetts General Hospital was laid, had spoken of "all classes of . . . citizens combining and concentrating their efforts."[142] That had been the dominant vision then, and occasionally during the long debate over the Athenaeum's status it slipped back into focus. Presumably Ticknor saw its relevance, but he was more concerned with other issues. To the followers of Alexandre Vattemare, on the other hand, it had been *the* issue. Vattemare's opening lecture on public libraries was delivered at the Boston Mercantile Library—a particularly happy choice, as it turned out. Established in 1820, the Mercantile Library had as its mission the encouragement of self-education among merchants' clerks and other ambitious young men. It must have been just such an audience that the eloquent, if somewhat bizarre, Frenchman addressed that evening in 1841, moving it to pass afterward a long set of enthusiastic resolutions. The resolutions touched on many points, but one of the chief reasons offered for "uniting our various Libraries and collections in Science and the Fine Arts," was that doing so "would benefit the great body of people . . . by breaking down the factitious distinctions which separate class from class."[143]

Such an argument could very well have come from the founders of the Massachusetts General Hospital. As philanthropists they too had hoped to break down class barriers—or at any rate soften their impact on everyday life. But by 1841 that goal was already beginning to give way to others, and over the next decade the shift became pronounced. If Vattemare's young admirers preferred to think of class distinctions as "factitious," no one reading Quincy's letter a dozen years later would have made the same mistake. Class distinctions were both real and formidable, and imbedded in institutions like the Athenaeum they were meant to survive, "in all time to come."

Quincy was probably just as happy to stop where he did in 1853, but the logic that leads from explaining social differences in terms of class to full-blown theories of class conflict is clear enough. Nor was it always so easy to resist that logic. One person who wrestled with the problem was Francis Bowen, Alford Professor of Moral Philosophy at Harvard. As Daniel Howe has pointed out, Bowen hoped to adapt the traditional tenets of Unitarianism to American Whig ideology and shape the whole into an explanation of "the changing economic conditions of the nineteenth century."[144] Borrowing heavily from classical economics, he nonetheless managed, in his *Political Economy*, to support the protective tariff. He waxed enthusiastic about cities and industrialization. He also took pains to point out that the different classes of society were "inseparably bound together by a community of interest."[145] Yet much of what he wrote seemed to imply precisely the opposite. A distinct inequality of wealth was essential if economic progress was to occur. The rich had a vital role to play, but as Bowen saw it their position in society was all too precarious. "In every community there is a secret feeling of bitterness rankling in the breasts of the poor against the rich, which is with difficulty kept down by the effects of moral and religious principle, and which, in times of great political excitement, becomes exasperated and menacing."[146]

Bowen's own loyalties in the face of the "menace" could be explained readily enough. Born poor, he had worked his way first through Phillips Exeter Academy, then through Harvard College, and gone on to teach at both places. He also served as editor of the *North American Review* from 1843 to 1854. Indeed the only rough patch in his career came when he failed to receive the McLean chair in history at Harvard, following public outcry over his spirited defense of the Austrian monarchy during the Revolution of 1848. He was finally appointed Alford Professor in 1854, and the *Political Economy* was published two years later, though the book was largely based on a course of Lowell Lectures delivered in 1850. Appropriately, Bowen dedicated his work to another self-made man: "To Nathan Appleton, one of the most eminent living representatives of a highly honored class, the merchant princes of Boston, who have earned success by sagacity, enterprise, and uprightness in all their undertakings, and have dignified it by the munificence of their charities, and by their liberal support of letters, science, and the arts."[147]

For his part, Appleton must have been delighted by the compliment. Certainly it offered eloquent proof of just how far he had traveled since the days of his youth. Yet beyond the flattering phrases of the dedication, Bowen's book told a rather different story. For ultimately the world described in the *Political Economy* seemed no more stable—or harmonious—than Isaac Appleton's New Ipswich. On the contrary, with the distance between classes grown greater than ever, the potential for conflict had only increased. And in that situation the possible fate of "princes" was bound to make their admirers uneasy, as plainly it did Bowen.

None of this implied for a moment, of course, that the need for philanthropy had diminished. Far from it. But after 1845 private generosity in Boston had increasingly come to take one of two distinct forms. The first was a more or less direct attempt to relieve suffering among the poor, especially "the deserving poor"—Abbott Lawrence's model lodging houses, for example. This was "charity," pure and simple, and the term was in fact used with growing frequency. The second type of response was a continued and often heightened involvement in certain kinds of educational and cultural activities. In such cases the vaguer term "philanthropy" seemed to apply best. Theoretically both charity and philanthropy were expected of anyone who wished to be considered a public benefactor, with the ideal being a nearly equal weighting of the two, though in practice not everyone managed the perfect parity Abbott Lawrence achieved.

Strong arguments were offered in behalf of each kind of response, but the rationale for charity was more obvious. Christian doctrine explicitly required the rich to share their bounty with the poor and downtrodden, and to those who did so the liberal religious persuasion of the day—which in one form or another claimed the allegiance of almost all of Boston's leading citizens—held out the hope of eternal life, or as Amos Lawrence put it, "the 'Well done'" promised to the faithful.[148] In addition, charity was supposed to provide the donor with an immediate sense of deep inner satisfaction. Always, too, there was the specter of what the community might become without the generosity of the rich. While charity did not "cure" poverty, it could act as a "balm," easing the pain of the distressed masses, who otherwise were seen as all too likely to rise up and take by force what they required for survival. The flood of Irish immigrants after 1845 gave particular point to such fears. And if many of the Irish themselves seemed immune to the workings of charity, that simply put a greater premium on seeking out those among the poor who could be helped, who "deserved" to be helped. Of course it might be difficult to distinguish. But in theory, at least, there was a considerable gulf between "poverty," which amounted to nothing more than "dependence on alms," and "pauperism"—a deep-seated condition, stemming from fundamental flaws in character. The former could be ameliorated even if the latter could not.

Philanthropy, meanwhile, relied on a different set of arguments. Depicting cultural and educational institutions as the guardians of "higher" values, their supporters were inclined to emphasize the special functions of such values in a democracy. Without them there would be nothing but unbridled self-interest to guide the average person in fulfilling his duties as a citizen. Amos Lawrence's concern about "character" was a corollary of this line of argument, and it figured prominently in much of what Ticknor said about public libraries. Occasionally, too, a case was made for the importance of advancing the frontiers of knowledge, either as something worthwhile for its own sake, or because of the benefits that would accrue to society. Finally, there was the matter of civic pride. Just at the time Josiah Quincy, Jr., and the city council were taking up the library issue in earnest, word came of John Jacob Astor's $400,000 bequest to New York City for a public library, giving a substantial push to their efforts.[149] If Boston was truly to merit the more exalted distinction its inhabitants claimed for it, then it had to have a great library, as well as a great university and a great hospital. Nothing less would do for the Athens of America, the Hub of the Universe, and it was up to the rich to do their part.

There was in all of this, surely, an unmistakable strain of defensiveness—a sense that an ample enough display of generosity would purchase not only the welfare of others, but their good opinion, plus a measure of security in a none-too-stable environment. Yet it would be a mistake to conclude that altruism played no part in the process. Christianity; the faith in "higher" values; the conviction that democracy, properly tutored, could be made to work; the belief that wealth was a "trust" to be administered for the good of society: each of these was taken seriously as a guide to action. They were never just elements of a convenient public posture. But because people rarely do things for one motive alone, it is possible to find defensiveness mixed with the altruism. And if one looks at results—as opposed to rhetoric —still other elements emerge, elements that in the long run may have mattered more than anything else.

Most of those other elements were not new. They had been characteristic of philanthropy in Boston since the early years of institutions like the Massachusetts General Hospital. With so much else changing after 1845, however, they tended to become more—not less—important. In that sense they were survivals, but survivals that found a ready home in the new environment.

One of them was the capital-pooling feature of philanthropic enterprises, which continued to concentrate ever-larger sums in the hands of trustees. At no point was there any disposition to change the established practice in that regard. Wherever possible capital amounts were kept intact and invested to produce regular income, which in turn was devoted to whatever purpose the donor had in mind. Even charity, as distinct from philanthropy, could be conducted on this basis, and was, in cases like the Appleton Fund for the Relief of the Insane and Abbott Lawrence's model lodging houses.

There is no way of calculating just how much money the combined endowments of Boston's major charitable and philanthropic institutions represented, but the total ran into the millions. In 1851 the treasurer of the hospital estimated its "invested property" at $200,000. The endowment of Harvard in 1840 was $646,235 and over the next three decades that figure more than tripled. In 1849 the Athenaeum's "productive property" was valued at $152,000, and its trustees also served as "visitors" of the trust created under the will of John Lowell, Jr., to endow the Lowell Institute. The original value of that trust was $250,000. Taking only these amounts, the total comes to well over a million dollars—a very large pool of capital by the standards of the time.[150]

Not surprisingly, trustees remained reluctant to sacrifice any of the control they exercised over the funds in their care. Technically their powers were the same as those of trustees acting under testamentary trusts: they held legal title to the property of the institution or philanthropy in question, and as far as the investment of the property was concerned their only obligation was to proceed as other "men of prudence" in the community did. In short their power was very nearly absolute, and as time passed their determination to keep it that way seemed to grow stronger. Particularly worrisome was anything that threatened to increase the involvement of the public, through government, in their deliberations. Thus the trustees of the hospital bypassed the commonwealth altogether in raising money in 1844. And when the Athenaeum's trustees came forward with their merger plan in 1848 it explicitly limited the city's share of directors to a minority of the reconstituted board. A similar arrangement had governed the makeup of the hospital's board from the beginning, but even that failed to persuade the Athenaeum's proprietors, and five years later Quincy's letter spoke openly about the impropriety of turning over the institution "and its property . . . to the care of a political body."

Though they jealously guarded their prerogatives against public interference, few trustees would have had any difficulty meeting the "prudent man" standard in a court of law. Most continued to rely on the Massachusetts Hospital Life Insurance Company, presumably the very model of prudence in financial affairs. Moreover, the flow of funds to the Massachusetts Hospital Life continued throughout the period when its deposits were being shifted so decisively into the textile industry. And even when endowment monies were not deposited with the Massachusetts Hospital Life, they still tended to gravitate toward Waltham-Lowell ventures. For example, after 1857, while Amos A. Lawrence was serving as treasurer of the university, a sizable portion of Harvard's endowment was invested directly in the Pacific Mills at Lawrence.[151]

Whether in fact so heavy a commitment to one group of companies in a single industry was prudent is debatable. Most modern trustees are conscious of the need to spread risks. But however dubious the policy, it followed logically from the realities of the situation. Control over charitable and philanthropic endowments had come to represent substantial power. With nothing to stop them, the men who exercised that power were free to do so for whatever ends they chose. If that meant binding the region's economy yet more tightly to what such men considered "safe" in terms of future development, then so be it. Prudence could be defined in more than one way, just as the power inherent in large pools of capital could be made to operate on several different levels at once.

So it was with a second form of power intimately associated with Boston's philanthropic enterprises: the power to set standards. Martin Green has argued cogently that the city's much vaunted literary culture was deeply and in not altogether salutary ways marked by the "social" norms of its upper classes.[152] If that was true, the impact elsewhere was even more palpable. As applied to thought and expression, a particular set of standards will usually leave room for differences of opinion. Unquestionably George Ticknor's vision of the proper uses of literature in a democracy was broader than Abbott Lawrence's, yet when such issues were translated into questions of institutional organization the space available for disagreement shrank considerably, as Ticknor discovered. For there, adhering to standards could—and often did—mean drawing hard-and-fast lines.

Nor were the lines drawn at places like the Athenaeum the only— or even the most important—barriers erected by Boston's philanthropists. Of far greater significance was the achievement in education and the professions. As standards were defined ever more precisely, and at the same time constantly raised at a small group of institutions, what resulted was a credentialing system of enormous potential influence. Though it was still possible to become a lawyer without formal legal education, those who attended law school enjoyed an obvious advantage over those who did not. And within New England, Harvard Law School, by virtue of its earlier entry into the field and superior resources, clearly occupied the premier position, as the university did in most other fields.

One of the great advantages of such a system was that power could be exercised through it quite subtly. An impressive degree of "openness" remained fully compatible with the protection of class interests. There was no need to resort to cruder forms of exclusion; admission to Harvard did not have to be restricted to the children of the rich alone. Poor boys like Francis Bowen, who made it over the requisite hurdles, could be left to absorb—through diligent performance of the tasks set before them, no less than through association with their professors and better-favored classmates—the proper attitudes.[153] Thus setting standards high enough made it possible to defend one's privileges in the very act of extending them to others—a democratic remedy for a democratic problem. Well might Abbott Lawrence seek to complete such a system by incorporating in it the one element it seemed to lack, training in practical science! Viewed in this light, too, the earnest dedication of Lawrence's brother Amos to the cause of country colleges and academies becomes all the more quixotic and poignant. With things as they were, what possible advantage—what conceivable security—could a sleepy college in a rural backwater offer the Boston Associates? The answer was none; Williams College was irrelevant.

As indeed was something else, which had once constituted a much more basic component of the Associates' philanthropic activities. For as philanthropy and charity together had come increasingly to express class interests and class needs, that older belief—the conviction that, properly managed, the generosity of the rich could result in the creation of true community—had necessarily faded. Though people still spoke of the need to bring disparate groups in the city together, there seemed little faith that it could be done on terms of genuine harmony. The best that could be hoped for was a kind of uneasy truce, and by mid-century even that seemed to be breaking down. If the growing preoccupation with class, as opposed to communitywide interests implied anything, it was this. And as a result, philanthropy, designed initially to prevent class divisions, was rapidly becoming one of the principal means of maintaining those divisions.

Yet even if one accepts such an analysis, it is difficult to explain the depth of the reaction. What exactly made the Associates so uneasy?

After all, a realistic assessment of conditions in Boston in 1850 would hardly have suggested that open class warfare was about to break out. To be sure, there were the Irish. And the very magnitude of the wealth of the city's "merchant princes"—so far beyond anything even the most fortunate of their fathers had achieved—made them appear all the more vulnerable. But neither explanation seems sufficient.

Unquestionably another source of the Associates' anxiety was business. The same years that saw the barriers rising at the Athenaeum and elsewhere also saw a marked—and sustained—decline in the profitability of Waltham-Lowell companies. Between 1844 and 1846 profits had averaged over 18 percent; by 1851 they had fallen below 1 percent. After that there was a brief upturn, but on balance the decade of the 1850s was a poor one from the standpoint of earnings. Even though dividends were kept up, they averaged much less than half of the 22 percent paid in 1847.[154] At the same time the economy in general continued to prosper, at least until 1857. The problem was confined to the textile industry, where an ever-increasing supply of finished goods put constant pressure on prices. Part of the difficulty lay in the tariff of 1846, but far more damaging was the enormous growth in the capacity of the American textile industry—something to which the Associates, with their vast expansion projects at places like Lawrence and Holyoke—were contributing not a little.

Meanwhile those projects themselves, after an impressive start, had come to look much less promising. With industry profits down, the mill sites and waterpower rights developed at such huge expense attracted few investors. For those still willing to put money in textile manufacturing, coastal towns like Newburyport and Fall River— where labor was abundant and where both raw cotton and coal for steam power could be brought in cheaply—offered brighter prospects. Consequently such towns flourished, while Lawrence and Holyoke limped along, half-built and likely to remain so for the foreseeable future. Indeed by 1858 the Hadley Falls Company, which had developed Holyoke, was facing bankruptcy.[155]

So much for whatever shape the Associates had hoped to give the region's economy by expanding the Waltham-Lowell system. Very simply the hope foundered on the hard realities of corporate profit-and-loss figures. And those figures told in other ways as well. In the early 1820s the Boston Company had earned an average profit of nine cents a yard on the cloth it produced; thirty years later, a half-a-cent a yard would have been considered adequate. Under the circumstances, treasurers and agents pressed for minor savings of every sort, which led in turn to a continual worsening of conditions in the mills. With wages constant or falling, the burden of work—the number of machines tended by individual workers—grew relentlessly. In the meantime other employment opportunities were opening up for the kinds of young native-born women who had once filled the mills. The net result was a dramatic change in the labor force. At the Hamilton Company, for example, the proportion of immigrant workers, most of them Irish, grew from under 4 percent in 1836 to more than 60 percent in 1860.[156]

Of course there was always a chance that business conditions would improve, and the Irish for their part turned out to be surprisingly tractable factory workers. So once again the Associates' fears might have seemed exaggerated—had it not been for yet another problem that arose during those years. Significantly, the early 1850s also marked a notably bleak juncture in the affairs of the Massachusetts Whig party. In the past the Whigs had suffered setbacks and recovered; this time there was to be no recovery. Though it would not be absolutely clear for a while longer, by 1854 the Massachusetts Whig party was moribund.

For the Associates the collapse of Whiggery constituted a major blow. From the start the Whig position on issues had been peculiarly tailored to the needs of the group, and for someone like Abbott Lawrence the party also offered a means of fulfilling—or trying to fulfill—personal ambitions that no amount of business success had ever completely satisfied. Nor would any of the various political combinations emerging after 1854 function nearly so well in those respects. The passing of the Whig party signaled a sharp decline in the Associates' influence over the politics of Massachusetts as well as of the nation at large. Added to the other developments of the period, the effect could only have been a pronounced increase in the level of anxiety felt by members of the group.

But to understand all of this it is necessary to explore the Associates' political activities more fully. If the story ended in defeat, it began on quite a different note. It began, in fact, with a string of impressive successes—impressive and also improbable, engineered as they were by a group of conservative gentlemen, operating amid the vagaries of Jacksonian politics.

6.

Politics and the Uses of Power

In 1831, when Amos Lawrence was writing his son letters warning against "foreign fancies" and extolling the virtues of American society, he remarked at one point, "the attempt to get up a 'Working-men's party' is a libel on the whole population, as it implies that there are among us large numbers who are not working-men."[1] Ironically, the life Lawrence himself led in later years might have been taken as evidence for the very "libel" he hoped to refute. But surely he would have resisted such an interpretation: "work" and "working-men" were terms he preferred to define quite broadly, just as he preferred a political system that softened most of the more obvious divisions in society. In both of those preferences he was one with the rest of the Boston Associates. When Andrew Jackson vetoed the bill rechartering the Second Bank of the United States, what most bothered members of the group was not the veto itself but the way Old Hickory chose to defend it. Daniel Webster spoke for them all when he rose in the Senate to condemn the president for "manifestly" seeking "to inflame the poor against the rich" and "wantonly" attacking "whole classes of people, for the purpose of turning against them the prejudices and resentments of other classes."[2]

Fully as troublesome as the yawning abyss of class conflict, too, were splits between east and west, city and country, modern and traditional economic activities. Without much difficulty all such divisions could be combined, and any system of political alignments based on the combination was certain to leave the Associates an isolated and embattled minority. What the group needed above all else was a politics that stressed harmony. In that respect the agenda was much the same as the one that had shaped projects like the Massachusetts General Hospital, and in the political arena the counterpart of the

hospital became the Whig party. First and last Massachusetts Whiggery was committed to blunting conflict, to drawing together the
myriad strands of the state's social and economic life in a way that
kept the whole running smoothly on track.

To be sure, the Whig party also worked tirelessly to protect large-
scale, corporate enterprise, ensuring that for twenty years the union
between wealth and Whiggery remained a central fact of Massachusetts politics. According to one study, of the 283 Bostonians identified
at the time as possessing fortunes of $100,000 or more, 86.5 percent
were Whigs, and the party fared still better among the millionaires in
the group. Of the 27 men in that category, only one preferred the
Democrats.[3] As for the Associates, to a man they backed the Whig
party: that was the perception of contemporaries, and none of the
available evidence challenges it. The connection even transcended
family ties. Joshua and David Sears were cousins, and both were rich,
but Joshua—Boston's lone Democratic millionaire—was not a member of the Associates group; David, a loyal Whig, was.

For most of the Associates, involvement in politics meant voting the
appropriate ticket, providing financial support for party activities, and
working behind the scenes to influence policy. In that sense the role
they played was less conspicuous than in philanthropy, but there
were exceptions. Both Nathan Appleton and Abbott Lawrence held
key positions in the inner councils of the Whig party. And like other
political leaders then and since, the two often had little choice but to
react to conditions as they found them. In deference to popular opinion they kept their overt demands on the political system to a minimum, or at least masked them as thoroughly as possible. They also
supported positions on some issues that had little to do with their
own immediate interests. As a result Whig party platforms rarely
amounted to a letter-perfect rendering of the Associates' point of
view. Yet precisely for that reason the unity celebrated by Whig
rhetoric was seldom without a basis in reality. Whatever the average
Massachusetts citizen thought of the owners of the Lowell mills, the
tens of thousands of voters who year after year elected Whig governors and returned Whig majorities to the legislature could believe,
and with some reason, that their interests too were served by the
party's perennial success at the polls.

Considering how much depended on that conviction, the pains the
Associates took to maintain it were understandable. But in making
the effort they also had solid precedents to follow. The Massachusetts
Whig party was no sudden, spontaneous growth. The landscape its
leaders cultivated so assiduously had long since been seeded by others. For more than a century groups with substantial interests at stake

had been proceeding in similar ways; like the Associates they had adopted harmony as a goal and worked to achieve it, often against imposing odds. The legislative compromises of the late colonial period, the Revolution itself, and the surprising success of the Massachusetts Federalist party were all proof that the interests of Boston businessmen could be reconciled with the needs of other, much larger groups. And in effect those earlier episodes, each of them intimately bound up with the history of every Associate family, defined a tradition—one that requires rather close examination. Because as it happened, both the Whig party and the role the Associates played in it fit the tradition remarkably well.

Or at any rate in the beginning they did. After 1845, as in philanthropy, other influences increasingly prevailed.

II

"I suppose there will be work for the Board of Ordnance at Cape Breton . . . I beg you will remember me at the Board, let nothing slip worth taking."[4]

Thus did Thomas Hancock, writing in 1745, soon after the fall of Louisbourg, instruct his London agent to go about the business of securing a contract to supply the garrison that would defend England's latest acquisition in the New World. Behind his words lay a keen understanding of political affairs in England as well as at home in Massachusetts, plus a network of contacts that spanned the Atlantic, and obviously a hearty desire to turn it all to profit. Nor without his insider's knowledge of politics and his contacts would Hancock's hopes of turning a profit have come to much. Both were essential to any merchant carrying on, as he did, "a large trade" in the eighteenth century, just as they were a hundred years later, to the Boston Associates.[5]

For at bottom, the problems confronting Hancock and the Associates in the political arena were the same. They were rich, and the wealth that distinguished them from all but a handful of their fellow citizens had been earned along the cutting edge of economic change. Yet given the unequal distribution of the fruits of change, that hardly endeared them to everyone. Also, their prosperity depended on a complex series of governmental sanctions and legal safeguards that were easily seen as special privileges, because that is exactly what they were. All of this, too, in the face of political institutions that imposed the need to seek—sooner or later, at almost every turn—the consent of the governed.

By the time Hancock was angling for military contracts, commerce had at least become an accepted part of Massachusetts life. Gone were the days when a Puritan merchant like Robert Keayne had had to confront an angry community and answer in court for "taking six-pence in the shilling profit."[6] Colonial governors in the eighteenth century, usually from commercial backgrounds themselves, tended to smile on whatever prospered trade, as did the Governor's Council, with its heavy preponderance of wealthy merchants. Still, the path was never free of obstacles. Competition among merchants for a limited supply of favors—of offices, contracts, and land grants—always had to be reckoned with. In the event, Hancock had to share the Louisbourg contract with Charles Apthorp, a member of Governor William Shirley's inner circle and reputedly the richest merchant in Massachusetts.[7]

The competition among colonial merchants for favors had its parallel in the nineteenth century in the scramble after corporate charters. And at all times such competition was a potent force for generating political activity in Massachusetts. Basically it was an insiders' game, played for high stakes in Boston by those who stood to profit directly from the outcome, but that was not always the case. Because the rewards were scarce, the participants—to improve their chances—regularly banded together in factional alliances, and when the conflict between factions became especially intense, it could produce far broader divisions, as the groups involved reached outward, beyond Boston, for support.

Certainly there were elements of this in each of the first two major party "systems" that developed in Massachusetts after 1800. Aptly labeled "the drawing room Orthodoxy of the rich," Federalism commanded the support of most families at or near the top of the social order, including the great majority of those that later made up the Associates' group, but there were always wealthy merchants willing to embrace the Jeffersonian "menace." As a rule Republican money was newer than Federalist money, and Republican merchants had fared less well in the state's initial distribution of corporate privileges in banking and transportation.[8] Similarly, when the Massachusetts Democratic party came into being a generation later, its first leader was David Henshaw, an arriviste drug manufacturer eager to channel his wealth into other fields.[9] And like the Republicans before them, the Democrats would mount, as a major thrust of their appeal to voters, a sweeping attack on monopoly privilege and the "aristocracy" it fostered.

But the most dramatic example of the extent to which competition among the rich and powerful could come to shape larger events occurred before 1800—in the struggle leading to the American Revolution. Beginning with the Stamp Act in 1765, Parliament's determination to bypass provincial assemblies in levying taxes split the Massachusetts commercial community as never before. For merchants whose fortunes were newer, who had not yet had time to consolidate their positions, the chance to influence the flow of revenue could still be vital. Even if there were other ways of obtaining the favors such men wanted, seldom was the governor in a position to be other than grateful for an offer of support in the annual haggling over taxes. So it was that John Hancock, the nephew and heir of Thomas, and in Newburyport Jonathan Jackson and his friend John Lowell, had come to stand on the "patriot" side of the developing breach, while the scions of older, better-established families like the Hutchinsons and the Olivers remained loyal.[10] But precisely because the wealth and power of Massachusetts were so evenly divided, it became impossible to limit the conflict to the methods merchants usually employed in the business of politics. The people at large had to be brought into the process, and as a result Massachusetts politics underwent a change as permanent as it was fundamental.

Before 1765 most voters had been content to concentrate on town affairs, leaving the government of the colony to others. Yet there had been breaks in the pattern even then—moments when issues like the money supply or taxation had sparked sudden bursts of interest across the normally unconcerned countryside. Typically, farmers favored easy money while merchants opposed whatever added to inflation, and both groups were eager to avoid as much of the burden of taxation as possible. Played out in the General Court, the conflict over currency and taxes saw different sides emerge victorious in different years, but overall the laurels went to the farmers. At critical points, country voters proved quite capable of turning out of office representatives who ignored their constituents' views. And properly "instructed" country representatives—by sheer intransigence—could bring the entire government of the colony to a halt. That had very nearly happened in 1741 and again in 1754, and in each case only a series of timely concessions to rural demands had ended the impasse.[11] On the other hand the adjustments in question were little more than temporary expedients. Revolutionary politics were to prove more demanding: there the goal had to be something close to a genuine accommodation among diverse interests and groups.

Ultimately the side that won—the party of John Hancock and John Adams, of Jonathan Jackson and John Lowell—tried half-a-dozen strategies for winning popular support, including a judicious use of "the mob." But to men with a large stake in society, who themselves finally turned to open revolt only with the greatest reluctance, crowds of angry citizens demanding rights remained an unnerving spectacle. Somehow it was necessary to tap what no amount of rioting in Boston ever could: the deep-seated sources of order that underlay Massachusetts life. And as it turned out, the solution lay in the principles the patriot leaders had articulated from the beginning of the struggle onward—in those principles and in the unerring instinct of the English for behaving as the perfect embodiment of everything the principles condemned.

The principles themselves had taken shape several generations earlier among a group of British thinkers who have since been identified as the "commonwealthmen." The commonwealthmen shared an abiding distrust of arbitrary power. To be legitimate, a government had to embody an implicit contract, involving mutual obligations, which found expression in a "mixed" constitution. Historically the great enemy of such a government had been arbitrary power, and the most likely place to find that, the commonwealthmen agreed, was in the executive. The effect was to discover virtue around the periphery of the system, while locating vice, with all its attendant potential for disorder, at the center.[12]

Recently, Daniel Howe has argued with great insight that the "country party" tradition—which the commonwealthmen all followed—proved invaluable to American Whigs in the nineteenth century, seeking as they were to promote a program that combined modern economic development with a deep commitment to existing patterns of social order.[13] In Massachusetts at the time of the Revolution, the country party tradition functioned in exactly the same way. It provided the sturdy bridge across which leaders from the eastern part of the colony traveled in their campaign to win support from thousands of people who had never been within half a day's ride of Boston. Actually the country party tradition was not so much antiurban as anti-"court"; nevertheless it retained a strong bias toward the kind of stable, ordered existence usually associated with rural communities. In such settings Protestant piety kept morals pure, while long-established social relationships made people both respectful of one another's rights and deferential to existing authority. But alien authority was another matter. It came as a thief in the night, shattering the time-honored patterns of community life; in the face of it the same people had every right to resist.

As a call to action, nothing could have been better calculated to strike a responsive chord across rural Massachusetts. In truth the pervasive "crisis" that beset so many of the colony's towns—the growing scarcity of land, the dislocations caused by the commercialization of agriculture—had little to do with British policy. Still, the effects were remarkably similar to those the country party tradition associated with subversion of the normal political order. And as time passed, even people who failed to see the connection would have been hard-pressed to explain how that older crisis, whatever its causes, could be resolved with all access to political power steadily diminishing. In that regard the ultimate folly of George III's ministers was the Government of Massachusetts Act, which granted the royal governor what amounted to dictatorial authority over every aspect of the colony's political life. Arbitrary power could do no more—except to send British regulars out to subdue the anxious countryside. And when that happened the farmers of Lexington and Concord were ready.[14]

Just as John Hancock was ready, fifteen months later, when the Continental Congress in Philadelphia finally voted in favor of independence, to sign, with a memorable flourish, the document that explained why. There, alongside the ringing phrases about self-evident truths and unalienable rights, were the facts of the case: the "long train of abuses and usurpations" by which George III had sought to establish his "absolute Despotism." If nothing else, the list made clear the foolishness of British colonial policy, but it also afforded a tantalizing glimpse of a political culture characterized by a deep—in fact a passionate—respect for government and all its works. Simply put, the king's great crime was that he had made government in America impossible. And by extension, independence had become necessary precisely because it offered the only way of restoring the country's political institutions—its assemblies and its courts, its laws and its lawmakers—to their full and accustomed vigor.

With such arguments did a group of essentially conservative gentlemen, speaking out of the country party tradition, succeed in convincing an equally conservative, largely rural population to persist in rebellion.

Altogether it was a stunning achievement. But ideologies forged to justify revolution do not always translate smoothly into guides to action once the conflict is over. The decades after independence were an uneasy period in Massachusetts, especially for those in power, who sometimes found themselves attacked by groups claiming to uphold the very principles that had sanctioned the Revolution. For a while in 1786—and more than once during the party battles of the Jeffersonian era—history almost seemed to be repeating itself. But sooner or later tempers always cooled, as political leaders again found ways of accommodating the interests of a broad cross-section of the electorate.[15]

The causes of what came to be called Shays' Rebellion were the predictable ones. Despite a sharp decline in agricultural prices following the Revolution, the General Court chose to increase taxes in order to service the huge debt incurred during the war. With no means of paying, many of the state's farmers were forced to borrow and then, when the situation failed to improve, faced losing everything. Meanwhile, the government resisted all but the mildest forms of relief, including proposals to tax foreign trade at a higher, more equitable rate. Finally, bands of outraged farmers—talking, as farmers in 1775 had, of the "Suppressing of tyrannical government"—marched on the courthouses to stop the rash of proceedings against debtors.[16]

Obviously something had gone wrong with the basic mechanisms designed to provide for the peace and proper ordering of society. In Boston the General Court blamed those who "affected to make a Distinction between the Government & People as though their Interests were different & even opposite."[17] But the rebels condemned the very shape and substance of the government. The point was well taken, for as Oscar and Mary Handlin have argued, the Massachusetts Constitution of 1780 "lodged power in the hands of a relatively small group of propertied farmers and merchants."[18] Yet the real problem was less the document itself than the ruthlessness with which those whose interests it promoted pressed their advantage. And beyond that, there was the alien culture they seemed to represent, with their insistence that commercial and financial obligations be honored at any cost in a society still overwhelmingly rural and agricultural.

An important component in the resolution of the crisis, too, was the willingness of such people to moderate their demands. In suppressing the rebellion the government acted decisively, sending out the militia to defeat the insurgents. But the following year the General Court hurried through a spate of relief measures with the full support of Governor John Hancock. Though proposals to issue paper money and scale down the public debt were defeated, payment of the debt was postponed and taxes were deferred for a year. At the same time partial relief was granted to imprisoned debtors, and a special commission pardoned most of the rebels.[19] In other words a compromise was reached, one that protected large property interests yet restricted the extent to which the state could be used to further those interests. It was a fine line, but the speed with which the government was restored to what Hancock called "its needed tranquility" suggested that most people were comfortable with the result. And that included the state's merchants, though accepting the implied limitation of their power was easier once the Articles of Confederation had been replaced by a new, much stronger federal constitution. The slow but sure strengthening of the economy also helped.

Unlike Shays' Rebellion, which had a relatively brief life, the turmoil surrounding the initial appearance of parties in Massachusetts politics stretched over an entire decade, in a series of skirmishes involving ever-higher levels of popular participation. In addition to their attack on monopoly privilege, the state's Jeffersonians stressed the peace issue—at least until 1812—as well as the whole question of religion. Because of the steady growth of dissenting sects, the favored position of Congregationalism as the established, tax-supported religion of the commonwealth was arousing increasing opposition, which the Republicans courted with great success. Taken together, in fact, the planks of the Republicans' platform gave them a formidable claim on the attention of the Massachusetts electorate, as results at the polls showed. In 1800 fewer than a third of the adult white males in the state had bothered to vote. By 1809, just under 64 percent of all adult white males were voting, which may well have been as high as 80 percent of those qualified to do so. And between 1804 and 1811 the Republicans carried the state fully half the time.[20]

In the long run, however, the supporters of Jefferson and Madison were not the chief beneficiaries of the growing interest of Massachusetts voters in state politics; the Federalists were. Before 1805 Federalist domination of the commonwealth could be taken for granted. In 1812 that pattern reasserted itself—and decisively. From then until 1823 the party never once failed to win the Massachusetts governorship, plus solid majorities in both houses of the General Court.

In part the Federalists' success was due to superior organization, but it was in the realm of issues that the contest was most sharply joined.[21] In 1811, after carrying the state for the fourth time in five years, the Republicans had moved to consolidate their position in a flurry of legislation, including a complete overhaul of the banking system, an act redistricting the state senate, and another defining in much more liberal terms the rights of religious dissenters. Of the three, the last was particularly objectionable to many ordinary voters across the state, and the Federalists were quick to respond, railing against those who sought to "encourage and multiply . . . fomenters of religious discord" by attacking "the regular parochial establishment."[22] In turn, Republican Governor Elbridge Gerry accused his opponents of trying to "beguile peaceable and happy citizens into a state of civil war,"[23] but speaking for the Federalists, Harrison Gray Otis had a ready reply: "We are sensible that this species of invective was a familiar expedient with some royal governors, the use of which compelled some of them . . . to spend the residue of their mournful days in foreign climes."[24]

So it went, and plainly the Federalists had the better of it. Yet the flood of votes that swept Gerry and his party from office the following year was not an unmixed blessing, as the sequel proved. By dramatizing the threat that Republican "reform" posed to the state's traditional religious and political life, the Federalists were indeed successful in attracting voters in rural areas like Hampshire and Franklin counties, but those rural voters had not entered the game as mere pawns. They were determined to make their views felt, even if it meant challenging the balance of power within the party itself.

The result was the event for which New England Federalism is better remembered than anything else: the Hartford Convention. The stimulus for calling a meeting of Northern representatives to coordinate "resistance" to the national government was the War of 1812. And opposition to "Mr. Madison's War" was strongest, as James Banner has demonstrated, not in Boston or along the coast, but in that bastion of rural Federalism, Old Hampshire County.[25] "A gigantic system of despotism" was how the Federalists of Hadley described the nation itself in their petition to the General Court—one of more than forty to reach Boston from outlying towns.[26] In Hatfield the memorialists predicted "the certain destruction of our moral virtues, the basis of our republican institutions,"[27] and in Wendell they spoke of "a history of repeated injuries and usurpations," adding, "Let the facts be submitted to a Candid World."[28]

Evoking the spirit and often the letter of the Declaration of Independence, the torrent of antiwar activity confronted Otis and the other members of the Federalist Central Committee with a stiff dilemma. The worst of the Republican reforms of 1811—or at any rate those that most annoyed the business community—had all been undone. The time had come for a respite. But the rural Federalists appeared more than willing to back up their antiwar rhetoric by keeping things in a state of constant turmoil until their demands were met. If the regular leadership failed to respond, it ran the risk of losing control altogether, and finally it was that danger that tipped the balance. Though Otis had begun by opposing a special convention, he ended by drafting the appeal that, in December 1814, brought twenty-six men from five New England states together in Hartford. He even served as a delegate and when the sessions were over traveled to Washington to put the case there as well. Unfortunately he arrived just as news of Andrew Jackson's great victory at New Orleans was filling the capital.[29]

Afterward Otis argued that the purpose of the Hartford Convention had been "rather to appease than produce excitement,"[30] which was true enough; just as it was true that the outcome amounted to little more than the "GREAT PAMPHLET" that George Cabot—another Massachusetts delegate—predicted would be the result.[31] Still, had men like Otis and Cabot had their way, there would have been no convention at all. Such was the price that had to be paid for the preservation of their political power. And the consequences did not end there, for the Hartford Convention also helped shape the legacy of Massachusetts Federalism in ways that made it still relevant, twenty years later, when the Boston Associates were flocking to join the Whig party.

Essentially, the legacy was a variant of the country party tradition that had figured so largely in the struggle leading to the Revolution. Together time and events had both broadened and deepened the tradition. Not only had the structure of politics changed, making it more difficult for leaders to ignore shifts in popular opinion, but a whole new set of issues had come to preoccupy voters. To succeed, the Federalists had to alter their approach accordingly. Yet true to the country party tradition, the vision of politics as a forum for battling tyranny and corruption at the center—whether in Boston or Washington—persisted. It was through that struggle, and the moral universe it defined, that the party's leaders sought to transcend all that separated their own interests from those of the population at large. While, too, the moralistic strain of Federalism tended to operate in tandem with much that was conservative, the party could and did speak out on an issue like peace, and at the time of the Missouri Compromise its leaders would take a forthright stand against the expansion of slavery.[32] So along with positions on trade and banking that appealed to merchants, Federalism also came to embrace a number of impulses that were frankly reformist. And those impulses as well would find their counterpart in Massachusetts Whiggery.

But before that happened there was to be a period of at least superficial calm in Massachusetts politics. In 1823 and 1824 the Republicans finally defeated the Federalists in a pair of briskly fought gubernatorial contests, and for the next ten years party competition languished as "amalgamation" brought most elements of the old parties together under the National Republican banner. Even after 1828, when the local supporters of Andrew Jackson became more active, the National Republicans remained the choice of most Massachusetts voters—or at any rate of those who bothered to go to the polls. The majority simply stayed home, as voters had a generation earlier, in the years before 1800.[33]

Yet soon enough party competition revived, and in that competition the Whigs were not only strikingly successful, but successful in many of the same ways the Federalists had been. Operating in a world where textile mills and railroads had replaced sailing ships and turnpikes as the chief harbingers of change, and where new issues arose with even greater frequency to trouble the political waters, the party had to work that much harder to persuade voters. Still, in its broad outlines, the resulting appeal was not at all unlike the synthesis the Federalists had come to a generation earlier. As Edward Everett—Whig governor of the state from 1836 to 1840, one of the Boston Associates' closest allies in politics, and the son-in-law of Peter Chardan Brooks, reputedly the richest man in the city and himself a member of the Associates group—wrote to Sir Robert Peel, "Little is . . . gained by resisting popular reforms; . . . everything is gained by measures of conciliation, which keep the great majority in good humor."[34]

III

In practical terms Everett's "measures of conciliation" were arrived at via an increasingly effective party structure. Like the Federalists, some Whigs had a penchant for depicting party organization as a threat to the body politic. In Massachusetts, where the Democrats regularly monopolized federal patronage and conducted party caucuses in the back rooms of the Commonwealth Bank, the point was not without relevance—another example of corruption at the center.[35] Yet during most years the Whigs' committee system, if more decorously managed than the Democrats', functioned with admirable efficiency to shape policy and get out the vote. Over time the legislative caucus gave way to the public nominating convention, but the change was a gradual one. As a rule power gravitated to a small group of eastern leaders, though the various county and town committees did provide a network for transmitting opinion upward from below. In addition, the Whigs could count on the support of a formidable array of newspapers, including three in Boston. Eventually, indeed, the party adopted almost the entire kit bag of innovations associated with the growth of political democracy. By 1840, for example, Whig "Young Men's Associations" were active throughout the state, adding—with their reading rooms, "lectures," and torchlight parades—to the mounting enthusiasm that produced the great party victories of that year.[36]

Thus organized, the Massachusetts Whigs could face with confidence the task of keeping "the great majority in good humor." Such was the lesson of the famous Log Cabin Campaign of 1840. But actually the added flourishes that went into electing "Tippecanoe and Tyler too" marked the culmination of a process under way as early as 1834. That was the year the Whig party first emerged in Massachusetts, and the event already had about it much the air of a modern mass movement, though characteristically the Whigs also managed to

evoke—in the very act of testing the waters of democratic politics—
strong echoes from the past.

The focus of the effort was a carefully orchestrated campaign denouncing the tyranny of "King Andrew" Jackson and in particular his
"removal" of federal deposits from the Second Bank of the United
States. Over twenty thousand signatures were collected on scores of
petitions, drafted at public meetings held throughout the state.[37] Not
since the War of 1812 had Massachusetts seen such an outpouring of
popular opposition to the policies of the national government, and as
on that other occasion the terms of the protest harkened back to a still
earlier conflict. Declared the petitioners of Springfield, for example,
"we regard the struggle which is now going on . . . as the struggle of
constitutional liberty against usurpation—of the sovereignty of the
people against the arbitrary will of one man."[38]

The immediate cause of the discontent expressed in such statements was real enough. Jackson's determination to end use of the BUS
as a depository for federal funds had led Nicholas Biddle to retaliate
by sharply contracting the bank's loans. The resulting distress—if
short-lived—was nonetheless acute. Privately Nathan Appleton and
his friends blamed Biddle and did their best, with no great success,
to persuade him to change his policy. Yet in public Appleton said
nothing to dispute the official Whig position, which held Jackson responsible for all of the nation's ills.[39]

One factor leading the Massachusetts Whigs to stress the withdrawal issue so heavily was the connection between the national
administration and the Commonwealth Bank. As both the unofficial
headquarters of the state Democratic organization and a "pet bank,"
the Commonwealth remained a favorite target for Whig invective
right up to the time when—having been refused aid by the Suffolk
Bank—it failed, causing the loss of thousands of dollars of government funds and raising serious questions of mismanagement and
fraud.[40] On the other hand, the Whigs had hardly mounted the anti-
withdrawal campaign for the sole purpose of dramatizing the shortcomings of Democratic banking practices. Their motives were more
complex and ultimately revolved around two other issues, both of
which had deeply touched the political life of the state. Those issues
were religion and Masonry.

In the years since the Religious Freedom Act of 1811, the relationship between religion and politics in Massachusetts had undergone a
complete transformation. Though dissenting sects continued to grow,
a more startling development was the addition of most orthodox
Congregationalists to the ranks of those demanding an end to all

formal ties between church and state. In scores of Congregational churches, the rise of dissent had been paralleled by a shift toward more liberal, "unitarian" doctrines. At the same time, a series of court decisions had denied any share of church property to conservatives who chose to secede from their churches rather than embrace the new "heresy." Then, in 1831 the Overseers of Harvard approved new statutes for the Theological School, further fueling fears that Unitarianism was becoming the established religion of the state. Reluctantly, the trinitarians turned to politics and the campaign for disestablishment as the only means of halting the drain on church membership and property. And in turning to politics, the orthodox forces faced a second painful choice. While the local National Republican party continued to oppose disestablishment, the Democrats' lingering association with Jeffersonian free thought made an alliance with them equally unpalatable.[41]

It was against this background that the disappearance of William Morgan, an obscure printer in western New York State, came to have a major impact on Massachusetts politics. At the time it was widely believed that Morgan had been murdered because he was threatening to reveal the secrets of Freemasonry. Whatever the facts, the result was a popular crusade against Masons and Masonry that spread throughout much of the northern United States. In Massachusetts the movement was relatively slow to take hold. Not until 1831—three years after the party appeared in the state—was there an Antimasonic candidate for governor, but from then on things moved quickly. Meanwhile, the campaign for religious disestablishment was also reaching critical proportions, and in November 1831 the *Boston Christian Herald*, a leading Antimasonic newspaper, came out in favor of disestablishment.[42]

The logic supporting a union between the enemies of Masonry and the opponents of religious establishment was inescapable. Both movements enjoyed impressive backing at the grass-roots level, and both were at odds with the regular party organizations in Massachusetts. In Antimasonry the orthodox would gain a viable political organization to back their cause, while for their part the Antimasons stood to gain votes—votes that would help make them, by 1833, the second strongest party in the state. But the ordinary arithmetic of election returns was only one factor moving the two groups together. At least as important was a complex calculus in which the forces of good were gathered to do battle against a vast network of evil, stretching to every corner of the state.

As palpable representations of evil, Masonry and Unitarianism not only served remarkably well, but were just closely enough linked to make a joint campaign against them plausible. Certainly Masonry, with its interlocking system of lodges and its elaborate rituals and secret oaths, had all the trappings of a dark, antirepublican conspiracy. And while not all Masons were Unitarians (or vice versa) a significant number were, especially among the rich and those prominent in public life, and even more especially within the leadership of the National Republican party. In their "Address to the Voters of Massachusetts" in 1833, the National Republicans dismissed the fears of the Antimasons as "altogether exaggerated and extravagant."[43] The charge missed the point. Freemasonry may not have been the threat its opponents claimed; still, opposition to it reflected feelings shared by large numbers of people around the state.

High on the list of causes, surely, was uncertainty about just where all the rapid social and economic change of the period was leading. Concern over the future of orthodoxy contributed directly to the strength of Antimasonry, and both movements drew on other anxieties as well. As a rule Antimasonic candidates did poorly in the larger cities but made strong showings in the adjacent countryside, where economic change was often less a given than a tantalizing—or, as the case may have been, a frightening—possibility.[44] With the General Court debating questions of corporate privilege and choosing from among competing railroad schemes, exactly where did the interests of the ordinary voter of Hampshire or Middlesex County lie? Would he be better or worse off with his daughter working in the mills at Lowell? As agricultural produce from everywhere moved more rapidly to market, how would his own crops fare? What price would have to be paid for progress?

Along with the uncertainty, too, went other emotions: guilt, perhaps, at being willing to abandon so much that was time-honored and familiar for the sake of personal gain, plus, paradoxically, a sense of powerlessness. For the guilt, religion offered its traditional solace, and for the sense of powerlessness, theories of conspiracy held out a ready explanation.[45] If the relevant decisions were being made by other people, they could bear the responsibility for the consequences. Or better yet, the victims could seize the levers of power for themselves. By the end of 1833 the Antimasons were still short of that goal, but they had at least succeeded in thoroughly disorganizing Massachusetts politics.

The principal losers were the National Republicans. In spite of mounting opposition, until 1832 they remained in control of the state government. Then came the decision to confront the protest against religious establishment and Masonry with no change in policy, or worse, a determination to defend what so many voters suddenly found abhorrent. Nothing could have been more ill-advised. In 1833, with former president John Quincy Adams as their gubernatorial candidate, the Antimasons received 29 percent of the vote. In the space of a year the National Republican total had fallen from 33,948 to 25,149, a decline of over 25 percent. After the election—since none of the various gubernatorial candidates received a majority—the contest went to the General Court, and there the National Republicans did manage to seat their candidate, John Davis. But the arrangement proved purely temporary. By 1834 the National Republican party had ceased to exist in Massachusetts, and in its place, as the state's principal anti-Jacksonian coalition, stood the Whig party.

Nor was the change—for all the speed with which it occurred—simply a clever bit of prestidigitation. Most of the leaders and many of the policies of the old National Republican organization reappeared under the Whig banner, but the new party approached some issues quite differently from its predecessor. Requiring a constitutional amendment, disestablishment had already passed by the end of 1833, sparing the Whigs the necessity of having to take an outright stand. Still, the party seemed more than willing to accept what had become an overwhelmingly popular reform—one the National Republicans had consistently opposed. When it came to Masonry, the difference was even more pronounced. In January 1834 the Grand Lodge of Massachusetts surrendered its charter. Then, with significant Whig backing, the General Court passed a law banning extrajudicial oaths. Finally, a group of Whig leaders used their personal influence to bring about the dissolution of many Masonic lodges around the state.[46] Designed to draw the greatest possible number of Antimasons into the Whig fold, the strategy was summed up by Edward Everett. Nothing would do, he wrote, but to "allow Masonry utterly, openly, and without qualification, to go down."[47]

However, even with religious establishment and Masonry allowed to "go down," the new Whig coalition required one last embellishment. In an environment in which symbolic issues and symbolic protests had achieved such importance through the opportunity they offered voters to express deep-seated anxieties, any party, to succeed, had to respond to that fact. Failure to do so had cost the National Republicans control of the state; the Whigs were not about to repeat the mistake. Hence the elaborate campaign against executive "tyranny" in Washington, which was gathering momentum steadily throughout the final stages of the Antimasonic crusade. If conscience-less villainy and plots to subvert the republic were wanted, the activities of "King Andrew" and his minions on the local scene provided more than enough evidence of both.

Or so the Whigs argued, and with great success, as it turned out. In the fall elections of 1834 John Davis carried the state easily, winning almost 45,000 votes—20,000 more than the year before. Though the Democratic vote also rose, the gain was modest by comparison. Meanwhile the Antimasonic total had fallen by over 40 percent. The following year the Antimasons suffered a second devastating defeat, effectively eliminating them as a significant force in Massachusetts politics. As a result, both of the major parties picked up votes, but the largest gains remained those won by the Whigs in 1834.[48]

During the months when Whig leaders were working simultaneously to close Masonic lodges and gather signatures on petitions condemning Jackson, the Boston Associates had smoothly, and with no apparent regret, turned from National Republicanism to Whiggery. They also made it clear that they planned to play a major role in the affairs of the new party. As always in such situations, there was a need for money. An especially important instance involved the Boston *Atlas*. In 1833 the paper had expressed its National Republican sympathies by heaping abuse on John Quincy Adams and the Antimasons. Afterwards, Edward Everett estimated that the attacks had netted Adams an extra 5,000 votes. While the figure may have been an exaggeration, changing the *Atlas*'s policy was essential. Late in the summer of 1834, an agreement was reached that obliged the paper's editors to follow the new Whig line—and abandon their assault on Antimasonry. In return, they were guaranteed regular financial assistance, with the funds to be supplied by the Lawrences.[49] And soon afterward, Abbott Lawrence—already emerging as the most politically active of the Associates—gave further proof of his dedication to the Whig cause by agreeing to accept the party's nomination to Congress from the Boston district. For anyone who wondered where the Associates' political preferences lay, Lawrence's decision to run answered the question unequivocally.

Some of the reasons for the Associates' conversion to Whiggery were obvious; others less so, but quite possibly more important. In the first category belonged all those questions of economic policy on which the new party seemed likely to be at least as accommodating as the National Republicans had been. By 1834, too, the Associates were committed to supporting Daniel Webster for the presidency two years hence, and Webster was most eager to build a strong local organization to cooperate with the Whig party on the national level. From Washington he wrote frequently, urging his Massachusetts backers to make peace with Antimasonry and focus instead on Jackson's high-handed abuse of executive power.[50]

Yet Webster's prodding counted for only so much. On every side attacks on privilege were growing. In addition to Antimasonry, a Workingmen's party had appeared in Massachusetts, which in 1833 polled over 3,000 votes. Made up largely of farmers and skilled craftsmen, the new party tended to concern itself more with traditional labor issues than the grievances of factory workers. Nevertheless, the Workingmen were outspoken in their condemnation of "associated wealth" and the disproportionate power it exercised in the state.[51] Well might Amos Lawrence claim "We are all workingmen." The problem was that by 1833 no political organization in Massachusetts seemed capable of reaching voters with such a message. National Republicanism had run hopelessly aground. Meanwhile, a group of younger Democratic leaders were actively courting both the Antimasons and the Workingmen.[52] In that year's election, a union of the three parties would have outpolled the National Republicans by a margin of better than seven to five. Even less than Webster, or Edward Everett and John Davis, could the Associates afford to let that happen. Not a few of them were Masons; many were Unitarians; and most had little use for Nicholas Biddle's BUS—still, they were only too happy to support, even to underwrite, the new Whig party.

But to say only this—to describe the group's response as purely an act of self-defense—undoubtedly misrepresents the reality. To someone like Amos Lawrence, at least, the ideological content of Whiggery mattered deeply. By accepting the popular verdict on religious establishment and Masonry, the Whigs were in effect reasserting the traditional harmonies of Massachusetts politics; to do that, in turn, was to depict the world as Lawrence genuinely wanted to believe it was. He had no desire to see himself as part of a selfish "aristocracy," conspiring to preserve its power at any cost. By the same token, it was easy to reject National Republicanism precisely because the party had come to behave like a faction bent on protecting narrow class interests. Nor did Lawrence wish to see economic change as altering in any fundamental way the organic social order he knew, an attitude which after all gave him a strong bond with groups like the Antimasons, torn as they were between welcoming change and fearing its consequences. To resolve that dilemma the Whigs would argue that change was desirable, but only if it could be controlled. And for good measure they managed to explain political conflict—in the manner of the country party tradition—not as a clash between interests or systems, but as a struggle between good and bad men. Character: for Lawrence as well as the Whigs it remained both the cornerstone of human history and the ultimate value.

IV

Like Amos Lawrence, Ralph Waldo Emerson set great store by character, describing it variously as "self-sufficingness . . . centrality, the impossibility of being displaced or overset," the "moral order seen through the medium of an individual nature," and "nature in the highest form."[53] Emerson also counted himself—if less wholeheartedly than those who financed and managed party affairs—a Whig in the political battles of his time. The Whigs had "the best men," and that settled the issue.[54] Ultimately, of course, Emerson's vision of political life extended far beyond the petty squabbles reported in the daily newspapers. The true mission of the state, he declared in his essay "Politics," was to educate the "wiseman," and with the appearance of the wiseman the state became unnecessary.[55] But most Whigs, including the Associates, stopped well short of such lofty flights. In some golden age in the future, government might prove superfluous; for the present its activities remained of the utmost importance, especially—the Associates were prone to feel—as those activities affected the economy.

On that front, the emergence of the Whig party in Massachusetts coincided with a continuing debate over "vested rights." A vigorous defense of such rights, as embodied in corporate charters, had been one of the main components of the old Federalist synthesis, and after 1823 the National Republicans had followed much the same line. But in one form or another the attack on economic "privilege" continued, until by 1830 the Federalist position—in its purer version—had been rejected by all three branches of state government. For the Associates, the state's action represented both an opportunity and a threat. Insofar as the flow of capital to certain kinds of projects was reduced, the amount of money available for investment in the textile industry grew. Yet most of the Associates' own enterprises operated under charters from the state, making some defense of corporate privileges imperative.

Central to these developments was the long dispute over the Charles River Bridge. Arising in 1823, it was not finally settled by the United States Supreme Court until 1837. The initial step had been a petition to the General Court. A year later a bill was introduced chartering a "free" bridge over the Charles to operate in direct competition with the toll bridge approved in 1785. Though the bill failed to pass—as did similar measures in each of the next two sessions—in 1827 the General Court reversed its position, only to have Governor Levi Lincoln veto the bill. Then the following year Lincoln changed *his* mind, and the free bridge sponsors won their charter. Two months later the proprietors of the 1785 bridge brought suit before the state supreme court, which also decided in favor of the free bridge, thereby paving the way for an appeal to the United States Supreme Court.[56]

Gathering momentum year by year, the Charles River Bridge dispute left a deep imprint on Massachusetts politics. Even before the turmoil over religious establishment and Masonry, it went far toward shattering the calm of amalgamation. David Henshaw, a key spokesman for the free bridge forces, was simultaneously emerging as the leader of the local Jacksonian Democrats. Levi Lincoln's veto of the 1827 bill marked the first time a Massachusetts governor had exercised that power, making all the more striking his *volte-face* a year later. In deciding the case, the justices of the state supreme court split evenly, half on the one side and half on the other. Of the two justices who supported the legality of a free bridge, Marcus Morton became the perennial Democratic candidate for governor and later twice carried the state. Meanwhile, argued time and again in the legislature, in petitions and pamphlets, and in newspapers throughout the state, the dispute raised many of the issues that would come into play a decade later, during Andrew Jackson's battle against the Second Bank of the United States—raised those issues, and resolved them much as Jackson and the Democrats in Washington would.

For essentially the Bank War and the Charles River Bridge dispute turned on the same question: the extent to which government, seeking to encourage economic change, ought to operate through exclusive grants of power to private investors. In claiming that their charter gave them a monopoly over the traffic between Boston and Charlestown—though the document itself contained no such provision—the proprietors of the 1785 bridge took the position that their interest in levying tolls on that traffic constituted a "vested right," which the state had contracted to protect in perpetuity, and which a free bridge would destroy. Against that view, the free bridge forces pressed the community's interest in cheaper transportation and the benefits that would follow from it. They also pointed out that the original investment in the 1785 bridge had long since been returned. If it had ever been necessary to protect the corporation against competition, that was scarcely true forty years later, by which time a single share in the Charles River Bridge costing $333 in 1785 had earned a clear profit of $7,000. Or, as one pamphleteer—probably David Henshaw—put it, in terms very close to those Jackson would use in his 1832 Veto Message: "To gain the road to improvement you must open the door to competition, and shut it to monopoly, the latter destroys, whilst the former nourishes improvement. The one benefits the few, at the expense of the many; the other benefits all at the expense of none."[57]

Competition versus monopoly, the welfare of society as a whole versus the prerogatives and inordinate profits of the few: with the contest defined in those terms, the outcome on the state level was never much in doubt. As one historian has remarked, "Whatever the validity or merit of their claims, politically the Charles River Bridge proprietors never could refute the charges that their claims to exclusive privileges constituted an intolerable stranglehold over the community."[58] When the case was decided by the Supreme Court in Washington, however, the proprietors lost on the much narrower grounds that a literal reading of their charter revealed no grant of monopoly privileges. In vain had Daniel Webster tried to persuade the Court to take a broad view of its responsibilities, to exercise its "enlightened conscience" and act to correct "improvident, inconsiderate, intemperate and hasty and sometimes ignorant legislation;"[59] even he held out scant hope that many of the justices would heed his appeal, which no doubt helped explain his "uneasy and moody" manner in court.[60]

But losing the case was not the only problem Webster faced at that moment; the increasing awkwardness of his position back home must also have bothered him. By 1837 the process of party formation had run its course in Massachusetts, and the truth was that neither of the two major parties offered the Websterian view of vested rights a comfortable home. The Democrats rejected it outright, and even the Whigs—Webster's own party—were at best equivocal on the subject. Thus, in Washington he faced a team of attorneys for the free bridge consisting of Senator John Davis and Simon Greenleaf, Royall Professor of Law at Harvard, both Massachusetts Whigs.[61] Nor when the decision was announced, did it provoke anything like a universal outcry from the local party press. On the contrary, the staunchly Whig *Boston Courier* seemed quite comfortable with the result. As for the notion that the Court was in the grip of "radical and revolutionary doctrines," the *Courier* flatly rejected all such claims of the "vested rights class."[62]

The *Courier*'s position indicated the willingness of powerful elements in the Massachusetts Whig party to live with a more modest interpretation of corporate privileges. It was significant that the financial support ensuring the *Courier*'s Whig loyalties came from Nathan Appleton. Ever a realist, Appleton had no taste for lost causes. He also had a limited stake in monopoly rights, since most of his own resources were invested in the Waltham-Lowell system, which required no such protection. Indeed, as a group the Boston Associates had little to gain from insisting on the more grandiose features of vested-rights doctrine. It became, then, a matter of working out practical alternatives, ways of protecting the group's interests that a majority of voters could be expected to approve. For the most part the necessary arrangements were made behind closed doors in Boston, at quiet meetings where few if any records were kept. Consequently, the clearest evidence of what was accomplished would remain the economic policies that the Whigs—with impressive unanimity—supported over the years.

The state's Democrats, meanwhile, found it all but impossible to agree with one another about corporations. Led by David Henshaw, one wing of the party seemed concerned with little beyond improving its own access to corporate privileges. In addition to backing various free bridge schemes, Henshaw had invested heavily in bank shares, especially those of the Commonwealth Bank. As Collector of the Port of Boston—and hence head of the state Democratic organization— he regularly railed against the city's "money aristocracy," but in substance he confined his attacks to the monopoly issue.[63] Other Massachusetts Democrats were more venturesome. Some favored a general law, establishing uniform procedures for incorporation. Yet what amounted to the opposite tack—the complete abolition of all corporate privileges—also had its supporters. And even after 1838, when a group of "radical" Democrats under Marcus Morton and George Bancroft succeeded in displacing Henshaw as party leader, it proved impossible to reach a consensus on the issue. During his first term as governor the following year, Morton did urge the legislature to enact a general incorporation law, but with his own party divided and the Whigs opposed, nothing came of the plan.[64]

Despite the failure of Morton's efforts, demands for general incorporation persisted over the next decade and a half. Yet taking their cue from the Associates, the Whigs continued to support the existing system, which required a separate legislative act for each new incorporation. In practice the General Court granted charters with ever-increasing liberality. Still, the extra time and effort involved in seeking a charter, plus the importance of cultivating the right political contacts, worked to check the number of requests. In effect the system defined a middle ground between the two conflicting alternatives that split the Democrats. Whereas eliminating all "artificial" props to economic development, including corporate privileges, might have slowed the rate of change substantially, retaining the forms but opening them to every comer threatened to have the reverse effect. With corporate privileges available for the asking, the state stood to lose a valuable means of controlling the pace and direction of future economic change.[65]

In general, the Whigs' approach to incorporation combined encouragement and restraint in different proportions, depending on the nature of the activity involved. In manufacturing little was done to check the number of incorporations, but the charters granted manufacturers contained the fewest special favors. Consequently incorporation tended to benefit only enterprises involving very large amounts of capital, at least until 1830. In that year the General Court passed a limited liability act, which restricted to the value of their shares the financial exposure of corporate stockholders.[66] The change—again strongly supported by the Associates—did make incorporation more attractive. In the two decades before 1830 the state had granted, on average, under ten charters a year to manufacturing concerns; during the next five years the rate more than doubled. In the textile industry alone, between 1830 and 1845, Massachusetts chartered 149 corporations, at least 20 of which were capitalized at $500,000 or more.[67] But even after 1830 the great majority of manufacturing firms remained unincorporated. As late as 1845 fewer than half the 568 textile "establishments" listed in the state *Statistics of Industry* were chartered.[68] Apparently for most smaller manufacturers the combination of the need to apply for a special act and the nebulous value of the advantages to be gained continued to tip the balance against incorporation.

In the field of transportation the situation was quite different. All railroads were incorporated and their promoters regularly requested elaborate grants of privilege in return for the risks they took, thus giving the state direct control over the rate of development. The pattern was set by the Associates' own Boston and Lowell. In 1830, at the height of the Charles River Bridge controversy, the state House of Representatives had balked at granting the corporation a monopoly. Thereupon the Associates withdrew their petition, unwilling, it was said, "to take a charter on terms which would subject them to all the expense of . . . building the first railroad without any chance of profit from it."[69] Faced with the prospect of losing the line altogether, the House then reconsidered its action and ended by awarding the Boston and Lowell a charter complete with a monopoly to run for thirty years, broad powers of eminent domain, freedom to set rates, and limited liability. Similar privileges were granted the Boston and Worcester as well as the Boston and Providence, and later the Western.[70]

Though all of these arrangements were made before the Massachusetts Whig party came into being, once in power the party supported them wholeheartedly. Thus in 1836, when the Associates requested

authorization for a $300,000 increase in the Boston and Lowell's capi-
talization, the Whigs succeeded in blocking a Democratic attempt to
eliminate the monopoly guarantee in the line's charter.[71] An even
more dramatic example of the party's special concern for railroads—
and another of the Associates' pet concerns—was the steady and
unprecedented flow of state aid to the Western. Initially the effort was
a bipartisan one, yet as time passed and costs continued to rise the
Democrats lost enthusiasm for the project, leaving the Whigs to carry
on alone. As a result, by 1842 the legislature had voted the Western a
total of $5 million in stock purchases and loans—more than twice the
amount invested in the corporation by private sources.[72]

The Whigs also backed state loans to several smaller lines. But at the
same time steps were taken to check what was already—by the middle
of the 1840s—threatening to become a full-scale epidemic of "railroad
fever." With appeals for cheaper, more direct service pouring in from
everywhere, the state-appointed directors of the Western consistently
supported policies that favored established manufacturing centers at
the expense not only of newly developed areas, but of the through
traffic which Boston shippers claimed was essential to revitalizing the
port.[73] And when those whose interests were adversely affected threw
their weight behind a scheme for a second line crossing the state from
east to west, the reaction among most Whigs was cool.[74]

Finally, in banking—no less than in manufacturing and transportation—the Whigs pursued an approach which, while it allowed for,
even fostered, expansion, also envisioned definite limits to the process. Typical was the party's handling of the Panic of 1837. Thanks to
one of the nation's strongest banking systems, Massachusetts suffered
less than most states in the aftermath of Jackson's Bank War, but
specie payments were suspended in Boston from May 1837 to May
1838, and during that time eleven banks failed. The state, however,
took little direct action. Instead Whig Governor Edward Everett's
strategy was to let the weaker banks—including David Henshaw's
Commonwealth—fall of their own weight. Then, with the crisis
largely over, Everett proposed, and the General Court approved, the
appointment of a commission to investigate the state's banks. Had
the commission been stronger, it might have had considerable impact,
but the act in question limited the body to only three members and
provided a very modest budget.[75] On the other hand, from the start
Everett and the Whigs had been able to assume the existence of a
powerful private agency working to promote sound banking in Massachusetts. Throughout the panic, the Associates' Suffolk system had
functioned efficiently—even ruthlessly—to hold individual banks to
account and hasten the resumption of specie payments. The Whigs

also, therefore, made a point of defending the Suffolk Bank and in 1838 moved decisively to halt an attempt in the General Court to curb the institution's power.[76]

The following year, with Morton in office, the Democrats launched a fresh campaign for banking reform, but once again the Whigs held the line. Characteristically, in his message to the legislature Morton advocated measures that seemed designed to achieve diametrically opposed objectives. While praising the national Democratic party's subtreasury system, with its tendency to curtail banking operations, he recommended a revision of state laws to permit "unrestrained liberty of Banking by individuals and unincorporated partnerships."[77] According to Morton, the change was necessary to break the "monopoly" enjoyed by the Commonwealth's chartered banks. But the Whigs—dismissing the governor's plan as a remedy "worse than the disease"—easily quashed it.[78]

Quite possibly if the Massachusetts Democrats had been able to settle on a consistent approach to economic issues, the party might have made greater headway against the Whigs. But even then it would have been an uphill struggle, for the Whig approach, if free of the contradictions that plagued the Democrats, was still remarkably flexible. Gone were the old rigidities of vested-rights doctrine, and in their place was a cluster of policies that attacked the problems of development—or seemed to—in something like piecemeal fashion. Because the policies varied, they presented no single convenient target. And they worked. Or at any rate large numbers of citizens could see around them tangible evidence that "progress" was occurring, evidence for which the Whigs were quick to take credit.

Actually, however, Whig economic strategy was never as flexible as it seemed; nor was its objective merely to generate ever-increasing rates of growth and expansion. Wherever possible the party held to existing procedures and worked through established institutions. Size was also crucial. Democrats like Morton might envision a world of small producers, operating freely as independent agents; time and again the Whigs bet on corporate enterprise, and in particular on large corporations, to carry forward the work of economic change.

A generation earlier the Federalists had made much the same choice, but the intervening years had seen a marked change in the legal status of corporations. Once considered quasi-public bodies, functioning in effect as arms of the state, they were rapidly losing that identity. Instead the tendency was to treat them as what they most often were: private associations, bent on earning profits for individual investors. Part of the change was the increasingly narrow interpretation given corporate privileges, as in the Charles River Bridge case. But equally important was the growing inclination of judges and legislators across the nation to deemphasize the public responsibilities of corporations.[79] In that sense the Massachusetts Whigs stood apart from the prevailing trend. While continuing to defend whatever remained of corporate privilege—post Charles River Bridge—the party also persisted in viewing the enterprises thus favored as something more than instruments of private gain. A prime example was the party's special solicitude for the Suffolk Bank.

Yet to see the Suffolk Bank as a quasi-public body was to read the evidence quite selectively. The service it performed in stabilizing New England's currency was wholly voluntary—was nowhere mandated in the Suffolk's charter. Rather the impetus had come from the stockholders and directors—had come, in fact, from the Boston Associates, as had so much else in Whig economic planning. And as in those other cases, the original purpose was less a public than a private one. Like limited liability or the Boston and Lowell Railroad, the Suffolk system mattered to the Associates chiefly as a means of protecting their investment in the textile industry.

For all of its apparent breadth and flexibility, then, the economic strategy of the Massachusetts Whig party depended, or much of it did, on a series of private initiatives undertaken largely to benefit a handful of the commonwealth's richest citizens. This was exactly what the Democrats charged, but making the charge stick was something else again. Just as the Associates shaped their own enterprises to maximize stability and order—even if doing so meant accepting a lower rate of financial return—Whig economic policy was keyed to achieving a similar balance. The pull in the system, the built-in restraints, always mattered at least as much as the push toward further expansion. Yet during the first decade of the party's existence the brakes had to be applied only intermittently. The state's economy was still relatively undeveloped, and after 1837 a nationwide depression held down the rate of growth. Thus the Whigs were free to concentrate on promoting change and in that role won the allegiance of many voters, who, for the moment, were more interested in results than anything else.

From the Associates' standpoint, meanwhile, the arrangement could hardly have been better. In the Waltham-Lowell system the group had created what its members wanted most—a satisfactory investment vehicle—and done so largely outside of the political arena. By 1834 all that remained was to lock in place the gains already made, and there the Whig party did yeoman service. For the most part the service was of a highly specific nature, but behind each year's carefully crafted legislative agenda lay the party's overall vision of economic reality—its commitment to measured, controlled growth, as opposed to simply letting the engines of change run on unchecked. That too was a vital element in the bond between the Associates and the Whigs, for it seemed to guarantee that as long as the party was in power, the group's achievement would remain secure.

V

But staying in power in Massachusetts continued to depend on far more than economic policy. The range of issues that moved voters grew steadily throughout the period, forcing constant revisions in party strategy. Also complicating matters for the Whigs was an unusually crowded roster of talented, ambitious leaders; keeping those leaders from coming into conflict with one another was never easy. At first the party managed quite well on both counts, winning control of the state for five years after 1833 without a break. Then twice over the next half decade—in 1839 and again in 1842—the Democrats had succeeded in placing their gubernatorial candidate, Marcus Morton, in office.[80] Even though those isolated Democratic victories produced no dramatic shifts in state economic policy, as a portent of things to come they were significant.

Decided by a *single vote* the election of 1839 was so close that anything could have determined the outcome, but the issue uppermost in the minds of many voters was temperance. For ten years the pressure to limit consumption of alcoholic beverages had been growing around the state. By 1838 it was strong enough to force consideration of a bill banning the sale of ardent spirits in quantities of less than fifteen gallons. Though the Whigs in the General Court were divided on the subject of the fifteen-gallon law, enough of them voted for it to ensure its passage. Reluctantly Edward Everett signed the measure, thereby—or so it was believed afterward—sealing both his party's fate and his own in the upcoming election.[81]

On the surface the Whig defeat in 1842 was less dramatic, and no single factor could have explained it. The inner councils of the party were split over Henry Clay's latest bid for the presidency. When the state convention that year endorsed Clay, Webster and his lieutenants retaliated by refusing to campaign for Whig candidates in Massachusetts. Also, a new third party, the Liberty party, dedicated to antislavery principles, had been gaining ground since 1840, mostly at the Whigs' expense. In the event, Marcus Morton received only a plurality at the polls but won the vote in the legislature, where the Liberty party held the balance of power.[82]

The following year, just as they had in 1840, the Whigs swept back into power with no apparent difficulty. But the weaknesses revealed by the party's second major defeat in four years could not be remedied by a single victory—or even a whole string of them. On the contrary, while George N. Briggs, the Whig candidate in 1843, managed to hold onto the governorship until 1850, the factors that would lead to the collapse of the party in Massachusetts were already at work. And ironically—considering all they had to lose—the Associates were not only playing, but would continue to play, a central role in the process.

For those familiar with the subtler workings of Massachusetts politics, the Whig state convention in 1843—the one that nominated George Briggs for the first time—was followed by two events of special significance. Within a week of the convention, Abbott Lawrence announced his intention to travel to Europe with his family for the summer, and early in November, Daniel Webster endorsed Briggs. Since it was already well known that the stolid Pittsfield lawyer's candidacy was acceptable to Webster, a public statement of some sort was expected, but characteristically Webster waited until the last minute.[83] Meanwhile, Lawrence had offered a variety of reasons for his trip abroad. Wrote his nephew, Amos A. Lawrence, "He says he is ill, and he cannot live as he does now, a contested election approaching, a crowd of strangers to whom he must pay attention, a diseased liver and other things induce him to take a journey to recruit himself."[84] But whatever Lawrence told others, his departure was more a strategic retreat than anything else. In a byzantine series of moves at the convention, his own candidate, the incumbent John Davis, had been forced to stand aside. Behind that contest, too, lay a much deeper and longer-lasting struggle between Lawrence and Webster themselves. At stake was no disagreement over issues: the prize for which the two men contended, purely and simply, was the leadership of the Massachusetts Whig party.[85]

From the founding of the party onward, Webster had taken it for granted that the position was his. His unique talents as an orator, as a lawyer, and as an advocate of the particular interests for which Whiggery stood in national politics, entitled him, he was convinced, to nothing less. Periodically, substantial cash contributions to maintain him in the princely style to which he had grown accustomed were also required, but those had always been forthcoming, chiefly as a result of the Associates' generosity.[86] As Thomas W. Ward, a member of the group and Baring Brothers' Boston agent, wrote his partners in London, one could deplore the great senator's "recklessness in pecuniary matters," but "the evil which might come from such a mighty intellect acting on the wrong side" made it imperative to keep Webster "right."[87] In addition to money, there were other forms of tribute. At the time of the Webster-Hayne debates, for example, Amos Lawrence had sent a handsome silver service "as testimony of my gratitude for your services to the country."[88] Yet what continued to matter more to Webster than anything else was the Massachusetts Whig party's support for his presidential ambitions, and it was there that he came into conflict with Abbott Lawrence.

Initially Webster's ambitions posed no problem for Lawrence. Quite the reverse. "This should be your destiny," Lawrence had written in 1835, "and your friends ought in justice to do for you all that may be required."[89] But as time passed and Lawrence's political involvement—and his own ambitions—grew, he came to feel differently. In 1836, running as the duly nominated presidential candidate of the Massachusetts Whig party, Webster received no electoral votes outside of the state. The suggestion was that his chances of ever winning the highest office in the land were slim. Why, then, should the local party continue to waste its influence by supporting him? In May 1838 Lawrence said as much to Webster, in an interview later described by Edward Everett to Robert Winthrop.[90] At about the same time, John Quincy Adams reported in his diary that Lawrence was backing Henry Clay for the top place on the Whig ticket two years hence. Presumably, given the opportunity, the Kentuckian would repay the favor.[91]

In choosing the course he had, Lawrence was setting himself apart from most of his fellow Associates. Few of them objected to nurturing Webster's grander ambitions, and fewer still had any interest in national political office themselves. During the colonial period, wealthy merchants might have looked on government service as an honorable and occasionally lucrative alternative to commerce, but much had changed since then. Most successful politicians in the early nineteenth century were lawyers. Equally important was the ability to appeal to voters in person. The leading figures in the Massachusetts Whig party—Webster himself, Edward Everett, Robert Winthrop, and Rufus Choate—were all accomplished orators. A generation earlier, several of the Associates, including Harrison Gray Otis, had played a large role in politics. Also, Nathan Appleton spent a brief period in Congress. But the usual pattern saw those members of the group who were politically active serving in local government or on the Whig state central committee. There was in all of this as well, perhaps, the suggestion that seeking office was not something a gentleman did. That was Amos Lawrence's opinion. But plainly his brother disagreed, and while Abbott Lawrence was neither a lawyer nor a particularly effective public speaker, he was adept at managing men and organizations—in itself an asset of no small value in the political milieu of the day.

Nevertheless the first round went to Webster. Having reached the conclusion himself that his chances for the Whig nomination in 1840 were hopeless, he threw his weight behind William Henry Harrison and managed to carry the Massachusetts Whigs with him. In return Tippecanoe appointed Webster secretary of state. And when Lawrence let it be known that he was willing to fill the resulting vacancy in the Senate, nothing came of the plan. Instead, the place went to Rufus Choate, one of Webster's closest allies in Massachusetts politics.[92]

But Lawrence could be patient when circumstances required. From 1838 on, his name was conspicuously absent from the lists of donors to the various funds collected on Webster's behalf.[93] Then fate played a hand, when Harrison died after only a month in office. In the turmoil that followed, Clay and his supporters, using the bank issue as a *casus belli*, launched an all-out attack on Harrison's successor, John Tyler. Since Webster remained in Tyler's cabinet when the other members resigned, he became fair game as well. The result was the 1842 Massachusetts Whig convention, which Lawrence himself presided over and which not only endorsed Clay, but denounced in no uncertain terms President John Tyler and all his works.[94] Furious at the implied condemnation of his own position, Webster stormed north and at a reception in Faneuil Hall—called to congratulate him for his part in the Webster-Ashburton negotiations—spent his time heaping abuse on the convention and everyone connected with it. "I am a Whig, I have always been a Whig," he declared at one point, "if there are any who would turn me out of the pale of that communion, let them see who will get out first."[95]

Even Webster's friends were shocked at the rancor of his outburst. Commented Robert Winthrop: "Nobody but W. could have taken the course he has with impunity."[96] On the other hand, the Whig defeat in the Massachusetts elections that fall seemed to suggest that without "Jupiter to get our wheel out of the mire of locofocoism," as one observer put it, referring to Webster, the party might continue to suffer at the polls.[97] Hence the nomination of Briggs in 1843—Webster's price for returning to the fold, and a definite setback for Lawrence. But the following year the score was evened when Henry Clay received the Whig presidential nomination, forcing Webster, if he wished to remain in the party's good graces, to campaign for his old rival.

There matters might have rested, had Lawrence and Webster chosen to let them, but Lawrence seemed quite unwilling to call a halt. Webster returned to the Senate early in 1845. Soon afterward Nathan

Appleton wrote to him, suggesting that he indicate a desire "to let by-gones be bygones," which Appleton would then pass on to "the other party."[98] Webster agreed and even sent a second version of the re-quested letter, when the first proved unsatisfactory.[99] Still, the hoped-for reconciliation turned out to be at best a partial affair. After a conversation with Lawrence, John Quincy Adams noted in his diary: "The intimate and cordial personal relations heretofore existing be-tween Mr. Webster and Mr. Lawrence are thus restored, but," Adams added, "it is very apparent that confidence between them never can be restored."[100]

At the time, a large annuity was being raised for Webster's benefit—half in New York and half in Boston—and contributions were lag-ging.[101] Otherwise he might well have refused Appleton's request. Appleton's motives were more complex.

By 1845 the rift between Webster and Lawrence had become a matter of general knowledge. For Appleton—twice connected by marriage with Webster and a close personal friend and business asso-ciate of Lawrence's—the situation must have been especially awk-ward. On top of that there was the damage to the Massachusetts Whig party, or more precisely to the sense of common purpose uniting the small group of men who normally managed party affairs. In his letter to Webster, Appleton had spoken only of "many reasons both public and private" for a reconciliation with Lawrence, but it was hardly necessary to say more.[102] Given the general direction of American politics, there were growing limits to what could be accomplished through quiet conversations in State Street offices and Beacon Hill drawing rooms; without unanimity on that front, party policy would be wholly at the mercy of "democratic" opinion.

One subject that must have been on Appleton's mind when he wrote to Webster was the tariff. No other issue in national politics mattered more to the Boston Associates. Ever since 1816 Appleton and his friends had stood firmly behind the protectionist system. In 1842, under Tyler, rates had been raised, but Clay's defeat by James K. Polk in the presidential election of 1844 promised a new round of tariff reductions. Actually the administration bill, which did not reach Con-gress until 1846, went further than that. All specific duties—the sine qua non of protection—were to be abolished and replaced by graded, ad valorem duties on broad categories of goods. Consulting often with Appleton and others at home, Webster worked long and hard in the Senate to substitute "a proper and *permanent*" compromise mea-sure that would at least have salvaged the principle of protection. In the end the administration bill passed by a single vote.[103]

But when Appleton took it upon himself to heal the breach between Webster and Lawrence, congressional action on the tariff still lay several months in the future. In the summer of 1845 another issue preoccupied most Whig leaders in Massachusetts, and that issue was Texas. From the time Andrew Jackson first recommended annexation of the fledgling republic, opposition to it had run high. Adding Texas to the Union would enlarge the area of slavery, and that made it widely unpopular in Massachusetts. Writing to Webster in 1841 on the subject, Tyler, who favored annexation, remarked: "Slavery, I know this is the objection."[104] Never the most prescient of observers, Tyler for once was right. Speaking in the House in Washington, Robert Winthrop was merely reiterating the settled conviction of the great majority of Bay Staters when he declared: "I have no hesitation in saying that I shall oppose the annexation of Texas, now and always, upon the ground that it involves an extension of domestic slavery . . . I am uncompromisingly opposed to . . . the addition of another inch of Slaveholding Territory to this Nation."[105]

For all the boldness of Winthrop's declaration, however, Texas had never been an easy issue for the Whigs. To be sure, they opposed annexation, but so did the abolitionists—Liberty party moderates and Garrisonian radicals alike—and for that reason Whig leaders differed as to the best way to proceed. Abbott Lawrence considered annexation "the most important matter we have had to deal with since the Independence of this country,"[106] yet he was loath to see Massachusetts Whiggery tainted by association with abolitionism. Clay's equivocation on annexation in the presidential campaign of 1844 further complicated the issue for Lawrence. Webster, on the other hand, chose to press opposition to annexation on every available front, and in the process he had forged an alliance with a number of younger Whig leaders in the state, including Charles Allen, Stephen Phillips, and Charles Francis Adams.[107]

Ambitious, energetic, and sincerely dedicated to a cause that they believed ruled out all halfway measures, the "Young Whigs," as historians have labeled them, consistently functioned as the vanguard of anti-Texas activities in Massachusetts.[108] As early as 1843 the General Court had passed a series of resolutions, drafted by Adams, vigorously opposing annexation. The following year Adams worked to commit his colleagues in the legislature to an even stronger statement, after word reached Boston, via a letter from Webster to Charles Allen, that a treaty with Texas was virtually complete.[109] And when Lawrence, in March 1844, called a meeting at his house to consider "whether any measures were expedient in regard to the annexation of Texas," Adams—annoyed that nothing substantive came of the meeting—noted in his diary: "The truth really is that the wealthy classes have become inactive."[110]

But Adams had spoken too hastily. The first stage of the Massachusetts anti-Texas movement climaxed with a large convention, held in Faneuil Hall on January 29, 1845, that enjoyed the support of all elements of the Whig party. Because Garrison and his followers were to attend, the members of the Whig caucus, which issued the call for the convention, decided not to use the party name. For the same reason, Abbott Lawrence stood aloof. Yet among the subscribers were "conservatives" Leverett Saltonstall, Josiah Quincy, George Ticknor, and, for the Associates, Peter Chardan Brooks. Also, the official address of the convention was drafted by Webster. Predictably, the abolitionists found the document inadequate, but with Stephen Phillips in the chair and Adams and the other Young Whigs working to persuade delegates on the floor, it passed overwhelmingly.[111]

Adams was delighted. Like many Whig leaders, he had been afraid that the Garrisonians might take over the convention and turn it to their own ends. Still, he had considered the risk worth taking, and the convention itself seemed to justify his faith. Afterward he was even left hoping that others might "have it in their power to follow up the thread thus held forth."[112] But far from winning new converts, the next stage of anti-Texas activity in Massachusetts found the ranks of the movement thinner and the Whig party—for the first time—openly split over the issue.

Given his party's commitment, and his own, to annexation, Polk's victory in 1844 had made congressional action on Texas a certainty. When the new president took office, the necessary bill had already been signed into law. Yet technically that still left Texas outside the Union. Admitting the former republic as a state would require additional legislation, which gave the anti-Texas forces in Massachusetts the better part of a year to continue their efforts, if they chose to. And by mid-autumn 1845, Adams and the other Young Whigs—working once again with the abolitionists—had organized for a final, massive offensive. A second convention in Faneuil Hall was planned, as well as others throughout the state, and a flood of petitions was released, which eventually produced over thirty thousand signatures.[113]

In all of their activities the Young Whigs took pains to appear as moderate as possible. They even succeeded in checking the more extreme enthusiasms of their abolitionist allies. Adams especially was determined to "walk on firmly and cautiously," and to be, as he put it—referring to the radicals' penchant for attacking the Whig party—"the cat's paw of no one."[114] But if he hoped thereby to unite the

Whigs behind continued opposition to Texas, the hope came to nothing. For some people Tyler's signature on the annexation bill settled the issue—certainly it did for the Associates.

Aware that much would depend on how Abbott Lawrence and Nathan Appleton reacted, Adams had written both men personally, urging each to add his "valuable name" to the Texas Committee's petition.[115] Their replies left no doubt as to where they stood. "A majority of the people have decided in favor of annexation," Lawrence wrote, "Texas now virtually composes a part of our Union."[116] Appleton's letter, if less abrupt, was just as emphatic. He had, he reminded Adams, opposed annexation "and I have contributed funds to oppose it, so long as there appeared to be a chance of preventing it." But now that Congress had acted, it seemed pointless to continue the struggle. "I cannot think it good policy to waste our efforts on the impossible."[117]

Whatever Adams thought of Appleton's position, it was not lightly held. Texas was a dead issue; so Appleton believed, and he was not likely to change his mind. He was also not unprepared for the dispute in which he found himself. Several weeks earlier, just as the anti-Texas movement in Massachusetts was mobilizing for its last great effort, he had offered his services as a peacemaker between Webster and Lawrence. To combat Lawrence's influence within the party, Webster had been cooperating with the Young Whigs. Plainly Appleton wanted to end that arrangement—to isolate the Young Whigs by reuniting the established leadership of the party. And at a Whig rally in November Webster did come out against "separate action" on the Texas issue. On the other hand he confined his criticism to the Liberty party and said nothing at all about the Young Whigs.[118]

But even if Webster had followed a line more to Appleton's liking, it would not have mattered. The Young Whigs were as eager to continue their crusade as Appleton seemed to be to stop it, and continue it they did, right up to the last minute. Thus within the space of a few months at the end of 1845 a disagreement over tactics had escalated into something much more serious. Part of the difficulty lay in conflicting personal ambitions, yet that was hardly a new problem in Massachusetts Whig politics. The crucial ingredient remained the issue of slavery, with all its potential for dramatizing the difference between workaday political expediency and high moral principle.

What determined political expediency in this case? One obvious answer was economic self-interest. Inevitably charges were made linking the role Appleton and Lawrence played in opposing further action on Texas to their involvement in the textile industry. Soon the terms "Cotton" and "Conscience" would come into general use to describe the two sides in the controversy, implying nothing if not a deep division over questions of the most fundamental importance. Even before then, however, the Young Whigs had indicated as much by taking the extraordinary step of publishing—complete with appropriate "strictures" of their own—the letters Appleton and Lawrence had sent Adams on the subject of Texas.[119] From that point there could be no easy return to Whig unity in Massachusetts, then or in the future.

VI

Texas was finally admitted to the Union on December 29, 1845. Six months later the nation was at war with Mexico, raising the possibility of vast new territorial gains to the south and further splitting the Massachusetts Whig party. Again the leaders of the party agreed on what might have seemed the essential issues: all of them opposed both the war and the prospect of expanding the area of slavery. Where opinions differed was over how strenuously to press those positions, with the two sides lined up much as they had been at the end of 1845. And there they would remain, as the rift in the party grew steadily wider.

Meanwhile, in Washington, the Bay State's Whig representatives struggled to preserve whatever middle ground was left. In the Senate, Webster condemned the Mexican War, yet rather than backing the Wilmot Proviso—which would have outlawed slavery in any territory acquired as a result of the conflict—he preferred leaving Mexico intact, thereby avoiding the issue altogether.[120] But such solutions rarely satisfied the Conscience Whigs, as Robert Winthrop had already discovered to his dismay. In his initial request for funds for the Mexican War, Polk had claimed that American blood had been shed on American soil and therefore that war existed "by the act of Mexico." Since the president had deliberately provoked Mexico by ordering troops into territory claimed by both countries, his view of the situation was immediately challenged. Nevertheless his language found its way into the preamble of the appropriations bill that was to stand in lieu of a declaration of war. In the House, Winthrop—having first tried and failed to change the preamble—finally voted for the bill, while all but one of his Massachusetts colleagues voted against it. By the end of the summer he was being relentlessly attacked in a series of articles published at home over the pseudonym "Boston."[121]

"Boston" turned out to be Charles Sumner, a recent recruit to the Conscience forces, with whom Winthrop had long been on cordial terms. Asked for an explanation, Sumner offered assurances that there was nothing personal in the attacks, yet his final flourish in the

"Boston" series suggested just the opposite. "Blood! blood! is on the hands of the representative from Boston," he declared, using the sort of vivid imagery that would one day make him famous. "Not all great Neptune's ocean can wash them clean."[122] Deeply offended, Winthrop wrote Sumner cutting off all further relations.

The "Boston" letters appeared in the *Daily Whig*, a paper Charles Francis Adams had begun editing as a vehicle for Whig antislavery opinion. Running concurrently with them was another series, attacking Abbott Lawrence, as well as a third, which had Nathan Appleton as its target. Written by Adams himself, the letters on Lawrence rehearsed his role in the Texas controversy in detail and accused him of thinking "more of sheep and cotton than of Man." According to Adams, Lawrence had "covered Old Massachusetts with shame," in his attempt "to keep down . . . the growing restiveness under the domination of the slave power."[123] As for Appleton, his "defection" from the anti-Texas movement had emboldened Polk to begin the Mexican War. Thus, the responsibility for the war was his, or so claimed John Gorham Palfrey—secretary of the commonwealth and a former member of the Harvard faculty—in his "Papers on the Slave Power."[124]

Lawrence chose not to reply to Adams publicly, but Appleton did send the editor of the *Whig* a letter, which later found its way into print. On the question of his responsibility for the war, he pointed out that the decision to publish his earlier letter refusing to sign the anti-Texas petition had been made by the Young Whigs themselves, without his approval. If the letter had done any harm, which he doubted, the fault was theirs, not his. He also repeated his reasons for not signing the petition—noting especially the prominent role played by abolitionists in the later stages of the anti-Texas movement. He then closed with a ringing affirmation on an altogether different subject: "I confess that I have always considered the Union of the States as the palladium of our safety, the only ark of security . . . Notwithstanding the Texas iniquity, notwithstanding the wicked Mexican War, notwithstanding the destructive tariff of 1846, I still cling to the Union of the States."[125]

In the battle waged in the party press in Boston throughout the summer of 1846, no one spoke of the Cotton Whigs with greater authority than Appleton. Behind his words lay all the weight of his commanding position in the party, plus his great wealth—much of it invested in the very industry on which the Conscience Whigs increasingly blamed the party's moral dereliction. Adams also considered Appleton "the ablest of all the combatants we have . . . to contend with,"[126] which was true. When moved to express his opinions, Abbott Lawrence could be more forceful, but his thinking lacked the subtlety of Appleton's.

Reduced to its essentials, the position of the Conscience Whigs was that "the Manufacturers" had hoped to trade their own refusal to take a more energetic stand against slavery for Southern concessions on the tariff. That was the accusation Appleton had to answer, and the facts of the case ruled out any simple, straightforward response. He could scarcely deny that the prosperity of the mills at Lowell, and hence his own, depended on the tariff, or that the tariff had been due to come up in Congress just as he and his friends were working to discourage further opposition to Texas. Were those facts connected? Appleton never attempted to refute the charge, no doubt because in all candor he could not have done so.

Instead he shifted the focus of the debate, bringing it to bear ultimately on "the Union of the States." For years it had been the standard position of Northern politicians that though slavery was, as Webster once had put it, "a great moral, social and political evil,"[127] the Constitution granted it protection and left to individual states the question of its existence. Rather than arguing the point, Garrison and his followers openly condemned both the Constitution and the Union. By allying themselves with the radicals, then, Adams and his friends were—as Appleton saw it—lending tacit support to disunionism. His response was to argue that preservation of the Union deserved priority over everything else. And preserving the Union, in turn, meant accepting the duly arrived-at decisions of the national government as binding—however little they accorded with one's personal interests or feelings. Significantly, in writing Adams, Appleton mentioned Texas, the Mexican War, and the tariff of 1846 in a single sentence, making it clear that he opposed each of them but put his dedication to the Union above all three. The suggestion was that while he and Adams might disagree about which of the three was more to be deplored, they could still find common ground in loyalty to the Union.

In effect what Appleton had done was to present a model of how he believed national politics ought to work. It was also a reasonably accurate rendering of the process that had, for more than ten years, blended the disparate components of Massachusetts Whiggery into a harmonious whole. Elite economic interests and the impulse toward moral reform had each played a role in shaping party policy; there had never been any need to choose between mutually exclusive alternatives. And if the resulting policy lacked clarity, what was the Union itself—"the palladium of our security"—but a vast and conveniently vague abstraction? The point was that, like the Union, the political process that sustained it could be whatever responsible men of good will, acting with due regard for one another's interests, chose to make it. Was Appleton bowing to Southern opinion on questions like Texas and the Mexican War? Not as long as there was any hope of affecting the outcome. But thereafter he would acquiesce in what he could not alter, and through it all slavery would remain but one issue among many, not *the* issue—the touchstone of party policy that the Conscience Whigs hoped to make it.

For their part, the Conscience Whigs rejected all of Appleton's arguments, considering him, as Adams put it in an editorial in the *Whig*, "not a safe guide in the construction of his neighbor's duties either to his country or his God."[128] So the controversy continued, though for the remainder of 1846 Appleton added nothing more to it. He also refrained from venting his annoyance at the Conscience Whigs in any of the more obvious ways he might have. As a result of his attack on Winthrop, Charles Sumner had found the doors of quite a few polite drawing rooms in Boston closed to him, but not Appleton's. Henry Wadsworth Longfellow, Appleton's son-in-law, counted Sumner among his closest friends, and Appleton himself had made something of a protegé of the younger man, steering occasional legal business his way. For the present those ties held.[129]

No doubt there were several reasons for Appleton's equanimity. He was not by nature a vindictive man. But more to the point, as serious as the dispute between the Cotton and Conscience Whigs had become, it had yet to disturb the delicate network of safeguards surrounding the Waltham-Lowell system. There, except for the tariff, the relevant issues were all local ones, and to date the Conscience Whigs had shown little if any inclination to delve into state economic policy. Nor had the dispute split the party in any formal sense—officially Adams and his friends remained within the Whig fold. Under the circumstances Appleton apparently thought it best not to stretch tempers any further.

That year's state election returns also pointed to the wisdom of such an approach. At the Whig convention in September, 1846—partly due to a dramatic entrance by Webster and Abbott Lawrence, walking arm in arm to the podium, moments before the vote—a set of unusually stiff antislavery resolutions proposed by the Conscience forces was defeated.[130] Yet in any contest with the Democrats, the Whig party continued to offer Massachusetts voters a clear choice on the issue of slavery. The same convention that rejected the Conscience resolutions overwhelmingly approved a platform pledging the party to "oppose at all times and with uncompromising zeal and firmness, any further addition of slaveholding States to the Union, out of whatever territory formed."[131] The Democrats' only response was to urge support for the Polk administration—a tactic that netted the party its lowest share of the vote since 1834, while the Whigs gained an additional 3,000 votes over the previous year's total despite a 4 percent decline in the number of ballots cast.[132] Obviously in Massachusetts antislavery politics made good sense. That being the case, too harsh a policy toward the Conscience Whigs could prove costly.

But restraint—on both sides—had its limits. The events of the next two years were to strain to the breaking point and finally shatter altogether any hope of reconciliation within the Massachusetts Whig party. As victorious American armies swept across Mexico, Congress angered everyone in the dispute by refusing to accept either the Wilmot Proviso or Webster's "no territory" formula, which the Cotton Whigs favored. And the Conscience Whigs were forced to witness as well the national party's choice of General Zachary Taylor—the hero of Buena Vista, a Southerner, and a slaveholder—as its presidential candidate. On June 10, 1848, with the guns that had sounded on Boston Common to celebrate Taylor's nomination barely still, the *Whig* issued a call for a meeting of all the "true hearted" at Worcester eighteen days later. Attended by over five thousand delegates, the Worcester convention formally rejected Taylor's candidacy, thereby confirming what most people already suspected: the Conscience Whigs were bolting the party.[133]

Speaking at Worcester, Charles Sumner argued that Taylor's nomination was the result of a vast conspiracy "between the cotton-planters and flesh-mongers of Louisiana and Mississippi and the cotton-spinners and traffickers of New England—between the lords of the lash and the lords of the loom."[134] Afterward Appleton, his patience at last exhausted, demanded to know what proof there was for such a charge. Sumner eventually replied, but with "very *skimble skamble stuff* in the way of evidence," Appleton thought.[135] His own explanation was simple: Sumner was lying. And this time Appleton stated his views in no uncertain terms. Yet once again the facts seemed to point to a different conclusion.

From the beginning, Taylor's principal Massachusetts backer had been Abbott Lawrence. As time passed Lawrence was also mentioned with growing regularity as a possible running mate for Old Rough and Ready—an honor he gave every sign of wanting. Meanwhile, against all odds, Webster continued to hope that the party's presidential nomination might come to him.[136] In that situation, the Conscience Whigs seemed to hold the balance of power between the Lawrence and Webster factions, though the advantage was more apparent than real, as the Whig state convention of 1847 showed.

By the time the delegates gathered in Springfield, the Conscience strategy was set. Just as Webster's name was about to be put in nomination, Stephen C. Phillips offered a motion stating that it was "inexpedient to recommend a nomination of candidates for the Presidency and Vice Presidency."[137] In the ensuing confusion, the chair's decision to accept a voice vote to table was challenged, but when the division was taken, the motion to table passed by a bare majority of ten, thus clearing the way for Webster's endorsement. Having struck at Webster and missed, the Conscience Whigs next turned to Lawrence, only to fail again. As soon as the platform was read, Palfrey rose with an amendment that would have put the Massachusetts Whig party on record as opposing any presidential candidate who was not an outspoken enemy of slavery. Clearly the intention was to discredit Taylor's candidacy, but the Lawrence camp—operating like a well-oiled machine—promptly quashed the move. Palfrey's amendment lost, and the platform passed intact.

That fall Charles Francis Adams voted for almost the entire Whig ticket, yet he did so convinced that it was the last time he would support the party in an election.[138] The Taylor-Lawrence forces, on the other hand, could not have been happier. Even though the Springfield convention had endorsed Webster, it amounted to little more than an empty courtesy. Few people believed that he stood any chance at all of winning the nomination. More to the point was the skill and efficiency with which Taylor's backers had handled the threat posed by the Conscience Whigs. As a result Lawrence's star continued to rise. In April of the following year Nathan Appleton was in Washington for talks with leading Taylor supporters there.[139] In May encouragement came from a group of prominent New York City Whigs: "We are now ready to strike for our friend and your friend, for the V. Presidency, and we write for the purpose of asking you to unite with us in furnishing the sinews of War."[140] Three weeks later, when the party's national convention opened in Philadelphia, a Taylor-Lawrence ticket seemed at least a distinct possibility.

But the Conscience Whigs were determined to block any such arrangement. Their days in the party might have been numbered; still Lawrence's "apostasy" was not to go unpunished. In due course the delegates at Philadelphia nominated Taylor. The next step should have been a vote to make the nomination unanimous, yet before that could happen Charles Allen of Massachusetts was on his feet declaring, "We spurn the nominee." Taylor's election could only mean "the rule of slavery for another four years," he continued; no man of conscience could sanction that. As for the chance that the vice-presidential nomination might fall to the Bay State, Allen was equally unyielding: "Massachusetts will spurn the bribe."[141]

Though most of those who heard Allen knew that he spoke for a minority of the Massachusetts delegation, evidently they preferred to take him at his word. When the balloting for vice-president began, Lawrence was already running behind Millard Fillmore. On the second ballot the New Yorker was nominated easily. At the time it seemed a clear victory for the Conscience forces, yet what continued to matter most to Allen and his friends was Taylor's nomination; because of it they were prepared to abandon the Whig party and would have done so whatever became of Lawrence's vice-presidential hopes.[142]

VII

The Whig Convention of 1848 produced a marked shift in the political climate of Massachusetts. Abbott Lawrence was left deeply disappointed by the outcome in Philadelphia, and so was Webster. But the most dramatic change remained the bolt of the Conscience Whigs. Since they had every intention of continuing their crusade against slavery, new political alignments began to emerge almost at once, and in the process familiar issues of all kinds took on fresh meaning. Increasingly, attacks on the South's peculiar institution were bolstered by challenges to the distribution of wealth and power at home in Massachusetts, with the Whig party—or what was left of it—bearing the brunt of both. For the Associates none of this boded well. Though the full extent of the damage would not be clear for a while longer, the party system that had protected the group's interest so effectively for fifteen years was on the verge of collapse.

Lawrence spent much of the summer of 1848 traveling in Canada. Then autumn brought Taylor's triumph at the polls, with its promise of rewards for his supporters. Hoping to enter the cabinet as secretary of the treasury, Lawrence eventually had to find what solace he could as American minister to the Court of St. James's. But the post—if no substitute for the vice-presidency—was at least an honorable one, and he filled it ably, despite the doubts of some about his "fitness . . . & that of his family, for doing the elegancies of such a station."[143]

Webster's situation was a good deal bleaker. At Philadelphia he had received a mere twenty-two votes for the presidential nomination. The Southern support he hoped to win simply never materialized. And once in power, Taylor's friends had debts enough to honor without worrying about Webster. As a result he found himself unable even to secure a minor federal appointment for his son and ultimately came to feel that his own future, no less than the nation's, depended on a permanent solution of the sectional controversy. In 1850 that conviction would lead him to support Henry Clay's sweeping compromise plan to eliminate slavery as an issue in national politics. And two years later, with sectional peace and the Union as his platform, he would make his final, unsuccessful bid for the presidency.[144]

From 1848 on, Webster's political course took shape in an environment dominated—at all levels—by the debate over slavery, but nowhere was slavery more intensely debated than in his own Massachusetts. The Conscience Whigs saw to that. Having rejected Taylor's nomination and declared their independence at Worcester in June 1848, they were ready by the end of the summer to go before the electorate as members of a brand-new political organization, dedicated to pressing the fight against slavery on every possible front.

In August, delegates from eighteen states met at Buffalo to establish the Free Soil party. As their presidential nominee they picked Martin Van Buren, a choice that aroused little enthusiasm in the Massachusetts delegation. But the fact that second place on the ticket went to Charles Francis Adams delighted the Bay Staters. They returned home eager to campaign throughout the state and did just that—with striking results. Winning 29 percent of the presidential vote, the new party performed better in Massachusetts than in any other state in the union except Vermont. And in the gubernatorial contest Stephen C. Phillips, the Free Soil candidate, outpolled his Democratic rival by almost eleven thousand votes. More impressive still, the Free Soilers cost the Whigs the statewide majority they had enjoyed since 1843.[145]

During the campaign of 1848 the Boston *Atlas*, which continued to speak for the Associates, regularly condemned the Conscience Whigs' "inconsistency" in supporting a long-time Democrat like Van Buren. And as Van Buren's running mate, Charles Francis Adams became a favorite target of the editors, who described him at one point as "a man who lives upon the reputation as well as the wealth of his ancestors."[146] But for the *Atlas* to make an issue of Adams' personal wealth—the result, in fact, of his marriage into the Brooks family—was after all a ticklish business. He himself remained convinced that the "property party," as he referred to what survived of Massachusetts Whiggery, was "destined to a heavy defeat from which it will not recover."[147] In 1848 that prediction might have seemed premature, but time proved otherwise.

From the standpoint of the Whigs generally—and the Associates in particular—the thing most to be feared was an alliance between the Massachusetts Free Soilers and the Democrats, since such an alliance would command a clear majority in the state. Yet already, by 1849 the signs along the political horizon were pointing in that direction. In November "combination" tickets appeared in many towns, especially those where the Free Soil vote was highest. When the ballots were counted, 130 representatives and 13 senators had won election under the joint auspices of the two parties.[148]

And even more disturbing than the fact of the emerging Free Soil–Democratic coalition was the ideological basis on which it was being forged. Determined to keep attention focused on slavery, Free Soil leaders like Adams and Palfrey believed that liberal positions on other issues would only dilute the party's moral authority. But most former Democrats in the Free Soil ranks disagreed, and their views found a ready advocate in Charles Sumner. As chairman of the party's state central committee, Sumner welcomed "full amalgamation" with the Democrats and seemed quite unbothered by the prospect of relying on more than a single issue, however pure, to win votes in Massachusetts. Soon after the election of 1848, he had surprised his friends by declaring privately that the republic was in greater danger "from the corruption of wealth than from mobs."[149] And for the Free Soil state convention of 1849 he drafted a set of resolutions that ended with a forthright denunciation of "the tendency of the legislation of the Commonwealth to consolidate wealth in corporations."[150]

As long as the debate over slavery ran on at full tilt, the Whigs could continue to stress the paramount importance of preserving the Union. But slavery and Union were issues in national politics; Sumner's attack on corporations was another matter. If that sort of "insidious appeal to class prejudices," as one Whig labeled it,[151] became part of the cement binding together a majority coalition of Free Soilers and Democrats in Massachusetts, where then could the Associates hope to find what Appleton had once called "the palladium of our safety"? What good would talk of the Union do when push came to shove in the State House in Boston over corporate charters or the activities of the Suffolk Bank? The answer of course was none.

Then in March of 1850, Webster threw his weight behind Clay's compromise, producing a fresh avalanche of antislavery protest in Massachusetts and a mixed reaction, at best, from the state's Whigs. The *Atlas* was highly critical. So was Robert Winthrop, who held his peace in public but remarked to Edward Everett, "If Gen. Taylor had said the same things precisely in his Message we should all have said—'so much for having a Southern President,' & W. himself would have led off in denouncing him."[152] Even after Taylor's death had removed the principal obstacle to the Compromise, only one Massachusetts Whig congressman voted for all of the necessary bills. Particularly objectionable was a new, much stiffer fugitive slave law.

Eventually, however, most conservative Whigs rallied behind Webster—and the Union. Talk of secession had become commonplace in the South, frightening many people. With the Compromise passed, tensions seemed to ease. By September 1850, Edward Everett's initial lukewarm response had turned into ardent enthusiasm. "I trust the country will have the discernment to appreciate and recompense the service," he wrote Webster.[153] Also typical was Samuel A. Eliot, the lone Whig in the Massachusetts congressional delegation to vote for the Compromise *in toto*. A member of the Associates' group and by his own admission a novice in politics, Eliot held the seat left vacant when Winthrop moved to the Senate after Webster, his personal fortunes like those of the Compromise suddenly altered by Taylor's death, became secretary of state. The fact that Eliot had beaten Sumner in the special election and gone on to vote for every one of "the peace measures" delighted Webster. Eliot became "a lion"—the very "personification of Boston, ever intelligent, ever patriotic, ever glorious Boston."[154]

But Boston was not the state, as anyone familiar with Massachusetts politics well knew. Antislavery feeling had always run higher outside the city than in it, and the Compromise had given the Free Soilers a stronger claim than ever on the antislavery vote. Meanwhile the party continued to move steadily nearer a full-fledged coalition with the Democrats. Again in 1850, the state elections failed to produce a majority, but for the third time in as many years the Free Soilers and Democrats together outpolled the Whigs. Between them the two parties also won control of the General Court and hence, under the terms of the Massachusetts constitution, the opportunity to distribute all of the major state offices, plus a full-term United States senatorship.

During the early weeks of 1851, the necessary bargain was struck: the Coalition became a reality. As their share the Democrats netted most of the state offices, including the governorship. Then, with significant Democratic backing, the other great prize, the Senate seat that had passed from Webster to Winthrop and which Winthrop wanted very much to keep, went to Charles Sumner. In short, the Whigs had been shut out of power completely.[155]

From the first the Associates had worked to block the Coalition. Scuttling Sumner's chances for the senatorship became a matter of the highest priority. "For heaven's sake keep him home," Samuel Eliot wrote Amos A. Lawrence from Washington,[156] to which Lawrence replied "Everything is being done . . . that can be."[157] In this case "everything" included a fund collected expressly "to defeat Sumner." The money was not "for influencing any member in an improper manner," Lawrence hastened to assure his friends;[158] rather it would

go for extra expenses—chartering special trains to bring absent legislators to Boston, for example, and paying their hotel bills while there.
But all to no avail, as it turned out. Sumner won and soon enough
left for Washington, despite the black arm bands that many Boston
businessmen wore in public the day after the final vote in the legislature; despite, too, Nathan Appleton's claim that the legislature's action represented "the most fatal blow to . . . popular suffrage" ever
inflicted.[159]

In the eyes of the Associates Sumner's election would remain the
surest proof of the charge repeatedly made, in public and private,
against the Coalition: that it was an immoral arrangement, entered
into for the sole purpose of winning office. Hence Appleton's strictures about the damage done to "popular suffrage." The voters had
rendered their verdict, giving the Whigs, if not the majority, at least a
plurality. But then the Democrats and Free Soilers, "with no principle
in common but the spoils of office," had seen fit to subvert that verdict
so that George Boutwell could become governor and Charles Sumner
could go to the Senate. Personal ambition and hunger for party power
were all that held the Coalition together.

Nor were Appleton and his friends alone in their opinion. Even
though he welcomed Sumner's election, Charles Francis Adams continued to see the Free Soil party's "unholy alliance" with the Democrats as a selfish strategy, lacking any real foundation in principle.[160]
And certainly much of the available evidence supported such an interpretation. In national politics the Democratic party had always been
more accommodating to the interests of slaveholders than the Whigs.
Time and again during the voting in Congress in 1850, northern
Democrats had provided the margin that ensured passage of the
Compromise, with all its hated concessions to "the Slave-power."
Most northern Whigs had resisted the siren call of Clay's "settlement," and none more stoutly than those from Massachusetts, except
of course Webster and Eliot. But Webster and Eliot *were* exceptions. If
the Bay State's Free Soilers had wanted to ally themselves with another party, surely a union with the Whigs would have made more
sense than one with the Democrats—at least on the grounds of antislavery principle. Or so ran the argument.

But for all its importance, antislavery principle was only one of
many elements present in the complex political mix of the period, and
those elements could be combined in more than one way. The harsh
words about corporations Sumner had inserted in the 1849 Free Soil
platform proved that. Whatever his motives, there was no inherent
contradiction between the position Sumner outlined and a strong
stand against slavery. Similarly, during the balloting in the legisla-

ture, widespread rumors had the coalitionists wooing votes for their candidates by pledging support for a large state loan to finance the Hoosac Tunnel, a project many Whigs had consistently opposed.[161] The rumors may or may not have been true, but a study of election returns shows that many of the Worcester County towns along the route the tunnel would serve had been producing healthy Free Soil majorities since 1848.[162] Presumably the voters in those towns—in addition to opposing slavery—had the usual interest in better railroad connections. If the two objectives could be pursued simultaneously, why not do so?

An analysis of the Free Soil vote is revealing in other ways as well. Of the 310 Massachusetts towns making legal returns in 1848, 69 had given the Free Soilers at least a plurality. How much of that vote came from former Democrats, and how much from former Whigs, it is impossible to tell with any precision, but more than half of the 69 towns—36, to be exact—had unfailingly returned Whig majorities up to 1848, while 6 others had voted Whig in most years. Of the 10 towns with the highest percentage of Free Soil vote, every one was normally a Whig town, and all were in Worcester County, a traditional Whig stronghold, which the Free Soilers also carried in 1848.[163]

What these figures suggest is how grave a blow, even before the Coalition, the Free Soilers had dealt Massachusetts Whiggery. Losing forty additional towns in any election would have been enough to cost the party its majority. But more, the movement of so many towns, so decisively, from the Whig to the Free Soil column argues that the Free Soil effort in Massachusetts was not just an antislavery phenomenon; it was also an anti-Whig phenomenon. And in that respect the union of former Whigs with former Democrats in the Free Soil party, and later the coalition between the Free Soilers and the Democrats, made excellent sense. What all of those groups had in common was a determination to see the power of the Massachusetts Whig party broken.

Equally significant was the geographical distribution of the Free Soil vote. Suffolk County, which included Boston, remained solidly Whig, but from Plymouth northward the ring of counties around Suffolk all contained pockets of Free Soil strength, with Worcester, again, leading the way. In addition the party did well in Franklin County, in the western part of the state.[164] The fact that the Free Soilers carried so many of Worcester's rising industrial centers indicated that something more than a simple rural-urban split was at work. On the other hand, quite a few small towns also returned Free Soil pluralities. And that trend continued under the Coalition, thanks to the question of annual representation. In 1840 an amendment to the state constitution had sharply restricted the years in which towns below a certain size could send representatives to the General Court. Despite the resentment caused by the amendment, the Whigs refused to consider any change, thereby giving their opponents yet another issue on which to campaign.[165]

Finally, raising levels of anti-Whig feeling even higher, were two other issues with broad appeal across the countryside—temperance and nativism. Over the years the movement to restrict consumption of alcoholic beverages had continued to grow, especially in rural areas. Though in principle the Whigs remained sympathetic to the cause of temperance, no new initiatives had followed the disastrous experiment with the fifteen-gallon law in 1839. In much the same way the party had associated itself, in vague terms, with the antiforeign, anti-Catholic impulses increasingly evident around the state. But some voters wanted more than mere rhetoric. In 1845 an American Republican party, pledged to immigration restriction, had cut sharply into Whig voting totals in Massachusetts. The campaign for greater representation for small towns also had distinct nativist overtones, since most immigrants lived in urban areas.[166]

In the long run the leaders of the Coalition would find it impossible to reconcile all of their supporters' competing demands. Any serious commitment to nativist "reform," for example, was sure to alienate the Irish, who usually voted Democratic, and the same was true of temperance. But for the moment such problems were more hypothetical than real. And however loudly the Associates might complain of "unprincipled alliances," the truth was that combining antislavery, economic reform, the restoration of annual representation, temperance, and nativism in a single party platform was only to follow—in reverse—the very logic on which the Whig party had for so long relied. From the founding of the party on, two considerations had taken precedence in shaping its strategy: protecting certain large-scale economic interests, preeminently those of the Associates; and maintaining, as the key to control of the state, a majority in Suffolk County. But it had always been necessary, too, to reach out to voters beyond Boston—to mobilize the periphery in support of the center. The great success of the coalitionists, on the other hand, lay in their ability, using many of the same issues the Whigs had, to mobilize the periphery *against* the center. By 1851 that process was complete.

The consequences were apparent almost immediately. In addition to electing Sumner to the Senate, the Massachusetts legislature in 1851 debated a series of landmark bills, including a constitutional amendment that would have cut Boston's representation in the General Court in half. At the last minute the amendment was defeated, but the leaders of the Coalition did manage to get a referendum on the question of calling a state constitutional convention added to the November ballot. Also passed were three other highly significant pieces of legislation: a bill altering the charter of Harvard College to give the state a larger voice in its affairs, a general incorporation law, and a free banking act.[167]

Together, the Coalition-sponsored reforms of 1851 signaled—and definitively—the end of an era in Massachusetts. Not only had the legislature sent "a one ideaed abolitionist agitator" to the United States Senate, but the political power of Boston was under attack, the autonomy of the state's oldest and richest cultural institution had been challenged, and the entire system by which the commonwealth restricted corporate privileges to those willing and able to obtain special legislation had been swept away. Amid the general wreckage of Whig policy, too, no group had suffered greater damage than the Associates. If the political power of Boston was to be reduced, so necessarily would theirs be; enlarging the role of the state at Harvard could only be accomplished at their expense; and what possible effect could general incorporation and free banking have, except to foster precisely the sort of uncontrolled economic expansion the group had always opposed?

Once before, the Associates had faced a situation like the one they confronted in 1851. Twenty years earlier, at the time of the Antimasonry crusade and the drive for religious disestablishment, a full-scale assault by the many on the power and privileges of the few had seemed imminent. But then, in a series of adroit moves, the leaders of the Massachusetts National Republican party had rallied under a new political banner and recast their appeal to the voters in terms that effectively cut the ground out from under their opponents. In those events the Associates played a central role. Yet in 1851 only a handful of Whig leaders in the state seemed interested in repeating the effort, and the Associates formed no part of that minority. On the contrary, while angry mobs in Boston fought to prevent the return of accused fugitive slaves, Amos A. Lawrence was writing the United States marshal charged with enforcing the law to offer his services "in any capacity 'during the war.' "[168]

And when it came to all those other vexing issues like annual representation and economic reform, official Whig opinion was even more rigid. The state convention in 1851 awarded the party's gubernatorial nomination to Robert Winthrop, who delighted in describing the Coalition's program as the "sort of reform practiced by certain daughters of antiquity upon their aged parent . . . cutting him up to pieces and boiling him in a cauldron, to make him young again."[169]

Among the resolutions adopted by the convention, one in particular seemed to epitomize the mood of the occasion: "Resolved, that reform in whatever is bad, conservatism in whatever is good, progress for whatever is better, and economy in all things, are the cornerstones of Massachusetts Whig Policy."[170]

Under the circumstances it would have been hard to imagine anything more foolhardy or unrealistic. The structure the Whigs hoped to preserve was already in shambles, and only a complete rebuilding on totally different foundations—"cornerstones" and all—could have salvaged any part of it. The delegates at Springfield might as well have been meeting on the moon.

VIII

Predictably, the Whigs' attachment to "conservatism in whatever" made scant headway with the voters. Again in 1851 the party lost to the Coalition in Massachusetts. But men like Nathan Appleton and Amos A. Lawrence did not give up easily. Throughout the next decade the Associates would struggle to recover their former footing in politics, and at times it almost looked as if they might succeed. Some lessons had been learned: new alliances were tried, as well as fresh approaches to the electorate. Yet finally none of it worked. The eve of the Civil War found the Associates no nearer their goal than ever. If anything, the intervening years had only widened the gulf that separated them from the great majority of voters in Massachusetts and everywhere else in the nation.

One of the experiments that seemed promising at first, only to turn out disastrously, was courting the Irish vote. As the Coalition moved through the rest of its reform agenda, the strains in its makeup became increasingly apparent. In 1852 the General Court passed, and Governor Boutwell signed, a version of the Maine Liquor Law, prohibiting the sale and manufacture of all intoxicating liquor except for medicinal purposes. Though most urban Democrats voted against the measure and many Whigs from rural areas voted for it, it was widely blamed on the Coalition. In the fall elections the Whigs ran John Clifford—an avowed "wet"—for governor and, stressing their sympathy with the Irish who particularly resented the law, regained control of the state.[171]

The following year the issue was different, but the same scenario played itself out. During the early months of 1853 the convention to revise the state's constitution met. The resulting document, along with many other changes, sharply readjusted representation in favor of small towns. In Boston the Irish Catholic press implored its readers to reject the convention's handiwork, a message Whig editors drove home with equal force. Declared the Worcester *Transcript:* "The main object . . . in the framing of this new constitution was to deprive the emigrants [*sic*] who live in our cities of their just and equal rights as American citizens."[172] And afterward, with the proposed constitution defeated and the Whigs again victorious, the Boston *Atlas* formally thanked the immigrants for their help, which the editors estimated had amounted to as many as ten thousand extra votes.[173]

At the time, much of the credit for engineering the Whigs' return to power in Massachusetts went to Abbott Lawrence. Back from England and finally rid of his old rival Webster, who died in 1852, he had thrown himself into political affairs with characteristic energy and openhandedness. In explaining the reasons for the defeat of the revised constitution, one Free Soil journalist put at the top of his list—right after the city of Boston—"Abbott Lawrence's wallet."[174] Exactly how much he spent, and on what, to guarantee the Whig victories of those years were matters of speculation, but it was well known that he consulted often with J. B. Fitzpatrick, the Catholic bishop of Boston.[175] And certainly the party's Irish strategy did have much the look of something Lawrence might have designed: it was bold; it took precise account of existing realities; and in the short run, at least, it seemed quite effective.

But in truth the strategy was never as successful as it appeared to be. Even with the added Irish support, Whig voting totals actually declined in both 1852 and 1853. The party won because the Democrats and Free Soilers suffered even greater losses, suggesting that the real reason for the Whig resurgence was the growing weakness of the Coalition. Worse still, the policy of courting the Irish vote had produced deep resentment among the voters—resentment that in 1854 helped fuel an astonishing outburst of nativist political activity around the state. Arising virtually overnight, the Native American or "Know-Nothing" party swept the fall elections that year, winning the governorship, all of the state's congressional seats, the entire state senate, and all but three seats in the state house of representatives.

The causes of the Know-Nothing triumph in Massachusetts were intimately bound up with the general political turmoil of the period. Disaffected rural Democrats, almost the entire Free Soil party, and untold numbers of Whigs all found a home, however briefly, in the movement. For Coalitionists angry at the defeat of the constitution, for native-born workers frightened by growing competition from immigrant labor, for temperance enthusiasts and the opponents of slavery, no less than for those who disliked foreigners, nativism offered an ideal protest vehicle: a way of freeing the political process from the grip of all existing party alignments—and politicians. Significantly, fewer than one in eight of the 354 Know-Nothings elected to the General Court in 1854 had any prior experience in office.[176] As Charles Sumner remarked, "The people were tired of the old parties and they made a new channel."[177]

Whether the Whigs could have prevented the spread of Know-Nothingism is debatable, but it was a fact that the party's earlier flirtation with the Irish made it the prime target for many voters. The consequences were devastating. Having lost in 1854, the Whigs fared even less well the next year, receiving barely 10 percent of the vote, and that was the last time the party contested a Massachusetts election.[178] Fortunately for his sake, Abbott Lawrence did not live to witness the ultimate outcome of his strategy. He died in August 1855, just two months before that final, ill-fated campaign.

With Lawrence gone—and Whiggery dead—the mantle of political leadership among the Associates passed to his nephew, Amos A. Lawrence. Neither as decisive nor as ambitious as his uncle, he had inherited many of the intellectual qualities and much of the idealism of his father, Amos Lawrence. But unlike his father, he was never content simply to observe the political scene; he remained convinced that there was an important role for a gentleman with his convictions and resources to play. The problem was discovering what that role might be, and little that he encountered in the decade of the 1850s seemed to offer any very clear solution.[179]

Given a choice, Lawrence would doubtless have preferred to concentrate on combating the forces of economic reform unleashed by the Coalition in Massachusetts. Yet any progress there presupposed control of the state government, and the same factors that had been the undoing of the Whigs continued to make that an elusive goal. Among other things, the slavery issue would not go away. And even though Lawrence counted himself as much an opponent of slavery as any man—and more than once acted forthrightly on his beliefs—like all of the Associates he persisted in putting his dedication to the Union above everything else.

Apart from the meteoric rise of the Know-Nothing party, the other signal event of 1854 was the Kansas-Nebraska Act. Furious at the stupidity and bad faith that "woke the sleeping tiger," once again thrusting slavery to the fore in national politics, Lawrence remarked, "You may rely upon it . . . the sentiment at this time among the powerful and conservative class of men is the same as it is in the country towns throughout New England."[180] And as if to prove his point, in what must have seemed an extraordinary *volte-face*, he offered to raise "any amount" of money to defend Anthony Burns, who had been seized in Boston and was about to be tried as a fugitive slave.[181]

Early in 1854 Lawrence also began his long association with the New England Emigrant Aid Company. Under the terms of the Kansas-Nebraska Act, the future of slavery in the two territories was to be determined by the settlers themselves. In passing the act Congress had willfully violated the Missouri Compromise—or so most Northerners, including Lawrence, believed—but at least "popular sovereignty" embodied a remedy of sorts. If the new territories were settled promptly by people who would vote to keep slavery out, the area could still be preserved for freedom. And that was the goal of the Emigrant Aid Company, which Lawrence served officially as treasurer and unofficially as chief fund raiser and policy planner. With his steady hand at the helm, an impressive sum of money was collected—not a little of it from old friends like William Appleton and Joseph Lyman—and hundreds of settlers were sent on their way to Kansas. Lawrence also took care that the company did not become a speculative venture, and he worked even harder to keep it out of politics and free from any taint of violence. But in the latter two respects events outran his control. As the situation in Kansas degenerated into open warfare, he found himself dashing off orders for "one hundred more of the Sharpes rifles at once."[182]

To have refused "the legitimate settlers" in Kansas the means to defend themselves against proslavery "border ruffians" would have been unconscionable, Lawrence believed. "When farmers turn soldiers, they must have *arms*," he wrote.[183] But he repeatedly stressed, too, that nothing should ever be done "to resist, or even to question the authority of the United States."[184] And in spite of the violence and the "appalling treachery" of the Buchanan administration in Washington, the situation did end as Lawrence hoped it would—with the admission of Kansas as a free state in January 1861. For his pains, the town of Lawrence, Kansas, was named after him, but that was more a source of embarrassment than anything else. The great thing was that popular sovereignty had worked: the Union stood; the Constitution and the laws made under it had been upheld—though what difference that made by 1861 was far from clear.

Meanwhile, another result of Lawrence's concern for "Bleeding Kansas" had been the formation of a highly improbable friendship. On May 22, 1856, three days after delivering an impassioned speech on "the Crime Against Kansas," Charles Sumner was brutally caned at his desk in the Senate by Preston S. Brooks, a representative from South Carolina.[185] Like most Massachusetts citizens Lawrence was outraged, but his response was to invite Sumner, who had been left badly injured by the attack, to rest at his home while traveling to Boston.[186] Considering its source, the gesture could hardly have been more surprising, which may have explained why Sumner accepted. In any case the cordial relations between the two men continued. By 1859 Lawrence was even proposing that Harvard award Sumner an honorary degree.[187]

But cordial relations and honorary degrees from Harvard were hardly the same as political cooperation or support. In issuing his invitation in 1856, Lawrence had carefully explained that he would understand if Sumner chose instead "to be with one of those who agree with you in regard to party politics."[188] The message was clear: whatever else they might have in common, Lawrence disagreed with Sumner about party politics. And that never changed. A world in which Lawrence felt compelled to arm someone like John Brown in an undeclared war half a continent away was still not one in which he could imagine voting Republican.

The Republican party had first appeared in Massachusetts—with Sumner as one of its founders—in 1854, at the height of the Know-Nothing crusade, and as long as the Know-Nothings commanded the support of most former Free Soilers, Republican ranks grew slowly. But within a year Know-Nothingism began to fade almost as quickly as it had materialized. By 1856 the Republicans were well organized and could claim to be the only party in the state unequivocally opposed to the further spread of slavery.[189] Yet for Lawrence—precisely because the party had committed itself to a position that doomed it to a "purely sectional" existence—any connection with the Republicans was out of the question. The rise of one sectional party was sure to beget another, and with the national political landscape thus demarcated, North and South, the Union would face a dangerous, quite possibly fatal, crisis. Nor were the Democrats, with their "indifference" to moral issues, any more appealing.[190]

In 1856 that left as the only possible alternative, the American party, an odd hybrid formed by joining the remnants of the Know-Nothing movement and what survived of conservative Whiggery. Surveying the political scene that year, both Nathan Appleton and Edward Everett agreed with Robert Winthrop that "nothing remained" but to support the American party's presidential nominee, Millard Fillmore. So did Lawrence, who proudly flew a Fillmore flag over his broad lawn in Brookline.[191] Two years later he even agreed to accept the American party's gubernatorial nomination and in his correspondence came out in favor of what he called "purer nationality" while condemning the use of public funds for sectarian education.[192] But the voters were simply not interested. As a candidate

Lawrence did so poorly that Horace Greeley's New York *Tribune* was able to comment with obvious relish, "Amos A. Lawrence . . . is left so out in the cold that he will one day be obliged to procure affidavits that he was ever a candidate at all."[193]

By then, too, the Panic of 1857 had occurred, requiring Lawrence and many of the Associates to devote much more energy than usual to business. Waltham-Lowell ventures—their earnings already falling—were particularly hard hit.[194] To further complicate matters, discontent among small stockholders had led to a series of embarrassing charges about the high profits earned by sales firms and the size of agents' salaries.[195] Turning from his other activities, Nathan Appleton hurriedly put together his *Introduction of the Power Loom and Origin of Lowell*, a history that he hoped would explain the true causes of "the present . . . depression of the cotton manufacture." In his opinion three factors were to blame: overproduction especially by companies "with inadequate capital"; the wars in China, which had disrupted the market there; and, predictably, "the tariff of 1846."[196]

"Our manufacturing interest is for the present completely broken down and discredited," wrote Lawrence.[197] Still, he continued to search for solid ground in the ever more rapidly swirling maelstrom of sectional conflict around him. Early in January 1859, he wrote Charles Robinson, the governor of Kansas, "We are ready for any sort of combination that will unite the opposition."[198] That "combination" turned out to be yet another new political party, the Constitutional Union party, which was organized at a meeting in Faneuil Hall in December 1859. In March of 1860 the Constitutional Unionists came forward with their candidates and a platform reading simply, "THE CONSTITUTION OF THE COUNTRY, THE UNION OF THE STATES, AND THE ENFORCEMENT OF THE LAWS,"—offered, as Edward Everett put it, "without note or comment."[199] Because of the important role Bay Staters played in forming the new party, second place on the ticket went to Everett, with John Bell of Tennessee as the presidential nominee.

For a while Lawrence held out high hopes for the Constitutional Union party. Once again he agreed to campaign as a gubernatorial candidate in Massachusetts. But his optimism began to fade when his personal choice for the party's presidential nomination, John Crittenden, refused the honor. There were to be other disappointments. The press was less than kind, and despite Lawrence's urging, even many of his conservative friends seemed reluctant to make more than a token effort. Then came the November elections. In Massachusetts and virtually everywhere else across the North, Lincoln and the Republicans carried the day, while most of the South fell to Breckenridge. Nationally none of the candidates received a majority, but

Lincoln did win more than enough electoral votes to guarantee his election. Bell and the Constitutional Unionists, on the other hand, finished a dismal fourth.[200]

Lawrence's worst fears had been realized: party divisions now mirrored the sectional split, with no effective middle ground. In rapid succession events played themselves out much as he had predicted they might. Between November 1860, and February 1861, six slave states responded to the Republican triumph by seceding from the Union and banding together to form the Confederate States of America. In Washington everything was in turmoil, yet from Illinois came word that Lincoln opposed any and all concessions to the South on the major point at issue: the future of slavery in the territories.

The time had come to resist the arrogant demands of the Slave Power: that was Lincoln's opinion, and he did not believe that acting on it would break up the Union. But Lawrence and most of the rest of Boston's conservative business leaders saw things very differently. Convinced that only extraordinary measures could save the Union, they rushed to support a compromise plan, sponsored by Crittenden in Washington, that would have extended the Missouri Compromise line to the Pacific. This time no effort was spared. A huge Union rally was organized in Faneuil Hall, and over twenty thousand signatures were collected on a petition endorsing the Crittenden Compromise. At the end of January, Lawrence, Edward Everett, and Robert Winthrop traveled to Washington to present the petition in person to Crittenden. Finally on February 12, the document, with its vast roll of signatures, was formally laid before the Senate.[201]

It was in every way an earnest undertaking, but also, tragically, a futile one. Even before the petition reached the Senate the three "Union-savers" from Boston had met with Charles Sumner, whose reaction was as blunt as it was devastating. All of their efforts were "mere *wind*—of no more use than a penny whistle in a tempest," as he put it.[202] And of course Sumner was right. The crisis had gone beyond the point where meetings in Faneuil Hall, however large, or judiciously worded petitions, however well supplied with the names of respectable gentlemen from Boston, could resolve it. It was just two months later that Lawrence's father-in-law, William Appleton— having raced South on a last desperate peace mission of his own and arrived in Charleston Harbor only hours before the guns opened fire on Fort Sumter—telegraphed the news to Boston: war had come.[203] Within another month Lawrence was busy coaching his neighbors in the manual of arms and complaining because only 75,000 Union volunteers had been called up, when five times that many were needed.[204] In spite of everything that he and others like him had done to prevent it, war had indeed come, and as always he meant to do his part.

IX

In a season so full of sad disappointments it would have been surprising if Amos A. Lawrence had paid much attention to election returns in individual towns across the state. But the results in one town would surely have caught his attention. In Groton, Massachusetts, with 68 percent of the ballots cast going to John Andrew, the Republican gubernatorial nominee, Lawrence himself had received only thirty-four votes—a mere 7 percent of the total.[205]

What made Groton significant was Lawrence's long association with the place. It was from Groton, after all, that his father and uncles had set out half a century earlier to make their way in the world. Members of the family still visited the Lawrence "homestead" often and continued to contribute generously to the local academy, which had been renamed in their honor. By rights Lawrence could claim to be something of a favorite son in Groton. But just as the family's circumstances had changed enormously in fifty years, Groton too was changing. And therein lay much of the explanation for the way its citizens voted in 1860, including the meager support they gave Lawrence's candidacy.

As late as 1843, anyone familiar with the town in the early years of the century would have found it little altered. The population had grown a bit, but most people still supported themselves by farming. There were a few professional men, and the usual crafts associated with an agricultural economy. The only other activity of note was the business of making palm hats, which earned enterprising farm families some much-needed extra cash. Yet for all its peaceful, timeless character, Groton existed even then as part of a larger world of change. In 1825 the Congregational Church had split, and seven years later a Baptist Society was organized. Boston was still half a day's travel away, but Lowell was much nearer. Then, in 1844, all distances began to shrink dramatically. The Fitchburg Railroad opened regular service through town, and by 1848 the Fitchburg had been joined by three other lines.[206]

The coming of the railroad altered everything. The junction point of the various lines in south Groton became the center of a bustling new community. For the first time significant industry developed. The state census for 1855 listed two paper mills and a plow factory in town.[207] All three were quite small; there were no major resources in Groton to attract Boston capital. But even starting from a modest base, substantial growth was possible. By 1865 the plow factory would be employing 125 workers and $150,000 in capital to manufacture goods worth $200,000.[208] Meanwhile, between 1840 and 1860 the town's population had grown by almost 50 percent, and in 1855 a Catholic mission had opened its doors in south Groton.[209]

In many ways the political shifts occurring in Groton paralleled those elsewhere in the state. In the early 1830s, reflecting the town's position on the periphery of change, the Antimasonic party did quite well, winning over 58 percent of the vote in 1832. No doubt the prevalence of religious dissent also contributed to the Antimasons' appeal. In any case Whiggery soon replaced Antimasonry as the dominant political persuasion, and for the next ten years the Whigs maintained a respectable majority against all comers.[210]

The initial break in the pattern of Whig success in Groton came—as in so many other places—with the rise of organized political antislavery activity. There was no great rush to the new movement; in 1848 the Free Soil gubernatorial candidate won only forty-two votes, just 10 percent of the total.[211] But the source of those votes was more important than their number. All, or almost all, seemed to come from the Whig side, thereby giving the Democrats a plurality, which in turn put the town solidly in the Coalition column for several years. Then as the Coalition declined—as, too, the forces of economic and social change continued to gather momentum in Groton—the majority of voters turned first to the Know-Nothing movement and finally to the Republican party.[212]

A decade of Whig domination, followed by fifteen years of constantly shifting political allegiance—that, broadly speaking, was the direction events took in Groton. And the fact that the second period coincided with a time of rapid change on other fronts suggests that there was indeed a connection; that things like the expanding transportation network, the development of industry, and the growing social and religious diversity of the town directly affected the way Grotonians voted. Also, once the Whig synthesis, with its dual commitment to limited economic development and modest levels of reform activity in areas like antislavery and temperance, had lost its hold on the voters, all attempts to rejuvenate it failed. In essence such a rejuvenation was the goal of both the American party—at least in its later guises—and the Constitutional Union party, and both were roundly rejected at the polls. Not the theme of Union, not popular sovereignty, not even the muted nativism of Amos Lawrence's campaign pronouncements during the late 1850s, succeeded in turning the tide. The citizens of Groton had found other issues to respond to.

Nor did it matter that those issues tended to resist easy synthesis. Under the Coalition, especially at the time of the convention to revise the state constitution, there had been a great deal of talk about reviving "the historical Massachusetts."[213] Similarly Know-Nothingism, with its vision of ethnic and religious homogeneity, seemed to harken back to an earlier, simpler era. Yet when their turn came, the Republicans frankly embraced change, particularly in the economic realm, and a majority in Groton supported all three movements. On one level the contradiction was obvious, but over and against it lay the persistent rejection of Whiggery. As confused as Grotonians may have been about what they wanted, they seemed to understand quite well what they did not want. Somehow in the face of the steadily accelerating social and economic change of those years the Whig party and what it stood for had ceased to appeal to anything more than a handful of voters. The question is why.

One factor, surely, was the failure of conservative Whig leaders to maintain the posture party ideology required of them. In Massachusetts, Whiggery had emerged as a resistance movement, one that responded to deep-seated anxieties in a citizenry poised between a familiar world that was passing and another not yet in place. By directing energies toward combating tyranny and corruption in Andrew Jackson's Washington, the party had given fresh meaning and purpose to political life at all levels. But once the forces of evil were defeated—as the Democrats were in 1840—the case became more complex. Where then did one find villains to resist?

The Conscience Whigs' solution had been to focus on the slaveholders of the South and their taste for territorial expansion. Within Massachusetts this seemed sensible enough, but beyond the borders of the commonwealth it threatened to have serious consequences. Party leaders like Webster and Abbott Lawrence who aspired to national political office could ill afford to alienate Southern Whigs. Nor, as a group, were the Associates willing to risk their interests in a political arena dominated by sectional conflict. Too much depended on the existing order of things in national politics and on the fragile consensus among "like-minded gentlemen" from all parts of the country that maintained it.

But protecting that system cost the Cotton Whigs dearly. Even at relatively low levels, the antislavery vote altered the political balance of power. Worse still, by refusing to take a more forthright stand

against slavery, the conservatives seemed bent on confirming what
their opponents had always charged: that their overriding objective in
politics was safeguarding their own class interests. Indeed, with only
a modest shift in perspective, the Cotton Whigs themselves could
be—and were—made to appear as the villains of the piece.

At the same time—and leading finally to the same result—the
battle against economic privilege was proceeding apace in Massachusetts. Hamstrung for a decade or more by the generally flourishing
condition of the commonwealth's economy, as well as by their own
internal disagreements over economic policy, the Democrats, after
1850, managed to win ever-widening support for measures that had
once excited little enthusiasm among the voters. In part the party
owed its success to union with the Free Soilers, yet the drive for
economic reform did not end with the victories on general incorporation and free banking in 1851, or even with the Coalition's defeat by
the Whigs in 1852. The Know-Nothings and the Republicans continued the trend. In 1854 the General Court approved a $2 million state
loan for building the Hoosac Tunnel.[214] The following year the Bank of
Mutual Redemption applied for and received a charter explicitly em-
powering it to collect the notes of other state banks and present them
for redemption. The service was precisely the one the Associates' own
Suffolk Bank had been performing, albeit without any authorization
in its charter, since 1818. But the stockholders of the Bank of Mutual
Redemption represented country banking interests, and they argued
that the Suffolk—lacking any state sanction for its practices—had
been engaged in what amounted to a criminal conspiracy. In time the
new institution's aggressive tactics and less restrictive approach led
the Suffolk to abandon the field altogether.[215]

Like general incorporation and free banking, state aid to the Hoosac
Tunnel and the establishment of the Bank of Mutual Redemption had
as their objective opening previously blocked avenues of economic
enterprise. What they all had in common was a thrust toward expansion. In much the same way, on the national level the Republican
party keyed its campaign promises to what would encourage growth,
and growth without the limits and restraints that had figured so
prominently in Whig ideology. In a place like Groton, too, policies
that encouraged continued, rapid, unrestrained growth had become
crucial. Success did not come easily for an enterprise like the town's
plow factory, undercapitalized, short of skilled labor, and forced to
compete with dozens of similar firms. The company was reorganized
three times before 1864, twice because the owners were forced to
sell.[216] It continued to grow only because the larger economy was
expanding, and on that expansion its survival depended.

Whether in the end the voters of Groton were more moved by the Republican party's opposition to slavery or its commitment to economic expansion is difficult to tell. The election returns for the town suggest that antislavery sentiment alone was not strong enough to change more than one in ten votes. But by another reckoning the question was moot, because the Republicans did make a point both of opposing slavery and of favoring expansionist economic policies. And on the second count, if not the first, their position on issues stood in stark contrast to that of the town's sometime-leading-citizen, Amos A. Lawrence.

Faced with serious problems of his own in the Waltham-Lowell system, Lawrence might have been expected to understand the anxieties of a Groton plow manufacturer. If nothing else the Republicans' tariff plank promised a welcome boost for falling textile prices. But just as he held aloof from Republicanism despite his abiding antipathy to slavery, Lawrence proved immune to the lure of higher Waltham-Lowell dividends implicit in the Republican platform. If those dividends were to come at the cost of unbridled economic expansion, evidently the price was too high.

Decades earlier, of course, Lawrence's father and uncles, along with the rest of the Associates, had made a similar choice. Over time the Waltham-Lowell system and the network of institutions that sustained it had grown and changed a great deal, but profits had never been more than a means to an end. Above all, it was to maximize the security and prestige of a particular group that the system had been established, and forty-five years later Lawrence seemed as thoroughly wedded to that vision as Francis Cabot Lowell had been. The difference was that time and events had stripped away much that obscured the true character of the vision. By 1861 the distance separating the Associates' interests from those of the great majority of their fellow citizens could hardly have been clearer. Faster, cheaper transportation, easier credit, higher tariffs—every one was of vital significance in Groton. To refuse to support them, as the Associates did, was to stand in the way of economic progress as surely as Southerners blocked moral progress by insisting that slavery be protected in the territories.

So the Associates were relegated to the ranks of the enemy, placed side by side with the likes of Preston Brooks and William Lowndes Yancy: the money power and the Slave Power. And the most Amos A. Lawrence could do in response was talk of the Union, a theme that held limited interest for voters wondering when the next bank would open in town or when the next railroad might reach them. In the midst of the campaign of 1860, the editors of the *Springfield Republican* had remarked of the Constitutional Union party's platform: "It might as well have taken the multiplication table and the decalogue for its platform as the Constitution and the Union."[217] The point was that no one disputed the importance of the Union, but neither was there any concerted movement in Massachusetts to abandon it. As an issue, the Union was simply irrelevant. Yet it was all the Associates had to offer—the ultimate abstraction, the sum total of everything that a group of anxious gentlemen could not afford to say.

So too with the political style the group continued to favor throughout the mounting turmoil of the 1850s. Oratory in the manner made famous by Daniel Webster, meetings in Faneuil Hall, petitions to Congress—such were the devices of a politics peculiarly tailored to the interests and talents of a self-conscious elite determined to command events to suit its own purposes, but by 1860 those devices had lost much of their ability to move the electorate. Instead, the shape of events was being hammered out in places like the Wigwam in Chicago, where the Republicans had held their national convention in 1860, there and in hundreds of editorial offices across the country where, thanks to the telegraph, news of Lincoln's nomination arrived within moments of the event itself. The fact that in time Lincoln achieved his own fame as an orator was ironic, but it hardly altered the case.

Similarly, a far greater irony—that four long years of civil war were about to give totally new meaning and substance to "the Union"—would change nothing, at least as far as the Associates were concerned. The group's political power was gone, and not even the tragedy of the "Brothers' War" could restore it.

Epilogue: The World They Made

In the Panic of 1857 five Waltham-Lowell companies failed—the Middlesex, the Bay State Mills, the Pemberton Mills, the Lawrence Machine Shop, and the Hadley Falls Company. Several others, including the Lyman Mills and the Hampden Mills at Holyoke and the Atlantic Cotton Mills and the Pacific Mills at Lawrence, came close to failing. Also, two of the four largest selling agents, Lawrence, Stone and Company and Charles H. Mills and Company, went bankrupt. From there the damage rippled outward, touching even as prudently managed an enterprise as the Massachusetts Hospital Life Insurance Company, which eventually had to write off several of its largest loans, among them those to Samuel Lawrence, brother of Amos and Abbott.[1]

During the Civil War, companies that could find supplies of raw cotton or had stockpiled them earlier did much better. In 1863 dividends of 25 percent were not unusual. Profits remained high in the five years after the War, too.[2] Still, one thing had become clear as directors, treasurers, and agents struggled to save what they could in the dark days of 1858: Waltham-Lowell ventures no longer enjoyed any charmed immunity from hard times. They faced the same risks other businesses did—were in fact quite like other businesses, except for their heavy concentration in what had grown to be an especially vulnerable industry. All of this could hardly have been farther from the intentions of the men who founded the system.

But by then most of the founders were gone. Francis Cabot Lowell had been dead for forty years, and Amos and Abbott Lawrence had both died earlier in the decade. Among the survivors, Nathan Appleton continued to play a leading role right up to his death in 1861. A few of the younger generation also remained active in the textile industry—notably Amos A. Lawrence and John Amory Lowell and his son Augustus. Yet most of the Associates' children chose other careers, and in time they, or those who made such decisions for them, were more likely to invest their money in other ways—in railroads or Western mining ventures, for example, or, later in the century, the telephone.[3]

Thus neither as a reliable investment outlet, nor as a means of defining group identity, did the Waltham-Lowell system outlast the Civil War. And on other fronts the hopes of the founders proved just as misplaced. The downward spiral of working conditions, and even more the quality of life in places like Lowell and Lawrence, continued in the years after 1850. An especially grim example of the general trend occurred at Lawrence in 1860. On January 10, while in full operation, the five-story Pemberton Mill collapsed to the ground in a matter of seconds, trapping hundreds of workers in the rubble. Then, as rescue efforts were proceeding, fire broke out. Ultimately 88 people lost their lives, and 116 others were seriously injured. A subsequent investigation identified a group of defective iron columns on the top floor of the mill as the cause of the disaster, but the investigation also revealed that the defect had first been noticed as early as 1854.[4]

The constant preoccupation with holding down costs that led to an incident like the one at the Pemberton Mill; the steady growth of a permanent labor force, largely propertyless and openly exploited; urban crowding, squalor, and disease: one by one they had been allowed to take their toll on everything that once had seemed so novel and promising at Waltham. Very simply, as an experiment in developing a distinctive kind of industrialization—one that combined modern factory production with the familiar patterns of traditional society—the Waltham-Lowell system was dead, the victim of a process of change the relentless logic of which the Associates chose, finally, not to resist.

Of course in their own defense they could have claimed—as Nathan Appleton did in 1858[5]—that many of the difficulties which befell their experiment stemmed from choices made by others. Had fewer people entered the textile industry, the consequences might have been different: without the tremendous growth in capacity that occurred after 1845, prices would doubtless have remained higher, perhaps reducing the pressure on owners and managers to monitor costs so closely. But the drive that led to the building of so many cotton mills across the North was part and parcel of the drive that shaped the entire process of industrialization in America. The profits were there for the taking; having demonstrated as much themselves, the Associates were in no position to deny those profits to others.

Equally futile was the attempt to hold down the overall rate of industrial development through government action—or inaction. The Associates tried that, and the only result was to cost the group its political power. For there was also a logic inherent in democratic politics; one that precluded confining to any very small group opportunities so attractive. In Massachusetts the turning point came as early as 1851. Thereafter there was no restraining the forces of change, or at any rate government could not be used to that end. On the contrary, in the eyes of most voters the proper role of the state had become to encourage and facilitate, in every way possible, the continued growth and expansion of the economy.

By any obvious standard, then, the Waltham-Lowell system failed to live up to the expectations of its founders. Despite the striking successes of the period up to 1845, the years afterward told an altogether different story. Indeed, with so many elements of the original vision already inoperative a decade and a half later, it is worth asking what—if anything—survived. The answer, surprisingly, is that a great deal survived. Because in the final analysis the Associates had achieved, for both themselves and their descendants, what had always mattered most: a secure and remarkably durable position at the top of the social order.

Despite its shortcomings, too, the Waltham-Lowell system was by no means irrelevant to that achievement. If the system failed to meet the test as a permanent investment vehicle, building the great mills and the network of institutions that supported them had still taught invaluable lessons, above all in the handling of capital. The key was the corporate form, providing as it did both an organizational structure and a way of pooling very large sums of money for the purposes of investment. The flexibility of the corporate form— its capacity to grow or contract as conditions warranted and the ease with which shares could be passed from individual to individual, even between generations, without attendant risk to the business itself—was also crucial.

In building the Waltham-Lowell system, the Associates had used every one of these features, yet it was in an enterprise like the Massachusetts Hospital Life Insurance Company that they gave the corporate form its fullest development. An investment trust for safeguarding private fortunes, a corporation that functioned by channeling capital to other corporations, the Hospital Life Insurance Company was an extraordinarily modern venture. As long as it favored the textile industry with so large a share of its investment funds, the potential of the arrangement was only partially fulfilled, but in time the officers of the company adopted a much broader strategy. As a result, it and other firms that followed its lead would help keep Boston one of the nation's prime sources of investment capital decade after decade, down to the present day. Throughout, the goal would be the free flow of pooled resources to areas of the maximum opportunity consistent with prudent management.

Meanwhile, as some of the leading beneficiaries of the skill and ingenuity of Boston's money managers, the Associates' children—to say nothing of their grandchildren and great-grandchildren—were free to arrange their lives as they chose. Since money was seldom a problem, large families remained the rule. Often, in each generation one son would enter business. Amos A. Lawrence, for example, had seven children, including two sons, the oldest of whom, Amory, followed his father as head of Lawrence and Company, the successor firm to A. and A. Lawrence. The second son, William, became Episcopal bishop of Massachusetts. Of the daughters, one married an Amory, one a Brooks, one a Loring, one a Cunningham, and one a Hemenway. Two of the sons-in-law were lawyers and one was a doctor, while the other two were described simply as "country gentlemen" by William Lawrence in his autobiography, *Memories of a Happy Life*. Of the two lawyers, one became a Supreme Court justice. Of the two "country gentlemen," one donated a gymnasium to Harvard.[6] All seven of the Lawrence children and their spouses, according to Bishop William, "tried throughout life to do their part by hard work, home-care, and public service."[7]

As it happened, much of the "hard work" and "public service" remained concentrated within a fairly narrow geographical area. After a happy childhood spent at his parents' "Cottage Farm" in Brookline and enlivened by the visits of luminaries like Charles Sumner and the Prince of Wales, William Lawrence himself attended Harvard and then studied for the ministry. His first parish—as it would be his son's—was Grace Church in Lawrence, Massachusetts, where he did what he could to improve working conditions in the mills. Next he went to Cambridge to take the Chair of Homilectics and Pastoral Care at the Episcopal Theological School. A few years later he became dean of the school and then, in 1893, at the age of forty-three, was consecrated bishop, a post he held for over thirty years and in which he was followed by his son-in-law, Charles L. Slattery.

Apart from his duties in the diocese, Lawrence devoted the lion's share of his energies to Harvard. At various times he served his alma mater as Preacher to the University, Chief Marshal at his twenty-fifth reunion, president of the Council of the *Harvard Graduates' Magazine*, president of the Alumni Association, and Overseer. In 1913, while Abbott Lawrence Lowell—the grandson of John Amory Lowell and Abbott Lawrence, and the brother of Amy, the poet, and Percival, the astronomer—was serving as president of the university, the Fellows of the Corporation elected Lawrence one of their number. Both before and afterward he was indefatigable in raising money for Harvard. One of his greatest successes was the campaign for funds to house the business school, an assignment he was pleased to accept out of "loyalty to the business traditions of my family and a conviction that this was a real missionary enterprise for the welfare of the country."[8]

Like his own parents, Lawrence had seven children, five daughters and two sons, both of whom found careers in the church. Except when his normal routine was interrupted by trips abroad, he spent the spring and autumn in Cambridge, winters in Boston, and the months of July and August at Bar Harbor, where he was one of the earliest members of the summer colony. There, in a rambling house that slept twenty-seven, the family would gather year after year—aunts, uncles, cousins, children, and grandchildren. A man of principle, Lawrence added his name to the appeal for a review of the verdict in the Sacco-Vanzetti trial. During his lifetime he received honorary degrees from no fewer than ten different colleges and universities, including Harvard, Yale, Princeton, and Cambridge in England. When he died at the age of ninety-one, he had just completed another major fund-raising campaign, this time for the Massachusetts General Hospital.

An Episcopal bishop who considered raising money for graduate education in business administration "a real missionary enterprise for the welfare of the country"—of such gentle anomalies were the lives of the Associates' descendants composed. In popular imagination they became "Proper Bostonians" or "Boston Brahmins," with their eccentricities and prejudices the subject of countless anecdotes.[9] In reality most of the anecdotes were apocryphal; at least according to historian Samuel Eliot Morison, himself a descendant of Harrison Gray Otis, a member of the Associates group. Rather, Morison suggests, what has most distinguished Boston's leading families—or those he knew as a young boy—from the rich of other American cities is their willingness to be content with wealth of relatively modest proportions and their tradition of service to society. "When a family had accumulated a certain fortune, instead of trying to build it up still further to become a Rockefeller or Carnegie or Huntington and then perhaps discharge its debt to society by some great foundation, it would step out of business or finance and try to accomplish something in literature, education, medical research, the arts, or public service."[10]

To a point such an analysis is correct, certainly. As time passed, the fortunes the Associates accumulated were to be increasingly dwarfed by those earned elsewhere. The tradition of service in Boston, too, as Digby Baltzell points out, has run especially deep.[11] But the institutional arrangements that pool and preserve Boston capital, and structure its transmission from generation to generation, are not at all unique. Neither is the control of certain key charitable, cultural, and educational institutions by a self-conscious elite—the sturdy foundation that still sustains so much of the city's tradition of service. Over the years the two together, operating in tandem, have become the norm in American society. Written into law and accepted by the public at large, they are in fact the principal means by which the existence of wealth is justified and finally sanctioned in the United States.

And it was the Associates who, more than any other single group of individuals, created that system. To be sure, someone like Amos Lawrence was far less wealthy than a Morgan or a Rockefeller, but Rockefeller himself understood full well what he owed Bishop Lawrence's forebears and gratefully acknowledged the debt. In 1917 the founder of Standard Oil and the Rockefeller Foundation remarked: "How clearly I remember reading when I was a boy The Life of Amos Lawrence [sic], the philanthropist. My employer gave me the book. I was sixteen years old . . . The Life of Amos Lawrence was a great inspiration to me."[12]

The accumulation of wealth, the cultivation of an appropriately modest style of life, the careful shepherding of family capital while most surplus income was given away to fund worthwhile projects— those were the lessons that a Rockefeller could learn from a Lawrence. The natural momentum of industrial development accomplished the rest—that and a political system prepared to accept the consequences. Nor was there any need for constant political activity by the wealthy to defend their own interests, at least as long as the necessary opportunities *seemed* to be available to everyone alike.

The Associates had assumed otherwise, but as it turned out, the loosening of restraints on economic expansion—the change they tried so hard to prevent—was anything but the opening skirmish in a concerted drive to redistribute wealth. Such an effort, after all, was no more likely to appeal to the struggling capitalists of Adams or Groton than it did to Nathan Appleton. Only much more slowly, in this century, have redistributive policies taken hold, and current American tax laws still grant highly preferential treatment to strategies aimed at the accumulation of capital in private hands. The laws are especially lenient, too, when it comes to funds earmarked for philanthropic purposes. Arguably, the Associates could have saved themselves the trouble and bothered less with politics. But as children of an earlier age, they persisted in believing that any gains made in this life had to be paid for by someone else's losses. For the most part their successors in the ranks of the very rich have adopted a more relaxed attitude, or at any rate have understood that such calculations are not so easily made in our own day, when great wealth has long since been transmuted from the solider stuff of land and merchants' cargoes into a miragelike tangle of impermanent values afloat on an ocean of paper, or—more illusive still—flickering across the display screens of innumerable computer terminals.

Beyond that, however, the line runs straight from Amos Lawrence to John D. Rockefeller to John Paul Getty. For better or worse, the world the Associates made is with us still.

Selected Business Corporations in Which the Boston Associates Were Active, 1813–1865

Associates	Textiles	Railroads	Banking	Insurance	M.H.L.I.
Amory, W.	Amoskeag Jackson Manchester Nashua Stark		Columbian	National	Direc.
Andrews, E.T.	Cocheco			Manufacturers Mass. Mutual	
Appleton, E.	Hamilton Merrimack Perkins				
Appleton, N.	Amoskeag Appleton Boott Boston Cabot Essex Hamilton Lawrence Manchester Merrimack Prescott Stark		Boston Suffolk		Pres. Direc. Fin. Com.
Appleton, S.	Appleton Hamilton Suffolk			American Boston	Vice P.
Appleton, W.	Amoskeag Appleton Chicopee Cocheco Dwight	Boston & Providence	Hamilton Suffolk	Boston	Vice P.

Associates	Textiles	Railroads	Banking	Insurance	M.H.L.I.
Appleton, W. *cont.*	Hamilton Lawrence Merrimack Perkins Stark Suffolk Tremont				
Batchelder, S.	Hamilton Laconia York				
Bond, G.	Cocheco				
Boott, J.W.	Hamilton Merrimack		Suffolk		
Boott, K.	Boott Merrimack				
Bowditch, N.	Merrimack				Direc. Actuary
Bromfield, J.	Appleton				
Brooks, E.	Boston		Merchants		
Brooks, P.C.	Cabot				Pres. Vice P.
Brooks, P.C., Jr.	Chicopee				Pres. Vice P.
Cabot, H.	Boott Cabot Chicopee Perkins Suffolk		Hamilton		
Cabot, R.C.	Lowell				
Cabot, S.	Cabot Dwight Perkins		Boston		
Cary, T.G.	Appleton Hamilton		Hamilton		
Chadwick, E.	Atlantic Hamilton Laconia Merrimack	Boston & Lowell	Suffolk	Merchants	Direc. Fin. Com.
Cotting, U.	Boston				
Crocker, S.	Hopewell Taunton				
Dean, O.	Manchester				
Dutton, W.	Boott Boston Hamilton Merrimack				
Dwight, E.	Cabot Chicopee	Western			

Associates	Textiles	Railroads	Banking	Insurance	M.H.L.I.
	Dwight				
	Hopewell				
	Taunton				
	Whittendon				
	York				
Edmands, J.W.	Atlantic		Suffolk	Merchants National	Direc.
Eliot, S.A.	Hopewell Whittendon				Vice P.
Francis, E.	Appleton Cocheco		Hamilton Suffolk	Mass. Mutual	Vice P. Direc.
Frothingham, S.	Manchester	Taunton Branch		National	
Gardiner, W.H.	Dwight			National	
Goodwin, O.	Massachusetts Perkins			National	
Gore, J.	Boston				
Gorham, B.	Boston Boott Merrimack				
Hallet, G.	Tremont				Direc.
Henshaw, S.	Stark	Conn. River	Merchants		
Howe, J.C.	Manchester		Boston		
Jackson, C.	Boston Lowell				Vice P.
Jackson, J.	Boston Lowell				
Jackson, P.T.	Amoskeag Appleton Boston Essex Great Falls Hadley Falls Hamilton Lowell Merrimack Prescott		Suffolk		Direc. Fin. Com.
Kuhn, G.	Boott Cabot Dwight Perkins			National New England Mutual	Direc.
Lawrence, Abbott	Boott Essex Massachusetts Tremont York		Hamilton Suffolk	Merchants	Direc. Fin. Com.
Lawrence, Amos	Tremont York		Suffolk	Boston	Direc. Fin. Com.

Associates	Textiles	Railroads	Banking	Insurance	M.H.L.I.
Lawrence, Amos A.	Essex		Suffolk		Direc.
Lawrence, S.	Essex				
Lee, J.	Hamilton				
Lee, T.	Lowell				
Livermore, I.	Manchester		City	National	
Lloyd, J.	Boston				
Lowell, F.C.	Boston				
Lowell, F.C., Jr.	Amoskeag Manchester Merrimack Stark			New England Mutual	Direc. Actuary
Lowell, J., Jr.	Appleton Hamilton Merrimack				Vice P. Direc.
Lowell, J.A.	Amoskeag Appleton Boott Boston Essex Hamilton Massachusetts	Boston & Lowell	Suffolk	Merchants National Mass. Mutual	Direc.
Lyman, G.W.	Appleton Boott Cabot Chicopee Essex Hadley Falls Hamilton Lowell Perkins Stark Suffolk	Boston & Lowell	Columbian		Pres. Vice P.
Lyman, T.	Essex				Vice P. Direc.
Mills, C.H.	Whittendon			American	Direc.
Mills, J.K.	Amoskeag Cabot Hadley Falls Hopewell	Boston & Providence Taunton Branch	Merchants		
Moody, P.	Boston Hamilton Merrimack				
Motley, T.	Hamilton				Vice P. Direc.
Nichols, B.R.	Lawrence Tremont		Suffolk	National	Direc.
Otis, H.G.	Cabot Chicopee			Boston	Vice P.

Associates	Textiles	Railroads	Banking	Insurance	M.H.L.I.
	Hopewell				
	Taunton				
Parker, D.P.	Appleton				Direc.
					Fin. Com.
Perkins, J.	Lowell				
Perkins, T.H.	Appleton			Boston	Vice P.
	Cabot				
	Dwight				
	Lowell				
Pratt, G.W.	Boott	Taunton			
	Tremont	Branch			
Pratt, W.	Hamilton				Vice P.
	Tremont				
Prescott, W.H.	Hamilton			Boston	Pres.
	Taunton				Direc.
Sargent, I.	Cabot	Conn. River	Globe	Boston	Direc.
	Chicopee				Fin. Com.
	Dwight				
	Hadley Falls				
	Perkins				
Sayles, W.	Manchester		Hamilton	National	
	Stark				
Sears, D.	Jackson				Vice P.
	Manchester				
	Nashua				
	Tremont				
Storrow, C.S.	Essex				
Sturgis, W.	Appleton	Boston &			Direc.
	Dwight	Lowell			Fin. Com.
	Hamilton	Boston &			
	Lowell	Providence			
	Perkins				
	Prescott				
Thorndike, I.	Appleton				
	Boston				
	Cabot				
	Hamilton				
	Lowell				
	Taunton				
	Thorndike				
Thorndike, I., Jr.	Appleton				Vice P.
	Boston				
	Cabot				
	Hamilton				
	Lowell				
	Taunton				
Tilden, J.	Amoskeag	Boston &	Columbian	Boston	Vice P.
	Suffolk	Lowell			Direc.
					Actuary

Associates	Textiles	Railroads	Banking	Insurance	M.H.L.I.
Wales, T.B.	Tremont	Nashua & Lowell Taunton Branch Western			Vice P.
Whitney, W.	Lowell			National	
Wolcott, J.H.	Boott				Vice P.

Sources: Vera Shlakman, *Economic History of a Factory Town: A Study of Chicopee, Massachusetts* (Northampton, 1935), pp. 39–42 and 243–247; Caroline F. Ware, *The Early New England Cotton Manufacture: A Study in Industrial Beginnings* (Boston, 1931), pp. 320–321; and Gerald T. White, *A History of the Massachusetts Hospital Life Insurance Company* (Cambridge, Mass., 1955), pp. 69 and 169–175.

Textiles. Listed are those companies in which the individuals in question were active as original stockholders, directors, and/or officers up to 1850.

Railroads. Listed are those lines operating in Massachusetts in which the individuals in question held directorships in the following years: The Boston and Lowell, 1847; the Boston and Providence, 1847; the Connecticut River, 1848; the Nashua and Lowell, 1847; the Taunton Branch, 1849; and the Western, 1837.

Banking. Listed are those Boston banks in which the individuals in question held directorships in 1848. Also included for the Suffolk Bank are the original directors (1818) and for the Hamilton Bank the directorate of 1831.

Insurance. Listed are those companies in which the individuals in question held directorships in 1846–47.

M.H.L.I. (Massachusetts Hospital Life Insurance Company). Listed are the positions held by the individuals in question from the founding of the company to 1865. Included are presidents, vice presidents, directors, members of the finance committee, and actuaries.

Notes

Abbreviations of manuscript collections cited throughout the notes to this book are: BL, Baker Library, Harvard Business School; MHS, Massachusetts Historical Society.

Introduction to Part I

1. Fernand Braudel, "Toward a Historical Economics," in Braudel's *On History* (Chicago, 1980), p. 84. It is one of the primary tasks of history, Braudel argues, to place such events "within the framework of a variety of contradictory possibilities, among which life finally made its choice." He continues: "For one possibility which was fulfilled, there were tens, hundreds, thousands, which disappeared . . . We must nonetheless somehow try to reintroduce them, because these vanishing movements are the multiple material and immaterial forces which have at every moment put the brakes on the great forward impetuses of evolution . . . It is indispensable that we know them."

1. Yankee Abroad

1. The best contemporary account of the development of the Waltham-Lowell system is Nathan Appleton's *Introduction of The Power Loom and Origin of Lowell* (Lowell, 1858). Caroline Ware's *Early New England Cotton Manufacture: A Study in Industrial Origins* (Boston, 1931), if not satisfactory in all respects, remains the clearest and most comprehensive scholarly treatment. Other works dealing with the subject are: Samuel Batchelder, *Introduction and Early Progress of the Cotton Manufacture in the United States* (Boston, 1863); John M. Chudd, *The Chicopee Manufacturing Company, 1823–1915* (Wilmington, 1974); John P. Coolidge, *Mill and Mansion: A Study of Architecture and Society in Lowell, Massachusetts, 1820–1865* (New York, 1942); David B. Cole, *Immigrant City: Lawrence, Massachusetts, 1845–1921* (Chapel Hill, 1963); George S. Gibb, *Saco-*

Lowell Shops: Textile Machinery Building in New England, 1813–1949 (Cambridge, Mass., 1950); Constance Green, *Holyoke, Massachusetts: Case History of the Industrial Revolution* (New Haven, 1939); Evelyn H. Knowlton, *Pepperell's Progress: The History of a Cotton Textile Company, 1844–1945* (Cambridge, Mass., 1948); Paul F. McGouldrick, *New England Textiles in the Nineteenth Century: Profits and Investment* (Cambridge, Mass., 1968); Vera Shlakman, *Economic History of a Factory Town: A Study of Chicopee, Massachusetts* (Northampton, 1935); Robert V. Spalding, "Boston Merchantile Community and the Promotion of the Textile Industry in New England, 1813–1860" (Ph.D. diss., Yale University, 1963); and Thomas Young, *American Cotton Industry* (London, 1902). On labor see especially Thomas Dublin, *Women at Work: The Transformation of Work and Community in Lowell, Massachusetts, 1826–1860* (New York, 1979) and Hannah Josephson, *Golden Threads: New England Mill Girls and Magnates* (New York, 1949).

There is no full-length biography of Francis Cabot Lowell. Ferris Greenslet's, *The Lowells and Their Seven Worlds* (Boston, 1946), which takes as its subject the family as a whole, contains some interesting leads, but the fullest treatment so far of Lowell's pioneering role in the textile industry is Robert Sobel's "Francis Cabot Lowell: The Patrician as Factory Master" in Sobel's *Entrepreneurs: Explorations within the American Business Tradition* (New York, 1974). See also Francis C. Lowell, "Address," in *Exercises at the Seventy-Fifth Anniversary of the Incorporation of the Town of Lowell* (Lowell, 1901).

2. Appleton, *Introduction of the Power Loom*, pp. 7–9. Evidently Lowell found a ready listener in Appleton, who was soon speaking in highly favorable terms of the prospects for textile manufacturing in the United States. Frances W. Gregory, *Nathan Appleton, Merchant and Entrepreneur, 1779–1861* (Charlottesville, 1975), pp. 70–71 and 141–146.

3. See Greenslet, *The Lowells*, particularly pp. 3–160.

4. The career of Thomas Hutchinson affords an especially striking example. See Bernard Bailyn, *The Ordeal of Thomas Hutchinson* (Cambridge, Mass., 1974). For a study of the corresponding phenomenon as it occurred in the outports of New England, and involved the Lowells specifically, see Benjamin W. Labaree, *Patriots and Partisans* (Cambridge, Mass., 1962), pp. 1–93.

On the place of merchants in colonial society, other valuable sources are, Bernard Bailyn, *New England Merchants of the Seventeenth Century* (Cambridge, Mass., 1955); James Henretta, "Economic Development and Social Structure in Colonial Boston," *William and Mary Quarterly*, 3rd ser., 22 (1965), 75–92; Alice H. Jones, "Wealth Estimates for the New England Colonies About 1770," *Journal of Economic History*, 32 (1972), 98–127; Allan Kulikoff, "The Progress of Inequality in Revolutionary Boston," *William and Mary Quarterly*, 3rd ser., 28 (1971), 375–441; and Jackson Turner Main, *The Social Structure of Revolutionary America* (Princeton, 1965).

5. The most comprehensive study of New England maritime commerce during the period remains Samuel Eliot Morison's *Maritime History of Massachusetts, 1783–1860* (Boston, 1921). See also Gregory, *Nathan Appleton*, pp. 13–137; Labaree, *Patriots and Partisans*; Kenneth W. Porter, *The Jacksons and the Lees: Two Generations of Massachusetts Merchants, 1765–1844*, 2 vols.

(Cambridge, Mass., 1973); and Carl Seaburg and Stanley Paterson, *Merchant Prince of Boston: Colonel T. H. Perkins, 1764–1854* (Cambridge, Mass., 1971).

6. Porter, *Jacksons and Lees*, I, 120 and 699–714. The cause of the firm's failure was overexpansion in the trade with India.

7. Lowell to Patrick Jackson, Nov. 16, 1811, Francis C. Lowell MSS, MHS.

8. Ibid.

9. Greenslet, *The Lowells*, pp. 81–82.

10. Lowell to William Cabot, May 29, 1811, Francis C. Lowell MSS, MHS.

11. Lowell to William Cabot, Jan. 2, 1812, Francis C. Lowell MSS, MHS.

12. Appleton to Eben Appleton, July 24, 1802, Nathan Appleton MSS, MHS.

Two important studies of early American responses to industrialization and its consequences are Thomas Bender, *Toward an Urban Vision: Ideas and Institutions in Nineteenth-Century America* (Lexington, 1975), which contains several chapters discussing the Waltham-Lowell system, and Leo Marx's wonderfully insightful *The Machine in the Garden: Technology and the Pastoral Ideal in America* (New York, 1964). On Jefferson's ideas in particular see Merrill Peterson's *Thomas Jefferson and the New Nation: A Biography* (New York, 1970).

13. For the details of Owen's life and thought see D. H. Cole, *Robert Owen* (Boston, 1925); and J. F. C. Harrison, *Quest for the New Moral World: Robert Owen and the Owenites in Britain and America* (New York, 1969).

Despite the superficial similarities, most recent scholars agree that New Lanark and Owen's ideas played little if any role in shaping the Waltham-Lowell system. See, for example, Bender, *Urban Vision*, pp. 35–36. However Gregory, in *Nathan Appleton*, reaches the opposite conclusion (see p. 45). As far as I know, no one else has ever attempted to determine what other Scottish examples—apart from New Lanark—might have influenced Lowell.

14. Appleton, Journal of 1810, Sept. 29, Nathan Appleton MSS, MHS. Visitors were not permitted in the buildings at New Lanark, but Appleton was able to see a certain amount through the windows.

15. See Robert Owen, *Statement Regarding the New Lanark Establishment* (Edinburgh, 1812).

16. Greenslet, *The Lowells*, pp. 94, 115, 132–133, and 148–149. On the intellectual community of which Charles Lowell was a member see Speculative Society of Edinburgh, *The History of the Speculative Society, 1764–1904* (Edinburgh, 1905) and Frances Hawes, *Henry Brougham: A Nineteenth-Century Portrait* (London, 1957).

17. The "memorandum" is undated and unsigned, but was obviously written by Charles Lowell. Francis C. Lowell MSS, MHS.

18. Lowell to William Cabot, May 29, 1811, Francis C. Lowell MSS, MHS.

19. Ibid.

20. In the following discussion I have relied particularly heavily on the information and analysis in N. T. Phillipson and Rosalind Mitchison, eds., *Scotland in the Age of Improvement: Essays in Scottish History in the Eighteenth Century* (Edinburgh, 1970). In addition see Roy H. Campbell, *Scotland Since 1707: The Rise of an Industrial Society* (New York, 1965); Anand Chitnis, *The*

Scottish Enlightenment: A Social History (London, 1976); James E. Handley, *The Agricultural Revolution in Scotland* (Glasgow, 1963); Henry Hamilton, *The Industrial Revolution in Scotland* (New York, 1966); Stewart Mechie, *The Church and Scottish Social Development, 1780–1870* (New York, 1960); John Prebble, *The Highland Clearances* (London, 1963); T. C. Smout, "Scottish Landowners and Economic Growth, 1650–1850," *Scottish Journal of Political Economy*, 11 (1964), 218–234.

Two other helpful sources, though they deal primarily with developments in England, are G. E. Mingay, *English Landed Society in the Eighteenth Century* (London, 1963); and Francis M. L. Thompson, *English Landed Society in the Nineteenth Century* (London, 1963). Also, here and elsewhere I have been much influenced by Lawrence Stone's work on the English landed elite. See Stone, *The Crisis of the Aristocracy, 1558–1641* (Oxford, 1965); and Lawrence Stone and Jeanne C. Fawtier Stone, *An Open Elite? England, 1540–1880* (Oxford, 1984).

21. Anne Grant, *Letters from the Mountains: Being the Real Correspondence of a Lady, Between the Years 1773 and 1807* (Boston, 1809), pp. 60–69.

22. "Memorandum respecting persons in Edinburgh," Francis C. Lowell MSS, MHS.

23. David Steuart Erskine, *The Earl of Buchan's Address to the Americans at Edinburgh on Washington's Birth-day, February 22d. 1811* (Edinburgh, 1811), pp. 7–8.

24. *Dictionary of National Biography*, s.v. "Erskine, David Steuart."

25. See T. C. Smout, "The Landowner and the Planned Village in Scotland, 1730–1830," in Phillipson and Mitchison, *Scotland in the Age of Improvement*, pp. 73–106. Among other things Smout points out how closely many of Robert Owen's schemes "fitted into the Scottish scene where he must have formulated them in the first place," to which he adds: "It was as though Owen had taken the landed preconceptions, added a dash of relish of his own, and turned them into a menacing and idealistic parody of what the landowners themselves intended." But Smout also considers the search for such connections "something of a red-herring," arguing: "Few landowners were philosophers, still fewer were conscious Utopians: most were practical men concerned, for reasons which seemed to them good and sufficient, with laying out and developing actual villages in the Scottish countryside." Ibid., pp. 80–81.

26. Sir John Sinclair, quoted in ibid., p. 79.

27. John Cockburn, quoted in ibid., p. 86.

28. Sir John Sinclair, quoted in ibid., p. 90.

29. "Memorandum respecting persons in Edinburgh," Francis C. Lowell MSS, MHS.

30. The phrase has been used as the title of a fine monograph on the subject: Eric Richards, *The Leviathan of Wealth: The Sutherland Fortune in the Industrial Revolution* (London, 1973). On the development of the Scottish properties in particular see pp. 149–297. In his analysis Richards tries to present a balanced view that avoids the extremes found in previous treatments, which he describes as follows: "The Sutherland policies are seen as *either* the draco-

nian, class-oriented actions of an alien aristocrat who sacrificed a dependent peasantry in the ruthless pursuit of capitalistic profits *or* the misinterpreted benevolence of an ideal landlord who was willing to forfeit his short-term ends in order to undertake his paternalistic duty of ameliorating the plight of his famine-doomed tenantry" (p. 160).

As Richards explains, the particular problem the Sutherland family confronted was that the income from the Bridgewater Canal had been settled on the Marquis of Stafford for a single generation only. The goal, therefore, was to use current resources to create additional sources of income for subsequent generations, and the strategies adopted to that end included extensive participation in railroad-building projects and the development of the countess's Scottish estates. Ultimately the goal was not achieved. The railroad investments returned their cost too slowly, and "economic expansion in Sutherland," Richards argues, "was largely frustrated by objective environmental conditions which were mostly created outside the region" (p. 297).

31. Lowell to Mrs. Samuel Gardner, July 5, 1811, Francis C. Lowell MSS, MHS. Queen Victoria is reputed to have said on visiting Stafford House in London, "I have come from my house to your palace." See Richards, *Leviathan of Wealth*, p. 17.

32. Richards, *Leviathan of Wealth*, p. 196. Richards is careful to point out that Stafford and his agents fully expected that, in addition to receiving the displaced tenants, the coastal settlements would, in time, contribute substantially to the estate's rental income.

T. C. Smout describes Helmsdale, one of the Sutherland villages, as an "outstanding" example of its type—"particularly ambitious and even splendid." All told over £14,000 went to create "a viable port and fishing community on what had formerly been a greenfield site." And whatever one might conclude about the Sutherland clearances, it is "only just," Smout feels, "to recognize that the Duke [as he became] was actually more lavish with capital to ameliorate social dislocation than any other landowner in the North of Scotland has ever been." See "The Landowner and the Planned Village," pp. 84 and 93.

33. Richards concludes that this figure is too high and puts the total at roughly £500,000, exclusive of additional land purchases in Sutherland, which accounted for another £554,000. *Leviathan of Wealth*, p. 232.

34. Great Britain, Board of Agriculture, *General View of the County of Sutherland . . . To Which is Annexed a Particular Account of the More Recent Improvements in that County by Captain John Henderson* (London, 1812).

35. Elizabeth, Countess of Sutherland, to Sir Walter Scott, October 22, 1811, quoted in Richards, *Leviathan of Wealth*, p. 177.

36. On Loch's early career and ideas see ibid., pp. 19–34. "The Sutherland Metternich" also produced his own description—and justification—of his employers' Scottish projects. James Loch, *Account of the Improvements on the Estates of the Marquis and Marchioness of Stafford* (London, 1820). An earlier edition was published anonymously.

37. Richards, *Leviathan of Wealth*, p. 33.

38. Loch to "Grant," July 1, 1816, quoted in ibid., p. 26.

39. See ibid., pp. 166–167. David Dale, Robert Owen's father-in-law and the founder of New Lanark, was also involved in the development of Spinningdale.

40. Appleton, *Introduction of the Power Loom*, pp. 7–9.

2. The Boston Company of Waltham

1. Vol. 1, Proprietors' Records, and vol. 2, Directors' Records, Boston Manufacturing Company MSS, BL.

Most studies of the Waltham-Lowell system pay relatively little attention to the Boston Company and concentrate instead on the development of Lowell ten years later. See, for example, Bender, *Urban Vision*. However, Caroline Ware, in *New England Cotton Manufacture*, pp. 60–78, devotes an entire chapter to the subject, as does Gregory in *Nathan Appleton*, pp. 141–172. Gregory's account, while it may overestimate Appleton's involvement during the company's first few years, is particularly detailed. See also Kenneth F. Mailloux, "The Boston Manufacturing Company of Waltham, Massachusetts, 1813–1848: The First Modern Factory in America" (Ph.D. diss. Boston University, 1957).

2. Appleton, *Introduction of the Power Loom*, pp. 7–9.

3. "The Articles of Agreement" are recorded in vol. 1, Proprietors' Records, Boston Manufacturing Company MSS, BL.

4. Appleton to Eben Appleton, Sept. 11, 1811, Nathan Appleton MSS, MHS. Appleton had already had at least a limited brush with the textile manufacturing business. In 1810 his older brother, Samuel, had bought a quarter interest in a small spinning mill in New Ipswich, New Hampshire, the brothers' boyhood home. While Samuel was in England, Nathan oversaw his investment. The firm was not especially successful, but Appleton blamed a "want of proper attention" to sound business principles. See Gregory, *Nathan Appleton*, pp. 143–144.

5. On British firms, see Seymour Shapiro, *Capital and the Cotton Industry in the Industrial Revolution* (Ithaca, 1967). Shapiro notes that the only major textile manufacturing concern operating on a joint-stock basis in Great Britain during the early nineteenth century was Robert Owen's at New Lanark. As a result of a law passed in 1725 after the South Sea Bubble affair, joint-stock companies were permitted to operate only under special charter and such charters could cost as much as £100,000. Ibid., pp. 156–163.

6. For an analysis of the evolution of the corporate form in Massachusetts see Oscar Handlin and Mary F. Handlin, *Commonwealth: A Study of the Role of Government in the American Economy: Massachusetts, 1774–1861* (New York, 1947). The use of the form by early manufacturing firms is discussed in detail in pp. 110–112 and 130–137. See also E. M. Dodd, *American Business Corporations until 1860, With Special Reference to Massachusetts* (Cambridge, Mass., 1960).

7. The petition is quoted in part in Ware, *New England Cotton Manufacture*, pp. 62–63. The act of incorporation was dated Feb. 23, 1813. Vol. 1, Proprietors' Records, Boston Manufacturing Company MSS, BL.

8. Vol. 1, Proprietors' Records, Boston Manufacturing Company MSS, BL. The date of the first subscription was Sept. 4, 1813. The other stockholders were Benjamin Gorham with three shares, Warren Dutton with two, and James Lloyd with five.

9. Appleton, *Introduction of the Power Loom*, pp. 7–8.

10. Vol. 1, Proprietors' Records, Boston Manufacturing Company MSS, BL. The dates of the second and third subscriptions were Oct. 3, 1815 and May 9, 1817.

11. Appleton, *Introduction of the Power Loom*, p. 10. The trade in Indian textiles is described at length in Porter, *Jacksons and Lees*, I, 27–39 and 51–75.

12. Appleton, *Introduction of the Power Loom*, pp. 11–12. Lowell and Jackson had estimated that 25 cents a yard would be sufficient for the first sale. By 1843 the price had fallen to $6\frac{1}{2}$ cents a yard but still netted a profit for the company. See Gregory, *Nathan Appleton*, p. 165.

13. Appleton, *Introduction of the Power Loom*, p. 12.

14. Ibid., p. 15.

15. For a general discussion of wages see Ware, *New England Cotton Manufacture*, pp. 236–248. Evidence presented by Ware indicates that in 1820, 45 percent of the work force in Massachusetts cotton mills consisted of children. The corresponding figure for Rhode Island was 55 percent. Eager to win the good opinion of the community, owners of "family" type mills did, in their advertisements for workers, try to demonstrate a concern for moral standards. "Families wishing a situation near to places of public worship will find this most delightful," announced one such owner. But meanwhile children working for Almy and Brown were regularly receiving no pay at all except the articles of clothing they were given as "apprentices." Ibid., pp. 210–211 and 203.

On the Rhode Island cotton textile industry, where "family" type mills were first established and continued to predominate, see also E. H. Cameron, *Samuel Slater: Father of American Manufactures* (N.p., 1960); Peter J. Coleman, *The Transformation of Rhode Island, 1790–1860* (Providence, 1963); James B. Hedges, *The Browns of Providence Plantations: The Nineteenth Century* (Providence, 1968); and Gary Kulik, "Pawtucket Village and the Strike of 1824: The Origins of Class Conflict in Rhode Island," *Radical History Review*, 17 (1978), 5–37.

Jonathan Prude, *The Coming of Industrial Order: Town and Factory Life in Rural Massachusetts, 1810–1860* (New York, 1983) is a fine study of the growth of the Massachusetts textile industry outside of places like Waltham and Lowell.

16. Smith Wilkinson, quoted in Ware, *New England Cotton Manufacture*, p. 200.

17. Appleton, *Introduction of the Power Loom*, pp. 15–16.

18. Ibid.

19. Ibid.

20. See McGouldrick, *New England Textiles*, p. 206.

21. Appleton to Samuel Appleton, Jan. 20, 1816, Nathan Appleton MSS, MHS.

22. Appleton, *Introduction of the Power Loom*, p. 13.

23. Ibid. On the impact of the tariff of 1816 on the trade in Indian cottons see Ware, *New England Cotton Manufacture*, p. 71, and Porter, *Jacksons and Lees*, I, 39. Porter's conclusion is that the act "by placing a prohibitive duty upon coarse foreign textiles, at one stroke made it impossible for East India merchants to deal profitably in what had hitherto been the principal staple of their trade." According to the *Report of the Committee of Merchants and Others, of Boston; on the Tariff* (Boston, 1820) the effective rate on Indian textiles had been raised to 83.5 percent.

24. See Sobel, "Francis Cabot Lowell," p. 33.

25. Robert B. Zevin, "The Growth of Cotton Textile Production after 1815," p. 40, in Zevin's *The Growth of Manufacturing in Early Nineteenth Century New England* (New York, 1975). Zevin's point that Lowell's interest in the power loom was by no means unique in New England at that time is well taken and coincides with my own view that too much is made of Lowell's technological abilities and too little attention is paid to his other contributions to the Waltham-Lowell system. If he had not developed a workable power loom, someone else soon would have. Indeed others did. Zevin's general argument—that the chief impetus behind the rapid, widespread adoption of power weaving in New England after 1815 was less a desire to save labor than a need to cut costs—also seems sound.

On sales of machinery by the Boston Company see Gregory, *Nathan Appleton*, pp. 157–158. Between 1817 and 1820 equipment was sold to nine different firms. The first power loom sold at $2,078, netting a profit of 20 percent. Gibb, *Saco-Lowell Shops*, pp. 40–41.

26. Vol. 2, Directors' Records, Boston Manufacturing Company MSS, BL. A committee having been appointed on Jan. 2, 1815, to determine Jackson's salary, the $3,000 figure was formally approved on Jan. 4, 1816.

27. Ibid. The increase was approved on Feb. 3, 1819.

28. There is no modern biography of Jackson. Among the available sources, the most useful is Porter, *Jacksons and Lees*. See also John A. Lowell, "Memoir of Patrick T. Jackson," in Nathan Appleton and John A. Lowell, *Correspondence between Nathan Appleton and J. A. Lowell in Relation to the Early History of the City of Lowell* (Boston, 1848).

29. Appleton, *Introduction of the Power Loom*, p. 11.

30. In addition to Gregory, *Nathan Appleton*, see Robert C. Winthrop, *Memoir of the Hon. Nathan Appleton, LL.D.* (Boston, 1861); and Louise Hall Tharp, *The Appletons of Beacon Hill* (Boston, 1973).

31. Vol. 1, Proprietors' Records, Boston Manufacturing Company MSS, BL. A committee had been appointed on Feb. 26, 1819, to investigate ways to increase the company's capital stock. The directors were authorized to petition the General Court for an increase in capitalization on Jan. 10, 1820, and the plan to dispose of the new shares was adopted on Jan. 25 of the same year. Meanwhile the proprietors, beginning on Aug. 6, 1819, had approved five loans, totalling $70,000, presumably to begin work on the expansion.

32. Ibid. The other new subscribers were J. W. Boott (with thirty shares), George Lee, Thomas Motley, Charles Thorndike, Edward Hobbs, Jr., and Thomas Borden.

33. Ware, *New England Cotton Manufacture*, pp. 140–141.

34. Gregory, *Nathan Appleton*, p. 281.

35. J. E. A. Smith, "Town of Pittsfield," in *History of Berkshire County, Massachusetts, with Biographical Sketches of Its Prominent Men* (New York, 1885), II, 337–338.

Surprisingly, Gregory does not mention the Pittsfield Woolen and Cotton Factory, though she does note that Thomas Gold wrote to Appleton in 1816 inquiring about the cost of power looms. *Nathan Appleton*, p. 157.

36. J. E. A. Smith, "Town of Pittsfield," p. 339.

37. Christopher D. Hardy, "The Reaction of Local Elites to Modernization: Berkshire County, Massachusetts, 1800–1860" (Honors thesis, Williams College, 1976) provides an impressive analysis of the changing composition of the county's economic elite.

38. Vol. 1, Proprietors' Records, Boston Manufacturing Company MSS, BL.

39. See note 23. On the intense antagonism of Boston merchants to the tariff see also Seaburg and Paterson, *Colonel T. H. Perkins*, p. 294; Samuel Eliot Morison, *Harrison Gray Otis, 1765–1848: The Urbane Federalist* (Boston, 1969), p. 448; and Thomas H. O'Connor, *Lords of the Loom: The Cotton Whigs and the Coming of the Civil War* (New York, 1968), pp. 18–25.

40. Jefferson to Benjamin Austin, Jan. 9, 1816, quoted in ibid., p. 18.

41. U.S. Congress, 16th Cong., 2d sess. House Report No. 34, p. 10.

3. Expansion

1. Charles Dickens, *American Notes for General Circulation* (London, 1842), I, 152–153. Dickens was but one of many distinguished Europeans and Americans to visit Lowell during the period. Among the others were Harriet Martineau, Michel Chevalier, Louis Kossuth, Henry Clay, Andrew Jackson, and James K. Polk. Like Dickens too, most such visitors—at least through the 1840s—were enthusiastic about what they saw. But there were always exceptions, and as time passed the unfavorable reactions became increasingly prevalent. See Bender, *Urban Vision*, pp. 40–51; Carl Siracusa, *A Mechanical People: Perceptions of the Industrial Order in Massachusetts* (Middletown, Conn., 1979); and Robert J. Topitzer, "Values about Industrialization: The Case of Lowell, Massachusetts, 1840–1860" (Ph.D. diss., University of New Hampshire, 1976).

2. Dickens, *American Notes*, pp. 154–163.

3. Ibid., pp. 164–165.

4. Lucy Larcom, *A New England Girlhood, Outlined from Memory* (Boston, 1889), p. 192.

5. Ibid., p. 12.

6. Ibid., p. 93.

7. U.S. Department of State, *Compendium . . . of the Sixth Census* (Washington, 1841), p. 10.

8. Massachusetts, *Statistical Tables: Exhibiting the Condition and Products of Certain Branches of Industry in Massachusetts, for the Year Ending April 1, 1837* (Boston, 1838), p. 31.

9. Appleton, *Introduction of the Power Loom*, pp. 19–28. Gregory, *Nathan Appleton*, pp. 173–193, provides a very detailed account of the founding of Lowell. See also Appleton and Lowell, *Correspondence in Relation to the Early History of Lowell*; Ware, *New England Cotton Manufacture*, pp. 79–85; Coolidge, *Mill and Mansion*, pp. 9–43; and Bender, *Urban Vision*, pp. 97–128.

10. Appleton, *Introduction of the Power Loom*, p. 24.

11. Ibid.

12. See Gregory, *Nathan Appleton*, pp. 183–185.

13. Appleton to Timothy Wiggin, Dec. 15, 1821, Appleton MSS, MHS. In the same letter, which was marked "Confidential," Appleton expressed his determination to hold on to "nearly all" of his textile manufacturing stock, even though, as he put it, "I am already offered a considerable advance if I will part with any."

14. The price initially charged the Hamilton Company was $26 per spindle for machinery and $4 per spindle for waterpower. Gregory, *Nathan Appleton*, p. 186.

15. Appleton, *Introduction of the Power Loom*, p. 15.

16. As advanced as the management structure of Waltham-Lowell companies was, it was still a far cry from modern industrial management structures, as Alfred D. Chandler, Jr., points out in *The Visible Hand: The Managerial Revolution in American Business* (Cambridge, Mass., 1977). Basically, Chandler contends, the companies were run "like partnerships," and the managerial methods used "adhered to those of the mercantile world that spawned them." See pp. 67–72.

17. The diversification of products in the Waltham-Lowell system had actually begun with the building of a bleachery by the Boston Manufacturing Company in 1819. The Merrimack Company included a printworks for producing calicoes. These developments, along with dyeing operations of various kinds, involved substantial outlays of capital and ultimately made a significant contribution to the growth of the chemical industry in the United States.

18. Gregory, *Nathan Appleton*, pp. 214–237.

19. Ibid. See also Ware, *New England Cotton Manufacture*, pp. 161–197.

20. Gregory, *Nathan Appleton*, pp. 169, 256, and 273–274.

21. McGouldrick, in *New England Textiles*, from which the foregoing data were drawn, provides by far the most systematic and complete analysis of profits and dividends in the Waltham-Lowell system. See especially pp. 73–138. In addition to the Boston and Merrimack Companies, those included in his sample (with the year of incorporation for each) are: the Hamilton (1826), the Nashua (1827), the Tremont (1832), the Suffolk (1832), the Lawrence (1834), the Dwight (1842), the Naumkeag (1846), the Pepperell (1851), and the Lyman (1854).

As invaluable as McGouldrick's data are, I do disagree with a number of his conclusions. In particular I question his contention that Waltham-Lowell investment and management policies were characterized by a high degree of "modernity." By that term he means those qualities of modern capitalism mentioned by Werner Sombart: "capacity for abstraction, rationality in relating means to ends, and separation of business and other goals in the course of operations." All of these, McGouldrick feels, characterized the controlling group of Waltham-Lowell policy makers. "Even if they did not consciously take long-run profit maximization as their guide," he argues, "they acted as if they did" (pp. 206–207).

My own view is that while Sombart's criteria for "modernity" may ultimately have come to characterize the management of the Waltham-Lowell system, that development occurred only very slowly, over a period of several decades.

22. According to Nathan Appleton, the desired ratio was two-thirds of capital in fixed assets with the remaining third kept liquid. Appleton, *Introduction of the Power Loom*, p. 30.

On the borrowing practices of Waltham-Lowell companies see McGouldrick, *New England Textiles*, pp. 14–18 and 154–207; and two excellent articles by Lance E. Davis: "Sources of Industrial Finance: The American Textile Industry: A Case Study," *Explorations in Entrepreneurial History*, 9 (1957), 189–203; and "The New England Textile Mills and the Capital Markets: A Study of Industrial Borrowing, 1840–1860," *Journal of Economic History*, 20 (1960), 1–30. On the subject of broad trends in capital mobilization, Davis concludes: "It appears that the historians of [the] New England textile industry have correctly assessed the importance of equity capital in industrial finance. At the same time they may have overemphasized the role of retained earnings (at least as far as the Massachusetts type mills are concerned) and have failed to acknowledge the contribution that was made by loan capital— particularly the long-term credit granted by credit intermediaries." Davis, "Sources of Industrial Finance," p. 203.

23. McGouldrick, *New England Textiles*, pp. 29–34 and 139–153. In general, textile mills required long production runs for efficient operation. At integrated mills, other factors making it difficult to scale down or shift production in the face of falling demand included the need to maintain a continuous flow from spinning through to the weaving process and the fact that changes in one usually required changes in the other, which were not always possible, given the machinery used. Also, waterpowered mills were less easily operated at partial capacity than modern factories, which rely mainly on electric power. And finally, in Waltham-Lowell mills the labor system tended to restrict flexibility in output, since the companies—in assuming the added expense of providing workers' housing—wedded themselves to a situation in which costs per unit of production rose sharply at levels under capacity.

24. Ibid., p. 33.

25. Technological innovation, increases in output and productivity, and changing wage rates in the early textile industry have been analyzed in a number of studies, including David Jeremy, "Innovation in American Textile Technology During the Early 19th Century," *Technology and Culture*, 14 (1973), 40–76; Lance E. Davis and H. Louis Stettler, III, "The New England Textile Industry, 1825–60: Trends and Fluctuations," in *Output Employment and Productivity in the United States after 1800*, Conference on Research in Income and Wealth (New York, 1966); T. Y. Shen, "A Quantitative Study of Capital and

Labor Productivity in U.S. Cotton Textiles, 1840–1940" (Ph.D. diss., Yale University, 1957); Robert B. Zevin, "The Use of a 'Long Run' Learning Function: With Application to a Massachusetts Cotton Textile Firm, 1823–1860," in Zevin, *The Growth of Manufacturing in Early Nineteenth Century New England;* and Robert G. Layer, *Earnings of Cotton Mill Operatives, 1825–1914* (Cambridge, Mass., 1955). See also Ware, *New England Cotton Manufacture,* pp. 268–273; McGouldrick, *New England Textiles,* pp. 29–43 and 139–153; and Dublin, *Women at Work,* pp. 86–144.

26. Ware, *New England Cotton Manufacture,* pp. 148–149.

27. Ibid., p. 150. The forty-three were divided as follows: ten Appletons, seven Lees, seven Lowells, six Abbotts, four Jacksons, three Lymans, three Lorings and three Bordens.

On Appleton's gifts to his children, see Gregory, *Nathan Appleton,* pp. 270–272.

28. By 1835, for example, Patrick T. Jackson owned stock in all of the following textile manufacturing companies: the Boston, the Merrimack, the Appleton, and the Lowell. In addition he was a stockholder in the Lowell Locks and Canals Company and had just under $90,000 invested in the Boston and Lowell Railroad. Similarly, Henry Lee, Jackson's brother-in-law, began buying stock in 1836 and over the next decade came to own shares in no fewer than twenty-three different textile and textile-related companies. Porter, *Jacksons and Lees,* I, 123–124 and 768–769.

29. The published sources dealing with the Lawrences are largely contemporary and contain little in the way of analysis. See Amos Lawrence, *Extracts from the Diary and Correspondence of the Late Amos Lawrence,* ed. William R. Lawrence (Boston, 1855); Nathan Appleton, *Memoir of Abbott Lawrence* (Boston, 1861); and Hamilton Hill, *Memoir of Abbott Lawrence* (Boston, 1883).

30. See Ware, *New England Cotton Manufacture,* pp. 320–321, for a list of principal subscribers to the first stock issues of ten Waltham-Lowell companies.

The fact that much of the capital invested in the Waltham-Lowell system came from individuals who had already earned substantial fortunes, usually in maritime commerce, distinguishes it sharply from the early British textile industry. Shapiro concludes that most British millowners came from the middle class. Almost none were members of the aristocracy or even the merchant class. The major exceptions were Scottish firms, which did to some extent involve both aristocrats and merchants as investors. See Shapiro, *Capital and the Cotton Industry,* pp. 163–178.

The high rate of payout of earnings practiced in the Waltham-Lowell system was also quite uncharacteristic of the British textile industry. British firms had a marked tendency to retain profits. Indeed Shapiro sees this as providing a "crucial" source of capital for the industry. Ibid., pp. 178–181 and 207.

31. Porter, *Jacksons and Lees,* I, 124–128. See also McGouldrick, *New England Textiles,* pp. 23–28. McGouldrick interprets the incident as evidence of a general distrust of management by stockholders, and in this case the point would seem to be well taken. On the other hand, earnings were falling sharply at the time, and management did respond quite quickly to the de-

mands of the "reforming party." Nor is McGouldrick able to point to another such incident until just before the Civil War. He also notes that the records of companies founded after 1840, unlike earlier ones, are largely silent on policy matters, leading him to conclude that by then the establishment of a textile mill had become "so routine that a reasonably well-capitalized business having competent supervisory personnel could perform satisfactorily without stockholder surveillance." McGouldrick, *New England Textiles*, pp. 26–27.

32. See Frederick C. Jaher, "Nineteenth-Century Elites in Boston and New York," *Journal of Social History*, 5 (1972), 32–77. Jaher concludes that, compared to the rich in New York, Boston's elite became involved in manufacturing earlier and maintained elite status longer. He also notes that the Boston group contained fewer individuals from long-established families and more who had been born in places other than the city itself. He draws his samples from tax assessment lists for both cities in the early period and uses *The* (New York) *Tribune Monthly* of June 1892 for the late nineteenth century. The dates of the lists in the case of Boston are 1835, 1845, and 1860 and the cut-off point for elite status is $100,000.

33. Robert C. Winthrop, speech of Aug. 20, 1855, *Addresses and Speeches of Robert C. Winthrop* (Boston, 1867), II, 210–212.

34. Porter, *Jacksons and Lees*, I, 768–769.

35. See Spalding, "Boston Mercantile Community," p. 59. None of the subsequent attempts to develop textile towns matched Lowell's success. Many indeed lost money, which tends to call into question Spalding's contention that it was the desire for quick profits from such promotional activities that provided the chief impetus for the expansion of the Waltham-Lowell system.

36. William Appleton, diary, Jan. 1835, *Selections from the Diaries of William Appleton, 1786–1862*, ed. Susan M. Loring (Boston, 1922), pp. 50–51.

37. Appleton, diary, Jan. 1, 1858, ibid., pp. 206–208.

38. Porter, *Jacksons and Lees*, I, 769.

39. Gregory, *Nathan Appleton*, pp. 270–271.

40. Henrietta Larson, "A China Trader Turns Investor: A Biographical Chapter in American Business History," *Harvard Business Review*, 7 (1934), 345–358.

41. Ware, *New England Cotton Manufacture*, p. 141.

42. For a more recent statement of the thesis see Sobel, "Francis Cabot Lowell." Gregory also follows much the same line in *Nathan Appleton*, though there is nothing at all in Appleton's own *Introduction of the Power Loom* to lend support to such an interpretation. He never mentions the depressed state of commerce and certainly does not offer it as a factor leading to the growth of the textile industry.

43. See Seaburg and Paterson, *Colonel T. H. Perkins*, pp. 263–317.

44. Henry Lee, quoted in Porter, *Jacksons and Lees*, I, 73.

45. Lawrence, diary, Jan. 1, 1826, quoted in *Diary and Correspondence of Amos Lawrence*, pp. 80–81.

46. Ibid. Apparently Lawrence managed to keep his resolution. The following year he was able to write: "The principles of business laid down a year ago have been very nearly practiced upon. Our responsibilities and anxieties

have greatly diminished, as also have the accustomed profits of business."
Lawrence, diary, Jan. 1, 1827, ibid., p. 81.

47. Appleton, quoted in Tharp, *Appletons of Beacon Hill*, p. 62.

48. Appleton, diary, June 7, 1822, *Diaries of William Appleton*, pp. 36–37.

49. Appleton, diary, June 20, 1822, ibid., p. 37.

50. Appleton, diary, Dec. 1, 1850, ibid., p. 144.

51. Appleton, diary, Jan. 1, 1856, ibid., p. 181.

52. Appleton, diary, Jan. 1, 1862, ibid., p. 248.

53. Appleton, diary, Jan., 1835, ibid., p. 45.

54. Appleton, diary, Jan. 1, 1858, ibid., pp. 206–208.

55. Perkins to Joshua Bates, Oct. 10, 1831, quoted in Seaburg and Paterson, *Colonel T. H. Perkins*, p. 374.

56. See Tharp, *Appletons of Beacon Hill*, pp. 246–262 and 319–335; and Frederic C. Jaher, "Businessman and Gentleman: Nathan and Thomas Gold Appleton—an Exploration in Inter-generational History," *Explorations in Entrepreneurial History*, 4 (1966), 17–39.

57. Lawrence to William R. Lawrence, July 27 and Aug. 27, 1829, *Diary and Correspondence of Amos Lawrence*, p. 90.

58. Ibid.

59. Lawrence to his wife, Dec. 23, 1833, ibid., p. 126.

60. Lawrence, diary, Jan. 1, 1852, ibid., p. 311.

For two interesting discussions of the values of Boston's economic elite see Paul Goodman, "Ethics and Enterprise: The Values of a Boston Elite, 1800–1860," *American Quarterly*, 18 (1966), 437–451, and Frederic C. Jaher, "The Boston Brahmins in the Age of Industrial Capitalism" in *Age of Industrialism in America: Essays in Social Structure and Cultural Values*, ed. F. C. Jaher (New York, 1968), pp. 188–262. Both authors argue that during the nineteenth century the upper levels of Boston's business establishment developed distinctive ways of thinking and talking about themselves and the world around them. The two disagree, however, about precisely when and why this happened. Jaher, who sees it occurring quite late in the period, explains it as a kind of defensive response made as "new forces and problems undermined the confidence of the class" (p. 197). He further argues that the chief consequence of the values thus derived was to make the situation that much worse. "Scattered energies, divided talent, and curtailed commitment grieviously disadvantaged the Boston Brahmins in the rationalized and competitive world of American business" (p. 243). Goodman, on the other hand, takes the view that the characteristic values of Boston's economic elite evolved much earlier and played a major role in shaping the group's business activities. In my opinion Goodman makes a stronger case with respect to timing, but given the limited range of material he considers he is unable to show either why the values in question developed when they did, or what specific impact they had in the realm of business enterprise. Jaher has expanded upon his argument in *The Urban Establishment: Upper Strata in Boston, New York, Charleston, Chicago, and Los Angeles* (Urbana, 1982).

My own interpretation of the changing values of Boston's economic elite has been influenced by a variety of sources, in addition to an extensive reading of the personal papers of members of the group. Two studies—both on topics somewhat removed from the subject itself—that have proved particularly helpful are Clifford Geertz, *Peddlers and Princes: Social Change and Economic Modernization in Two Indonesian Towns* (Chicago, 1963); and Anthony F. C. Wallace, *Rockdale: The Growth of an American Village in the Early Industrial Revolution* (New York, 1978).

61. Lawrence to George Shattuck, July 2, 1833, quoted in Spalding, "Boston Mercantile Community," p. 53.

62. The best source on the developing labor movement at Lowell is Dublin, *Women at Work*. See especially pp. 86–131. Other studies which treat the subject in some detail are Ware, *New England Cotton Manufacture* and Josephson, *Golden Threads*.

63. On the physical transformation of Lowell and the general deterioration of living and working conditions see Coolidge, *Mill and Mansion*, pp. 58–103; Bender, *Urban Vision*, pp. 95–128; and Dublin, *Women at Work*, pp. 132–144.

64. Coolidge provides a particularly forceful statement of this point of view in *Mill and Mansion*, pp. 9–27. Cf. Bender, *Urban Vision*, pp. 110–111.

65. An examination of the personal papers of many of the major investors in Waltham-Lowell companies reveals little about their attitude toward the changes occurring at Lowell. Indeed, one is tempted to conclude that they were simply oblivious to what was happening. Bender demonstrates that this was by no means true of the mill agents on the spot in Lowell, or of local civic leaders (*Urban Vision*, pp. 110–126), but their concerns were hardly ever echoed by the owners. Typically, in his *Introduction of the Power Loom*, Appleton writes only of the growth of Lowell and says nothing about the consequences of that growth.

66. See McGouldrick, *New England Textiles*, pp. 73–120.

67. On the politics surrounding what eventually became the Hoosac Tunnel see Edward C. Kirkland, *Men, Cities, and Transportation: A Study in New England History, 1820–1900* (Cambridge, Mass., 1948), I, 387–432.

68. The development of Lawrence as a textile manufacturing center is described in Donald B. Cole, *Immigrant City*, pp. 17–26. On Holyoke, see Green, *Holyoke*, pp. 18–30.

69. Green, *Holyoke*, pp. 27–29.

70. Lawrence, quoted in William Lawrence, *Life of Amos A. Lawrence, With Extracts from His Diary and Correspondence* (Boston, 1889), pp. 23–24.

4. Transportation, Banking, and Insurance

1. Shlakman, *History of a Factory Town*, pp. 30–47. In addition to being the first historian to use the term "the Boston Associates," Shlakman initiated the systematic analysis of the phenomenon she used the term to describe. Since then, a number of other studies have appeared that contribute in important ways to an understanding of the subject, including Robert K. Lamb, "The Entrepreneur and the Community," in *Men in Business*, ed. William Miller (New York, 1962); Edward Pessen, *Riches, Class, and Power before the Civil War*

(Lexington, Mass., 1973); Ronald Story, *The Forging of an Aristocracy: Harvard and the Boston Upper Class, 1800–1870* (Middletown, Conn., 1980); Peter D. Hall, *The Organization of American Culture, 1700–1900: Private Institutions, Elites, and the Origins of American Nationality* (New York, 1982); and Jaher, *Urban Establishment.*

Though they differ considerably on points of detail, all these authors agree that the first half of the nineteenth century saw a marked trend toward the consolidation of wealth and power in the hands of Boston's economic elite, leading ultimately to the emergence of something like a distinct upper class. In each case the Associates and their activities are seen as a vital part of that process, but only Lamb focuses on the group per se. Of the three most recent studies, Story's and Hall's concentrate primarily on cultural institutions and attitudes; they also rely on existing analyses of the business interests of the elite, as does Jaher. None of the three discusses political developments after 1830 in any detail.

2. The information in this and the following paragraphs was drawn from a variety of sources, including: Shlakman, *History of a Factory Town*, especially table 1, "Officers and Principal Stockholders of Specified Cotton Mills Before 1850," pp. 39–42, and Appendix A, "Financial and Transportation Interests of the Boston Associates," pp. 243–247; Ware, *New England Cotton Manufacture*, Appendix K, "Some of the Promoters and Original Stockholders of the Waltham and Lowell Companies," pp. 320–321; and Gerald T. White, *A History of the Massachusetts Hospital Life Insurance Company* (Cambridge, Mass., 1955), table 5, "Membership of the Committee of Finance in the Period 1838–1878," p. 69, and Appendix 1, "Officers of the Massachusetts Hospital Life Insurance Company from its Organization," pp. 169–176. On family relationships among the Associates see Mary C. Crawford, *Famous Families of Massachusetts*, 2 vols. (Boston, 1930).

3. Gregory, *Nathan Appleton*, p. 198.

4. White, *Massachusetts Hospital Life Insurance Company*, pp. 27, 32, and 82–84. The company finally wrote its last life insurance policy in 1867.

5. Handlin and Handlin, *Commonwealth*, pp. 108–110 and 114–120.

6. Morton J. Horwitz, *The Transformation of American Law, 1780–1860* (Cambridge, Mass., 1981), p. xv. See also pp. 63–139. Among other things Horwitz takes issue with the Handlins—and other "consensus" historians who have done similar work—for failing to ask "in whose interest" the pattern of governmental action documented in their studies was forged. "To a surprisingly great extent, they treated all instances of state intervention as equally proving their point, as indeed such evidence would tend to do, given the qualitatively undifferentiated questions they tended to ask" (p. xiv).

7. For a general description of prerailroad transportation projects in New England, see Kirkland, *Men, Cities and Transportation*, I, 32–91.

8. Handlin and Handlin, *Commonwealth*, pp. 109–110 and 114–115; and Stanley J. Kutler, *Privilege and Creative Destruction: The Charles River Bridge Case* (New York, 1978), pp. 8–13.

9. On the building and subsequent history of the Middlesex Canal, see Christopher Roberts, *The Middlesex Canal, 1793–1860* (Cambridge, Mass., 1938).

10. The most thoroughgoing analysis of the Charles River Bridge case is Kutler, *Privilege and Creative Destruction*. See also Horwitz, *Transformation of American Law*, pp. 130–139.

11. Seaburg and Paterson, *Colonel T. H. Perkins*, pp. 330–344. In addition to quarrying and transporting stone for the Bunker Hill Monument, the Granite Railway made a profitable business of providing building material for many other imposing structures in Boston and elsewhere along the East Coast. Perkins stepped down as president in 1834, and the line eventually became part of the Old Colony system and later of the New York, New Haven, and Hartford Railroad. See pp. 423–424.

12. For example Kirkland, in *Men, Cities, and Transportation*, tells the story of the coming of the railroad to Massachusetts chiefly in terms of Boston's attempts to improve communications to the West. See especially vol. 1, pp. 92–124.

This view, however, has been effectively challenged by Stephen Salsbury in *The State, the Investor, and the Railroad: The Boston & Albany, 1825–1867* (Cambridge, Mass., 1967). New England's first transsectional railroad, he contends, "was not primarily a response to the Erie Canal . . . but the result of a concerted drive by manufacturing groups who wanted transportation to inland factory sites" (p. 36).

In so arguing, Salsbury takes issue too—and with good reason—with Jules Rubin's view that the inherent conservatism of Bostonians delayed the state's response to the Erie Canal. (See Rubin, *Canal or Railroad? Imitation and Innovation in Response to the Erie Canal in Philadelphia, Baltimore, and Boston*, Transactions of The American Philosophical Society, n.s., 51 (1961).) Again, Salsbury argues, the building of a railroad to the West awaited the growth of manufacturing in the interior. Earlier discussions of a canal in Massachusetts got nowhere because the chances for profit were too slim to attract private capital and rural opposition in the legislature effectively blocked state aid. Salsbury, *The Boston & Albany*, pp. 34–44.

Finally, Salsbury also rejects the notion—put forth by, among others, Albert Fishlow, in *American Railroads and the Transformation of the Antebellum Economy* (Cambridge, Mass., 1965)—that railroads contributed little to American industrial growth during the period. Taking the example of the Lowell mills specifically, Salsbury argues that the fact that they could have done without rail transport (p. 245) proves little, and it ignores the major role played by millowners in promoting early railroads. Salsbury, *The Boston & Albany*, pp. 336–337, n. 12.

13. Elias Derby, "Progress of Railroads in Massachusetts," *Hunt's Merchants Magazine and Commercial Review*, 14 (1846), 30.

14. Lawrence to William R. Lawrence, Jan. 16, 1831, quoted in *Diary and Correspondence of Amos Lawrence*, p. 103. At roughly the same time William Appleton was writing in his diary: "The year has been one of unprecedented prosperity in the Country, and particularly so to enterprising Merchants and Manufacturers." Appleton, diary, Jan. 1, 1831, *Diaries of William Appleton*, p. 38.

15. See Salsbury, *The Boston & Albany*, pp. 62–111 and 133–181.

16. For a brief account of the Boston & Lowell see Kirkland, *Men, Cities and Transportation*, I, 111–112.

17. Salsbury, *The Boston & Albany*, pp. 95–96.

18. Josiah Quincy, Jr., quoted in Charles F. Adams, Jr., "The Canal and Railroad Enterprise of Boston," in *The Memorial History of Boston, Including Suffolk County, Massachusetts, 1630–1880*, ed. Justin Winsor (Boston, 1881), IV, 131.

For Lawrence's address at the rally see the *Boston Commercial Gazette*, Oct. 8, 1835.

19. Salsbury, *The Boston & Albany*, pp. 138–141 and 275.

20. Ibid., Appendix D, "Comparison of Stock Prices and Rates of Dividends, 1835–1867: Boston and Worcester and Western Railroads," p. 310.

21. Appleton, quoted in Gregory, *Nathan Appleton*, p. 277.

22. Salsbury, *The Boston & Albany*, pp. 182–273.

23. Ibid., pp. 259–269.

24. Ibid., p. 82.

25. Ibid., pp. 154, 221, and 302–303.

26. The best general account of American banking during the period remains Bray Hammond, *Banks and Politics in America: From the Revolution to the Civil War* (Princeton, 1957). Other studies providing useful information include: N. S. B. Gras, *Massachusetts First National Bank of Boston* (Cambridge, Mass., 1937); Handlin and Handlin, *Commonwealth*; Henry P. Kidder and Francis H. Peabody, "Finance in Boston," in Winsor, *Memorial History of Boston*, IV, 151–178; and David R. Whitney, *The Suffolk Bank* (Cambridge, Mass., 1878).

27. Gras, *Massachusetts First National Bank*, pp. 12–13.

28. Handlin and Handlin, *Commonwealth*, pp. 120–130 and 174–178.

29. Gregory, *Nathan Appleton*, pp. 271 and 280–283.

30. Ibid.

31. Hammond, *Banks and Politics*, pp. 172–183 and 549–551; and Handlin and Handlin, *Commonwealth*, pp. 125–130 and 176–177.

32. Whitney, *Suffolk Bank*, pp. 6–57.

33. Kidder and Peabody, "Finance in Boston," pp. 162–163; and Handlin and Handlin, *Commonwealth*, pp. 181–182.

34. Shlakman, *History of a Factory Town*, pp. 243–244.

35. Appleton to George Ticknor, Feb. 4, 1853, Nathan Appleton MSS, MHS.

36. Lawrence to Leverett Saltonstall, Aug. 2, 1841, Saltonstall MSS, MHS; Appleton to Thomas Appleton, July 13, Aug. 15, and Sept. 16, 1841, Nathan Appleton MSS, MHS.

37. Appleton's major published piece on banking—which does bear his name—is *Remarks on Currency and Banking Having Reference to the Present Derangement of the Circulating Medium in the United States* (Boston, 1841). A selection of shorter articles is contained in Scrapbooks, vols. 1 and 2, Nathan Appleton MSS, MHS. His argument in the former could not have been clearer on the subject of national banks: "A great central power, independent of the general or state governments, is an anomaly in our system. Such a power over

the currency is the most tremendous which can be established. Without the assurance that it will be managed by men, free from the common imperfections of human nature, we are safer without it." Appleton, *Remarks on Currency and Banking,* p. 36.

38. Gregory, *Nathan Appleton,* p. 218.

39. Ibid., pp. 229–237.

40. Davis, "New England Textile Mills and the Capital Markets," pp. 5–6. The companies in the sample include the Amoskeag, the Boston, the Dwight, the Cabot, the Perkins, the Lawrence, the Lyman, and the Massachusetts, and there are eight categories of lenders: commercial banks, savings banks, trust companies, insurance companies, individuals (including trust accounts personally held), cotton mercantile firms, manufacturing companies, and miscellaneous institutions.

41. See Gregory, *Nathan Appleton,* pp. 197 and 270–272. Though Gregory herself does not make the point, the data she presents show Appleton's investments in manufacturing companies rising steadily throughout the period he was reducing his commitments to Paige & Co.

42. Osborne Howes, Jr., "The Rise and Progress of Insurance in Boston," in Winsor, *Memorial History of Boston,* IV, 179–184.

43. Gregory, *Nathan Appleton,* p. 284; Shlakman, *History of a Factory Town,* pp. 44 and 245–246.

44. Gregory, *Nathan Appleton,* pp. 271 and 283–285.

45. Davis, "New England Textile Mills and the Capital Markets," p. 6.

46. Kidder and Peabody, "Finance in Boston," pp. 160–161; Handlin and Handlin, *Commonwealth,* p. 182; Davis, "New England Textile Mills and the Capital Markets," p. 6. On Boston's first savings bank, see also Walter Muir Whitehill, *The Provident Institution for Savings in the Town of Boston, 1816–1966* (Boston, 1966).

47. White, *Massachusetts Hospital Life Insurance Company,* pp. 73 and 93.

48. Ibid., p. 90. In Davis's study the Massachusetts Hospital Life figures as "the largest single lender" of funds to the eight companies for periods of a year or longer. Davis, "New England Textile Mills and the Capital Markets," p. 8.

49. Lowell to Samuel Appleton, Dec. 26, 1834, quoted in White, *Massachusetts Hospital Life Insurance Company,* pp. 199–200, n. 7. See also Nathaniel Bowditch to Judah Hays, Aug. 4, 1824, quoted in ibid., p. 34, which makes much the same point. Bowditch—the noted mathematician, astronomer, and author of the *Practical Navigator*—was the company's first chief executive. Ibid., pp. 23–25.

50. Ibid., p. 3. For a lengthy and provocative discussion of the development of trusts as a way of protecting family capital see also Peter D. Hall, "Family Structure and Class Consolidation among the Boston Brahmins" (Ph.D. diss., State University of New York at Stony Brook, 1973), pp. 195–322. Hall's argument is that trusts played a crucial role in a process of class consolidation in Boston that was already far advanced by the early years of the nineteenth century. Though his point about the importance of trusts is well taken, in general he tends to rush the timetable of the process he is

describing. Class consolidation among Boston's economic elite may have been well along by 1850: that was not the case thirty years earlier. Second, Hall's analysis depicts a group of individuals moving step by step, with utter assurance, to achieve a position of dominance definable in strikingly modern terms. Again I disagree. Planning and forethought there were aplenty; but there was also a great deal of gradual evolution—as well as shifting of focus over time —in the efforts of the elite to achieve its goals. To take only a single example: the Massachusetts Hospital Life Insurance Company did not begin concentrating its investments so heavily in the textile industry until more than twenty years *after* it was founded. Nor is there any evidence to indicate that its founders saw it initially as a major source of capital for industrial ventures. The change was just that: a change in policy as well as practice—unforeseen and unforeseeable. To interpret it otherwise is to confound results and intentions.

A briefer statement of Hall's argument, along with a discussion of the use of trusts in states other than Massachusetts, appears in his *Organization of American Culture*, pp. 114–124.

51. White, *Massachusetts Hospital Life Insurance Company*, pp. 60–61. On the duration of trusts see Guy Newhall, *Future Interests and the Rule against Perpetuities in Massachusetts* (Boston, 1942).

52. Lowell to Samuel Appleton, Dec. 26, 1834, quoted in White, *Massachusetts Hospital Life Insurance Company*, pp. 199–200, n. 7.

On private trustees see Augustus P. Loring, *A Trustee's Handbook* (Boston, 1898); and Donald Holbrook, *The Boston Trustee* (Boston, 1937).

53. See White, *Massachusetts Hospital Life Insurance Company*, Appendix 3, "Resources and Liabilities of the Massachusetts Hospital Life Insurance Company 1824–1900," pp. 190–194.

54. Ibid., pp. 34–35.

55. The initial, descriptive portions—omitting the application and contract forms, etc.—of *Proposals of the Massachusetts Hospital Life Insurance Company to Make Insurance on Lives, to Grant Annuities on Lives and in Trust, and Endowments for Children* are reprinted as Appendix 2, ibid., pp. 177–189.

56. My calculations are based on the data in ibid., p. 38n.

57. Stockholders Record Book, Massachusetts Hospital Life Insurance Company, Feb. 3, 1823, quoted in ibid., p. 14.

58. See ibid., Appendix 1, pp. 169–176.

59. Ibid., pp. 41–54.

60. Ibid., pp. 49–51.

61. Ibid., pp. 48 and 53.

62. Ibid., pp. 89–98. For another analysis of the connections between the Massachusetts Hospital Life and the Waltham-Lowell system, see Gregory, *Nathan Appleton*, pp. 287–290. Appleton was a member of the Committee of Finance and subsequently president of the company during the period the Massachusetts Hospital Life's funds were shifted so heavily into the textile industry. Considering all of the available evidence, Gregory's conclusion that "Appleton's handling of the finances of the MHLI Co. reveals his ability to direct the fortunes of one company without letting them be affected by its ties to his other ventures," seems curious.

63. White, *Massachusetts Hospital Life Insurance Company*, p. 89.

64. Ibid., pp. 88–89; Salsbury, *The Boston & Albany*, pp. 153–154.

5. Philanthropy and the Uses of Wealth

1. The Jackson-Warren letter, dated Aug. 20, 1810, is reprinted in N. I. Bowditch, *A History of the Massachusetts General Hospital (to August 5, 1851) Second Edition, with a Continuation to 1872* (New York, 1972, Arno Press reprint), pp. 3–9, n.

There is no comprehensive history of the Massachusetts General Hospital. However, Bowditch's work is invaluable, containing as it does a record of all actions taken by the hospital trustees as well as lists of officers and donors. Several comparable studies covering later periods include Nathaniel Faxon, *The Massachusetts General Hospital, 1935–1955* (Cambridge, Mass., 1959); Grace W. Myers, *History of the Massachusetts General Hospital, 1872–1900* (Boston, 1929); and Frederic A. Washburn, *The Massachusetts General Hospital: Its Development, 1900–1935* (Boston, 1939). See also Massachusetts General Hospital, *Massachusetts General Hospital: Memorial and Historical Volume* (Boston, 1921).

Other specialized studies which provide useful information are John B. Blake, *Public Health in the Town of Boston, 1630–1822* (Cambridge, Mass., 1959); Thomas F. Harrington, *The Harvard Medical School* (New York, 1905); Rhoda Traux, *The Doctors Warren of Boston* (Boston, 1968); and Henry Viets, *A Brief History of Medicine in Massachusetts* (Boston, 1930).

On medicine and the medical profession in general during the period see Daniel Calhoun, *Professional Lives in America: Structure and Aspiration, 1750–1850* (Cambridge, Mass., 1965); Joseph Kett, *The Formation of the American Medical Profession: The Role of Institutions, 1780–1860* (New Haven, 1968); William G. Rothstein, *American Physicians in the Nineteenth Century* (Baltimore, 1972); and Richard H. Shrock, *Medicine and Society in America, 1660–1860* (New York, 1960).

Bostonians were relatively late in building modern medical care facilities. By the time Massachusetts General Hospital was founded, New York and Philadelphia already had hospitals.

2. Jackson-Warren letter, in Bowditch, *Massachusetts General Hospital*, p. 4, n.

3. The charter was dated Feb. 25, 1811, but ten years passed before the necessary funds were collected and the first building was open. Ibid., pp. 3–55. For Bowditch's account of the activities of the visiting committee see pp. 383–409.

4. Ibid., p. 170.

5. The "Donation Book" was nonetheless a subject of great interest to the trustees, who appointed a special committee to oversee its preparation and entered a five-page report on the subject in their records. Ibid., pp. 82 and 172–173.

6. Ibid., p. 25 and "Officers of the Hospital from Its Foundation," pp. 417–422.

7. These calculations are based on data in the various lists of subscribers and donors that appear in ibid., pp. 423–445.

8. Lawrence, *Diary and Correspondence of Amos Lawrence*, pp. 28, 30, and 36–37.

9. Tharp, *Appletons of Beacon Hill*, pp. 14–27, provides the fullest account of the earlier generations of the Appleton family. See also Gregory, *Nathan Appleton*, pp. 1–6.

10. On the founding of New Ipswich Academy see [Frederic Kidder and Augustus A. Gould] *The History of New Ipswich, From Its First Grant in 1736 to the Present Time . . .* (Boston, 1852), pp. 197–202.

11. Gregory, *Nathan Appleton*, p. 6.

12. The Appleton genealogy is recorded in [Kidder and Gould] *History of New Ipswich*, pp. 294–306.

13. Three fine studies that develop this thesis are Kenneth A. Lockridge, *A New England Town, the First Hundred Years: Dedham, Massachusetts, 1636–1736* (New York, 1970); Robert A. Gross, *The Minutemen and Their World* (New York, 1976); and Patricia J. Tracy, *Jonathan Edwards, Pastor: Religion and Society in Eighteenth Century Northampton* (New York, 1980). Other important analyses of changing patterns of community life in colonial New England include Richard Bushman, *From Puritan to Yankee: Character and the Social Order in Connecticut, 1690–1765* (New York, 1970); David H. Flaherty, *Privacy in Colonial New England* (Charlottesville, 1973); Philip Greven, *Four Generations: Population, Land, and Family in Colonial Andover, Massachusetts* (Ithaca, 1970); James Henretta, "Families and Farms: *Mentalité* in Pre-Industrial America," *William and Mary Quarterly*, 3rd ser., 35 (1978), 3–32; and John J. Waters, "Patrimony, Succession, and Social Stability: Guilford, Connecticut in the Eighteenth Century," in *Perspectives in American History*, 10 (1976).

14. See Labaree, *Patriots and Partisans*, pp. 1–15; and Greenslet, *The Lowells*, pp. 26–27.

15. Tharp, *Appletons of Beacon Hill*, pp. 20–22.

16. For an interesting discussion of the relationship between changing social and economic conditions and the coming of the Revolution see Kenneth A. Lockridge, "Social Change and the Meaning of the American Revolution," *Journal of Social History*, 6 (1973), 403–439. Gross, in *Minutemen*, shows how such considerations worked to shape events in a single town.

17. Gregory, *Nathan Appleton*, p. 6.

18. Tharp, *Appletons of Beacon Hill*, p. 23.

19. Ibid., pp. 23–27.

20. [Kidder and Gould], *History of New Ipswich*, pp. 118–119, 131–132, and 205–209.

21. The Kidder and Gould *History of New Ipswich*, published in 1852, is probably itself a good example of how the Appletons wished to remember the town—and to have it remembered by others. Dedicated to Samuel Appleton, the book was clearly financed by him as well. The activities of the family receive extensive coverage, and despite considerable evidence presented to the contrary, the final years of the preceding century are described as a period of great prosperity: "the town was in a flourishing condition, and in many

respects was in as effective a condition as it has ever been since." Ibid., pp. 119–120.

Some sense of the uses the family made of the volume is suggested by the copy in the Williams College Library, which seems to have been a gift and is inscribed, in a rather shaky hand: "For Williams College Library, From Samuel Appleton, aged 86 yrs. 4 mos. & 13 days."

22. Porter, *Jacksons and Lees*, pp. 346–390; and Labaree, *Patriots and Partisans*, pp. 67–92. Labaree demonstrates that in general the commercial elite of Newburyport fared quite badly in the aftermath of the Revolution, most of them eventually being displaced by a rising generation of self-made merchants. See pp. 94–119 and 207–219—"Biographical Sketches"—as well.

23. Lowell to William Cabot, Jan. 2, 1812, Francis C. Lowell MSS, MHS.

24. Lawrence to William R. Lawrence, Aug. 27, 1829, *Diary and Correspondence of Amos Lawrence*, p. 90.

25. Lawrence to William R. Lawrence, Jan. 16, 1831, ibid., p. 103.

26. John Adams, quoted in Greenslet, *The Lowells*, p. 52.

27. Ibid.

28. Morison, *Harrison Gray Otis*, pp. 193–203 and 218–223. See also Allen Chamberlain, *Beacon Hill, Its Ancient Pastures and Early Mansions* (Boston, 1925); Harold Kirker and James Kirker, *Bulfinch's Boston, 1787–1817* (New York, 1964); William H. Pierson, Jr., *American Buildings and Their Architects: The Colonial and Neo-Classical Styles* (Garden City, N.Y., 1976), pp. 240–268; and Walter M. Whitehill, *Boston: A Topographical History* (Boston, 1963).

29. Modern judgments tend to confirm this view. Writes William Pierson, Jr.: "As the century progressed, and the sonorous tones of an aggressive romanticism began to demand an audience, Beacon Hill remained aloof. In a rising tide of abundance, it became an island of restrained classicism, serene and secure in the strength of its Bulfinchian heritage." *American Buildings*, p. 259.

30. For an especially thoughtful analysis of the unique place of literature in Boston see Martin Green, *The Problem of Boston: Some Readings in Cultural History* (New York, 1966). Two other studies which deal with the subject are Van Wyck Brooks, *The Flowering of New England* (New York, 1952) and David B. Tyack, *George Ticknor and the Boston Brahmins* (Cambridge, Mass., 1967).

31. The "Memoir" is reprinted in its entirety in Josiah Quincy, *The History of the Boston Athenaeum, with Biographical Notices of its Deceased Founders* (Cambridge, Mass., 1851), pp. 25–43.

32. Ibid., pp. 32–34.

33. Ibid., p. 36.

34. Ibid., pp. 41–43.

35. The original subscribers are listed in ibid., pp. 43–45. Also, two complete lists—one arranged chronologically and the other alphabetically—of all proprietors from the founding through the end of 1850 appear in pp. 243–263. My calculations are based on those lists.

On the high level of affluence characteristic of Athenaeum proprietors in general see Ronald Story, "Class and Culture in Boston: The Athenaeum, 1807–1860," *American Quarterly*, 27 (1975), 178–199.

36. "Memoir," quoted in Quincy, *History of the Boston Athenaeum*, p. 38.

37. The rules and regulations are reprinted in ibid., pp. 48–53.

38. "Memoir," quoted in ibid., pp. 37–38. On William Roscoe see Story, "Class and Culture in Boston," pp. 184–186.

39. Quincy's address is reprinted in full in Bowditch, *Massachusetts General Hospital*, pp. 41–44.

40. Ibid., p. 42.

41. Ibid., pp. 7–25.

42. Bowditch's analysis appears in ibid., pp. 432–433.

43. Ibid., pp. 215–345. On the Perkins Institution and Howe's work there see Seaburg and Paterson, *Colonel T. H. Perkins*, pp. 377–384; and Harold Schwartz, *Samuel Gridley Howe, Social Reformer* (Cambridge 1956). Bowditch's lengthy account of the first use of ether—and of the ensuing protracted dispute as to who deserved credit for the discovery—is in fact one of the few times when he describes medical practices at the hospital in any detail at all. The bulk of his history is taken up instead with subjects like fund-raising, numbers of patients, and trustee visits to the wards. This would seem to suggest two things, both no doubt true: that as a nonprofessional he did not consider himself sufficiently knowledgeable to discuss medical matters; and second, that in his opinion what remained most notable about the institution was indeed the high level of community involvement which characterized it—a point he makes time and again.

44. Peter D. Hall also contrasts the intensely local outlook of Boston's philanthropists with patterns found elsewhere in the nation, but he draws the contrast rather differently than I have here. See Hall, *Organization of American Culture*, especially pp. 178–180.

On the benevolent societies and their organizers and sponsors two important sources are: Clifford S. Griffin, *Their Brothers' Keepers: Moral Stewardship in the United States 1800–1865* (New Brunswick, N.J., 1960); and Bertram Wyatt-Brown, *Lewis Tappan and the Evangelical War against Slavery* (Cleveland, 1969).

45. Bowditch, *Massachusetts General Hospital*, p. 447.

46. Ibid., p. 446.

47. Bowditch in his history even lists the weeks when trustees *failed* to visit the hospital or the asylum. Up to 1850 there were barely a dozen such instances in each case. Ibid., pp. 383–384. Interestingly, just under half the omitted visits fell in the period 1834–1841, a time of more or less acute financial dislocation. Five omissions (the most for any single year) occurred in one month—August—of 1837 alone. At that point all banks had suspended specie payments and the panic precipitated by the Bank War was at its height.

48. Eliot, quoted in ibid., p. 119.

49. Ibid., p. 72.

50. Ibid., pp. 421–422 and 731–733. On the perpetuation of the pattern see Traux, *The Doctors Warren*. Martin Green argues that "no other of the world's great hospitals has a record like this." Green, *Problem of Boston*, p. 49.

51. The standard general history of Harvard is Samuel Eliot Morison, *Three Centuries of Harvard* (Cambridge, Mass., 1936). Other useful sources are: Josiah Quincy, *The History of Harvard University*, 2 vols. (Cambridge, Mass.,

1840); Harvard University, *Historical Register of Harvard University, 1636–1936* (Cambridge, Mass., 1937); and Seymour E. Harris, *Economics of Harvard* (New York, 1970).

Ronald Story, in his *Harvard and the Boston Upper Class,* provides a trenchant analysis of the multiple ties between Harvard and Boston's economic elite during the period. The extensive use of information gathered from probate records is especially impressive. On the same subject see also Hall, *Organization of American Culture,* pp. 178–206.

In addition there are several studies that help place developments at Harvard in the broader context of the history of American higher education in general, including Bernard Bailyn, *Education in the Forming of American Society* (New York, 1960); Frederick Rudolph, *The American College and University* (New York, 1962); Lawrence Veysey, *The Emergence of the American University* (Chicago, 1965); and John S. Whitehead, *The Separation of College and State: Columbia, Dartmouth, Harvard, and Yale* (New Haven, 1973).

52. Morison, *Three Centuries of Harvard,* pp. 158–159. For a fuller treatment see Story, *Harvard and the Boston Upper Class,* pp. 24–56.

53. The Fellows of the Corporation are listed in Harvard, *Historical Register,* pp. 5–9.

54. Harris, *Economics of Harvard,* pp. 237–247. See also Whitehead, *Separation of College and State.*

55. Francis Bowen, quoted in Harris, *Economics of Harvard,* p. 238.

56. Ibid., pp. 279–280 and 292–295.

On the sources of this private support Story offers the following conclusions: "Approximately 80 percent of the Massachusetts millionaires of the antebellum period contributed $1,000 or more to Harvard, as did 68 percent of the directors of the largest New England textile firms and 52 percent of the Boston Athenaeum board of trustees. The names of some 90 percent of the wealthiest 200 Boston families of 1848 appear on the Harvard subscription or individual contributor's lists, as do those of 85 percent of the antebellum directors of the three leading Boston financial institutions," Story, *Harvard and the Boston Upper Class,* p. 31.

Comparing the groups Story cites, it is interesting to note that the one in which the Boston Associates would have been most prominent—directors of large textile firms—has a lower percentage of contributors than those defined simply in terms of wealth. Though Story does not comment on the fact, the suggestion would seem to be that the Associates, if still very generous to Harvard, were marginally less so than Boston's rich in general were.

57. Lists of subscribers for the projects in question appear in Quincy, *History of Harvard,* II, 542–553, 564–565, and 637.

58. Ibid., II, 412.

59. Ibid., II, 412–413. In his letter presenting the Ebeling Library, Thorndike wrote: "I have to request that your Corporation will be pleased to accept this library, with my best wishes that it may be found conducive to the great end we all have in view, the extention of knowledge in our country." Ibid., II, 596–597. On Thorndike's life and career, see also J. D. Forbes, *Israel Thorndike: Federalist Financier* (New York, 1953).

60. *Report of the Visiting Committee of Harvard Made to the Overseers,* Jan. 1849, quoted in Harris, *Economics of Harvard,* p. 239. The report also described Harvard as "the El Dorado of Education," ibid., p. 231.

61. See Harvard, *Historical Register,* pp. 43–65, "Holders of Endowed Professorships," and 97–478, "Officers of Government and Instruction." A glance at the listings under the names Lowell, Jackson, Thorndike, Appleton, Lawrence, Perkins, and Bowditch will suggest something of the dimensions and persistence of the phenomenon.

62. Bowditch, *Massachusetts General Hospital,* p. 62.

63. White, *Massachusetts Hospital Life Insurance Company,* pp. 39–40.

64. Bowditch, *Massachusetts General Hospital,* pp. 179–183.

65. A list of subscribers—with Bowditch's analysis—appears in ibid., pp. 434–438. My calculations are based on those data.

66. Ibid., pp. 42 and 433.

67. Ibid., pp. 6–7.

68. Oscar Handlin, *Boston's Immigrants: A Study in Acculturation* (Cambridge, Mass., 1959), pp. 51–52 and 243.

69. Ibid., pp. 124–150.

70. Jackson and Warren, quoted in Bowditch, *Massachusetts General Hospital,* p. 5n.

71. Ibid., pp. 124 and 384–393; and Massachusetts General Hospital, *Memorial and Historical Volume,* pp. 118–119.

There are two studies of the McLean Asylum, neither of which adds significantly to the information contained in the sources cited above. The two are Morrill Wyman, *The Early History of the McLean Asylum for the Insane* (Cambridge, Mass., 1877); and Nina F. Little, *Early Years of the McLean Hospital* (Boston, 1972), which consists largely of the journal of a medical student who served as apothecary of the institution in 1825.

On the care and treatment of the mentally ill in general during the period see Norman Dain, *Concepts of Insanity in the United States, 1789–1805* (New Brunswick, N.J., 1964); Albert Deutsh, *The Mentally Ill in America: A History of Their Care and Treatment from Colonial Times* (Garden City, N.Y., 1938); Gerald H. Grob, *The State and the Mentally Ill: A History of the Worcester State Hospital in Massachusetts, 1830–1920* (Chapel Hill, N.C., 1966); and David Rothman, *The Discovery of the Asylum: Social Order and Disorder in the New Republic* (Boston, 1971).

72. Bowditch, *Massachusetts General Hospital,* p. 82; Massachusetts General Hospital, *Memorial and Historical Volume,* pp. 120–121.

73. Massachusetts General Hospital, *Memorial and Historical Volume,* pp. 120–121.

74. Ibid., p. 119.

75. Bowditch, *Massachusetts General Hospital,* p. 174.

76. Ibid.

77. Massachusetts General Hospital, *Memorial and Historical Volume,* p. 123. Perhaps as a consequence of Bell's concern, at about this time hospital officials and trustee reports, in presenting statistics on patients, began distinguishing between "Americans" and "foreigners." See Bowditch, *Massachusetts General Hospital,* pp. 354, 360, and 366.

78. Massachusetts General Hospital, *Memorial and Historical Volume*, p. 121.

79. Bowditch, *Massachusetts General Hospital*, p. 364.

80. Ibid., pp. 485–486; Massachusetts General Hospital, *Memorial and Historical Volume*, p. 120.

81. Bowditch, *Massachusetts General Hospital*, p. 364.

82. Lawrence to William R. Lawrence, Jan. 31, 1830, *Diary and Correspondence of Amos Lawrence*, pp. 91–92.

83. Ibid., pp. 169–174.

84. Lawrence to William R. Lawrence, Nov. 12, 1852, ibid., pp. 332–333.

85. Lawrence to William R. Lawrence, Jan. 31, 1830, ibid., pp. 91–92.

86. Lawrence to "Sister M.," Apr. 19, 1843, ibid., pp. 166–168. See also pp. 139–140.

87. Webster, speech of June 17, 1843, *The Writings and Speeches of Daniel Webster* ed. James W. McIntyre (Boston, 1903), I, 259–283. For an analysis of the occasion and Webster's speech, see Robert F. Dalzell, Jr., *Daniel Webster and the Trial of American Nationalism, 1843–1852* (Boston, 1973), pp. 1–16.

88. Lawrence to J. Hamilton, July 23, 1849, *Diary and Correspondence of Amos Lawrence*, p. 270.

89. Lawrence to J. Hamilton, Apr. 8, 1851, ibid., pp. 294–296.

90. Lawrence, quoted in ibid., p. 223.

91. Ibid., pp. 221–224; Samuel A. Green, "Groton," in *History of Middlesex County, Massachusetts, with Biographical Sketches of Many of its Pioneers and Prominent Men*, ed. D. Hamilton Hurd (Philadelphia, 1890), II, 526.

92. There are several histories of Williams College, including Calvin Durfee, *A History of Williams College* (Boston, 1860); Arthur L. Perry, *Williamstown and Williams College* (Williamstown, 1899); and Leverett W. Spring, *A History of Williams College* (Boston, 1917). Hopkins' life and career are admirably detailed in Frederick Rudolph, *Mark Hopkins and the Log: Williams College, 1836–1872* (New Haven, 1956).

93. On the Lowell Institute see Harriette R. Smith, *The History of the Lowell Institute* (Boston, 1898); and Edward Weeks, *The Lowells and Their Institute* (Boston, 1966). Lowell's will further stipulated that his bequest should be administered by a single trustee, preferably a member of the Lowell family. In the twenty years before 1860, the institute sponsored more than a hundred different lecture series and attracted a total audience of several hundred thousand people.

94. Lawrence to Robert Trumbull, Nov. 2, 1841, *Diary and Correspondence of Amos Lawrence*, pp. 160–161. See also Lawrence to "My Friend," June 11, 1847, ibid., pp. 246–247, in which he states: "I offer it as my opinion that the Unitarianism growing up among us the few years past has so much philosophy as to endanger the Christian character of our denomination, and to make us mere rationalists of the German school, which I dread more than anything in the way of religious practice."

On the theological and social doctrines of Unitarianism a useful study is Daniel W. Howe, *The Unitarian Conscience: Harvard Moral Philosophy, 1805–1861* (Cambridge, Mass., 1970). See also Conrad Wright, *The Beginnings* of

Unitarianism in America (Boston, 1966). Digby Baltzell, in *Puritan Boston and Quaker Philadelphia: Two Protestant Ethics and the Spirit of Class Authority and Leadership* (New York, 1980), provides an insightful discussion of the role of religion in shaping the attitudes and behavior of Boston's elite over the years.

95. Rudolph, *Hopkins*, p. 176.

96. Ibid.

97. Lawrence to Hopkins, Jan. 26, 1846, *Diary and Correspondence of Amos Lawrence*, p. 213.

98. Rudolph, *Hopkins*, p. 177.

99. Hopkins, sermon delivered at Williams College, Feb. 21, 1853, quoted in Lawrence, *Diary and Correspondence of Amos Lawrence*, p. 290.

Lawrence's very substantial donations to Williams College and to the academy at Groton, as well as his brother's to the latter institution and those of the Appletons to New Ipswich Academy, would seem to raise an interesting issue. While there is nothing to suggest that this sort of philanthropy was typical of Boston's economic elite as a whole, it did exist and it stands in rather striking contrast to the pattern of highly concentrated, carefully calculated giving to Harvard detailed in Story's *Harvard and the Boston Upper Class*. For all the dominance of that pattern, clearly there were others. See note 56 for further evidence on the point.

100. Hopkins, sermon of Feb. 21, 1853, *Diary and Correspondence of Amos Lawrence*, p. 291.

101. Rudolph, *Hopkins*, p. 178.

102. Lawrence to Hopkins, Nov. 11, 1850, quoted in ibid., p. 187.

103. Lawrence to Hopkins, June 12, 1848. *Diary and Correspondence of Amos Lawrence*, p. 259.

104. Hopkins, sermon of Feb. 21, 1853, quoted in ibid., p. 349.

105. Lawrence's son describes his activities in this regard in ibid., pp. 92–94. See also Rudolph, *Hopkins*, pp. 178–180.

106. Hopkins, sermon of Feb. 21, 1853, *Diary and Correspondence of Amos Lawrence*, p. 348.

107. Amos A. Lawrence, diary, Jan. 24, 1842, Amos A. Lawrence MSS, MHS.

108. Lawrence to [no name or date], *Diary and Correspondence of Amos Lawrence*, p. 257.

109. Lawrence to William J. Hubbard, Aug. 14, 1844, quoted in Hill, *Memoir of Abbott Lawrence*, p. 105.

110. Lawrence to [no name], July 25, 1845, quoted in ibid., p. 106.

111. Quincy, *History of Harvard*, II, 545–553 and 637; Bowditch, *Massachusetts General Hospital*, p. 436.

112. Hill, *Memoir of Abbott Lawrence*, pp. 106–107.

113. Ibid., pp. 108–116; Morison, *Three Centuries of Harvard*, pp. 279–280; Harris, *Economics of Harvard*, pp. 287–288. Presumably in recognition of his generosity, Lawrence, who was to serve as an Overseer from 1854 to 1855, was awarded an honorary degree by Harvard in 1854. Harvard, *Historical Register*, p. 294.

114. Lawrence to Samuel A. Eliot, June 7, 1847, quoted in Hill, *Memoir of Abbott Lawrence*, pp. 109–114.

115. Lawrence to Abbott Lawrence, June 9, 1847, *Diary and Correspondence of Amos Lawrence*, pp. 244–248.

116. Morison, *Three Centuries of Harvard*, p. 279. See also Lawrence to "a friend" [no date], *Diary and Correspondence of Amos Lawrence*, p. 245.

117. Morison, *Three Centuries of Harvard*, pp. 279–280; Harris, *Economics of Harvard*, p. 288. Agassiz was the first European-trained scientist on the Harvard faculty, and he turned the Lawrence Scientific School into an institution for study in the natural sciences. On his life and career see Edward Lurie, *Louis Agassiz: A Life in Science* (Chicago, 1960). In addition to teaching at Harvard, Agassiz married a granddaughter of Thomas H. Perkins. On his ties to the Boston elite, see Story, *Harvard and the Boston Upper Class*, pp. 84–87.

118. Hill, *Memoir of Abbott Lawrence*, pp. 114 and 126–127. By 1876, in addition to building and maintaining a group of houses on East Canton Street in Boston, the trustees had distributed over $17,000 to various charities in the city. Ibid.

119. Daphne Bennett, *King without a Crown: Albert, Prince Consort of England, 1819–1861* (Philadelphia, 1977), p. 168; Hermione Hobhouse, *Prince Albert: His Life and Work* (London, 1983), pp. 57–58. Albert's interest in the housing problems of the poor found its chief outlet through the activities of the Society for Improving the Condition of the Labouring Class, of which he became president in 1844. The society was responsible for building several model housing complexes in London, and in 1851 Albert arranged for the construction of a pair of cottages in Hyde Park, near the site of the Crystal Palace, where thousands of people visited them during the Great Exhibition. As minister to Great Britain, Lawrence played a major role in organizing American participation in the exhibition—the first world's fair and the most successful of all of Albert's various projects.

120. Hill, *Memoir of Abbott Lawrence*, pp. 107 and 126.

121. Amos Lawrence's son calculated that his father spent $639,000 for charitable purposes during the last twenty-three years of his life. *Diary and Correspondence of Amos Lawrence*, pp. 311–312.

122. Winthrop, speech of Aug. 20, 1855, *Addresses and Speeches*, II, 210–212.

123. Walter M. Whitehill, *Boston Public Library: A Centennial History* (Cambridge, Mass., 1956), pp. 34–35 and 41.

Whitehill's history remains the standard source on the Boston Public Library, but his account of the founding of the institution should be supplemented by three other studies that contain important information: Justin Winsor, "Libraries in Boston," in Winsor, *Memorial History of Boston*, IV, 279–294; Horace G. Wadlin, *The Public Library of the City of Boston: A History* (Boston, 1911); and Jesse Shera, *Foundations of the Public Library: The Origins of the Public Library Movement in New England, 1629–1855* (Chicago, 1949).

124. See Tyack, *George Ticknor*.

Considering the importance of Ticknor's role in bringing the Boston Public Library into being, it is surprising that Tyack devotes only five pages (208–

212) to the subject. For another discussion of Ticknor as well as the library see Green, *The Problem of Boston*, pp. 80–101.

125. Parker, quoted in Green, *The Problem of Boston*, p. 84.

126. Ibid., p. 101.

127. Ticknor to Daniel Webster, Feb. 2, 1826, quoted in Whitehill, *Boston Public Library*, pp. 2–3.

128. See Quincy, *Boston Athenaeum*, pp. 94–99. In January 1826 a committee was created to consider, among other things, the feasibility "of uniting, in the Athenaeum, the principal circulating libraries of this city." Ticknor served on the committee, and presumably it was there that he worked to have his plan adopted—unsuccessfully, as it turned out. The committee did recommend that the Athenaeum "join" to its holdings those of the Boston Medical Library and the Massachusetts Scientific Society, and the recommendation was accepted. "Union" went no farther than that, however, and nothing at all was done about admitting the general public.

When the committee was established the Athenaeum's finances were at a temporary low ebb, but between then and the time the committee made its final report, substantial contributions from Thomas H. and James Perkins plus a drive for new members remedied the difficulty. Ibid., pp. 97–105.

129. Whitehill, *Boston Public Library*, pp. 3–11; Wadlin, *Public Library of Boston*, pp. 1–5; Shera, *Foundations of the Public Library*, pp. 172–174. See also Josiah P. Quincy, "The Character and Services of Alexandre Vattemare," *Massachusetts Historical Society, Proceedings*, 21 (1884), 260–272.

130. Circular letter [no date], quoted in Whitehill. *Boston Public Library*, p. 7.

131. Committee report [no date], quoted in ibid., p. 8.

132. Committee report of August, 1848, quoted in Quincy, *Boston Athenaeum*, p. 186. See also ibid., pp. 204–205; and Whitehill, *Boston Public Library*, pp. 11–15.

133. Quincy, *Boston Athenaeum*, p. 186.

134. Whitehill, *Boston Public Library*, pp. 19–35; Wadlin, *Public Library of Boston*, pp. 11–46.

135. Boston, City Doc. No. 37, *Report of the Trustees of the Public Library of the City of Boston, July, 1852* (Boston, 1852), pp. 16–17. Ticknor was the principal author of the report.

136. Ibid., p. 15.

137. Whitehill, *Boston Public Library*, p. 38.

138. Ticknor's letter, which appeared in the *Daily Advertiser* of Mar. 14, 1853, was subsequently republished in pamphlet form under the title *Union of the Boston Athenaeum and the Boston Public Library* (Boston, 1853).

139. Whitehill, *Boston Public Library*, pp. 39–40.

140. Josiah Quincy, *An Appeal in Behalf of the Boston Athenaeum, Address to the Proprietors* (Boston, 1853).

141. Whitehill, *Boston Public Library*, p. 40.

142. Quincy, address of July 4, 1818, quoted in Bowditch, *Massachusetts General Hospital*, p. 42, n.

Quincy had also been surprisingly receptive to Vattemare's ideas a dozen years earlier, writing to his son: "In short I see but few obstacles, and a great advantage in the scheme proposed, and I am not for rejecting it, on the consideration that it did not originate with us. I hope some meeting may be had and an attempt made. We can never hope to succeed in anything, if we begin with a preconception that it is unattainable." Quincy to Josiah Quincy, Jr., Apr. 14, 1841, quoted in Shera, *Foundations of the Public Library*, pp. 173–174.

143. The resolutions are reprinted in full in Wadlin, *Public Library of Boston*, pp. 2–5.

144. See Howe, *Unitarian Conscience*, pp. 226–231; also Joseph Dorfman, *The Economic Mind in American Civilization* (New York, 1946), II, 835–844.

145. Francis Bowen, *The Principles of Political Economy Applied to the Condition, the Resources, and the Institutions of the American People* (1856), p. 18.

146. Bowen, "French Ideas of Democracy and Community of Goods," *North American Review*, 69 (1849), 324–325.

147. Bowen, *Principles of Political Economy*, p. iii. See also Gregory, *Nathan Appleton*, p. vi, where Bowen's dedication is reprinted.

148. Lawrence to G. W. Blagden, Nov. 4, 1847, *Diary and Correspondence of Amos Lawrence*, p. 316.

149. Whitehill, *Boston Public Library*, p. 14; Wadlin, *Public Library of Boston*, p. 13.

150. Bowditch, *Massachusetts General Hospital*, p. 448; Harris, *Economics of Harvard*, p. 270; Quincy, *Boston Athenaeum*, p. 211.

For two contemporary estimates—one made in 1845 and the other fifteen years later by the same person—of total contributions to Boston "charities" see Samuel A. Eliot, "Public and Private Charities in Boston," *North American Review*, 61 (1845), 145–159; and Samuel A. Eliot, "Charities of Boston," ibid., 91 (1860), 154–157. Relying largely on Eliot's figures, Story concludes that "Bostonians expended at least ten million dollars in charitable funds between 1800 and 1860, approximately 70 percent of it on more or less permanent, endowed institutions and societies." Story, *Harvard and the Boston Upper Class*, p. 8. Of course only a portion of the money contributed to endowed institutions actually went into endowment.

151. Harris, *Economics of Harvard*, p. 368. Harris points out that "today one might consider this a conflict of interest," since Lawrence at that point had very substantial investments of his own in the Pacific Mills.

152. Green's *Problem of Boston* is in fact a sustained—and generally quite compelling—amplification of this thesis.

153. For an interesting description of how the process worked in detail at Harvard, see Story, *Harvard and the Boston Upper Class*, pp. 89–134.

154. McGouldrick, *New England Textiles*, pp. 81 and 251; Ware, *New England Cotton Manufacture*, pp. 151–153.

155. Green, *Holyoke*, pp. 34–41 and 55–65. Green's account of the failure of the Hadley Falls Company is particularly thorough and provides a telling picture of conditions in the textile industry in general during the period.

156. Dublin, *Women at Work*, pp. 138–164. At towns established after 1845 the labor force was heavily composed of immigrants from the beginning. See Cole, *Immigrant City*, pp. 26–41; and Green, *Holyoke*, pp. 30–32 and 48–50.

6. Politics and the Uses of Power

1. Lawrence to William R. Lawrence, Jan. 16, 1831, *Diary and Correspondence of Amos Lawrence*, pp. 103–104. The definition of "working-man" that Lawrence offered his son underscored the point. "He is a working-man whose mind is employed, whether in making researches into the meaning of hieroglyphics or in demonstrating any invention in the arts, just as much as he who cuts down the forests, or holds the plough, or swings the sledgehammer," ibid.

2. Webster, speech of July 11, 1832, *Writings and Speeches*, VI, 179–180.

3. Robert Rich, " 'A Wilderness of Whigs': The Wealthy Men of Boston," *Journal of Social History*, 6 (1971), 261–276.

The closeness of the ties between Boston's economic elite and the Whig party has been repeatedly stressed in studies of Massachusetts politics during the period. See for example Kinley J. Brauer, *Cotton versus Conscience: Massachusetts Whig Politics and Southwestern Expansion, 1843–1848* (Lexington, Ky., 1967), pp. 7–29; O'Connor, *Lords of the Loom*, pp. 28–41; and—for a more recent view—Ronald P. Formisano, *The Transformation of Political Culture: Massachusetts Parties, 1790s–1840s* (New York, 1983), pp. 283–288 and 314–315.

4. Thomas Hancock to Christopher Kilby, July 15, 1745, quoted in Robert Zemsky, *Merchants, Farmers, and River Gods: An Essay on Eighteenth-Century American Politics* (Boston, 1971), p. 196.

5. Though the standard source on Thomas Hancock is W. T. Baxter, *The House of Hancock: Business in Boston, 1724–1775* (Cambridge, Mass., 1945), Zemsky's chapter-long analysis of the connections between Hancock's commercial and political activities provides an especially revealing picture of how the two operated together in colonial Massachusetts. See *Merchants, Farmers, and River Gods*, pp. 178–215. On the early stages of the evolution of the system see Bailyn, *New England Merchants*, particularly the final three chapters.

6. Keayne's troubles had arisen over a sale of sixpenny nails for 10d. during the first decade of Massachusetts Bay Colony's settlement. Fined by the General Court and censured by his congregation, he nursed his resentment as long as he lived, eventually producing, as his final will and testament, an *Apologia* that ran to over a hundred pages and included—along with instructions for various philanthropic bequests—an elaborate defense of his commercial dealings. See Bernard Bailyn, "The *Apologia* of Robert Keayne," *William and Mary Quarterly*, 3rd ser., 7 (1950), 568–577.

7. Zemsky, *Merchants, Farmers, and River Gods*, pp. 196–205. As Zemsky points out, Hancock's ultimate interest in securing the Louisbourg contract—and presumably Apthorp's as well—was less in the profits to be made by selling provisions to the British garrison than in providing himself with a supply of reliable bills of exchange to use in commercial transactions with London.

8. On the connections between Federalism and the social and economic elite of Massachusetts see James M. Banner, Jr., *To the Hartford Convention: The Federalists and the Origins of Party Politics in Massachusetts, 1789–1815* (New York, 1970), pp. 122–197. Paul Goodman, in *The Democratic-Republicans of*

Massachusetts: Politics in a Young Republic (Cambridge, Mass., 1964), pp. 70–86 and 97–127, provides a corresponding analysis for the state's Jeffersonians. Typical of Republican merchants were the Crowninshields of Salem. In the 1790s they were challenging the position of the Derbys as the port's leading traders; under Monroe, Benjamin Crowninshield served as secretary of the navy. In the meantime the family had purchased the Derby country seat, and—in a Republican "reform" of the state banking system, which occurred in 1811 and allowed all existing charters to lapse—they had secured one of only two new grants of banking privileges in Massachusetts. Another example was a group of newly risen merchants led by William King of Bath, Maine. While championing the rights of squatters in the district, King and his associates managed to parlay their political influence into title to three Maine townships, plus a string of other "benefits"; Goodman, *Democratic-Republicans*, pp. 108–115, 122–127, 155–162, and 178–181.

9. On Henshaw's early business and political activities, see Arthur B. Darling, *Political Changes in Massachusetts, 1824–1848: A Study of Liberal Movements in Politics* (New Haven, 1925), pp. 40–84; and Arthur M. Schlesinger, Jr., *The Age of Jackson* (Boston, 1945), pp. 146–148.

10. Of the many studies of the Revolution in Massachusetts, the one that gives the clearest sense of the role such factors played in the conflict is Bernard Bailyn's *Thomas Hutchinson*. There are several biographies of Hancock, the most recent being Herbert S. Allan, *John Hancock: Patriot in Purple* (New York, 1948); and William M. Fowler, Jr., *The Baron of Beacon Hill: A Biography of John Hancock* (Boston, 1980). On Newburyport, see Labaree, *Patriots and Partisans*, pp. 16–41. The striking unanimity with which Newburyport's merchants supported the patriot cause may well have been due to the fact that the town was the most recently established of the colony's major ports, which in turn would have given its merchants less opportunity than those elsewhere to translate their economic success into political influence.

11. Zemsky, *Merchants, Farmers, and River Gods*, pp. 99–156 and 216–283.

12. See Bernard Bailyn, *The Ideological Origins of the American Revolution* (Cambridge, Mass., 1967), especially pp. 34–54. Other studies that illuminate in important ways the ideology in question—including the "country party" tradition—are Caroline Robbins, *The Eighteenth Century Commonwealthman: Studies in the Transmission, Development and Circumstance of English Liberal Thought from the Restoration of Charles II until the War with the Thirteen Colonies* (Cambridge, Mass., 1961); Isaac Kramnick, *Bolingbroke and His Circle: The Politics of Nostalgia in the Age of Walpole* (Cambridge, Mass., 1968); and J. G. A. Pocock, *The Machiavellian Moment: Florentine Political Thought and the Atlantic Republican Tradition* (Princeton, 1975).

13. Daniel Howe, *The Political Culture of the American Whigs* (Chicago, 1979), pp. 76–95. In taking the position he does, Howe is well aware that it might "at first seem anomalous" to link the American Whigs, who favored industrialization and economic development, to the country party tradition. Certainly in the hands of someone like Bolingbroke, country party ideology was uncompromisingly antimodern. But the point that Howe repeatedly stresses in discussing the Whigs' commitment to modernization is how thor-

oughly tied it was to a belief in traditional social values and institutions. Indeed for many Whigs, he argues, the hope was that economic modernization could actually be made to function as a "substitute" for social change. Ibid., pp. 7–8.

14. For a thoughtful analysis of how local conditions, revolutionary ideology, and British policy worked together to shape events in a single town see Gross, *Minutemen*.

15. On Massachusetts politics in the years immediately following the Revolution, a particularly useful study is Van Beck Hall, *Politics without Parties: Massachusetts, 1780–1791* (Pittsburgh, 1972). On the Jeffersonian era see the sources cited in notes 20 to 32.

16. The most extensive recent account of Shays' Rebellion is David P. Szatmary, *Shays' Rebellion: The Making of an Agrarian Insurrection* (Amherst, 1980). Szatmary appropriately stresses the growing radicalism of the Shaysites' demands, but his treatment of the final stages of the conflict is less satisfactory, omitting as it does any discussion of several important steps taken in Boston to calm the protest. See also Marion Starkey, *A Little Rebellion* (New York, 1955); Handlin and Handlin, *Commonwealth*, pp. 33–52; and Goodman, *Democratic-Republicans*, pp. 10–16.

17. "Address of the General Court to the People," [no date], quoted in Handlin and Handlin, *Commonwealth*, p. 46.

18. Ibid., p. 29. On the Constitution of 1780, see also Labaree, *Patriots and Partisans*, pp. 42–57; and Ronald M. Peters, Jr., *The Massachusetts Constitution of 1780: A Social Compact* (Amherst, 1978).

19. Handlin and Handlin, *Commonwealth*, pp. 49–52; Goodman, *Democratic-Republicans*, pp. 15–16.

20. Goodman, *Democratic-Republicans*, pp. 128–153. On the growth of religious dissent and its impact on politics see ibid., pp. 86–96; Jacob C. Meyer, *Church and State in Massachusetts from 1740 to 1833* (Cleveland 1930); William G. McLoughlin, *New England Dissent, 1630–1833: The Baptists and the Separation of Church and State*, II (Cambridge, Mass., 1971); Banner, *To the Hartford Convention*, pp. 197–215; and Formisano, *Transformation of Political Culture*, pp. 153–159.

21. The extent to which political parties during the Jeffersonian era came to resemble modern American political parties remains a topic of lively debate among historians. For two rather different views of the subject see Banner, *To the Hartford Convention*, pp. 216–267; and Formisano, *Transformation of Political Culture*, pp. 84–148. On balance Formisano makes the stronger case. As impressive as the Federalists' organizational achievement seems when compared to what had preceded it in Massachusetts, it still fell far short of being truly modern—or democratic—in structure, style, and intent. Indeed much the same can be said of most aspects of politics during the period. As Formisano argues: "Political life in the early national period is not understood primarily by looking ahead to a triumphant arrival of organization and democracy. Political structures as they emerged were a synthesis of old and new" (p. 148). David H. Fischer offers an interpretation similar to Banner's in *The Revolution in American Conservatism: The Federalist Party in the Era of Jeffersonian Democracy* (New York, 1965).

22. *Massachusetts Spy*, July 31 and Aug. 1, 1811, quoted in Goodman, *Democratic-Republicans*, p. 165. On the Religious Freedom Act and the other Republican reforms of 1811 and their political consequences see ibid., pp. 165–181; Banner, *To the Hartford Convention*, pp. 212–215 and 275–279; and Formisano, *Transformation of Political Culture*, pp. 72–76.

23. Gerry, speech of June 7, 1811, quoted in Morison, *Harrison Gray Otis*, p. 315.

24. Otis, quoted in ibid., p. 315.

25. Banner, *To the Hartford Convention*, pp. 313–318.

26. Hadley memorial, quoted in ibid., p. 317.

27. Hatfield memorial, quoted in ibid., p. 317.

28. Wendell memorial, quoted in ibid., p. 317.

29. Morison, *Harrison Gray Otis*, pp. 353–399; Banner, *To the Hartford Convention*, pp. 318–350.

30. Otis to Mrs. Willard [no date], quoted in Banner, *To the Hartford Convention*, p. 332. See also Morison, *Harrison Gray Otis*, pp. 353–354 and 381.

31. Cabot, quoted in Banner, *To the Hartford Convention*, p. 334. The remark was made in a conversation with Edmund Quincy.

32. On Massachusetts Federalism and the Missouri Compromise, see Morison, *Harrison Gray Otis*, pp. 424–432; also Shaw Livermore, Jr., *The Twilight of Federalism: The Disintegration of the Federalist Party, 1815–1830* (Princeton, 1962); and, for a discussion of Federalist attitudes toward slavery in general, Banner, *To the Hartford Convention*, pp. 99–109. Banner correctly stresses that while the party did oppose the expansion of slavery, at no point did it champion the cause of abolition per se.

33. For an analysis of the elections of 1823 and 1824 see Formisano, *Transformation of Political Culture*, pp. 120–125 and 168–170. On the early phases of Jacksonian political activity in Massachusetts see ibid., pp. 246–249; and Darling, *Political Changes in Massachusetts*, pp. 55–84.

Even though the period lacked the focus of strong two-party competition, Formisano argues that it was still one in which a great deal of significant political activity occurred, as various groups around the state maneuvered to press their interests and grievances to the fore. Ultimately, he contends, this "creative chaos" had a major impact on the rise of mass political parties in Massachusetts. *Transformation of Political Culture*, pp. 173–244.

34. Everett to Sir Robert Peel, Jan. 8, 1850, quoted in Handlin and Handlin, *Commonwealth*, p. 215.

35. On the connections between the Commonwealth Bank and the Democratic party, see Darling, *Political Changes in Massachusetts*, pp. 15, 137–138, and 178–179.

36. The development of Whig organization through the election of 1840 is described in Formisano, *Transformation of Political Culture*, pp. 250–267. In addition see Robert J. Haws, "Massachusetts Whigs, 1833–1854" (Ph.D. diss., University of Nebraska, 1973), pp. 9–112. Haws emphasizes the lingering antiparty bias of most Whig leaders during this period, while Formisano sees the general political milieu of the time as "far less overtly antipartisan" than the Jeffersonian era had been. Cf. Howe, *Political Culture of the American Whigs*,

pp. 50–55, which also stresses Whig antipartyism, though Howe does concede that "as time went by, most Whigs became reconciled to the idea of party," so long as the basis for party was issues and not patronage.

37. Haws, "Massachusetts Whigs," pp. 46–47; Formisano, *Transformation of Political Culture*, pp. 252–253.

38. Springfield memorial, quoted in Haws, "Massachusetts Whigs," p. 47.

39. On Appleton's stance in this phase of the Bank War see p. 95.

40. Darling, *Political Changes in Massachusetts*, pp. 178–179 and 224–229.

41. Haws, "Massachusetts Whigs," pp. 20–22 and 27–28; Darling, *Political Changes in Massachusetts*, pp. 22–30; and Formisano, *Transformation of Political Culture*, pp. 168–169. For additional background on the religious and legal issues, see Wright, *Beginnings of Unitarianism in America*; Meyer, *Church and State in Massachusetts*, pp. 184–220; and Leonard Levy, *The Law of the Commonwealth and Chief Justice Shaw: The Evolution of American Law, 1830–1860* (Cambridge, Mass., 1957), pp. 24–42.

42. In the absence of a badly needed book-length study of the subject, the fullest treatments of the Antimasonic movement in Massachusetts are Darling, *Political Changes in Massachusetts*, pp. 85–129; and Formisano, *Transformation of Political Culture*, pp. 197–221. Formisano aptly describes Antimasonry as "middle-class moral populism" (p. 220). On the connections between Antimasonry and religious orthodoxy, see pp. 217–221; and Haws, "Massachusetts Whigs," pp. 23–30.

43. *Columbian Centinel*, Oct. 19, 1833, quoted in Haws, "Massachusetts Whigs," p. 42.

44. For detailed analysis of the Antimasonic vote see Darling, *Political Changes in Massachusetts*, pp. 97, n. 21; 104, n. 37; 115, n. 58; and 127, n. 81; and Formisano, *Transformation of Political Culture*, pp. 206, 210, 212–213, 434, nn. 34 and 35; 436, n. 51; and 437, n. 62.

45. On the widespread use of the conspiracy paradigm in American politics during the period, see Howe, *Political Culture of the American Whigs*, pp. 79–81. Howe rejects the notion, put forth by Richard Hofstadter among others, that a belief in conspiracy is necessarily "paranoid" and that historically it "has a greater affinity for bad causes than good." His conclusion is that "we must overcome this reaction if we are to take American political discourse during the early and middle periods of our history with the seriousness it deserves . . . The paradigm seems paranoid only to those who have imperfectly mastered the language of politics in pre–Civil War America" (pp. 80–81).

46. The efforts of Whig leaders to win Antimasonic support are described in Formisano, *Transformation of Political Culture*, pp. 214–217 and 254; and Haws, "Massachusetts Whigs," pp. 43–45 and 48.

47. Everett to Caleb Cushing, Mar. 2, 1834, quoted in Darling, *Political Changes in Massachusetts*, p. 119.

48. See ibid., pp. 191–193, including nn. 37 and 38. Darling attempts to demonstrate that the Democrats gained very substantial support from former Antimasons, as does Richard McCormick in *The Second American Party System*

(Chapel Hill, N.C., 1966), pp. 48–49, but Formisano concludes that this was not in fact the case. See *Transformation of Political Culture*, pp. 254 and 256.

49. Haws, "Massachusetts Whigs," pp. 49–50.

50. On Webster's role see Sydney Nathans, *Daniel Webster and Jacksonian Democracy* (Baltimore, 1973), pp. 83–89.

51. The Massachusetts Workingmen's movement and party are treated in a number of studies. The chapter on the subject in Formisano's *Transformation of Political Culture* (pp. 222–244) is both balanced and insightful. See also Darling, *Political Changes in Massachusetts*, pp. 97–100, 102, 116, and 188–189; Schlesinger, *Age of Jackson*, pp. 148–154 and 167–170; and—for a sense of the broader context in which the Massachusetts movement operated—Edward Pessen, *Most Uncommon Jacksonians: The Radical Leaders of the Early Labor Movement* (Albany, 1967).

52. Darling, *Political Changes in Massachusetts*, pp. 121–122 and 124–126.

53. Ralph Waldo Emerson, "Character," in *Essays, Second Series* (Boston, 1876), pp. 95, 99, and 105.

54. Ralph Waldo Emerson, "Politics," ibid., p. 209.

55. Ibid., pp. 215–216.

56. Kutler, *Privilege and Creative Destruction*, pp. 1–53. On the impact of the free bridge controversy on Massachusetts politics, see also Darling, *Political Changes in Massachusetts*, pp. 49–55; and Formisano, *Transformation of Political Culture*, pp. 190–195.

57. *An Appeal to the Good Sense of the Legislature and the Community in Favor of a New Bridge to South Boston*, quoted in Kutler, *Privilege and Creative Destruction*, p. 22. The pamphlet was written in defense of another free bridge proposal—one to link Sea Street in Boston to new lands in South Boston—pending at the same time. Henshaw was one of the principal promoters of the project. See Darling, *Political Changes in Massachusetts*, pp. 49–50.

58. Kutler, *Privilege and Creative Destruction*, p. 155.

59. Webster, quoted in ibid., p. 79.

60. Simon Greenleaf to Charles Sumner [no date], quoted in ibid., p. 79. Webster had written his son earlier that he expected to lose the case. Ibid.

61. See ibid., pp. 76–77.

62. *Boston Courier* [no date], quoted in ibid., p. 128. The ties between the *Courier* and the Whigs had been cemented in 1834 with promises of financial support from Nathan Appleton and editorial assistance from Robert Winthrop. See Haws, "Massachusetts Whigs," pp. 50–51.

63. On Henshaw's attitude toward corporations see Darling, *Political Changes in Massachusetts*, pp. 48–50, 134–139, and 197–199; Schlesinger, *Age of Jackson*, pp. 147–148, 170–172, and 175–176; and—for a somewhat different view—Formisano, *Transformation of Political Culture*, pp. 272–273. Formisano stresses that for all Henshaw's involvement in banking and other enterprises, he still took positions on a variety of issues, including monopoly privilege, that no Whig would have found acceptable.

64. The fullest account of the internal struggle for control of the state Democratic organization is to be found in Darling, *Political Changes in Massa-*

chusetts, though Darling's Turnerian convictions led him to oversimplify the contest as one between "city" and "country." See pp. 83 and 173–215, and— on Morton's first term in office and his attempts at reform—pp. 251–273. On the movement for a general incorporation law see also Handlin and Handlin, *Commonwealth,* pp. 233–235.

65. Handlin and Handlin, *Commonwealth,* pp. 173–194. Also, for a thoughtful analysis of Whig economic policy in general, which emphasizes its commitment to controlling as well as stimulating change and takes as one of its examples Nathan Appleton, see Howe, *Political Culture of the American Whigs,* pp. 96–149.

66. Handlin and Handlin, *Commonwealth,* pp. 155–161. On the Associates' support for a limited liability law see Ware, *New England Cotton Manufacture,* pp. 147–148.

67. Handlin and Handlin, *Commonwealth,* pp. 174 n. 2; and Ware, *New England Cotton Manufacture,* Appendix A, "Textile Manufacturing Companies Incorporated in the State of Massachusetts, through 1845," pp. 301–302.

68. These calculations are based on the data provided in Ware, *New England Cotton Manufacture* and in Massachusetts, *Statistics of the Condition and Products of Certain Branches of Industry in Massachusetts, for the Year Ending April 1, 1845* (Boston, 1846), pp. 329–335.

69. *Boston Daily Advertiser,* June 10, 1830, quoted in Salsbury, *The Boston & Albany,* p. 338, n. 17. See also Kutler, *Privilege and Creative Destruction,* p. 51.

70. Kutler, *Privilege and Creative Destruction,* pp. 156–157; Kirkland, *Men, Cities, and Transportation,* I, 116–119 and 126; Salsbury, *The Boston & Albany,* pp. 85–86 and 133.

71. Haws, "Massachusetts Whigs," p. 128.

72. Salsbury, *The Boston & Albany,* pp. 133–156 and 223–225.

73. Ibid., pp. 206–244.

74. Kirkland, *Men, Cities, and Transportation,* I, 387–398.

75. Haws, "Massachusetts Whigs," pp. 130–132.

76. Handlin and Handlin, *Commonwealth,* p. 182.

77. Morton, *Message to the General Court,* Jan. 22, 1840, quoted in Darling, *Political Changes in Massachusetts,* p. 253.

78. *Answer of the Whig Members of Both Houses to the Address of Governor Morton,* quoted in ibid., p. 253. In 1843, while serving his second term as governor, Morton changed his tack on banking and proposed that the board of bank commissioners be abolished; that the books of all banks be opened for inspection by the stockholders; and that statements of loans by banks to their directors be published. Also, his message to the legislature that year again recommended a general incorporation law. But the Whigs managed to block every one of these reforms. Ibid., pp. 296–297 and 299.

79. For two discussions, from rather different perspectives, of these developments see Handlin and Handlin, *Commonwealth,* pp. 144–194; and Horwitz, *Transformation of American Law,* pp. 109–139. While Horwitz, in his introduction, raises a number of questions about the Handlins' approach (see Chapter 4, note 6), Formisano points out that the end results of the two studies are not all that different. He also suggests—appropriately, it seems to me—

that Horwitz himself may have been unduly imprecise in answering the crucial question of who benefited from the changes in American law occurring at the time. Formisano, *Transformation of Political Culture*, pp. 317–318 and 474, n. 33.

80. On the elections of 1839 and 1842, see Darling, *Political Changes in Massachusetts*, pp. 239–250 and 286–293; and Haws, "Massachusetts Whigs," pp. 132–140 and 159–165.

81. There are several studies that treat the temperance movement during the period, including George F. Clark, *History of the Temperance Reform in Massachusetts, 1813–1883* (Boston, 1888); Joseph Gusfield, *Symbolic Crusade: Status Politics and the American Temperance Movement* (Urbana, 1966); and Ian R. Tyrell, *Sobering Up: From Temperance to Prohibition in Antebellum America, 1800–1860* (Westport, Conn., 1979). Once in office the Democrats repealed the fifteen-gallon law, but temperance remained very much an issue in Massachusetts.

82. There is no separate study of the Massachusetts Liberty party, which embraced the cause of immediate emancipation but broke with the Garrisonians over the means to that end. In general, historians have paid surprisingly little attention to the subject. On the growth of the party's vote in the state through 1842, see Darling, *Political Changes in Massachusetts*, pp. 270, n. 25; 281, n. 47; and 289–291, nn. 66 and 67.

83. Webster, speech of Nov. 9, 1843, *Writings and Speeches*, III, 159–185.

84. Lawrence, diary, June 10, 1843, Amos A. Lawrence MSS, MHS.

85. The conflict between Lawrence and Webster is discussed at length in a number of studies, including Nathans, *Daniel Webster and Jacksonian Democracy*, pp. 195–200; Haws, "Massachusetts Whigs," pp. 142–170; and Dalzell, *Daniel Webster*, pp. 61–97.

86. For a list of the contributors to a $2,500 fund collected in Webster's behalf in 1838—almost all of whom were members of the Associates group— see "Boston. Dec. 11, 1838—The following Amts. paid over to Hon. Dan. Webster," Thomas W. Ward MSS, MHS. This was neither the first nor the last time the Associates came to Webster's rescue. Eventually, to spare everyone involved the embarrassment attendant upon the constant appeals for small loans and gifts, as well as to counteract Webster's chronic financial irresponsibility, a fund of $37,000 was deposited in his name at the Massachusetts Hospital Life Insurance Company, with stipulations that the income be paid to him during his lifetime and that the principal revert to the donors on his death. The list of donors contained forty names, including several Appletons and Lowells, William Amory, Josiah Quincy, Jr., and William H. Prescott. See David Sears to Webster, Mar. 21, 1846, Webster, *Writings and Speeches*, XVI 445–446. Unfortunately financial security continued to elude Webster. Shortly before his death he asked to have the payments maintained for his widow's benefit, and the donors agreed.

87. Ward to Baring Brothers, Apr. 29, 1839, Daniel Webster MSS, Dartmouth College; Ward to Joshua Bates, Apr. 15, 1839 and Feb. 27, 1843, Thomas W. Ward MSS, MHS.

88. Lawrence to Webster, Oct. 23, 1830, *Diary and Correspondence of Amos Lawrence*, p. 102.

89. Lawrence to Webster, Jan. 5, 1835, quoted in George T. Curtis, *Life of Daniel Webster* (New York, 1872), I, 503–504.

90. Everett to Winthrop, May 21, 1838, Robert C. Winthrop MSS, MHS.

91. John Quincy Adams, *Memoirs*, ed. Charles F. Adams (Philadelphia, 1874), X, 43.

92. Webster's decision to support Harrison and his role in the campaign of 1840 are described in Dalzell, *Daniel Webster*, pp. 67–70; and Nathans, *Daniel Webster and Jacksonian Democracy*, pp. 123–144. On Lawrence's senatorial ambitions and his disappointment at not being chosen, see Winthrop to Everett, Dec. 30, 1840, Edward Everett MSS, MHS.; and John Clifford to Winthrop, Jan. 20, Feb. 21, and Mar. 31, 1841, Robert C. Winthrop MSS, MHS.

93. When Ward was collecting the $2,500 fund for Webster, Lawrence wrote explicitly refusing to contribute. Lawrence to Ward, Apr. 29, 1839, Thomas W. Ward, MSS, MHS. Thereafter Lawrence's name never appeared on any list of Webster contributors. He did, however, occasionally open his purse to help other leading American political figures. For example, in 1845 he both made a large gift to Henry Clay and offered John C. Calhoun a loan of $30,000. Clay accepted the gift, but Calhoun refused the loan because he thought the interest was too high. Clay to Lawrence, Mar. 20, 1845, MS in Houghton Library, Harvard; Calhoun to Lawrence, Apr. 9 and May 13, 1845, ibid.; and Lawrence to Calhoun, Apr. 30, 1845, ibid.

94. Nathans, *Daniel Webster and Jacksonian Democracy*, pp. 148–197; Dalzell, *Daniel Webster*, pp. 30–58 and 70–74.

95. Webster, speech of Sept. 3, 1842, *Writings and Speeches*, III, 117–140.

96. Winthrop to Everett, Oct. 15, 1842, Edward Everett MSS, MHS.

97. C. P. Curtis to Webster, Mar. 23, 1843, Daniel Webster MSS, Library of Congress.

98. Appleton to Webster, Aug. 4, 1845, Nathan Appleton MSS, MHS.

99. Webster to Appleton, Aug. 8 and Sept. 11, 1845, ibid.

100. Adams, *Memoirs*, XII, 213–214. Adams, who had never had any use for Webster, consistently sided with Lawrence. On the relations between the two men he commented further: "All Webster's political systems are interwoven with the exploration of a gold-mine for himself, and all his confidential intimacies with Lawrence have been devices to screw from him, or, by his agency, from others, money by the fifty or hundred thousand dollars at a time." Ibid.

101. The original goal had been $100,000—half to be raised in Boston and half in New York. The result was the $37,000 fund deposited at the Massachusetts Hospital Life Insurance Company. See note 86. Thomas W. Ward remarked that for the sake of Webster's "influence" it was best that the larger amount had not been forthcoming. Ward to Joshua Bates, Jan. 15, 1846, Thomas W. Ward MSS, MHS.

102. Appleton to Webster, Aug. 4, 1845, Nathan Appleton MSS, MHS.

103. Dalzell, *Daniel Webster*, pp. 109–113. Most of the Boston business community supported Webster's efforts to bring about a compromise on the tariff issue, once it became clear that there was no hope of defeating the administration bill outright. Abbott Lawrence, however, thought that if there

was going to be a compromise it should be presented by a Democrat. Lawrence to John J. Crittenden, July 24, 1846, John J. Crittenden, MSS, Library of Congress. On the effects of the Tariff of 1846 on the cotton textile industry, which were severe, see McGouldrick, *New England Textiles*, pp. 119–120.

104. Tyler to Webster, Oct. 11, 1841, Daniel Webster MSS, Library of Congress.

105. Winthrop, speech of Jan. 6, 1845, *Addresses and Speeches*, p. 441.

106. Lawrence to Francis Granger, Mar. 2, 1844, quoted in Brauer, *Cotton versus Conscience*, p. 69. Later the same year Amos Lawrence wrote: "If Texas can be kept off, there will be hope for our government. All other questions are insignificant in comparison with this. The damning sin of adding it to this nation to extend slavery will be as certain to destroy us as death is to overtake us." Lawrence to [no name or date], *Diary and Correspondence of Amos Lawrence*, p. 192.

107. Dalzell, *Daniel Webster*, pp. 85–97.

108. The "Young Whigs" are extensively treated in a number of studies, including David Donald, *Charles Sumner and the Coming of the Civil War* (New York, 1960); Martin B. Duberman, *Charles Francis Adams, 1807–1886* (Boston, 1961); Frank O. Gatell, *John Gorham Palfrey and the New England Conscience* (Cambridge, Mass., 1963); and Brauer, *Cotton versus Conscience*. The development, over time, of a more conservative position on the Texas issue—embraced principally by the Boston Associates—is also discussed in these studies, as well as in O'Connor, *Lords of the Loom*. Though the arguments vary, there is a general tendency to let stand the Young Whigs' claim that the chief cause of the Associates' growing opposition to the anti-Texas movement was concern over the tariff. As an explanation of what happened in 1844–45 this is probably accurate enough, but to extend it further poses serious problems. No single factor can explain the Associates' political behavior in the decade and a half before the Civil War, and certainly not the tariff.

109. Webster to Allen, Mar. 13, 1844, *Writings and Speeches*, XVI, 417. On Adams' activities in the legislature, see Duberman, *Charles Francis Adams*, pp. 84–85 and 87–89.

110. Adams, diary, Mar. 10 and 21, 1844, Charles Francis Adams MSS, MHS.

111. On the first anti-Texas convention and the maneuvering that preceded it, see Brauer, *Cotton versus Conscience*, pp. 115–125. Brauer's account, which is very thorough, emphasizes the extent to which—even at this point—most "conservatives" worked to distance themselves from the movement. Except in the case of Lawrence, however, the evidence would not seem to support such an interpretation.

112. Adams, diary, Jan. 30, 1845, Charles Francis Adams MSS, MHS.

113. Duberman, *Charles Francis Adams*, pp. 101–109; Brauer, *Cotton versus Conscience*, pp. 135–158.

114. Adams, diary, Dec. 9, 1845, Charles Francis Adams MSS, MHS.

115. Adams to Lawrence, Nov. 13, 1848, ibid.

116. Lawrence to Adams, Nov. 17, 1845, ibid.

117. Appleton to Adams, John G. Palfrey, and Charles Sumner, Nathan Appleton MSS, MHS.

118. Webster, speech of Nov. 7, 1845, *Writings and Speeches*, XIII, 310–324.

119. Brauer, *Cotton versus Conscience*, pp. 152–153. Adams himself supplied the remarks on Lawrence's letter, while Charles Sumner commented on Appleton's. All four documents were published together in the *Free State Rally* on Nov. 27, 1845.

120. Dalzell, *Daniel Webster*, pp. 122–130.

121. As Winthrop saw it, the choice he had was to vote for the bill, or to refuse supplies to an American army under fire in the field.

122. Boston *Whig*, Aug. 13, 1846. On Sumner's somewhat tardy entry into the Young Whig fold and the background of the "Boston" letters, see Donald, *Charles Sumner and the Coming of the Civil War*, pp. 130–144.

123. Altogether Adams produced thirteen of his "Sagitta" letters. The series ran in the *Whig* from mid-June through mid-September 1846.

124. Palfrey's twenty-four "Papers on the Slave Power" appeared in the *Whig* during July, August, and September of 1846. Subsequently they were published together in a pamphlet under the same title. By then there had been an exchange of letters between Palfrey and Appleton on the subject, and since Palfrey refused to include those letters in his pamphlet, Appleton produced one of his own: *Correspondence between Nathan Appleton and John G. Palfrey: Intended as a Supplement to Mr. Palfrey's Pamphlet on the Slave Power* (Boston, 1846).

125. Appleton's letter to Adams, dated Aug. 8, 1846, was published in the *Whig* on Aug. 14, 1846.

126. Adams, diary, Aug. 11, 1846, Charles Francis Adams MSS, MHS.

127. Webster, speech of Mar. 15, 1837, *Writings and Speeches*, II, 193–230.

128. Boston *Whig*, Aug. 14, 1846.

129. On the growing distance between Sumner and most of the rest of the Boston elite, see Donald, *Charles Sumner and the Coming of the Civil War*, pp. 149–154.

130. Ibid., pp. 146–147; Duberman, *Charles Francis Adams*, pp. 113–118; Brauer, *Cotton versus Conscience*, pp. 181–194; and Dalzell, *Daniel Webster*, pp. 117–122.

131. "Report of the Whig State Convention," Boston *Whig*, Sept. 24, 1846.

132. Darling, *Political Changes in Massachusetts*, pp. 339, n. 64, and pp. 340–341.

133. See Duberman, *Charles Francis Adams*, pp. 122–143; Donald, *Charles Sumner and the Coming of the Civil War*, pp. 155–166; and Brauer, *Cotton versus Conscience*, pp. 206–239.

134. Sumner, speech of June 28, 1848, quoted in Donald, *Charles Sumner and the Coming of the Civil War*, p. 166.

135. Appleton to Sumner [no date], quoted in ibid., p. 170.

136. Dalzell, *Daniel Webster*, pp. 125–152.

137. Phillips, quoted in Brauer, *Cotton versus Conscience*, p. 217.

138. Adams, diary, Nov. 8, 1847, Charles Francis Adams, MSS, MHS.

139. The trip was made at Lawrence's request. Among the Taylor men he asked Appleton to see was John J. Crittenden. Lawrence to Appleton, Apr. 18, 1848, MS in Houghton Library, Harvard.

140. Hugh Maxwell, M. H. Grinnell, J. D. Hall, and S. Draper to Appleton, May 16, 1848, Nathan Appleton MSS, MHS. Meanwhile Sumner, naively hoping that he might succeed, had tried to persuade Lawrence to withdraw from the Taylor movement, to which Lawrence replied: *"What can I do about it; I AM IN UP TO THE EYES."* Donald, *Charles Sumner and the Coming of the Civil War,* pp. 162–163.

141. Allen, quoted in Holman Hamilton, *Zackary Taylor: Soldier in the White House* (Indianapolis, 1951), p. 95.

142. Despite the tendency—then and since—to assume that Allen's outburst was the cause of Lawrence's defeat, Brauer argues convincingly that other factors were probably more important, in particular local politics and Clay's disaffection with Lawrence. *Cotton versus Conscience,* pp. 234–236.

143. Winthrop to John P. Kennedy, June 30, 1849, Robert C. Winthrop MSS, MHS. On Lawrence's service as minister to Great Britain, see Hill, *Memoir of Abbott Lawrence,* pp. 80–98.

144. Dalzell, *Daniel Webster,* pp. 157–304.

145. Darling, *Political Changes in Massachusetts,* pp. 348–359; Brauer, *Cotton versus Conscience,* pp. 229–245; Duberman, *Charles Francis Adams,* pp. 139–157; and Donald, *Charles Sumner and the Coming of the Civil War,* pp. 164–169.

146. Boston *Atlas,* [no date], quoted in Duberman, *Charles Francis Adams,* p. 158.

147. Adams, diary, Oct. 4, 1848, Charles Francis Adams MSS, MHS.

148. Duberman, *Charles Francis Adams,* pp. 158–162.

149. Sumner, quoted in Donald, *Charles Sumner and the Coming of the Civil War,* p. 180.

150. Ibid., p. 182.

151. Cornelius C. Felton to John G. Palfrey, Sept. 13, 1849, quoted in ibid., p. 182. On the "loco-foco" tone of the 1849 Free Soil platform, see also Duberman, *Charles Francis Adams,* p. 160.

152. Winthrop to Everett, Mar. 17, 1850, Edward Everett MSS, MHS.

153. Everett to Webster, Sept. 13, 1850, Edward Everett MSS, MHS. In some quarters strong support for Webster's position had been forthcoming from the start. Within three weeks of the Seventh of March speech an "Address of Thanks and Congratulations" had been signed by some three hundred of Boston's most prominent citizens, including many of the Associates. Edward Curtis to Peter Harvey, Apr. 4, 1850, Daniel Webster MSS, Library of Congress; C. P. Curtis to Webster, Apr. 5, 1850, ibid.; Winthrop to Everett, Apr. 7, 1850, Edward Everett MSS, MHS. See also David Van Tassel, "Gentlemen of Property and Standing: Compromise Sentiment in Boston in 1850," *New England Quarterly,* 23 (1950), 307–319.

Despite conservative support, however, the Compromise continued to divide the Massachusetts Whigs, with Webster and his backers on one side and George Morey, Chairman of the Whig state central committee, and the rest of the regular party organization on the other. The breach was not finally healed until 1852. Dalzell, *Daniel Webster,* pp. 214–222, 228–234, and 241–242; Haws, "Massachusetts Whigs," pp. 219–222 and 226–233.

154. Webster to Franklin Haven, Sept. 12, 1850, *Writings and Speeches,* XVIII, 388.

155. Donald, *Charles Sumner and the Coming of the Civil War*, pp. 186–202; Duberman, *Charles Francis Adams*, pp. 170–174.

156. Eliot to Lawrence, Jan. 23, 1851, Amos A. Lawrence MSS, MHS.

157. Lawrence to Eliot, Feb. 10, 1851, ibid.

158. Lawrence to William Appleton, Feb. 10, 1851, ibid.; Lawrence to Ezra Lincoln, Feb. 10, 1851, ibid.; also Lawrence, appeal for funds "to defeat Sumner," Mar. 14, 1851, ibid.

159. Appleton to Fanny Longfellow, May 23, 1851, quoted in Donald, *Charles Sumner and the Coming of the Civil War*, p. 203.

160. See Duberman, *Charles Francis Adams*, pp. 173–174.

161. Donald, *Charles Sumner and the Coming of the Civil War*, p. 198.

162. The town-by-town election returns are available in the Massachusetts State Archives. My analysis here and below is based on those returns and the data provided in Darling, *Political Changes in Massachusetts*, pp. 354–358, nn. 87 and 88.

163. Ibid.

164. Ibid.

165. The 1840 amendment also contributed directly to the coalition's victory in 1850, since, under the terms of the amendment, all towns were entitled to send representatives to the legislature for one year at the beginning of each decade, and the coalition won many of the extra seats in 1850 by appealing to voters' dissatisfaction with the existing system in towns not regularly represented. On the complex issue of annual representation and its political impact before as well as after 1850, see Kevin Sweeney, "Rum, Romanism, Representation, and Reform: Coalition Politics in Massachusetts, 1847–1853," *Civil War History*, 22 (1976), pp. 116–137.

In the absence of the sort of comprehensive coverage provided by Darling and Formisano for the preceding decades, Sweeney's analysis of Massachusetts politics during these years is invaluable. Other useful studies—all unpublished—include: William G. Bean, "Party Transformations in Massachusetts with Special Reference to the Antecedents of Republicanism, 1848–1860" (Ph.D. diss., Harvard University, 1922); Godfrey Anderson, "The Slavery Issue as a Factor in Massachusetts Politics from the Compromise of 1850 to the Outbreak of the Civil War" (Ph.D. diss., University of Chicago, 1922); and Robert O. McCabe, "The Twilight of the Second Party System in Massachusetts: The Collapse of the Massachusetts Whig Party" (Honors thesis, Harvard University, 1974).

Of the countless studies of American politics in general during this period, two especially have stimulated my thinking: Eric Foner, *Free Soil, Free Labor, Free Men: The Ideology of the Republican Party before the Civil War* (New York, 1970); and Michael F. Holt, *The Political Crisis of the 1850s* (New York, 1978). Both are broadly and imaginatively conceived, yet the two authors reach very different conclusions. Foner puts slavery at the center of the political breakdown that led to the Civil War; Holt stresses the critical importance of other issues as well. My own opinion is that Holt's view comes nearer the truth. Certainly the example of Massachusetts bears out his argument. Nevertheless on many points Foner's analysis is unexceptionable.

166. A helpful introduction to the subject of nativism and Massachusetts politics in the 1850s is William G. Bean, "Puritan versus Celt, 1850–1860," *New England Quarterly*, 7 (1934), 70–89. On temperance and nativism together as factors in the coalition's initial success—and eventual demise—see Sweeney, "Rum, Romanism, Representation, and Reform."

167. The most detailed account of the coalition legislature of 1851 appears in Bean, "Party Transformations in Massachusetts," pp. 64–100. See also Handlin and Handlin, *Commonwealth*, pp. 234–235; and—on the bill aimed at Harvard, which was part of a larger campaign against the institution, carried on by the coalition over several years—Story, *Harvard and the Boston Upper Class*, pp. 140–142.

In addition to the other reforms enacted in 1851, the legislature also lowered the amount of capitalization required for incorporation. Gregory, *Nathan Appleton*, p. 265. And the following year, in yet another move striking at the Associates' interests, a special legislative committee undertook an investigation of charges of political coercion at Lowell. The committee concluded that the charges, if not completely accurate, were by no means unfounded: employment at Lowell for male workers was sometimes made directly contingent on voting the Whig ticket. Formisano, *Transformation of Political Culture*, pp. 285–286 and 336–337. As a result of the issues that led to the investigation, the legislature passed a secret ballot act that year, which the Whigs effectively nullified when they returned to power in 1853. See Michel Brunet, "The Secret Ballot Issue in Massachusetts Politics from 1851 to 1853," *New England Quarterly*, 25 (1952), 354–362.

In spite of repeated Whig attempts to repeal them, however, the general incorporation and free banking laws remained on the books.

168. Lawrence to Charles Devens, Feb. 17, 1851, Amos A. Lawrence MSS, MHS.

169. Winthrop, quoted in McCabe, "Collapse of the Massachusetts Whig Party," p. 81.

170. *Proceedings of the Whig State Convention Held at Springfield, Massachusetts* (Boston, 1851), p. 22.

171. Sweeney, "Rum, Romanism, Representation, and Reform," pp. 128–132. On the passage of the liquor law see also Bean, "Party Transformations in Massachusetts," pp. 113–117; and, on the role of the Boston Irish in the election of 1852, Handlin, *Boston's Immigrants*, pp. 195–196. Handlin cites contemporary estimates of the number of Irish voting Whig in both 1852 and 1853, but Sweeney's analysis indicates that these were exaggerated. His conclusion is that Democratic losses consistently counted for more than Whig gains throughout the state.

172. Worcester *Transcript*, Oct. 8, 1853, quoted in an earlier, unpublished version of Sweeney's article. On the other provisions of the proposed constitution, and its rejection by the voters, see Samuel Shapiro, "The Conservative Dilemma: The Massachusetts Constitutional Convention of 1853," *New England Quarterly*, 33 (1960), 207–224; Handlin, *Boston's Immigrants*, pp. 196–197; and Sweeney, "Rum, Romanism, Representation, and Reform," pp. 133–137.

173. Ibid., p. 136.

174. Evening *Post*, [no date], quoted in McCabe, "Collapse of the Massachusetts Whig Party," p. 110. Among the other items on the list were: "3. The Roman Catholic vote. 4. The entire party opposition of the Whigs. 5. The rum vote. 19. The opposition of Harvard College and the Unitarians. 20. The opposition of old-foggy Whigs. 21. The opposition of the liberal Whigs. 22. Hatred of niggers and Free Soilers. 23. The opposition of the large cities."

175. Handlin, *Boston's Immigrants*, p. 197.

176. Virginia C. Purdy, "Portrait of a Know-Nothing Legislature: The Massachusetts General Court of 1855" (Ph.D. diss., George Washington University, 1970), p. 149. Other studies of Know-Nothingism in Massachusetts include John R. Mulkern, "The Know-Nothing Party in Massachusetts" (Ph.D. diss., Boston University, 1963); and Dale Baum, "Know-Nothingism and the Republican Majority in Massachusetts: The Political Realignment of the 1850s," *Journal of American History*, 64 (1978), 959–986. Based on the evidence presented by Purdy and Mulkern, Formisano suggests that, along with an animus against foreigners, the Know-Nothings "brought to fruition perhaps the most sweeping single impulse of democratization and utilitarian reform in the history of Massachusetts." *Transformation of Political Culture*, p. 24. On the other hand, Baum attempts to prove—not altogether successfully, it seems to me—that the movement had only a limited impact and contributed little to the subsequent rise of the Republican party in the state.

177. Sumner to Mrs. Hamilton Fish, Nov. 15, 1854, quoted in Donald, *Charles Sumner and the Coming of the Civil War*, p. 269.

178. The Know-Nothings carried the state again in 1855.

179. The only full-length treatment of Lawrence is William Lawrence, *Life of Amos A. Lawrence, with Extracts from his Diary and Correspondence* (Boston, 1889). On his political activities during the 1850s see also O'Connor, *Lords of the Loom*, pp. 93–153, *passim*.

180. Lawrence to Andrews [?], May 26, 1854, quoted in Duberman, *Charles Francis Adams*, pp. 189–190.

181. O'Connor, *Lords of the Loom*, p. 100.

182. Lawrence to Thomas H. Webb, July 20, 1855, *Amos A. Lawrence with Extracts from his Diary and Correspondence*, p. 96.

183. Ibid.

184. Lawrence to Franklin Pierce, December 10, 1855, ibid., p. 104. Pierce, in addition to being president of the United States, was a distant relative of Lawrence's. See also Lawrence to Charles Robinson, Aug. 10, 1855, ibid., pp. 100–101, in which he states: "However wrong in our opinion, there never can be good reason for resisting our own government, unless it attempts to destroy the power of the people through the elections, that is, to take away the power of creating a new administration every four years." Robinson was the Emigrant Aid Company's agent in Kansas, and the letter accompanied its first shipment of rifles to the territory.

185. See Donald, *Charles Sumner and the Coming of the Civil War*, pp. 278–311.

186. Lawrence to Sumner, Oct. 10, 1856, *Amos A. Lawrence with Extracts from his Diary and Correspondence*, p. 141. In explaining the invitation, Lawrence wrote: "Mr. Sumner's speech on the 'Kansas Crime' alone entitles him to the gratitude of every man who has an American heart, whatever may be his politics. He will always have mine, and shall be welcome to my house as long as I have one." Lawrence to Henry W. Longfellow, [no date], ibid., p. 142.

187. Ibid., p. 146.

188. Lawrence to Sumner, Oct. 10, 1856, ibid., p. 141.

189. Donald, *Charles Sumner and the Coming of the Civil War*, pp. 266–277 and 318–322; Duberman, *Charles Francis Adams*, pp. 189–209; and Bean, "Party Transformations in Massachusetts," pp. 327–353. Unwilling to embrace nativism openly, yet equally anxious not to lose nativist support for their national ticket through a contest with the Know-Nothings on the local level, the Republicans made no gubernatorial nomination in 1856. However Frémont, the Republican presidential nominee, ran very well in the state, receiving almost 60 percent of the total vote. On the political sources of the growing Republican vote in Massachusetts, see Baum, "Know-Nothingism and the Republican Majority in Massachusetts," pp. 966–977. Unfortunately Baum's analysis does not include the 1856 presidential vote.

190. For an interesting perspective on Lawrence's antipathy to "the formation of sectional parties," see Lawrence to Jefferson Davis, Dec. 22, 1859, *Amos A. Lawrence, with Extracts from his Diary and Correspondence*, pp. 136–138. At the 1856 Republican state convention in Springfield, Lawrence had been chosen as a Frémont presidential elector but declined the nomination. Ibid., p. 140.

191. The Fillmore flag was flying the day Sumner visited, and to further underline his views Lawrence refused the seat which had been saved for him in the barouche that was to carry Sumner on his triumphal entry into Boston. Lawrence, diary, Nov. 3, 1856, ibid., pp. 142–143.

192. This was the third time Lawrence had been asked to run as the American party's gubernatorial candidate in Massachusetts, but in both 1856 and 1857 he refused to be considered for the nomination. Lawrence to Jefferson Davis, Dec. 22, 1859, ibid., 136–138. On the rapidly changing composition of the American party's following in Massachusetts, see Baum, "Know-Nothingism and the Republican Majority in Massachusetts," pp. 967–973.

193. New York *Tribune*, [no date], quoted in O'Connor, *Lords of the Loom*, p. 129.

194. Ware, *New England Cotton Manufacture*, pp. 113–114 and 151–153; McGouldrick, *New England Textiles*, pp. 74–75, 96, and 103; and White, *Massachusetts Hospital Life Insurance Company*, pp. 94–95.

195. Stockholder discontent with Waltham-Lowell companies, which first assumed significant proportions during the Panic of 1857, continued to grow thereafter. Several years later Dr. James C. Ayer, a successful manufacturer of patent medicine who also owned stock in the Merrimack Company, published a pamphlet describing a wide variety of abuses, including nepotism, excessive payments to cotton brokers and selling houses, concealment and

falsification of company records, and conflicts of interest. Ayer, *Some Usages and Abuses in the Management of Our Manufacturing Corporations* (Lowell, 1863).

A second set of charges leveled at the companies—most notably by Erastus Bigelow, the founder of the largest carpet factory in New England—accused them of inhibiting future growth through a failure to retain earnings. "We draw our capital from other sources than manufacturing and pay out the earnings if there happen to be any. The manufacturing interest is thus made subject to other interests, on which it must depend not only for extension but for support." Bigelow, *Remarks on the Depressed Condition of Manufactures in Massachusetts* (Boston, 1858).

196. Appleton, *Introduction of the Power Loom*, pp. 30–36.

197. Lawrence to Charles Robinson, Oct. 19, 1857, quoted in O'Connor, *Lords of the Loom*, p. 126.

198. Lawrence to Robinson, Jan. 7, 1859, quoted in ibid., p. 132. Later that year Lawrence refused to run again as the American party gubernatorial candidate. Meanwhile John Brown's raid at Harpers Ferry had occurred. The two men had come to know one another through the Emigrant Aid Company. Lawrence had contributed money to help defray Brown's personal expenses, and he had organized a subscription to buy a farm in New York for Brown's family. The rifles used in the Harpers Ferry raid were part of a shipment from the Emigrant Aid Company. At different times Lawrence described Brown as "a calm, temperate, and pious man," "a true representative of the Puritanic warrior," "a desperate abolitionist," "a brave man," and "a Puritan whose mind has become disordered by hardship and illness." When a subscription was being raised for Brown's legal defense after Harpers Ferry, Lawrence contributed without hesitation, and he wrote Governor Wise of Virginia urging him "to insist on a fair trial." During the trial, he thought Brown carried himself "wonderfully well" and after it was all over remarked in his diary: "Old Brown hanged with great ceremony. He died grandly. Nevertheless he must be called a fanatic." John Brown to Lawrence, Mar. 11, 1857; Lawrence to Brown, Mar. 20, 1857; Brown to Lawrence, Apr. 16, 1857; Lawrence to Governor Wise, Oct. 26, 1859; and Lawrence, diary, Jan. 6 and 7, 1857, May 28, Oct. 18, 21, 24, 26, Nov. 1, 5, 22, 25, 29, and Dec. 3, 1859, *Amos A. Lawrence, with Extracts from his Diary and Correspondence*, pp. 123–136.

It is interesting to compare Lawrence's attitude toward John Brown—and his efforts in his behalf—with those of other Massachusetts political figures. Both Sumner and Adams, for example, successfully avoided involving themselves in the entire affair. Donald, *Charles Sumner and the Coming of the Civil War*, pp. 349–351; and Duberman, *Charles Francis Adams*, p. 213.

199. Initially Lawrence had been dubious about the "Union" efforts in Boston. Not wishing "to help the Democrats," he refused to serve as an officer of the Faneuil Hall meeting in December, but then the following day he changed his mind and was glad he had, commenting afterward: "A grand affair. The crowd was very great even on the outside. Ex-Governor Lincoln presided . . . Mr. Everett spoke as well as I ever heard him. Then Caleb Cushing. The enthusiasm was tremendous whenever the *Union* was alluded

to." Lawrence, diary, Dec. 5 and 6, 1859, *Amos A. Lawrence, with Extracts from his Diary and Correspondence*, p. 134. Three months later he was busy writing "influential men throughout the state" and organizing " 'Union' clubs in the towns and cities" in preparation for the Constitutional Union convention. See ibid., pp. 144–145.

200. For an analysis of the Constitutional Union vote in Massachusetts see Baum, "Know-Nothingism and the Republican Majority in Massachusetts," pp. 977–979. Bell received only 13 percent of the popular vote, "the vast bulk" of which came from former Know-Nothings, Baum concludes.

201. Also circulated in Boston and sent on to Washington was a second petition, which did not mention the Crittenden plan but simply urged that every effort be made to achieve "pacific settlement of our present difficulties." O'Connor, *Lords of the Loom*, p. 146.

202. Sumner, quoted in Donald, *Charles Sumner and the Coming of the Civil War*, p. 370.

203. See O'Connor, *Lords of the Loom*, pp. 154–155.

204. Lawrence, diary, Mar. 21, 22, and 24, 1861, and Lawrence to William H. Seward, Apr. 1, 1861, *Amos A. Lawrence, with Extracts from his Diary and Correspondence*, pp. 169–171.

205. Election returns for Groton, 1860, MSS, Massachusetts State Archives.

206. Green, "Groton," in Hurd, *History of Middlesex County*, II, 501–570, passim. See also George J. Burns, "Ayer," ibid., pp. 639–688. The town of Ayer, which included south Groton was "set-off" from Groton as a separate town in 1871.

207. Massachusetts, *Statistical Information Relating to Certain Branches of Industry in Massachusetts, for the Year Ending June 1, 1855* (Boston, 1856), pp. 309–310.

208. Massachusetts, *Statistical Information Relating to Certain Branches of Industry in Massachusetts, for the Year Ending May 1, 1865* (Boston, 1866), pp. 353–355.

209. The population of Groton between 1790 and 1860 was as follows: in 1790, 1,840; in 1800, 1,802; in 1810, 1,886; in 1820, 1,897; in 1830, 1,925; in 1840, 2,139; in 1850, 2,515; and in 1860, 3,193. Green, "Groton," in Hurd, *History of Middlesex County*, II, 543.

210. Election returns for Groton, 1832, 1836, 1840, and 1844, MSS, Massachusetts State Archives.

For an interesting attempt to identify the social bases of Massachusetts political parties through a close analysis of data for individual towns, see Paul Goodman, "The Politics of Industrialism: Massachusetts, 1830–1870," in *Uprooted Americans: Essays to Honor Oscar Handlin*, ed. Richard Bushman et al. (Boston, 1979). Goodman found that the Whigs made their strongest showing in large cities, fishing towns, and towns with only Congregational churches. The Democrats, on the other hand, tended to carry the towns "least touched by industrial and commercial development" and those where religious dissenters were particularly numerous. Towns that fell between the two extremes usually, but not always, voted Whig. In rough terms Groton—with some developing industry and a certain amount of religious diversity—would seem to fit the pattern as one of those towns that generally produced Whig majorities, though not without a contest.

211. Election returns for Groton, 1848, MSS, Massachusetts State Archives.

212. Election returns for Groton, 1852, 1856, and 1860, ibid.

213. See Sweeney, "Rum, Romanism, Representation, and Reform," pp. 126 and 134.

214. Kirkland, *Men, Cities, and Transportation*, I, 397–398. Actually the loan was passed by the last Whig legislature in a desperate attempt to stave off defeat in that fall's elections.

215. Handlin and Handlin, *Commonwealth*, p. 182; Hammond, *Banks and Politics in America*, pp. 554–556.

216. Burns, "Ayer," in Hurd, *History of Middlesex County*, II, 667–668.

The differences between Whig and Republican economic policies are discussed with considerable insight in Howe, *Political Culture of the American Whigs*. See especially pp. 280–281 and 301–303.

217. *Springfield Republican*, [no date], quoted in O'Connor, *Lords of the Loom*, p. 141.

Epilogue

1. White, *Massachusetts Hospital Life Insurance Company*, p. 95. As the list suggests, hardest hit were newer companies, particularly those at Holyoke and Lawrence. On their financial weakness and the problems they faced in 1857, see Green, *Holyoke*, pp. 55–65; and Gregory, *Nathan Appleton*, pp. 204–208.

2. McGouldrick, *New England Textiles*, pp. 81 and 251.

3. On the extension of Boston capital—and business enterprise—into different regions and new industries, see A. M. Johnson and B. E. Supple, *Boston Capitalists and Western Railroads: A Study in the Nineteenth Century Investment Process* (Cambridge, Mass., 1967); William B. Gates, *Michigan Copper and Boston Dollars: An Economic History of the Michigan Copper Mining Industry* (Cambridge, Mass., 1951); Vincent F. Carosso, *Investment Banking in America* (Cambridge, Mass., 1964); and Gabriel Kolko, "Brahmins and Businessmen: A Hypothesis on the Social Basis of Success in America," in *The Critical Spirit: Essays in Honor of Herbert Marcuse*, ed. Barrington Moore and Kurt Wolfe (Boston, 1967).

4. Cole, *Immigrant City*, pp. 31–32; Lawrence, diary, Jan. 10, 11, and 12, 1860, *Amos A. Lawrence, with Extracts from his Diary and Correspondence*, p. 163.

5. Appleton, *Introduction of the Power Loom*, pp. 30–36.

6. William Lawrence, *Memories of a Happy Life* (Boston, 1926), p. 143. On Lawrence's life see also *Dictionary of American Biography*, suppl. 3, s.v. "William Lawrence"; and the autobiography written by his daughter, Marian Lawrence Peabody, *To Be Young Was Very Heaven* (Boston, 1967). Amos A. Lawrence had become an Episcopalian soon after his marriage, thereby abandoning the Unitarianism that had increasingly troubled his father and paving the way for his son's future career in the church.

7. Lawrence, *Memories of a Happy Life*, p. 25.

8. Ibid., p. 418.

9. For an example of this sort of approach to the subject see Cleveland Amory, *The Proper Bostonians* (New York, 1947).

10. Samuel Eliot Morison, *One Boy's Boston, 1887–1901* (Boston, 1962), p. 68.

11. Baltzell, *Puritan Boston and Quaker Philadelphia*.

12. John D. Rockefeller, quoted in Lawrence, *Memories of a Happy Life*, p. 140. The remark was reported to Lawrence in a letter written while he was working on his autobiography, but he indicates neither the name of the writer nor the date.

Index

Harvard Studies in Business History

(Some of these titles may be out of print. Write to Harvard University Press for information and ordering.)